POLARITY, PATRIOTISM, AND DISSENT IN
GREAT WAR CANADA, 1914–1919

Compared with the idea that Canada was a nation forged in victory on Vimy Ridge, the reality of dissent and repression at home strikes a sour note. Through censorship, conscription, and internment, the government of Canada worked more ruthlessly than either Great Britain or the United States to suppress opposition to the war effort during the First World War.

Polarity, Patriotism, and Dissent in Great War Canada, 1914–1919 examines the basis for those repressive policies. Brock Millman, an expert on wartime dissent in both the United Kingdom and Canada, argues that Canadian policy was driven first and foremost by a fear that opposition to the war among French Canadians and immigrant communities would provoke social tensions – and possibly even a vigilante backlash from the war's most fervent supporters in British Canada.

Highlighting the class and ethnic divisions which characterized public support for the war, *Polarity, Patriotism, and Dissent in Great War Canada, 1914–1919* offers a broad and much-needed re-examination of Canadian government policy on the home front.

BROCK MILLMAN is an assistant professor in the Department of History at Western University.

BROCK MILLMAN

Polarity, Patriotism, and Dissent in Great War Canada, 1914–1919

UNIVERSITY OF TORONTO PRESS
Toronto Buffalo London

© University of Toronto Press 2016
Toronto Buffalo London
www.utppublishing.com
Printed in Canada

ISBN 978-1-4426-4725-1 (cloth)
ISBN 978-1-4426-1538-0 (paper)

∞ Printed on acid-free, 100% post-consumer recycled paper with vegetable-based inks

---

Library and Archives Canadian Cataloguing in Publication Data

Millman, Brock, 1963–, author
Polarity, patriotism, and dissent in Great War Canada, 1914–1919 / Brock Millman.

Includes bibliographical references and index.
ISBN 978-1-4426-4725-1 (bound)   ISBN 978-1-4426-1538-0 (paperback)

1. World War, 1914–1918 – Protest movements – Canada.   2. Dissenters – Canada – History – 20th century.   3. Peace movements – Canada – History – 20th century.   4. Patriotism – Canada – History – 20th century.   5. Social conflict – Canada – History – 20th century.   6. World War, 1914–1918 – Social aspects – Canada.   7. Canada – Politics and government – 1911–1921.   I. Title.

FC557.M58 2016   940.3'71   C2015-906780-4

The author acknowledges the assistance of the J.B. Smallman Publication Fund, and the Faculty of Social Science, University of Western Ontario.

University of Toronto Press acknowledges the financial assistance to its publishing program of the Canada Council for the Arts and the Ontario Arts Council, an agency of the Government of Ontario.

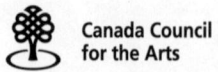

History is unjust to the living, and impartial to none save the dead. At the back of events whose course we are watching today, however, lays [sic] the province of the immaterial forces which have brought them about; for the phenomena of the visible world are rooted in a world invisible, wherein the feelings and beliefs which rule us are wrought to their perfection. This province of causes is the only one which I now propose to investigate.

As I have often said, it is not the philosopher's business to scrutinize the rational value of the motives which actuate mankind, but rather the influence which they exert; for, if the battles which have been fought over illusions that were totally devoid of rational value were to be erased from history, there would not be many left.

Gustav Le Bon, *The Psychology of the Great War*, 1917

I do not know whether you know Mariposa. If not, it is of no consequence, for if you know Canada at all, you are probably well acquainted with a dozen towns like it.

There it lies in the sunlight, sloping up from the little lake that spreads out at the foot the hillside on which the town is built. There is a wharf beside the lake, and lying alongside of it a steamer that is tied to the wharf with two ropes of about the same size as they use on the Lusitania. The steamer goes nowhere in particular, for the lake is land-locked and there is no navigation for the Mariposa Belle except to "run trips" on the lake on the first of July and the Queen's Birthday, and to take excursions of the Knights of Pythias and the Sons of Temperance to and from the Local Option Townships.

In point of geography the lake is called Lake Wissonotti and the river running out of it is the Ossawippi, just as the main street of Mariposa is called Missinaba Street and the county Missinaba County. But these names do not really matter. Nobody uses them. People simply speak of the "lake" and the "river" and "main street", much in the same way as they always call the Continental Hotel, "Pete Robinson's" and the Pharmaceutical Hall, "Eliot's Drug Store". But I suppose this is just the same in every one else's town as in mine, so I need lay no stress on it.

Steven Leacock, *Sunshine Sketches of a Little Town*, 1912

There has [sic] only got to be two parties in this fight, and the time has come for those two parties to line up, and the line up is going to be this, all who are for the war have got to get on one side and all who are against the war on the other (Applause). The politician who attempts to wonder about in no man's land must be ruthlessly destroyed (hear hear).

John Milton Godfrey, 1917

To the soldiers of the Fourth Canadian Division

Contents

List of Figures and Tables xi

Preface xiii

Introduction: Trouble in Mariposa   3

1 "They Exceed in Stringency Anything We Know Here": State-Orchestrated Repression in Great War Canada   12

2 "Because They Are Totally and Exclusively Canadian": A Clash of Canadas   34

3 "A Cleavage in the Population of This Country along Racial Lines": French and New Canada   58

4 "A Life and Death Struggle for Christian Civilization": The Great British Canadian Crusade   82

5 "Down with King Borden and His Boches. Long Live the Jails!" Intercommunal Riot as Social Control, 1916–1917: The Case of Quebec   109

6 "We Cheerfully Accept the Burden Laid upon Us": Intercommunal Riot as Social Control in British Canada, 1916–1917   127

7 "The Politician Who Attempts to Wander About in No Man's Land Must Be Ruthlessly Destroyed": The Election of 1917   147

8 "Absolute Masters of All Authority": Intercommunal Violence, 1918   183

9 1919: The War at Home Continues: When the Boys Came Home   209

Conclusion   245

Appendix A: Opinion and Punishment   255

Appendix B: "War Crimes" in Canada during the First World War   260

Appendix C: Great War Timeline   267

Notes   283

Bibliography   341

Index   355

Figures and Tables

Figures

4.1 Meeting of LOL 2533, Forest Lawn, Alberta, uniformed members in attendance 93
4.2 Election poster for Roberta Macadams 98
4.3 The GWVA, a potent force on the Canadian home front 103
5.1 Anti-conscription march in Montreal, 1916 111
6.1 Calgary firemen attacking German soldiers hanged in effigy 135
6.2 The saloon of the Riverside Hotel after the riot 137
6.3 Riverside Bar 138
7.1 Unionist poster from the 1917 election 175
8.1 Anti-IWW poster 193
9.1 The boys come home 228
9.2 Winnipeg veterans attending an anti-Bolshevik, anti-alien rally 232
9.3 Winnipeg special policemen 236

Tables

1.1 Offence by year and type 18
1.2 Total "war crimes" by province and year 19
1.3 "War crimes" by province, by year, weighted for population 20
1.4 Total number of "war crime" convictions per year/percentage of the population, less convictions under the Alien Restriction Regulations 20

Preface

This book began life as a consideration of the way in which the government of Canada restrained dissent in Great War Canada. In conception, it was to have been something like an earlier work regarding the management of Great War dissent in Britain. I quickly discovered, however, that the patterns found in Canada were very different – both in the way in which dissent was managed, and in the way in which it was conceived and recorded. In Britain, the great problem for a historian was identifying exactly what had happened. Once that was ascertained, the "whys" were relatively easy. In the Canadian case, since the repression of dissent was openly orchestrated by the federal government, the general "what" was the easy part. Finding answers for the question "why" the Canadian mechanism took this pattern proved more difficult. What was to have been the primary concern of this book, therefore, is summarized in the first chapter. The rest seeks to explain the seemingly odd patterns illustrated there.

This book is, I think, not structured according to any pre-existing theory. I am aware of certain resonances between my work and that of others; I am also cognizant of some oppositions. I consider in general, however, that, like lawyers, historians go to theory when they do not have facts. I have tried to do the best I can here with the facts as I was able to ascertain them. I ask pardon for this contribution from a newcomer to the writing of Canadian history and indulgence for any minor errors and omissions that may survive.

POLARITY, PATRIOTISM, AND DISSENT
IN GREAT WAR CANADA, 1914–1919

Introduction: Trouble in Mariposa

> I think too, you should in all your speeches emphasize the supreme issue, namely, to keep a united Canada, and to avoid the set of things that has happened in both Ireland and Russia.
>
> W.L Mackenzie King to Sir Wilfrid Laurier, November 1917[1]

The First World War did not end with the military victory of either opposing coalition. Rather, from 1916 all combatant nations faced a time of severe strain as each attempted to shoulder a burden become unimaginably weighty. National resolve was tested when societies began to fracture as the war was differentially experienced and interpreted by individuals, communities, and social segments. Within a year it was obvious that some nations on each side were not up to the task. Thereafter they were sustained by their allies or collapsed altogether. In the end, the Entente powers won the war more because they endured longer than because they fought better; some allies collapsed along the way, while others were plainly towed to victory. All combatants, victors and vanquished, steadfast until the end or foundered along the way, were profoundly affected by the experience and by those things that had been done during the war to maintain the war effort. In some aspects of the life of some combatant nations – the political history of the United Kingdom, for example – the Great War was the single most significant passage in the twentieth century.

A major factor determining which nations lasted and which collapsed was the relative effectiveness of the mechanism adopted to deal with dissent at home, a critical issue by 1917. This is, however, an aspect of the war which has not received the attention it merits, even in consideration of those cases in which dissent at home exercised a profound, and obvious, influence on wartime outcomes. We know that there were two Russian revolutions, for example. Certainly there were long-term causes, and just as certainly there were immediate war impacts. Might the Czarist order have acted more effectively at home, thereby preserving itself while making a greater contribution to the Allied cause? It probably could have done so. The failure to maintain an adequate food supply to the cities, in the winter of 1916–17, and to restrain war-accentuated dissent were probably more directly connected to the ensuing revolution than the failure of the 1916 offensive, or some long-term inadequacy. Similarly, the final straw breaking Germany's back in 1918 was the palpable failure of the home front rather than heavy, but not necessarily mortal, blows received at the front. On the other hand, we know that the French and Italian armies almost collapsed in 1917. Why "almost" and not "absolutely," as the Austro-Hungarian, Ottoman, and German armies did a year later? Outside Ireland, the government of the United Kingdom does not appear to have been as severely challenged. Was this, however, because no internal threat arose, or because His Majesty's government managed either to pre-empt or to defeat it?[2] In Canada too there were obvious signs of trouble at home in the latter war years, but there was again no obvious failure. Was dissent too weak, or was the government too clever (or at least sufficiently strong, and determined) for the national effort to be effectively challenged?

Some aspects of the management of the Great War Canadian home front have received some attention (conscription, internment, labour unrest, and, recently, censorship). As is generally the case elsewhere, however, these things are studied discretely without much attempt to associate them, or to place them within a greater Canadian reality with roots in prewar history and wartime society and ramifications for the postwar future. The tone in general is critical, and apologies have been demanded and recently extended. Little attempt is made to understand the context in which decisions were made and the nature of the challenges and choices faced by the government. Even so, the predominant focus of writing concerning the Canadian Great War remains the front, notwithstanding the fact that some of the more significant wartime outcomes had very little to do with what was happening in France and Belgium and rather a lot to do with what was happening on the streets of Brandon, Manitoba, London, Ontario, and Quebec City. To indicate only one obvious example, the Conservative Party is not severely challenged in the province of Quebec because of anything that happened in France and Belgium.

The following is a modest effort to make more sense of things at home: to establish, first, what the government of Canada did generally to maintain order at home, and then to ascertain why this was the path and these the methods chosen. The narrative will move from a general overview of government efforts at home to control dissent and maximize national effectiveness in the fight, and then through general to specific context – describing the society of Great War Canada, before turning to some particularly enlightening aspects of wartime social interaction. In the process the rationale behind government activities should become clear.

The general argument, in brief, follows. It will be accepted from the beginning that some regime to control dissent was inevitable. Canada would have been unique among combatants if it had had none, and would probably not have participated very effectively in the war after 1916. While mechanisms to control dissent were inevitable, there was considerable variation among combatants as particular threats emerged and were assessed, tools chosen, and local cultural preferences manifested. At a minimum, any government response had to be consistent with the nature of a particular dissent; otherwise it would surely fail and might well prove provocative. Revolutions are not killed with kindness. Unrest, on the other hand, is seldom stilled with free employment of a heavy hand. For some, a real constraint was the fact that in a democracy opponents expect as a right tolerance of what, in most times, would simply be expression of timely political opinion – advocacy, not seditious incitement. The religious, similarly, can be cajoled. It is notorious that they often gather strength and conviction from actual repression, as Tertullian observed long ago. Dissent expressed as a social critique, appealing to one or another social stratum, must be dealt with differently from a dissent which finds a communal host. Members of a community, coherent as a society and geographically, can be encouraged to help. Actual repression invites attempted secession and civil war. As the war progresses, every measure of war management – every departure from peacetime practice, whether it be control of manpower, industrial restructuring, economic realignment, or whatever – provides at once provocation of some constituency, opportunity to ameliorate some grievances, and tools which can be used, in the extreme, to suppress those who cannot be convinced. Control, if sometimes provocative, is power. The aim, of course, is always to ensure maximum effectiveness in the war while laying up as little trouble for the future as possible, either for the nation, for the government, or for the governing party. Such is the arithmetic of the war at home.

Even a cursory examination of the Canadian case indicates some odd patterns. Some measures of control were stringent, probably out of keeping both with the actual threat and, more importantly, with the immediate war-related requirement perceived by Ottawa. The arithmetic, quite simply, did not work sometimes. It is true that obvious regional disparities remained in how rigorously the war regime was imposed. It is also true, however, that efforts were in train, in 1918, to eliminate these. The Canadian mechanism for censorship was uniquely stringent. The enforcement of Canadian conscription in some areas of the country, and (if the war had continued for another year) probably in the entire country, was harsh relative to the systems introduced in kindred political systems. The regulation of Enemy Aliens in Canada was relatively benign; on the other hand, it also appears to have been excessive to requirement. While it is true that the Canadian state has always been strong, jealous of its prerogatives, and intolerant of opposition, the arithmetic of the thing still did not work. Aggregated wartime dissent in Canada, while obvious and sometimes violent, was not in the end very strong – or, at least, it lacked the resolution to seek a politically dominant position whatever the cost. Whatever the government may have gained by one or another measure of repression often appears to have been outweighed by its costs, present and prospective. Let us set aside for a moment the possibility that government policy was simply wrong. If it were not, then there was something about the nature of Canadian society and the way in which it was affected by the war which made relatively repressive policies seem necessary to the government of the day, in the day.

If there is an arithmetic to the management of dissent, there is also a mathematics. In any state, but particularly in a democracy, there are always two target communities when the questions arise: "What should the government do to win the war?" and subsequently, "What should the government do to manage dissent at home?" There are those about whom the government must worry (styled "dissenters" in what follows), and those whose support is essential to the prosecution of the war (hereafter "patriots," following wartime usage); those who are the object of its attentions and substance of government suspicions, and its collaborators and sometimes agents. Any government must go at least far enough to contain dissent, but can neither go further nor much less far than its supporters demand. It must always, in any case, credibly simulate sympathy with the desires of the patriotic constituency. Quite plainly, in Canada, the most vocal wartime "patriots" were "British Canadians," and most dissenters were, or were perceived to be, French and "New" Canadians. Positions and intercommunal animosities had been amplified by the war. Tolerance of dissent was simply not in the cards. The failure of the government to satisfy British Canada, in essence, might well have constituted acceptance by default of intercommunal attacks. The adoption of a policy of pragmatic tolerance, even, would probably have been the anteroom to profound civil strife, already germinating in the middle war years. The government, therefore, was compelled to act with a heavier hand than it probably considered necessary, or even advisable. It had little choice but to satisfy the minimum requirements of communally defined patriotism, growing increasingly hysterical as the war entered its latter, terrible years. At a minimum, this involved repressive practice directed at malcontents, generally understood during the war to be members of other communities, conceived as being hosts to dissent. A different government would have faced identical challenges, and a failure to credibly meet them would have been the real mistake. Quite plainly, there was no viable successor to the Borden government. Laurier, not Borden, ruled out the possibility of National Union. The only possible replacement, therefore, was a dissenting-Laurier minority, in the aftermath of the emergence of which profound civil disturbance could be safely predicted. In either event – if the government became irrelevant or disintegrated and was replaced – Canada might well have been destroyed as communities turned on one another. It need hardly be added that Canada's contribution to the Allied cause would have suffered in the process. If there was a danger of permanently alienating some members of those communities opposed to the war, or which found themselves the particular object of British Canadian venom, this danger paled beside the immediate danger of civil strife at home if the government failed to make some credible simulation of doing what its most convinced, largely British Canadian supporters deemed necessary. Such was the unfortunate mathematics of total war in Great War Canada.

Canada's repressive mechanism, therefore, was only designed in part to meet the challenge of Canadian dissent. It was also intended to satisfy British Canada, growing increasingly frantic as the burden of the war was felt and disproportionately shouldered, that the Borden government would do whatever had to be done to win the war, however drastic or distasteful. Volunteer assistance, too evidently available by the second half of 1916, was simply not required.

Before proceeding to demonstration, some preliminary definitions are required.

While, perhaps, the terms "British Canada" (and therefore "British Canadian") may produce some pause, any historian of the period works with or against contemporary categories in attempting to explain what transpired. The term has the excellent advantage of being consistent with Great War thinking and sanctified by use in Canadian censuses at the time. It describes a collective of very disparate and often squabbling elements: the native born, and emigrants from all of the constituent nations of the United Kingdom, from the other Dominions, and of British origin from the United States, however recently arrived; members of the principal Protestant denominations in Canada and the Irish faction of the Canadian Catholic communion; Grits, Radicals, and Tories mixed together higgledy-piggledy. While this group was marvellously disparate, the line drawn around this cluster together, in contemporary imaginations, was far more important than the differences between elements. During the Great War this line became the most significant factor in Canadian national life. By employing "British Canada" to describe this aggregate, as well, confusion with current usage – "anglophone" or "English Canada," for our purposes nearly useless categories – is avoided. If the term is to be truly helpful, of course, we must include in the conglomerate – perhaps as honorary members – those members of other communities who had been assimilated to British Canada linguistically, culturally, and ideologically.

On the other hand, what British Canada was not, exactly, was simply British. The term should not be taken to describe a conglomerated ethnicity precisely. The English then as now were, of all of Canada's constituent communities, the most enthusiastic miscegenationists, and the products of mixed unions almost universally considered themselves, and were considered, "British." On the other hand, some sorts of "British" newcomer – the "remittance man," the "labour agitator" – were well known, and intensely disliked even before the war began. Some British and American immigrants, especially, were prominent among the war's opponents. American "wobblies," or voluble Yankees ill disposed to accept that in Canada things were done differently, were widely despised. Indeed, during the war itself, and in its immediate aftermath, Canada took steps to legally separate itself from these – by amending the Immigration Act, for example, in 1919 to make it possible to define offensive labour agitators as less than fully "British" so that the Dominion could then deport them as foreigners of doubtful allegiance.

We should note, as well, that wartime patterns overlay existing regional differentiation. British Columbia and the Maritime provinces, while certainly "British" and "Canadian," were different, characterized in large measure by patterns unique to themselves. In what follows, therefore, "British Canada" should be taken to mean primarily Ontario and the provinces formed from the old North West – Manitoba, Saskatchewan, and Alberta. These provinces had been recently settled in large measure by internal immigration from Ontario, and exhibited during the war, sometimes in an exaggerated manner, patterns brought with people from the Central Canadian heartland. While contemporary Westerners might object to being lumped in with Ontario as part of the same social-cultural continuum, and maintain that the West was even then an entity distinct to itself, we would do well to remember that the sod in the West was only just being broken in 1914. Many of the settlers, and almost all of the local elites, were transplanted from Ontario and points east. One generation is not a long time to differentiate.

"French Canadians" and "French Canada" require no explanation, though these terms will be employed here essentially to describe the critical mass of French Canadians in Quebec. Profuse apologies are tendered in advance to Acadians, Franco-Ontarians, and French Canadians resident elsewhere. However, as a general rule, during the Great War these other subspecies of French Canadian behaved by turns like their compatriots in Quebec and like the British Canadians among whom they lived, depending on the issue. They appear to have joined the army as volunteers in similar proportions to their British Canadian neighbours and were capable of launching vociferous defences of their patriotism when it was questioned. Moreover, the criteria they employed to describe that patriotism would be familiar to any Orangeman. Indeed, as enthusiastic volunteers, they were sometimes quick to denounce perceived disloyalty in other Canadians. They tended to oppose conscription loudly, however, like the *Québécois*. As conscription was the most important issue dividing British and French Canada, generalization does less violence to the model that will emerge than might normally be the case.

"New Canadians," on the other hand, presents more of a poser. We do not now commonly use it; the term was pejorative, and employed at the time to describe all the members of the enormous variety of cultures imported into Canada during the period of massive immigration which immediately preceded the war – those cultures, in any case, which were not understood in 1914 as native to the country by members of those communities already established. The term, however, has again the excellent advantage of being sanctified by period use, and alternatives are much less precise.

"Alien," for example, might be taken to include all Americans. "Alien Enemy" is confusing, since common usage does not now, and did not then, equate to legal definition.[3] Period writing on the subject was not always clear on the distinction, nor does modern perception account for it. Moreover, the definition of who might be an Alien Enemy changed in the course of the war as various classes of Ottoman, Austrian-Hungarian, Russian, and German subjects were perceived to have shifted their loyalties. The term would also exclude members of some groups – those from Southern Europe or Poles, for example – not liked much better than Germans and generally included on the debit side of the ledger in wartime discourse on the nature of the demographic challenge facing British Canada. Confusion is inevitable. "Foreigner," while certainly used, carried legal connotations that confuse the issue. A German Canadian born in Canada was not a "foreigner." He was a British subject. He was, however, a New Canadian. "Newcomer" would generally be thought to label all the new arrivals, including, for example, immigrants from the United Kingdom (the largest single source of "newcomers"), who, provided they were of the right stuff, were taken to be acceptable members of the British Canadian community the moment they got off the boat.[4] Aliens "of other European birth," the census category into which most New Canadians then fell, while more properly descriptive, is clumsy – and in any case would exclude those many "New Canadians" born here or who arrived in the Dominion following secondary emigration from the United States and elsewhere.

The principal disadvantage of "New Canadian," of course, is obvious. The term describes an incredibly divergent grouping that exhibited a medley of responses to the war – the British Columbia Japanese fighting, literally, for the right to military service lumped together with Finnish social democrats, some of whom surely and earnestly hoped for revolution in their adopted as in their birth homeland. Since, however, the focus remains on British Canada in what follows, undue distortion is not apprehended. When a reader thinks, "But that just was not true in regard to this particular group; its patterns were different," he should continue to ask whether the distinction or the difference would have been noticed by the majority of other Canadians. The answer, generally, must be "no." Government policy was often informed, and more often impelled, by the same prodigal freemasonry.

"Patriot" is used here in the general wartime sense – somebody who supports the war effort, and is actively engaged in its prosecution. No moral quality should be assumed, and certainly none is assigned or implied here. "Dissenter" is preferred to wartime categories to describe opponents of the war ("traitor," for example) as plainly more neutral and inclusive. Invariably in wartime, "patriotic" and "dissenting" parties emerge, and equally inevitably are confirmed in their position in the course of the conflict. Initial enthusiasm becomes ardent commitment as threats are perceived and real sacrifices are made with more demanded. Opposition to the war or some element of war management tends to become total as costs are appreciated, and on occasion, as repression is experienced. The longer the war goes on, the more total dissent becomes, and the more obvious is the ensuing polarity. Dissent must be carefully handled as an integral part of war management because, of course, it alone represents an immediate threat to the war effort. If defeat is avoided, the nettle harvest the patriots sow might sometimes be anticipated, but it is seldom reaped during the war. A sitting wartime government cannot be expected to attempt to mediate impartially between the groups, however much tolerance it may demonstrate. A government at war desires victory. Patriots support the war effort, although they are sometimes singularly troublesome in calling for more vigorous prosecution or more stringent controls, as they always do.[5] Dissent, not patriotism, can place victory in jeopardy. In wartime, until late in the game, the general perception is that the peace can look after itself. Almost invariably this is a mistake.

1 "They Exceed in Stringency Anything We Know Here": State-Orchestrated Repression in Great War Canada

I want to say to the people of Canada this, free speech is one thing and sedition and treason is another thing. Look at the people of the United States. I admire them for the way they are putting down sedition and treason in their own country, and it is an example for us.

Mayor of Toronto Tommy Church, August 1917[1]

Let us begin by attempting to establish the quantity and quality of Canadian repression of some types of wartime dissent. The aim here is to establish not whether "repression" existed (it did inevitably), but whether Canadian practice was truly "repressive"; also whether any patterns can be established which might provide clues to motive. First, however, some more definitions are clearly necessary.

"Repression" and "repressive" are slippery and emotive concepts often used and more often implied. Each actually requires explanation beyond that provided by a dictionary, and "repressive" only means anything when valid comparisons are provided. A wartime policy constituted repression when it was not "business as usual" and when it contained mechanisms to mute, intimidate, punish, and otherwise silence opposition either to the war in general or to some item of wartime management in particular. If the real purpose of a policy can be construed to have been its probable effects on dissidents, then it was repression especially. A policy of conscription, for example, in itself did not necessarily constitute "repression." Conscription is nearly inevitable during a total war. The men must be found, or the war must be ended. Eventually that is the choice. The subordinate mechanisms put in place to make conscription effective by enforcing compliance and punishing opponents are invariably repression. Not all measures of repression are, however, truly "repressive"; many inevitably follow from the policies they are designed to safeguard. Opponents of conscription, for example, will always face repression wherever conscription is instituted, or the policy will not work at all. National registration (conscription without compulsion) always fails, everywhere attempted. A man who cannot be convinced to volunteer is unlikely to offer himself up if made to feel some shame and offered a "pretty please." "How many" opponents are intentionally impacted, "how harshly," and "how unusual" this treatment might be relative to that meted out to anti-conscriptionists in other comparable systems must be ascertained before the judgment that a policy is "repressive" can be tendered. The judgment that a measure was "repressive," therefore, qualifies its implementation as having been characterized by an exceptional degree of ruthlessness.

Measures of repression considered here are those wartime departures designed to ensure compliance with critical aspects of home front management (manpower controls especially), to restrain the expression of unacceptable or dangerous opinion (censorship, broadly defined), and the regulatory mechanism designed to control residents of doubtful allegiance (general anti-war dissidents and Alien Enemies inevitably occupying pride of place here). For our purposes, the logical comparisons are to British and American practice. Let us begin by indicating that, compared to these others, the government of Canada acted with exceptional vigour in specific directions, though ostensibly odd instances of relative tolerance remained.

While period statistics lack some detail, and while criminal statistics must always be used with care,[2] it is possible from open sources to provide an aggregate figure which indicates something like the total number of Canadian residents tried, by one method or another, for one or another act of opposition to the war. Appendix B summarizes this information and indicates something like the scale of wartime state repression in Canada. Round numbers are adequate for our task here, and alas, space constraints permit no fuller demonstration.

Between 1914 and 1919 approximately 7,000 Alien Enemies were convicted of offences against the Alien Restriction Regulations (ARRs) imposed under the authority of the War Measures Act (WMA) introduced in 1914.[3] Most of those so convicted were fined or received a short prison sentence, served in a local lock-up. Meanwhile, about 8,579 Alien Enemies were ordered detained, although this figure needs to be refined if it is to be useful:[4] 8,579 Alien Enemies were not detained for the duration, but at any time, and for any time, during the war. Most were not very long in the camps, and were released as soon as they were found productive employment. Some (about 817) were not detained by Canadian authorities, but were despatched to Canada from elsewhere in the British Empire.[5] At any one time about 2,000 Alien Enemies appear to have been behind the wire, including those brought to Canada from elsewhere.[6] At the end of the war, when the internment regime was ended, about 1,900 Alien Enemies were ultimately expelled as incorrigibles. We should note, of course, that most of those interned appear to have been either enemy army reservists resident in Canada (and therefore, properly speaking, POWs)[7] or individuals who were held to have indicated by some action or gesture that they were actually hostile to the Crown (and who were therefore "Alien Enemies" as comprehended by the law). Some Alien Enemy indigents were interned as a form of relief, but these do not appear to have been many.[8] About 81,144 Alien Enemies (of, perhaps, 800,000 subjects of enemy powers resident in Canada) were ultimately required to register with police.[9] All Alien Enemies, however defined, were subject to an exceptionally rigorous wartime judicial regime which effectively stripped them of most legal rights and safeguards, the right to habeas corpus in particular.[10] This could be a considerable handicap in Canada, where the courts were particularly active in orchestrating repression, and may well account, in part, for what appears to be the over-representation of New Canadians convicted of other species of wartime offence. In general, however, the wartime regime introduced to manage Alien Enemies was probably for most a cause of anxiety rather than anything more serious. Most Alien Enemies, however defined, were regulated but not harried in most jurisdictions for most of the war.

The scope of state repression visited on Canadians opposed to conscription is more easily ascertained, because this form of opposition was ultimately a crime, recorded as such, and because those guilty of it were almost by definition British subjects, which precluded recourse to extra-legal or administrative repression. The catalogue of those facing prosecution for this species of crime, therefore, is apt to constitute a relatively inclusive count of dissenters impacted by this form of repression. Great War statistics indicate that about 10,000 Canadian residents were convicted under the Militia Act for opposition to efforts to generate an effective Canadian army. About 1,500 of these were ultimately imprisoned, most of them for two years, as Military Services Act (MSA) evaders. Some few Canadians appear to have received more severe punishments. The MSA permitted imprisonment for up to five years, with the concurrence of the attorney general of Canada, and some opponents appear to have gone this route and received this sentence, although no aggregate figures survive. There appear to have been relatively few conscientious objectors (COs) in Canada, probably because members of the most obvious pools apt to produce COs – the peace churches – were excluded from the operation of the MSA from the outset.[11] Some hundreds of Canadians, nevertheless, were imprisoned in Canada when their conscientious objection was refused. As well, some hundreds of Canadians – Desmond Morton has 645 – were enrolled in the army, whether willing or not, and were subsequently detained in Britain for refusing lawful orders.[12] There was not much exceptional here, either in the number of individuals impacted or the way in which they were treated. Likewise, the mechanism by which Canada identified and selected conscripts was not unusual.[13] The powers assumed by the federal government in 1918 to enforce the MSA locally, however, represented a real departure for home front Canada, and some of them were of doubtful constitutionality. The assumption by the federal government of the power to unilaterally cancel exemptions and the federalization of policing and enforcement in the spring of 1918 were particularly problematic. Constitutional issues notwithstanding, the new powers were used, and an enforcement mechanism had emerged by the end of the war which must have made – and which was designed to make – the lives of the non-compliant extremely difficult.[14]

The scale of the repression visited on opponents of other sorts of manpower control, however, is more difficult to ascertain. It is true that the government ultimately assembled some frightening powers: nationalization and militarization of critical industries if this were deemed necessary;[15] the federalization of law enforcement when provincial efforts were insufficient;[16] pre-emptive detention for labour organizers judged to be hostile to the war effort;[17] the outright proscription of a long list of working-class and socialist organizations deemed to be dangerous;[18] immediate, mandatory enlistment to the army of any agitator advocating or participating in a strike or lockout, for example.[19] Most such powers, however, do not appear to have been actually used very widely, whatever Order-in-Council might have provided. For example, while conscription appears to have been occasionally used as a threat – if you strike, you will lose MSA exemption and will be imprisoned if you will not serve – it does not appear to have actually been employed as a weapon by being focused at individuals, or at particular classes of dissenter, as was probably the case in Great War Britain.[20] In this aspect of home front management, the Canadian government appears to have been in the game of assembling powers and then holding them in reserve against, it seems, some more ultimate contingency than actually developed. Perhaps the powers were simply important because they could be the source of credible threats. No Canadians appear to have been actually imprisoned for violation of the WMA following from opposition to government attempts to control or restructure workplaces (manpower controls more broadly defined), although any attempt at effective opposition to such measures was probably illegal already under peacetime Canadian law.[21] Even in 1918, when the government did begin to move to organize industries and workplaces judged to be critical to the Allied war effort, its agents, faced with local opposition, generally restricted their repression to the occasional utterance of warnings, albeit bloodcurdling warnings. The threat to expropriate a particular workplace and militarize its operation obviously represented rather a significant departure from early war *laissez-faire*, and could only be taken seriously by both workers and employers. No such threat, however, appears to have been actually acted upon.

Censorship, in the end, was the answer of choice to most problems, and Canadian practice was uniquely harsh. By 1917, expressions of opinion critical of government efforts or which were considered harmful to the war effort in any fashion would most certainly bring any sort of dissenter to the attention of the censorship authorities and generally of the police and the courts shortly thereafter.[22] At least six thousand persons were sentenced for actions contrary to the WMA or various Orders-in-Council. In general, many such malefactors appear to have expressed (or to have harboured) opposition to the war or to some necessary element of wartime management. Those who failed to heed warnings, and who were censored by the mechanism provided by Canadian courts, appear to have been dealt with quite ruthlessly: substantial fines and imprisonment were not unusual. If opposition took the form of actual libel – dissent expressed in print – then presses could be seized,[23] and the charge in Canada not uncommonly was Criminal Code sedition. Canadian courts, called upon to arraign dissidents, were easily convinced and punitive. Some interesting precedents ultimately emerged. A man observing a recruiting meeting failed to raise his hand when asked to do so to demonstrate support for the war effort. The result? A beating administered by outraged patriots followed by thirty days in the jug for interfering with a recruiting meeting.[24] A man was convicted for criminal sedition despite the fact that the objectionable words in question had been uttered after the war was already over (unbeknownst to the speaker).[25] This conviction was repeatedly upheld on appeal. A speaker was convicted for sedition in that he should have known that his expression of opinion was certain to lead to serious civil disorder – disorder not committed or advocated by him, but directed against him by enraged patriots.[26] A railroad worker was fined $2,000 and jailed for three years for distributing prohibited literature, and for being suspected of being a Bolshevik.[27] This list could be attenuated to considerably greater length, but the point is obvious: in seeking to advocate their views, Canadian dissenters trod lightly, necessarily. It should be added that late war regulations delineated an entirely exceptional range of media as being of interest to the censors, and indicated rather inclusively objectionable subjects and sources.[28] In the extreme, Canadians could be (and were) convicted of expressing the temperance message over-vigorously.[29] Indeed, they could be convicted for testifying in court to the accuracy of a temperance advocate's facts, if the facts were sufficiently inconvenient. The army believed temperance advocacy to be prejudicial to recruiting and in some forms tantamount to crypto-nativist anti-imperialism, unacceptable within the context of the Great War.[30] Other Canadians were convicted for possessing banned material, even if it could not be established that they had read the thing, much less agreed with it. Canadian law uniquely held that possession of banned material could be held to indicate agreement with what it contained and signal the attempt to disseminate the message.[31] What the material might actually contain was irrelevant. It was illegal because the censor had said so.[32] Possession alone could be taken, by 1918, to constitute sedition and, if a Canadian were unfortunate enough to consort with a wretch in possession of such filth, conspiracy. More demonstrations could be piled up, but this selection should suffice to establish that the Canadian censorship regime was thoroughgoing in conception as in practice. By 1917 it would have been rather hard for a Canadian to express any opinion in any way, in any medium, or to be considered to harbour any thought conceivably prejudicial to the government's war policy and not be in danger of prosecution, apt to lead to rather heavy punishment. It could be dangerous, even, to be acquainted with such a person, particularly if he were a member of one of a number of organizations that, from time to time, found themselves the particular objects of government loathing.

18 Polarity, Patriotism, and Dissent in Great War Canada, 1914–1919

Table 1.1. Offence by year and type

	War Measures Act Summary Procedure	Alien Restriction Regulation	War Measures Act	Militia Act	Sedition	Treason
1912	0	0	0	19	0	0
1913	0	0	0	13	0	0
1914	0	0	0	27	1	0
1915	0	0	0	74	7	15
1916	0	0	156	725	31	4
1917	0	2,467	31	765	15	1
1918	2,582	2,832	15	3,713	21	4
1919	1,207	1,072	0	3,990	19	0

Note: Table indicates global "war crimes" by type. The latter war "spike" is obvious ... even impressive.

Meanwhile, several hundred more persons were tried for more serious offences with application to the war – treason, sedition – under the Criminal Code, as amplified, interpreted, and enforced during the war emergency. Most of the traitors were apprehended attempting to assist Alien Enemies in making their escape from the Dominion – this defined as "treason" by a 1915 decision unique to Canada.[33] Sedition trials were far more common in Canada than elsewhere in the Common Law area and can be thought to have constituted a particularly severe form of censorship: indeed, it is very difficult from period records to ascertain where censorship left off and sedition began, so thoroughly was regulation for censorship informed by notions of what constituted criminal sedition, and so perfectly did the censors come to define what sedition meant. It is probable that many others were tried for Criminal Code offences rooted in opposition to the war – for "breach of the peace," violation of the Master and Servant Act (i.e., striking), rioting, or even common assault following a fist fight – although no assumed figures will be included here, since war-related offences cannot now be separated from the others.[34]

There were, therefore, at least 24,000 wartime political trials[35] in Canada – trials of those who found themselves at odds with some element of war management. Given the remarkable decline in other crimes registered during the war, Canadian courts in some particularly engaged jurisdictions[36] must have experienced a significantly increased burden of business, particularly in the bitterly divisive latter war years. Sentences ranged all the way from minor fines to, in at least one case, life imprisonment.[37] Amy Shaw indicates that some conscientious objectors received sentences of life imprisonment, and that the incident of this sort of sentence increased the longer the war progressed.[38] To be clear, Shaw's "lifers" were objectors who, having found their way into the army and on a boat to France, found themselves subject to the Army Act while in an active theatre of war. Those under consideration here appeared before civilian courts, properly constituted. Most of these trials took place in the war's last years, with a crescendo reached in most categories in the last years of the war emergency, 1917–19.

Regional differences in the rigour with which opposition to the war was punished were striking. The vast majority of "war crimes" trials occurred in British Canada as defined in the Introduction. In respect of some species of charge – offences against the Militia Act or prosecution for Criminal Code sedition, for example – the proportion registered in this part of Canada was higher still, as tables 1.2, 1.3, and 1.4 illustrate.

Table 1.2. Total "war crimes" by province and year

	PEI	NS	NB	PQ	ON	MN	SK	AL	BC
1912	0	0	0	8	4	0	2	3	4
1913	0	0	0	0	7	1	1	0	2
1914	0	0	0	0	16	1	1	2	4
1915	0	2	14	14	60	6	9	6	4
1916	0	32	21	163	548	37	41	51	24
1917	0	35	22	161	1822	216	724	345	92
1918	1	104	27	110	4,462	389	1,604	857	1,452
1919	15	91	58	2,639	2,706	289	663	365	380

Note: Regional differentiations are obvious and illustrate dramatically the very different wartime environments existing in Canada's various regions. The 1919 "spike" in prosecutions in Quebec requires explanation. These were MSA evaders, tried under the Militia Act. Since the 1919 judicial statistical year covered the period September 1918–September 1919, in the main this was not repression but book clearing. As appendix B indicates, the typical punishment received, at this juncture, in this jurisdiction, was a small fine.

Table 1.3. "War crimes" by province, by year, weighted for population

	PEI	NS	NB	PQ	ON	MN	SK	AL	BC	Canada
1914	0	0	0	0	0.46	0.16	0.15	0.39	0.74	0.24
1915	0	0.29	2.87	0.5	1.71	0.94	1.32	1.16	0.74	1.25
1916	0	4.68	3.07	5.86	15.62	5.78	6	9.83	4.4	9.17
1917	0	5.12	4.51	5.79	51.95	33.75	106	66.47	16.88	42.46
1918	0.77	15.23	5.53	3.95	127.23	60.78	234.85	165.13	266.42	90.06
1919	11.53	13.32	11.89	94.83	77.16	45.16	97.07	70.33	69.72	72.06

Note: Table 1.3 weighs for population, by dividing the total number of war crimes by the percentage that the population of each province constituted of the Canadian whole. The Canadian average, from totals, is provided for comparison.

Table 1.4. Total number of "war crime" convictions per year/percentage of the population, less convictions under the Alien Restriction Regulations

	PEI	NS	NB	PQ	ON	MN	SK	AL	BC	Canada
1914	0	0	0	0	0.46	0.16	0.15	0.39	0.74	0.24
1915	0	0.29	2.87	0.5	1.71	0.94	1.32	1.16	0.74	1.15
1916	0	4.69	4.3	5.86	15.63	5.8	6	9.82	4.4	9.17
1917	0	5.12	4.5	5.75	11.17	11.88	6.8	7.13	8.07	17.79
1918	0.77	13.03	5.33	3.95	113.94	51.72	118.89	92.49	244.03	61.74
1919	11.54	13.03	11.89	94.83	58.86	26.56	75.84	50.29	58.9	61.34

Note: Table 1.4 indicates something like the relative willingness of Canadians in the various provinces to persecute their neighbours, other than those subject to an exceptional legal regime. The similarity between the patterns existing in Ontario and the West – in "British Canada" as here defined – is striking, as is the relative disengagement of the Maritime provinces and Quebec, by this measure. BC's remarkable late/postwar showing corresponded to a rash of WMA summary procedure prosecutions concurrent with the "Red scare" – particularly intense in British Columbia.

Even though Alien Enemies were not liable for military service (and, therefore, could not normally be tried under the Militia Act), and even if prosecution for violation of Alien Restriction Regulations (ARRs) is excluded, it seems likely that half of those convicted were New Canadians. New Canadians were particularly at risk if they were thought to be opposed, or if they expressed themselves in opposition to, the war in general or any element of war management. In this case, they would, by definition, be held to have forfeited the King's protection and to be his actual enemies, required to register with police and free only at the discretion of local Alien Registrars and police authorities.

There was repression in wartime Canada, as in all combatant states. Twenty-four thousand Canadians, at least, had special cause to know this. Was Canadian prosecution of dissidents and the non-compliant particularly ruthless? Was Canadian practice actually repressive? Consider how the scale of Canadian repression measured against that of the most persuasive comparatives. To a certain extent, comparison of quantity here can speak to quality, and even suggest intention.

During the Great War, the population of the United Kingdom was approximately six times greater than that of Canada; that of the United States, then as now, twelve times. One hundred and forty-four thousand war trials – most in a two-year period, in half the country – would surely have raised eyebrows in the United Kingdom, though "how high" would be difficult to calculate exactly now. Consolidated warrelated criminal statistics were not kept in British jurisdictions during the war. Wartime British practice was to register war-specific charges under the applicable peacetime statute when this was possible, and only after the war did Home Office statisticians attempt to sort things out. Some things, however, are quite clear. In its regulatory and judicial treatment of Alien Enemies, Britain was much harsher than Canada. There were, in the course of the war emergency, 54,784 crimes successfully prosecuted under the Alien Restriction Act in England and Wales alone; that is, Britain's much smaller immigrant community was the object of about eight times more successful prosecutions. Similarly, in 1914, there were only 322,124 resident aliens in the United Kingdom, of whom 13,546 men (12,318 British born) and 10,505 women were subsequently classified as Alien Enemies.[39] Nevertheless, by the end of the war, Britain had interned 65,000 people – considerably more than it had initially classified as Alien Enemies. On the other hand, Canada was much less tolerant of anti-conscriptionists, in British Canada anyway. Statistics indicate 2,021 British convictions in the judicial years 1915–17 for offences under the National Registration Act. There were, as we have seen, approximately 10,000 Canadian convictions under the Militia Act in the course of the war. In the end, something like 5,000 Britons went to prison or detention for refusing to serve, with about 1,543 "absolutists" refusing subsequent offers of pardon. During the war years, nearly 1,500 Canadians were committed to prison for violations of the Militia Act, with, it seems probable, hundreds of others intimidated into the army or otherwise punished. Canadians refusing orders once deemed to be enlisted, in any case, remained in the glasshouse long after their British comrades had been returned to civilian jurisdiction or paroled as harmless. Likewise, Defence of the Realm Act (DORA: the British equivalent of the WMA) prosecutions appear to have been relatively few, setting aside those fined, for example, under the Highway Act or various municipal by-laws for crimes like "driving with lights on during a black-out" – although there appears to have been a prodigious number of these. The director of public prosecution, generally responsible for handling the prosecution of dissidents, simply harried very few Britons and those not very vigorously. In the judicial district of England and Wales, for example, he sought and successfully prosecuted on behalf of the government only 169 persons in the course of the war. A total of 199 Englishmen and Welshmen were convicted in court of "offences against the state and public order." There were no sedition trials. Two traitors were convicted (one in 1914 and another in 1916) ... but they were actual traitors, and were accordingly executed. In the end, HMG sought very few prosecutions, and tended to consider and reconsider every major act of repression individually at the highest level.[40] Keep in mind, once again, that there were only about six and a half million British subjects in Canada, and that the great majority of convictions, and the most ruthless sentencing, occurred in a community of perhaps four million persons (i.e., British Canada). The relative forbearance of HMG in dealing with wartime dissidents by this comparison is what is truly striking.[41] Only in its treatment of Alien Enemies did British ruthlessness exceed Canada's, and that by a considerable margin.

Consolidated American statistics for wartime offences do not exist, since criminal justice rests in state jurisdiction. As a consequence, consolidated statistics concerning "war crimes" do not exist. However, Alexander Mitchell Palmer, Woodrow Wilson's attorney general, reported 877 convictions of 1,956 prosecutions commenced under the Espionage and Seditions Acts by 1920. Meanwhile, pre-emptive raids directed by Palmer ("the Palmer raids") started in November 1919 – just as the situation in Canada was returning to normal – and netted by January 1920 approximately 16,000 suspected anarchists and communists, of whom 249 were deported (compare to about 1,900 "incorrigibles" ultimately kicked out of Canada).[42] There were, it seems, some thousands of Americans prosecuted for offences against the Selective Services Act, though the aggregate number is difficult to establish. In the United States, what the Act meant was essentially how it was locally interpreted. As in Britain, however, the most effective American repression of dissent remained "out of doors"; indeed, one American magistrate released a man charged under the Espionage Act for making anti-war statements on the grounds that the most likely consequence of this particular disloyal speech in the venue chosen would not have been the disaffection of the listeners but a broken head.[43] Some Americans, certainly, received stinging sentences for expressions of prohibited opinion – fifteen or even twenty years. It did not matter. All such sentences were commuted when the legislation under which they were registered was repealed. Even while such sentences were being imposed, public and privy misgivings were already very apparent among many of the most influential inhabitants of the American government. In any case, it must be conceded that 288,000 "war crimes" trials in the United States would scarcely have been taken as evidence that America had what it took to see the fight for liberty through to a successful conclusion. Legal action on this scale probably would have invited rebellion.

To assert that Canada's wartime domestic regime in general was relatively repressive in scale is true: a matter of record. Its treatment of the opponents of conscription and of "thought criminals" (i.e., those who fell afoul of censorship regulation, or some other statute with implication for expression or opinion) was particularly rigorous, and, in this aspect of war management, contemporaries at home and in allied nations suspected by 1918 that something unusual was happening. The consolidated Canadian censorship regulations, C.P. Scott of the the *Manchester Guardian* considered,

> [e]xceed in stringency anything we know here. The public will be allowed to know – and so far as the Government is able to control it, to think – only what happens to suit the purpose of the small group of individuals who for the time being are Masters of the Machine of State.
>
> Such an arrangement could, perhaps, be defended if Governments never were ignorant and never made mistakes. We know from our own experiences that neither of these assumptions can be made.
>
> They are deliberately intensifying the evils of censorship in Canada ...
>
> Under such *ukases* it is possible for the Government to suppress any opinion that is distasteful to it. The public is allowed to know only so far as the Government wishes.[44]

The Canadian response: monitor the Canadian papers that had printed Scott's remonstrance, in however abbreviated a form – an opinion which, had it been expressed in Canada, would certainly have led to police action and which might well have ended with seizure of the *Guardian* press and premises. In any case action, almost certainly, would have been taken against Scott for breach of censorship, in criticizing censorship. Rodolphe Lemieux, previously Liberal minister of labour and no civil rights activist – he was the author of the notorious Lemieux Act, after all – concurred with Scott's assessment, and emphatically, poignantly regretted his modest part in permitting the formulation of legislation turned to such repressive purpose:

> I need not say that my heart is in this war, but I regret that I ever gave my assent to the War Measures Act as it has been framed and applied. The country is being shorn of its liberties; Parliament of its constitutional rights. It is being shorn of its privileges and it ancient usages. The constitution has become a by-word in Canada. The country is governed by Order-in-Council passed before, during and after session of Parliament under the shadow pretension of winning the war.[45]

Only in its treatment of Alien Enemies would it be possible to register a verdict of "not guilty" to the charge that Canada acted in an unusually repressive fashion, if formal, state-organized, judicial, or regulatory proceedings are taken as the measure of repression. It may be, on the other hand, that Canada's Alien Enemies were repressed with great relative ruthlessness, but not formally by the state.

Let us turn to the question of motivation, the central issue in what follows. There was repression in Canada, and in some aspects of its practice Canada acted exceptionally repressively. Why did the government of Canada choose this path?

We should start by remembering that some decisions were not Canada's to make. Some issues could simply not be addressed by the Canadian government in isolation. The impact of the imperial imperative on Canadian treatment of Alien Enemies, for example, is obvious. Canadian citizenship policy, including the denaturalization of Alien Enemies, their loss of all substantial legal rights in 1914, their 1917 exclusion from voters' lists under the Wartime Elections Act (1917), and even the internment of certain classifications of Alien Enemies (army reservists for example), followed from common imperial policies, produced at a time when it was obnoxious for any dominion to have policies regarding such matters unique to itself. Canadians were, during the Great War, British subjects in the fullest sense of the term. The Common Law was a seamless whole to an extent that modern Canadians would find curious. In consideration of such issues, Canada did not choose a repressive policy but rather implemented one negotiated elsewhere, which in the context of Canadian conditions became more repressive than might have been considered necessary. As a consequence, it is probably true that, left to its own devices, Canada might well have devised a regime for Alien Enemies still less rigorous than the comparatively tolerant policy actually introduced.

Similarly, the example of the United States was always persuasive then as now. The fact of neutral America, prior to April 1917, almost certainly inhibited Canadian action in some sectors of national mobilization – war-driven social-economic restructuring and effective propaganda, for example – which might have provided alternatives to those repressive practices preferred, particularly censorship. Moreover, with the American entry to the war, some elements of American practice, or perhaps more appropriately the fact of American executive (and shortly thereafter public) hysteria, powerfully influenced Canadian public assessment of what was appropriate – what constituted suitable policy. In particular, the latter war agitation to crush all species of dissent, pre-emptively if necessary, and to make conscription truly effective nationwide owed much to the American example and Canadian shame that the Dominion had not already instituted such thoroughgoing solutions itself. The postwar revision of the immigration and sedition laws in 1919, as well, was quite plainly influenced in detail by the highly persuasive example set south of the border.

Other Canadian policies appear to have followed from intelligence provided from London or Washington perhaps describing American or British reality, but with little Canadian implication, though this was not always appreciated at the time. For example, the great Bolshevik scare of 1917–19 (and the resultant restrictive alien and labour regimes that developed in response) appears to have resulted in large measure from the Canadian government's over-credulous acceptance of intelligence assessments produced elsewhere. While Canadian police authorities, through 1918, continued to insist that there was no evidence of real danger,[46] London and Washington said otherwise, and with the prime minister in London and American authorities so vocal, they got the better hearing. The curious late war, early postwar delusion that revolution was actually imminent, and that Bolsheviki-cum-Wobblies were behind it, was American. No less an authority than the American attorney general, Palmer, went so far as to set a date – May Day 1920 – for the North American instalment of the World Revolution. Nightmares not of Canada's dreaming sometimes powerfully affected government policy, and not for the last time.

In some cases, Canadian policy appears to have been an amalgam of local preference impacted by offshore example and inhibition. The relative absence of economic, workplace, and manpower (other than conscription) controls, for example, is curious. No doubt government lassitude here derived in part from the fact that the government simply did not identify a place for itself in the economic organization of the home front until the last year of the war, so that the war ended before restructuring was possible and therefore repression necessary. On the other hand, the United States was neutral until April 1917, and it must have been difficult to imagine how a dependent, integrated, export-based, and much smaller economy could be effectively regulated given that fact. Perhaps also a penny-pinching government had gathered from British practice that repression of labour dissidents worked best when accompanied by amelioration – sometimes expensive amelioration – of working-class grievances. Since the government really had no intention of spending money to ameliorate anything, perhaps it seemed better to leave the economy to sort itself out insofar as possible. Censorship of such few labour dissidents as might emerge was probably the best, and was certainly the cheapest, policy. On the other hand, it might well be that no Canadians were prosecuted overtly for opposition to workplace or labour control because Canadian provisions for censorship were sufficiently severe to render repression specific to the workplace unnecessary. What was the point of imprisoning a striker as a striker, for example, if it were already an offence simply to advocate a work stoppage, irrespective of its ever taking place? If the intent and advocacy were illegal, then why worry about the action? Some kinds of repression common elsewhere, in other words, may not have been used in Canada because other tools were selected. Some tools may not have been available because the government of Canada never placed them in its box, from preference for others.

All of this notwithstanding, it should be noted that with few exceptions the general pattern was for the Canadian government acting at home to assume domestic powers greater than those ever achieved by the "total war" Lloyd George government or the "win the war" Wilson administration, and to use them in a much more openly ruthless fashion. Indeed, a striking, and revealing, feature of the repression of dissent in Canada was that government never attempted to disguise what was happening. "Repression," in internal correspondence, is described as just that. The word was used openly without, it seems, many misgivings public or private, official or unofficial, that the employment of intentionally repressive practices might not be appropriate.

In comparison, British alterations to peacetime practice were introduced as lamentable wartime deviations when they were admitted at all. After the war, Britain quickly disassembled most of its regulatory machinery, many of the most important features of which were permissive not prohibitive – what the government permitted its supporters to do rather than what it prohibited its opponents from doing. To parade dissent openly, publicly, was always to invite a broken head from some enraged patriot, with the British government restricting its role to public pleas that it had no responsibility for protecting dissenters from the consequences of advocating their beliefs, while conspiring to ensure that those consequences were realized. Leaders of dissenting opinion and the apparatus of dissent were the primary targets of HMG's regulatory attention, rather than individual malcontents. Silencing these would render dissent, however widespread, ineffective, leaving the government to get on with the business of winning the war. With peace, tolerance would return, the majesty of the King's justice unsullied in the meantime.

In the United States, during and after the war, there was a concerted attempt to maintain the illusion that the government had done as little as possible to violate constitutional rights, and that patriotic organization (including censorship and propaganda) was the work of volunteers. The Wilson government agitated for the power to deal with domestic enemies from 1915. Congress, however, could not be easily convinced. The resultant structure was ramshackle – "official vigilantism" perhaps its best description. The emergency safely over, repressive Acts – the Espionage Act, the Sedition Act, state ordinances dealing with sabotage – were repealed and the imprisoned released. The whole episode, it appears, had been a monstrous aberration, even a mistake, during which, happily, a practicable doctrine of freedom of expression had been defined. In acting repressively during the war, it appears, America had actually been reaffirming its basic convictions, even if, at the time, these were embodied in a few minority opinions and overturned judgments.[47] In short, the British and Americans, with their governments, were more than a little ashamed of the mechanisms of repression necessitated by the war.

In contrast, the government of Canada does not appear to have been ashamed, ever. There were no paroles and certainly no apologies until very recently. While difficult to disentangle in retrospect, the thing was simple for Great War patriots. Any form of opposition to the war was crime – likely sedition, if not treason – and all necessitated legal action. The only thing, really, was to decide which flail to select. The general effect of Canadian wartime regulation was that power was echeloned – several mechanisms constructed and the appropriate one to answer a particular incident of dissent chosen from the lot. Often the rationale behind new regulation was not so much to create new powers as to facilitate prosecution while reducing all "war crimes" to matters of fact. A jury was not asked whether an opinion was objectionable, but whether a man possessed a book the police had found in his possession; not whether an evader should be exempted, but whether he had, in fact, reported, notification having been delivered by post to his declared residence. In the event, the weapon chosen to combat a particular offence was selected to ensure the speediest conviction, and the most appropriate punishment, publicly administered. In most of Canada, the most dangerous enemy of a wartime dissenter was an activist magistrate. In Britain and the United States, the fists of angry patriots were apt to impose the most extreme sanction. The nature of the forum in which dissenters were typically arraigned speaks volumes about the extent of inhibition, on the one hand, and its absence on the other.

In this regard, a striking, and enlightening, feature of the wartime mechanism for dealing with dissent is how much of it had been previewed in peace; the extent to which emergency measures simply defined the wartime operation of powers the government always had. Much wartime repression followed from mechanisms built into the Canadian legal system to deal with nineteenth-century challenges to the emerging Canadian state. The Militia Act, for example, provided for the routine punishment of opponents, and opponents were routinely punished. The Criminal Code retained the charge of "sedition," and the seditious were arraigned. At times of crisis, traitors were dealt with according to their deserts. Similarly, some wartime innovations were ultimately grafted onto the postwar legal system as useful weapons to be held in reserve against some future threat. Some still survive there. British historians concerned with the Great War home front have tended to forget that a major part of the war at home was the battle against dissent, so stealthy was the campaign against it. American legalists have almost uniformly indicated wartime measures as a regrettable departure from the norm. Canadian legal historians of wartime repression, often of a liberal inclination, have generally noted – often with some outrage – that most of what Canada did during the war was consistent with its prewar and postwar, wartime and peacetime practice, intentionally repressive throughout.[48]

The attitude of the Canadian government to censorship was particularly revealing. The government frankly admitted that it was acting repressively to control thought and expression, and that it did not approve of certain ideas expressed in any form – would not permit even the possession (quite apart from the production) of publications held to carry the contagion; did not approve of Canadian residents thinking certain things; was capable even of taking action against those who failed to say the appropriate, approved things. It did not seek to manage expression of dissent or to counter-mobilize the population until very late in the day. It invited opponents – all opponents, and not just opposition leaders or activists – to take notice that they had best keep their thoughts to themselves. Better still if they cleansed their minds of antiwar pollution before some act or omission brought them before a magistrate. In Canada, regulation for censorship was informed by, amplified, and explicated Criminal Code provision for sedition – a crime, the very anteroom to treason, to be denounced and publicly punished by whatever means proved most convenient to the state. Tolerance of such opinion was not a virtue but war-losing, nation-breaking lassitude. Free speech was not a right, which alas might have to be abridged in wartime, but a privilege the extent of which would be defined by the government's timely apprehension of danger, in wartime as in peacetime.

Canada's wartime regime was, therefore, also relatively and intentionally repressive in quality. In some areas, more people were more harshly affected, with greater evident relish. Canada acted repressively because it wanted to; it had always planned to if necessary. Some general reasons for this preference can be adduced, rooted in Canadian history and in the nature of Canada, and therefore not specific to the Great War itself.

Perhaps the Canada of 1914 was, in some measure, the Canada of the "peace, order and good government" myth. It is revealing, for example, that Canada did not just punish certain kinds of dissident with greater vigour and enthusiasm in wartime than kindred systems: it harried all criminals at all times with unusual gusto. In 1914, for example, in the United Kingdom, there were 14,671 criminal indictments and 11,699 convictions, with a further 94,243 summary trials and 43,972 summary convictions. Britain punished a total of 58,653 criminals in all venues for all offences.[49] In little Canada, that same judicial year, magistrates tried 28,007 Canadians for statutory offences and convicted 21,438, with another 161,597 convicted summarily – a total of 183,035 convictions.[50] In the year immediately before the war, therefore, Canada, with one-fifth the population of the United Kingdom, labelled three times as many of its inhabitants "criminal." A Canadian was fifteen times more likely than a Briton to be branded "criminal" in 1914. Canada may never have been a police state, but Edwardian Canada appears to have been a well-policed state without much of a sense of humour when an infraction of the law was apprehended. Therefore, Canada was relatively more active in punishing "war criminals" probably in part because it punished all criminals with greater vigour than kindred systems. Canadians apparently believed that crime merited punishment. Canadian action against dissent was repressive because Canada *preferred* repression. It was simply in Canada's nature to make this choice. Peace and order implied law and order, which necessitated, it seems, vigilant courts and the punishment of the recalcitrant and wicked – functions, no doubt, of good government. Tolerance of wartime opponents rather than repression of dissent would require explanation as the exception to business as usual. If this is so, it is the relative forbearance of the Canadian government, faced with the terrible crisis of the war, which is astounding.

We should remember as well, in this regard, that Canadian laws – indeed, the Canadian legal system – had been conceived in a distinct context, and the particular characteristics of this context became more important during the war. Henry Kissinger wrote that "[c]ohesive societies can regulate themselves through custom which reveals that disputes are peripheral. Societies which contain fundamental schisms must rely on law, the definition of a compulsory relationship."[51] Canada was, quite simply, a much less coherent society than Britain, in particular, and therefore could less afford tolerance and required more openly coercive legal mechanisms. Canada, unlike Britain, needed to mandate a central body of belief. It was compelled to be a compulsory society if it were to gel at all. Britain disliked new departures because the greater the recourse to exceptional legal action, the more it became clear that really significant division had emerged. America was very diverse, but tended to deny the implications of that fact (self-evident, universal, inalienable rights are difficult to reconcile with the fact of diversity and variable response), and therefore in times of emergency employed exceptional regimes, thereafter repudiated. Great War Canada assumed that any question of significance would produce dangerous divides as a matter of course. Therefore, Canadian law was broadly defined and included provision for emergency. Canadian statutes designed to meet the eventuality of conflict, or the operation of which would probably lead to conflict, routinely contained mechanisms for the repression of dissent. Canadian laws had not been calculated to reinforce consensus but assumed social conflict and were therefore designed to preserve the supremacy of the established system against threats within and without.[52] In 1914 Canada knew how to deal with the seditious, treacherous, and reluctant because it had encountered them, named them so, and dealt with them before. The events of 1775, 1812, and 1837 were powerful folk memories, particularly in British Canada. There were many alive in 1914 who had served with the Canadian militia during the Fenian raids (1866-70) – invasion from without accompanied by treachery within. Some who had served against Louis Riel in Saskatchewan in 1885 saw service again in this war. Principle, in Canada, could look after itself: defence of well-established practice and loyalties was the thing. In the nineteenth century, the final consequence of a challenge to the state had typically been a trial in which societal norms and political expectations were reaffirmed. Political trials, Kenneth McNaught writes, were essentially dramas designed to demonstrate the certainty of the state and the cost of opposition. The accused, in exchange for clemency, were expected to participate in this drama – and invariably did. The people of British Canada, in particular, had always constituted a most gratifyingly appreciative audience at such performances, repeated many times through 1920.[53] Herbert Marx considers, finally, that the relatively harsh nature of Canadian wartime regulation derived in part from the diversity of Canada, particularly the fact that in Canada the Crown is divisible and powers are shared between levels of government. Effective wartime government, however, is unified and central. Canadian federalism – governmental incoherence rooted in diversity – in essence reinforced the disposition of the central government to assert itself more overtly in an emergency than some other, closely kindred systems seemingly required.[54] Marx's opinion should not be easily set aside. He was, after all, a professor of constitutional law in Quebec during the 1970 "Quebec Crisis," subsequently justice minister of the province, and then a judge on the Quebec Superior Court. Lack of coherence – in this case, governmental incoherence derived from Canadian diversity – made and sometimes makes the repressive choice the only choice. This is a significant argument, and one we will have good cause to remember shortly.

As war dissent began to emerge, therefore, it found the Canadian legal system already armed with what it took to be the remedy. Such dissent found agents of that system, in British Canada anyway, willing, wanting, and waiting to administer the corrective. It found the federal government predetermined that it would see its writ run – against inevitable enemies necessarily, against patriots and provinces if need be; whatever the constitution might suggest and however much other levels of government might protest. Repression of dissent was something to be expected. Once again, it would have been odd if wartime dissenters had been tolerated.

However, to understand that Canadian wartime practice was simply an amplification of peacetime practice only gets us so far. There is the fact, for example, of massive regional differentiation in the ruthlessness with which wartime repression was administered. Why were there many, many more prosecutions in Ontario than in Quebec, even for species of war crime in consideration of which we might anticipate the reverse? Why were Alien Enemies in Canada far less likely to be interned for violation of ARRs, but far more likely to face prosecution for breach of censorship than appears to have been the case elsewhere? Why was censorship so exceptionally ruthless in Canada, while there was little provision for propaganda, the "positive" side of the equation, in the battle for public space? Why harry anti-conscriptionists so vigorously, but employ so little compulsion against other species of manpower dissident? In a total war is a man who will not parade more dangerous than one seeking to organize a strike? Lloyd George surely did not think so. How to account for the "spikes" – the 1917–18 spike in ARR convictions obvious across British Canada, the 1918–19 spike in WMA prosecutions especially notable in British Columbia, the postwar spike in Militia Act convictions in Quebec – illustrating regional differentiation and marking particularly ruthless enforcement of various elements of the wartime legal regime locally, when these are so obviously disassociated from any real requirement or actual increase in the scale or effectiveness of dissent? These are only a few of the more striking features of Canadian practice for which general explanations cannot account, and for answer to which we will have to look to specific context – to the wartime patterns particular to Great War Canada.

Finally, there are also problems with the arithmetic of the thing. In a total war, governments make choices designed to maximize national clout. Some aspects of Canadian practice, however, had very problematic secondary effects. The arithmetic quite plainly did not work. The costs were simply too heavy, the impact too immediately divisive and likely to be lasting. Satisfaction in crime well punished was much. It could not be, however, sufficient recompense for national disarray evident with gloomy prognoses for the future. What is the point of a system of repression to make conscription effective if, for example, it requires more men to operate than it produces, as was probably the case with the MSA in parts of Canada? It was this sort of arithmetic which prevented Lloyd George from introducing conscription to Ireland, while allowing the number of exemptions granted to elements of Britain's disgruntled working class to increase throughout his tenure in office, and particularly during the last desperate year of the war. Borden, in comparison, hitched up his britches and not only introduced the MSA but actually sought to enforce it, from Sea to Sea and from the River even unto the end of the Earth, come what might. This decision requires explanation if it were not simply an error. Similarly, how could a Canadian government define "victory" as a maximum effort for Britain accompanied by the permanent alienation of parts of Canada? How would it be if, having worked very hard to convince New Canadians to come to Canada, the government adopted wartime policies which slowed or even reversed the flow? Why would a sitting government, more to the point, accept policies which even its supporters, convinced partisans, indicated as likely to produce a reaction which would keep the party which introduced them out of office for a generation? The implementation of such a system must be a mistake, unless there are other considerations – a higher mathematics – which make the decision comprehensible.

Let us turn, in what follows, to the particular context in which a disposition to act repressively developed and was embodied as it was. Doing so will make the "higher mathematics" obvious. Robert Borden did not make mistakes. He did the best he could in the circumstances in which his government found itself, wartime Canada being what it was.

2 "Because They Are Totally and Exclusively Canadian": A Clash of Canadas

I would draw your attention to the fact that we have conditions to contend with in Canada which do not exist in the United Kingdom. There you have a small area peopled with a homogenous population; here we have a huge territory with a comparatively scarce population including settlements of people of Alien Enemy birth.

Colonel F.E. Chambers, chief censor, 30 September 1917[1]

We must look within Canadian society for the reasons for the patterns informing Canada's management of dissent at home during the Great War. Canadian society gave Great War dissent a particular form, while constituting the general context in which it developed and conditioning also the nature of any response. Canadian patterns were different, therefore, because Canada was different, productive of a different type of dissent and a particular reaction. Let us start with some generalization which will be amply justified in what follows.

What made Canadian dissent different from that found in Britain or the United States was its strong regional, sectarian, and communal flavour. In Britain, social and ideological cleavages underlay most dissent. In the United States, there were notoriously disaffected communities that opposed entry to the war, the Germans and the Irish particularly. These were, however, dispersed across the nation, though there was a heavy concentration of German Americans in the Midwest and Irish Americans in the principal cities of the East Coast. The United States, however, does not have a Quebec. The American West was not in the process of being settled, but rather had been settled in the course of the previous century. The United States did not have in 1917, therefore, an Alberta or Saskatchewan. Canada, in the basic facts of its composition, was far more like South Africa or Ireland than like either of the two greater English-speaking powers with which it normally compared itself. While there certainly were ideological and class factors predisposing Canadians to support or oppose the war, basic tribal affiliation was a much more important factor, and to a much greater extent than was the case in the United States or the United Kingdom, outside Ireland: the regional reality of Canada produced a situation in which opponents and supporters of the war tended to be geographically concentrated. Both were spokesmen for relatively self-contained communities to which they could look for succour, rather than leaders of disgruntled but dispersed and vulnerable minorities. As in Ireland or South Africa, a situation rapidly developed in which dissent often appeared less dangerous than growing polarity. The German army would never march through Ottawa. Unrestrained intercommunal violence would destroy Canada just as surely.

The vigorous reaction of the Borden government was, therefore, an attempt not simply to contain dissent but to avoid intercommunal violence by giving British Canada – the burning bit between its teeth – the minimum it was willing to accept. By 1916, the Borden government was not leading the charge but being driven by British Canadian opinion, which demanded action and which was demonstrating that it was quite capable of taking matters into its own hands. The possibility of alienating French Canada or New Canadians appeared less dangerous than the near certainty that British Canada, in the absence of sufficiently strong action by the government, would simply act in a way that could only prove fatal to the nation. To a sympathetic observer, British Canada's major motives might seem to have been a combination of exultation, resolution, loyalty, horror, despair, and fear intermingled, and in aggregate quite understandable, remembering context. If these motives were allowed free play within a fractured Canadian society, however, the emerging nation would die just as surely as it would if British Canada were motivated solely by the basest passions. Canada was not alone in facing this sort of reality, or in adopting a government-directed policy of repression to head off intercommunal conflict. Gerhard Fischer has identified the same dynamic as having influenced Great War Australia's treatment of its relatively small Alien Enemy population.[2] The message the Australian government wished to send by repression of its Alien Enemy community was that *it* was in control ... so no freelance action against dissent was necessary. What made Canada different, of course, was the urgency and scale of the problem. Such is the argument in what follows.

Wartime dissent in Canada did not derive from class divisions. Indeed both class and ideological divisions tended to parallel communal differences. This is important because elsewhere class identity played a large role in determining whether or not an individual chose to support or oppose the war. In Great War Canada, however, there were effectively no classes. Donald Avery is certainly correct, for example, in writing about the "ethno-class divide" at the root of the 1919 Winnipeg General Strike;[3] John Porter considers further that if Canada were a mosaic – we are told now that it was and is – it was a vertical mosaic in which certain groups expected, demanded, and received a privileged position in a social hierarchy largely defined by community.[4] More than half a century after the First World War ended, it was still difficult for Wallace Clements to differentiate between ethnicity and social class when considering economic mobility in Canada.[5] In 1914, more than we might commonly assume, ethnic identity transcended and subsumed class. A consequence of this fact was that there could not be an effective challenge to the war arising from war-accentuated class differences, because there were not self-conscious, unified, cross-community classes. Differences in wealth and function there certainly were. The notion that these, however, should have been decisive in shaping identity or political action was contrary to the accepted common sense in Canada's dominant communities and therefore to the reality into which New Canadians immigrated.

Nor were there many disposed to interpret reality differently, and these were unlikely to be very influential. For one thing, there were very few socialists positioned to make much of a difference. The audience prepared to accept the message of those who existed was small in numbers and influence. Most actual socialists were immigrants, and therefore debarred from effective connection with Canadians of other communities, who, in any case, were poorly prepared to understand their message. Difficulties might be expected even when attempting to attract members of their own communities. Period Canadians of all flavours quite plainly tended to interpret social tension through the lens of communal rather than class identity. An immigrant New Canadian was "radical" (later, a "Bolshevik") not because he was working class or even because he was a social democrat or a misunderstood Wobbly, but because he was a foreigner. The boss was hateful not because he was a member of an exploitive class, but because he was a "bloke." They were like that. Wages were low not because it is in the nature of capitalism to exploit, but because members of other, less reputable communities depressed wages, or because, variously, members of other, better-placed communities monopolized privileged positions. Notions that an individual might have common interests with a member of another community simply would not have occurred to most Canadians in the period of the Great War.

The absence of truly effective classes in French Canada should not surprise anyone. French Canada was united by culture, language, and religion. Those outside were outsiders. The Catholic Church was powerful, and for Rome politics based on "class solidarity" was a dangerous illusion. The notion that working-class politics should be based on "class interest" or "solidarity" against other classes was actually anathema – a diabolical lie sold to the credulous by the evil. Piux IX and Leo XIII, with their message of social integration, were far more influential than Karl Marx. The ideal in French Canada was integrative: everyone happy in their station doing what was appropriate, giving what they could, getting what was necessary, respecting those deemed worthy of respect, protecting the common heritage – the whole process of social interaction conducted under the tutelage of the Church. Not all French Canadian Catholics would concur with this vision, of course, and not everyone in Quebec was a French Canadian or a Catholic. A critical mass, however, were prepared to accept this vision as absolutely "gospel." Those prepared to break ranks were, most considered, radicals infected by foreigners or atheists. They were, in any case, utterly unable to reach appreciable numbers of French Canadians as, for that matter, were foreigners and atheists.

The situation in British Canada was similar but requires some explanation, if only because British Canadians were a more diverse group and because political radicalism was almost as much a part of British Canadian history as integrative Toryism, even in Ontario.

In the nineteenth century, British Protestants quickly became a majority in Upper Canada. The native-born population when not assimilated was segregated. Other groups were small and peripheral to British Canadian society. Some of them (Waterloo County Mennonites, for example, who had been in Canada for some time) mainly wished to be left alone.[6] The Methodist, Anglican, and Presbyterian churches were dominant and, while in a state of chronic and sometimes ruthless competition, established among themselves an unofficial but effective establishment with far-reaching cultural ramifications. With the exception of the Baptists, then concentrated in the Maritime provinces, other Protestant denominations – not even to mention religions – were trace elements. There were, of course, Irish Catholics. In British Canada, however, Irish Catholics tended to assume most of the attitudes of their fellow Britons, even when these placed them in conflict with their co-religionists.[7] French Canadians, the only significant minority left outside the "British" condominium, were less than 3 per cent of the Ontario population, and concentrated in a few enclaves. While it cannot be said that any single type of Briton was dominant, the British corporately dominated the province, and the cultural institutions – particularly the churches – unique to each section of this omnibus identity worked hard to inculcate the principal components of an emerging British Canadian nationalism: the ideal of an ordered and orderly society, loyal to the Crown and distrustful of the United States. Without obvious, institutionalized acceptance of these ideals, chances of social betterment were limited.[8]

As is generally the case where community is more important than class, "nepotism" was one of the principal organizational mechanisms of society.[9] A member of nineteenth-century British Canadian society did not generally better his lot by uniting with class comrades and opposing other self-interested social groups, but by affiliating with the more powerful members of his own community – "ethnarchs," "patriarchs," or *"padrones,"* in effect, rather than simply "bosses." Integrative organizations – the churches, fraternal organizations, the militia, and the political parties – were extremely important in British Canada for precisely this reason. Loyal membership defined an individual as a worthy member of the community upon whom patronage would not be wasted. Through the course of the century as the British omnibus community defined itself against external threats (most particularly against the United States), a garrison mentality developed. Canada would remain "British" because Canadians were "British." Intracommunal divisions remained important, but were far less significant than this basic consensus. Ontario became Orange, and became as well the most important source of internal immigrants as Canada expanded. The early twentieth-century success of Robert Borden and the Tory party depended on this dynamic.

With agricultural depression in the United Kingdom from 1870, and with the closure of the American frontier in the 1890s, Canada for the first time began to become the destination of choice for British emigrants. No emigrant population is a faithful reflection of the motherland. Not every sort of person chooses to leave. In the nineteenth century, those who left had significantly more choice than at present. New homelands were chosen with care. Those who chose – and were chosen – to come to Canada, in general, were a good fit with existing society and accentuated rather than diluted its basic characteristics. For many, the idea that Canada was "British" was critical. "British North America," America without the republic and what went with it, had an attractive ring to it, particularly in the latter nineteenth century, Britain's great jingo age. Many were farmers, attracted by the idea of getting more land than they could easily have at home. Most others were possessed of those sorts of skills urgently required in a nation moving for the first time into the industrial age. Most were churchgoers, members of those denominations (particularly Anglican) already dominant in British Canada. The social and cultural institutions already powerful in British Canada, in part because of their transatlantic connections, identified and assisted with the immigration to Canada of deserving and acceptable Britons. "Acceptable," in this case, normally meant "similar" to the existing stock of British Canadians – hardworking, deferential, and loyal Ulsterman, Scots, and skilled workers from Northern England always preferred.[10] Upon arrival, most, in any case, quickly joined organizations which at once facilitated their transition, helped them to maintain their "Britishness," and put them in touch with native-born Canadians who might be predisposed to fellowship. On the other side of the coin, so completely did British immigrants come to dominate some skilled trades that in many communities it became almost impossible for a working-class Canadian to enter a trade without the requisite memberships and affiliations necessary to establish "British" identity. In workplaces dominated by immigrant, Northern English members of the Amalgamated Society of Engineers (CPR repair yards) or Ulstermen (Eaton's), for example, native-born Canadians could be required to demonstrate, or at least simulate effectively, kinship with relative newcomers as a condition of employment.[11] The end of the process was that Ontario, the heartland of British Canada, the scene of most of the new industrialization, and therefore the destination of most British immigration, already Orange and British, became steadily more so, contrary to what we might expect. In Western Canada, Ontario immigrants provided local elites. Ontario patterns became British Canadian patterns – the Maritime provinces and British Columbia, of course, always excluded, although here often local patterns developed little different from those prevailing in the

Ontario heartland of British Canada. Robert Rutherdale's description of wartime Lethbridge is enlightening in this regard:

> The overwhelming majority of the population had arrived within the previous fifteen years, comprising a polyglot conglomerate of communities that often remained separated by differences of language and religion. Local politics and businesses, however, remained under the control an Anglo-Protestant majority, conforming in the broad pattern of Anglo conformity and nativism in Alberta at this time.[12]

As New Canadians began to arrive in the later nineteenth century – first as a trickle, then with a rush – nepotism did not stop. Rather, British Canada commenced attempts to either assimilate them when this seemed possible (as with the Germans and the Dutch) or submerge them when it was not. Tory ideals in Ontario, like Catholic principles in Quebec, were integrative. If you were "in," then class or ethnicity need not be a decisive consideration at least insofar as it might affect your children's future prospects, and it was assumed that everybody would want "in." In Mariposa, you were "in" or not; if not, not respectable. "We" are consolidated on the inside, looking after our own; "they" are on the outside, denied access to the patronage chains so critical to improvement, even survival, in a society like early twentieth-century British Canada. The more of "them" there are, the more tightly "we" need to hold together; the more important become those characteristics that define "us." Nepotism (favouring our own), an essential prop to communal cohesion, begins to become what has been styled "democratic discrimination" (handicapping "them") – the apparently inconsistent maintenance of democratic, even egalitarian practice and ideology within a community which actively excludes other groups.[13] A self-evident community begins to become a continuously buttressed rigidity within a class society, the most important characteristic of which is not the relatively advantaged or disadvantaged status of individuals but a sense of common identity from which most else followed. Communities began to demonstrate class characteristics. The chance that follow-on groups of immigrants might change these patterns was small. While society retained some fluidity, new members of the elite tended to come from the same communities that had produced their predecessors.

> As each new district or colony was settled the structure of power underwent a change that can well be likened to a jelly setting. Those who were

in at the top remained there, those who were down the scale, or who came late, had to work that much harder to join the power elite. For members of a new ethnic group this would be particularly difficult, even more so because they had to take on the business methods and social characteristics of the ruling elite in order to advance.[14]

In the end, if a New Canadian tried hard enough he could find a relatively comfortable place for his family within this reality. In the process, however, he would almost necessarily become British.

Even among working-class people, communal differences were extremely important, even decisive, in shaping sense of self and social place. The chance that skilled British Canadian labourers, humble though their standard of living might be by modern standards, would perceive any motivating, common interest with "bohunk" navvies was extremely remote. Even in those workplaces in which there appeared to be but little difference between workers – among "bunkhouse men" doing the heavy work in the lumber and railroad industries, for example – British Canadians provided almost all skilled and semi-skilled workers, relegating the New Canadians among whom they lived and worked to the heaviest and dirtiest sort of labour. Who held the spike and who swung the hammer mattered more than we might think. For somebody inside such a local system, the differences between types of worker were among the most basic facts of Canadian society.

In summary, it is probable that British Canada was more self-consciously British, more religious and priggish, and more aggressively Protestant in the reign of King George V than it ever had been during the long Victorian noon. In 1914, Ontario was more, not less, the Ulster of North America than it had been at Confederation. The approved churches were more, not less, powerful and effectively established than they had been in Upper Canada. British Canada became steadily more, not less, militantly British even as it became ever more demographically Canadian. In many Edwardian Mariposas, the Holy Trinity was composed of the Orange Lodge, the Anglican Church, and the Tory party – coequal, co-eternal, consubstantial, incomprehensible, exactly in the manner described by St Athanasius. Except that a man believed this, he could not be saved.

So what? In Canada, there could not be in 1914 anything approaching an aware and coherent working class – a social group which elsewhere provided the mass for effective dissent. There were, of course, relatively disadvantaged people in all communities. Those who were

"British" or "French," however, tended to look to affiliation with social betters from their own community to improve their lot. The idea of solidarity with those similarly disadvantaged from other communities was impossible. There were, as well, relatively advantaged and disadvantaged communal groups that tended to amalgamate what might have been elsewhere concepts of social "class" or social justice to religious, political-ideological, and ethnic identities. Insofar as general labour radicalism emerges, however, it tends to develop from a momentary and local convergence of different interests among members of diverse communities rather than from a permanent amalgamation of common interests perceived to exist among brothers.[15] Such patterns did not quickly fade. At least one historian, David Bright, writing about immediately postwar Calgary, has indicated that, if class consciousness existed in Calgary (and it did), it coexisted and interpenetrated broader cultural affiliations like religion, community, and language, and competed moreover with a widespread desire not to combine against class enemies but to better one's lot by hard work and obedience to authority. Unity among "people like us" was plainly more important than solidarity with members of some other tribe, particularly if help from kindred was anticipated.[16]

In Britain, Germany, Russia, and Italy, radical and war-radicalized labour has often, and correctly, been identified as one of the more potent sources of opposition to the war. In Canada it was a negligible force. Organized – which normally meant, in 1914, "skilled" – labour in Canada was "British."[17] British immigrants, once again, dominated the skilled trades. Many had been deliberately recruited by Canadian manufacturers, often cooperating with British unions anxious to keep wages high by encouraging the immigration of part of their membership. Often these workers established, in their Canadian workplace, union locals that continued to be affiliated with the British parent. French Canadians tended to be suspicious of unions. New Canadians, in general, had limited hope of entering skilled, organized trades. The upshot was that, in 1914, the great majority of active trade unionists were politically moderate British, or British descended, Ontarians.[18] Perhaps half were Orangemen (the LOL, like the churches, once again, acting as an important labour exchange). For many of these men, political affiliation – Liberal and Conservative – was much more important than social-political activism. Both of Canada's major parties actively proselytized among Canada's workers.[19] Communal affiliation was, of course, more important still. The shifting flotsam of unskilled workers who did the heavy lifting, and to whom we might normally look for effective labour radicalism, were in 1914 very often single men attempting to make enough money to homestead. By 1914, a significant proportion were New Canadians disassociated from British or French Canada. They had therefore very little contact, through 1918, with organized labour movements of any kind.[20] It was unlikely that there would be much of a challenge from this quarter. If anything, the response of existing trade unionists to the war was even more disproportionate than that of the community from which they sprang. In 1916, Alderman J. Gibbons of Toronto, a prominent labour leader, anticipated little opposition to conscription from Ontario labour, whatever some ideologically impelled leaders might say. One-third of all union men were already in service. One-third, he said, had tried to join and been rejected for one reason or another. The remainder were too old to go. All remembered their brothers in France, and would do the right thing by them.[21] This complex of facts was undoubtedly one of the reasons why labour opposition to the war was so muted in Canada, despite manifest, sometimes shocking, provocation.[22]

Even so, Canadian workers were thinly organized – there were only 100,000 Canadian trade unionists in 1914, less than 2 per cent of the Canadian population. Undoubtedly the affiliative nature of period Canadian society had retarded what was elsewhere one of the principal social/political characteristics of the age, the growing tendency of working people to organize one way or the other and to seek political power. And while Canadian unions tripled in membership during the war, they immediately declined in the postwar years as old patterns re-emerged. Labour organizations were, moreover, also divided and unclear on the way forward. Quebec workers tended to heed the church and were suspicious of trade unionism from the outset. British Canadian workers were unsure whether to follow a British or American path. Should they organize to produce change by forming working-class political parties, or simply to pursue workplace issues? If the latter, should they heed Sam Gompers and the American Federation of Labour (AFL), or Big Bill Heywood and the International Workers of the World (IWW)? Should they do something else entirely? Such splits often assumed a regional colouration. In Ontario and the East, the great question was whether the labour movement should form craft or industrial unions, political parties (as in Britain), or a unified labour organization like the AFL. In the West, on the other hand, the ideas of the IWW appear to have received a better hearing – though this is by no means as uniform a process as some would have it – gaining entry through penetration of the militant Western Federation of Miners into the British Columbia and Alberta mines.[23]

Insofar as the British and French Canada's working class had a perceived "class interest," as in much of the United States and Australia, it consisted of keeping cheaper labour out. Foreigners, inured to hard work and long hours for a small wage, made the possibility of a "family wage" and social progress for the native-born ever more remote. As everywhere, working-class Canadians, perceiving a threat from outgroups, responded with more aggressive and hostile nativism.[24] The desire of Canadian business to access sources of cheaper foreign labour, quite plainly, was one of the most emotive working-class issues of the age. Anti-foreign rioting was not new to Canada. Some outbreaks – the anti-Asian riots that rocked Vancouver in 1907 especially – are notorious. These were, however, not momentary, regional aberrations rooted in simple bigotry, but the product of deeply held convictions common to many working people in British and French Canada. The wonder is not that such incidents occurred but that there were not more of them, and that the Dominion government continued to encourage immigration, violence notwithstanding. Sergeant William Varley, the soldier-labour candidate of Northeast Toronto during the war, spoke for many working-class nativists when he asserted that "aliens in Canada are a very real problem" that was soon going to have to be dealt with ... "for all time to come." It would not do merely to intern aliens or conscript them, for at the end of the war, during the transitional period, they would flood the labour market.[25] The answer was obvious. Victory for the British Canadian working class would not be complete without the expulsion of alien labour. For Varley, and the many who felt like him, wartime "class interest" was inextricably associated with the national/ethnic interest: victory in the war abroad and in the social-communal conflict at home.

Such wartime strikes as occurred focused mainly on the "right to organize" – just being established – or followed from simple misery. The Canadian cost of living nearly doubled in the course of the war, while wages in many sectors of the economy simply did not keep pace. The hourly rate for workers in the benchmark building trades, meanwhile, did not change through 1915 and then increased slowly.[26] Only in 1921 was something like the 1913 balance restored.[27] In the course of the war, therefore, workers lost approximately 40 per cent of their purchasing power. The government, meanwhile, ignored workplace issues in a way that would have horrified Lloyd George. Relative to provocation, Canadian labour remained remarkably quiet. Its agenda was not ultimate, but ameliorative. Trade unionists Canada had, even sometimes angry trade unionists. Opposition to the war itself, however, as a source of misery would not have occurred to many as a viable or even permissible policy. Accentuated dislike of New Canadians who appeared to be doing relatively better out of the war and loathing of war profiteers bloated on blood-money came much more naturally.

So, if the trade unions were a weak reed with which to construct a working-class opposition, how about socialist-political groups? Despite the considerable historical interest they have aroused, radical political groups were few, local, transitory, and small. There was the IWW, already mentioned. The government certainly feared it, but however many adherents it may have had, it does not appear to have acted very effectively at all, at least during the war, even in British Columbia, where it is supposed to have been strong. There was, as elsewhere, a whole mosaic of avowedly "socialist" groups. These, however, in Canada were often composed in large measure of New Canadians bringing with them perspectives and politics originating in the Old World. Indeed, during the Great War period effective socialist organization was sometimes not easily distinguishable from communal organization. For example, the first Ukrainian socialists organized in Canada under the leadership of Kyrilo Genyk not officially for political, but for cultural action. The most significant early Ukrainian cultural organization in Canada, the Taras Shevchenko Reading Society, founded in 1903, was socialist inspired.[28] Matthew Popovich – shortly thereafter one of the fathers of the Canadian Communist Party – chose a 1917 meeting of this organization to welcome the Russian Revolution as the first step to world socialism. The assembled poetry lovers passed the following resolution:

> We Ukrainian workers, gathered in a mass meeting in Winnipeg, send fraternal greetings to the revolutionary Russian workers on the occasion of the splendid victory of the revolution over autocratic tsarism and the collapse of the Prison House of the Nations, from which, without any doubt, the Ukrainian people will now be free. We are confident that our Russian comrades will not confine themselves to a radical change of the political structure of Russia, but will carry forward the struggle for the complete victory of the working people over all their enemies.[29]

It is unlikely that such an appeal, made in this forum, can have had much attraction for the workers from either of Canada's two dominant communities, without whose active support no effective challenge to the war or to Canadian society could be mounted. It is doubtful, indeed, that any were present when the resolution was read. For most, the forum in which the thing was done would have been enough to damn the project generally. The situation did not change quickly. Ninety per cent of the membership of the future Communist Party of Canada would be Ukrainian, Finnish, or Jewish.[30] The seeming inability of the wartime government to distinguish between the political and cultural organizations of New Canadians can sometimes be understood.

What about other sorts of political objection? Certainly there were Canadian liberals, as in Britain, opposed at minimum to the significant illiberal distortions introduced into national life by the war. Many liberals in all communities disapproved, for example, of conscription, as of compulsion and limitation of choice of all kinds. In both British and French Canada, however, community proved more powerful. Most French Canadian Liberals opposed elements of war management less because they were liberal by conviction than because they happened to be Liberal or became so because the Liberal Party, under the leadership of Wilfrid Laurier, dissented. French Canadians in essence voted Liberal in 1917 because the party advocated that policy, which this community favoured. The community did not favour the policy because of a preference for the party and its ideology. Had it been the Liberals (as in Britain) who introduced conscription and the Tories who were in opposition, French Canadians quite possibly would have been as militantly *Bleus* as they became convinced *Rouges*. Most prewar British Canadian Liberals similarly rejected the party lead for the opposite reason. It is revealing, in this regard, that the leaders of the Canadian National Service League, as of the latter war "win the war" movement, were renegade Liberals. The Grit-Tory, *Bleu-Rouge* divides increasingly became, as the war wore on, a French *Rouge*–British Tory divide, with the ethnic identifier most important. Canada might produce a Wilfrid Laurier. It would never produce a Trevelyan, a Snowden, a Morel, or a Ponsonby. Mackenzie King or perhaps Mitch Hepburn somewhat later was about as close as it came.

In Canada, therefore, effective opposition to the war could never form around socialist-political, working-class-labour, or liberal ideological movements. Insofar as there was a self-aware, politically motivated working class, it tended to be composed of New Canadians incapable of effectively combining except on issues of momentary, local import with British or French Canadian workers who were far more disposed to regard New Canadians as competitors than comrades. Socialists were peripheral and too closely identified with New Canada to make much of a running in either French or British Canada. French Canadians tended to support the Liberals not because of a profound sense of loyalty to liberal principles but because they fell into step behind the party that gave most active voice to war dissent, rooted in perceived communal interest. Most British Canadians, whatever their prewar affiliation and ultimate political convictions might have been, were for the duration of the war equally convinced Tories, since the Conservative Party was viewed as furthering community interest best by promising the greatest vigour in pursuit of victory – "victory" understood by the British Canadian working class as at once a national, communal, and class interest.

Nor would effective opposition to the war develop from a religious-based critique as it sometimes did elsewhere. British Nonconformists, for example, were prominent among the war's opponents. Canadian Lutherans, Mormons, and Pentecostals were always sceptical. On the other hand, Canada's dominant denominations – Catholic, Methodist, Presbyterian, and Anglican (listed in order, by number of adherents) – were hardly pacific by doctrine, during the First World War anyway. Indeed their Canadian practice at this juncture was highly bellicose. Taken as a group, clergymen from all these persuasions were among the war's most convinced supporters: its most enthusiastic performers on the recruiting platform, and men who appear to have demonstrated their engagement by giving their sons to the army in gross disproportion. Outright pacifists, with a religious objection to the war, were rare and did not possess the power that, for example, members of the Society of Friends did in both the United Kingdom and the United States. Moreover the objection of the largest pacifistic sects was understood and tolerated.[31] Once this was allowed, members of these communities – Mennonites, Doukhobors, and Quakers – lapsed almost uniformly into quietism for the duration.[32] Amy Shaw has demonstrated as well that for the "peace churches" obedience to authority was as fundamental a principle of religion as non-violence. Once the government signalled that it was prepared to excuse members of these denominations from combatant service, cooperation was normal. Even the 1917 loss of voting rights was considered to be a small price to pay for the right to opt out of the war, which had been conceded in the MSA. Those denominations that produced the majority of Canada's conscientious objectors had, in 1914, no more than a few thousand adherents each. Some – the Jehovah's Witnesses, for example – were the more generally disliked the better they were known. Even taken together, these sects could not mount any effective challenge to the war.

Canada's Jewish community might have presented a problem. It was small, but it was vocal and politically engaged. Fifteen hundred Montreal Jews, for example, expressed their opposition to conscription in May 1917[33] – though more probably as newly arrived *Bundists* (Jewish socialists) than as Jews. The good news for the government, however, was that these opponents were not yet British subjects and could not be enlisted in any case. They were, more importantly, utterly incapable of expanding their objection into a more broadly based opposition against conscription, particularly in Quebec. Alliance with a substantial number of anti-conscriptionist French Canadians, which might have made this critique effective, was impossible. In the end, it is doubtful that the government was much more discouraged by the news that Montreal's Jews disapproved of conscription than heartened by the assurance of a Montreal Italian Protestant minister, Pastor de Pierro, that 99 per cent of his congregation supported it – or indeed by the intelligence that Toronto's more assimilated Jewish community, of like mind with their neighbours, heartily approved of the great crusade.[34]

Canada had no socialist or labour movements opposed to the war, capable of mobilizing anything like mass support in British or French Canada. It contained no substantial, influential community of individuals opposing the war from profound political or religious conviction. Canada could never produce, therefore, an equivalent of Britain's Union of Democratic Control (UDC) or No Conscription Fellowship (NCF) – organized communities of dissidents brought together by the fundamental belief that war, this war, or some war measure was simply wrong. While there was certainly dissent in Canada, it did not follow a British pattern and therefore required different handling.

In Canada anti-war dissent arose from differences in notions about what being Canadian meant, these notions based on communally defined perceptions, experiences, and interests. In 1914, Canada was less a unified Dominion beginning to emerge from imperial tutelage than a number of communities – three significant to the war; two of them largely self-contained – each possessed of its own patriotism and none disposed to take the patriotism of the others very seriously. This was Canada's tragedy. Prewar controversies centring on how the Dominion related to the Empire had already revealed how quickly and completely this issue, above all others, could divide. Differences between these communities were already well established. To make matters worse, by 1914 Canada was in the midst of some dramatic and traumatic transformations of a type which everywhere, and in all times, inflame identity differences. So disturbing were some of these processes that intercommunal clashes might well have become politically decisive even if the war had not intervened to make them so.

One of the most important of these was rapid urbanization, which, as elsewhere, raised questions of nation and identity in a far more forcible fashion than had previously been the case. A French Canadian living on the land in the Beauce or a British Canadian resident in one or another Mariposa was unlikely to actually much hate any "other," whatever a particular communal mythology might suggest as appropriate. How could they? They came into contact with few obvious others. In most of British Canada the only substantial community of "others" were Irish Catholics – in all respects but religion very like their neighbours. Since the conquest there had been a resident British population in Quebec, but the French Canadian population tended to be rural and the British Canadians were, in most of the province, city dwellers. In the twenty years before the war, however, Canada ceased to be a country of farms and hamlets very quickly. By 1921 fully half of the Canadian population lived in cities. Ontario and Quebec already had urban majorities by 1914.[35] The change in Quebec came remarkably quickly and was particularly dramatic and disruptive. In 1890, Quebec had been one-third urban. By 1900, it was half urban, and by 1911 only a third of the population remained on the land. The flight to the city accelerated during the war. In less than a single generation, in effect, one-third of the population of Quebec had pulled up stakes and moved to town. The population of Montreal nearly doubled between 1901 and 1921, from 328,172 to 618,566.[36] The social reality of French Canada had changed fundamentally, as indeed had the demography of Quebec towns and cities.

The Canadian population, meanwhile, was growing very quickly as immigration, for the first time in Canadian history, began to outpace emigration: 331,288 immigrants arrived in 1911, 375,456 in 1912, 400,870 in 1913, nearly half a million in 1914.[37] The transformation in some respects was almost marvellous. In 1871 Canada was 92.62 per cent of "British" or French origin – about an equivalent proportion of each.[38] Virtually all residents were British subjects. There was a net outflow of emigrants from Canada. In 1921, there were, approximately, four million "British" Canadians, many of them recent arrivals, two million French Canadians, and two million members of New Canadian communities – "Germans" and "Austrians" heavily represented.[39] Still more outlandish "others" were beginning to arrive in some localities in substantial numbers. The proportion of the Canadian population that was foreign born was higher than at any time before or since.[40] Many of the newcomers settled in cities, just as uprooted rural folk began to crowd in.[41] Canada was plainly a society – or rather a set of societies – in rapid flux.[42]

As elsewhere, rapid population growth coupled to urbanization and immigration produced much greater differentials in wealth than had existed before, with the lowest social segments suffering relative pauperization. Indeed, the standard of living for the poorest sectors of the Canadian population – regardless of who they were or where they had come from – was probably declining in the years before the war, and this process accelerated during the war.[43] British and French Canadians obviously felt that wages were falling because of the "unfair" competition of immigrant groups. Anger smouldered in the cabbage towns and "lower cities" across the country. "Poor white" syndrome flourished. New Canadian slum-dwellers, still more relatively disadvantaged of course, analysed the question differently. Canadian society was, in 1914, two ethnically based communities, one of them (British Canada) beginning to show the first signs of dissolution, existing within a broader context in which the characteristics of a class society were all too apparently emerging and resonating with, and impacting upon, communal identities.

As elsewhere, these processes were linked together – rapid population growth, ethnic mixing, urbanization, and pauperization – and produced an explosive mix. Canada's constituent communities, in a more forcible way than previously, confronted questions of status and identity. A French Canadian living in Montreal and working sometimes in English for British managers beside New Canadians with whom he had little in common, whose politics and habits were hateful, and whose presence in his workplace tended to depress wages below what he considered equitable, confronted different questions from his forefathers working on the land and living in an entirely French Canadian milieu. The questions "What am I?" "Who are we?" "What does the society of which I am a member owe me?" "How does this society relate to the state?" and "How do I ensure that my children are like me?" could only emerge in a much more urgent and ambiguous form than had been the case for the *habitants*. Anxiety was heightened by the disquieting flow of French Canadians south to the lumber camps and mill towns of the United States, there to be absorbed. What future could a culture as distinct as that of French Canada have in the face of entirely inimical demographic facts – the emigration of French Canadians combined with the immigration of Britons and New Canadians apt to be assimilated into British Canada? Would French Canadians become a peripheralized minority of helots and navvies in their own fatherland? In French Canada, anxiety was beginning to produce nationalism of a new stripe.

British Canada was likewise disquieted. British Canada was a staid, religious, and intolerant place in 1914. What need of tolerance when a near consensus had emerged on the most important issues? Both its virtues and its vices were those of the unpopular variety, and most British Canadians shared them. Mariposa might have been Stephen Leacock's joke but it was drawn true to life, reflective of many local realities. Hard work and serious attention to the business of life were much admired. Religion confounded with politics provided real answers. Temperance was in the air. Intemperance, associated with vice of all kind, was uniformly, publicly deplored, if sometimes secretly indulged. Mariposa was earnest and hypocritical by turns. One thing few doubted, however, was that British Canadians were the finest people in the world and the luckiest citizens of the best-favoured Dominion, of the greatest Empire the world had ever known – an Empire which Canada's paragons would inherit in the fullness of time, and which would not simply fade away. The New Jerusalem was building.[44]

There was some room in this vision for ambiguity, but not so much as would have been necessary if the New Canadians were to have had an easy time adjusting to their new surroundings. While the preferred image of New Canadians was of solid, sod-busting frontier folk, many, by 1914, were concentrated in ghettoes in major urban areas, growing explosively. Some arrived in the Dominion with plainly subversive ideas – "subversive" having a rather more generous meaning in 1914 than at present. Many did not appear to recognize the fact that they had been done a great favour in being allowed to come to Canada in the first place and were there, for the moment, on a trial basis and not by right. Some, indeed, showed no interest in assimilation at all, and, it seemed, only wanted to make as much money as possible as quickly as possible. When it looked at the New Canadians, British Canada did not generally see solid, hardworking farm folk. It saw itself invaded, overrun by foreigners of often disgusting and frightening habits – people, plainly, who did not understand what Canada was about and who had no real interest in finding out or fitting in. Opinions changed quickly. "For many Anglo-Saxons, the image of the typical foreigner," Avery writes, "was no longer that of a placid, hardworking peasant wearing a sheepskin coat; but rather the disturbing vision of some swarthy 'bohunk or Polack,' eyes glazed with cheap liquor, ready to commit a heinous crime"[45] and probably a member of some criminal, or subversive organization, it might be added. Indeed, even before they began to arrive in Canada in appreciable numbers, many types of New Canadian were already associated in British Canadian minds with radical politics and crime, based on the American experience. The United States, John A. Macdonald thought, "is a great country, but it will have its vicissitudes and revolutions. Look at the mass of foreign ignorance and vice which has flooded the country with socialism, atheism and all other isms."[46] Obviously Canada would have to do better. New Canadians bore watching, required training, and might need occasional, salutary correction if they were to constitute any sort of useful reinforcement for the garrison.

There was more. Canada, in 1914, remained colonial in many ways: incomplete in itself, requiring a greater international reference to provide context. What made the situation in 1914 particularly problematic, however, was that each of Canada's constituent communities had a different reference. An international event of the magnitude of the First World War could not but be particularly divisive, its impacts appreciated differently. "What does Canada mean?" was and remains inextricably tied to the question "How does Canada fit in the world?" Canadians were already divided on the first question. Attempts to address the second drove them still further apart. As war impacts became heavier, answers were required more urgently and were supplied more shrilly and emphatically.

For British Canadians, the greater reality was and could only be the British Empire. In fighting for the Empire, Canadians were not less but more truly Canadian – imperialists, as Stephen Leacock said, because they *would not be colonial*. Insofar as French Canada, more sufficient in itself, looked to the outer world, one reference was Britain; another was Rome. French Canada was quite capable of moderating its participation in the war, as in the Empire in general, perceiving that there could be for Canada worse things than failure to achieve total Entente victory. In any case, the Pope was opposed to the war. He was trying to arrange, not greater participation by Catholics to ensure an Entente victory, but peace. New Canadians could only see whatever fatherland they had left, not so very long before. What was Britain? They were of course thankful to the Dominion for the ability to improve their lot but would have been unnatural human beings if they had perceived what for many involved the real possibility of contributing to the extinction of kin with anything other than mixed feelings. To British Canada, the position adopted by the others looked very much like treachery; worse, the abnegation of what it meant to be a real Canadian. For French and New Canadians, of course, British Canada, in calling so stridently for total victory whatever the price, was ceasing to be Canadian at all. It was simply British; or worse, "*tête carré*" – square headed – insofar as its militancy was taken to imply exactly the type of militarism it claimed to be fighting.

If the wartime chasms emerging between Canada's communities were widened by disparate reference to greater, idealized communities, it might be as well that local loyalties – more primal and much closer to home – were also at work to the same dangerous purpose. A recent addition to nationalist theory has been provided by Paul Stern's "proto-theory" of nationalism in which he reverses traditional flows of dependency. Most theorists have it that nationalism (loyalty to the "tribe") is either something natural (in which case diverse nationalisms in Canada are to be expected, since we are dealing with not one but several confederate tribes) or something rationally learned (citizens expect to get something concrete from the nation and deport themselves accordingly). In either case, other, subordinate loyalties are described as achieving success insofar as they are able to tap into a primordial, national identity. Englishmen are in great disproportion adherents of the Church of England because, being English, they view the "national" church as their obvious affiliation or because the perks afforded by membership in the national church are some of those offered for loyalty to the nation. According to Stern, however, it is the other loyalties that are most important – love of community, love of family, love of church. Englishmen choose to be English, in effect, not least because England plays host to the mother church of the Anglican communion, organized from local congregations to which loyalties are precedent and much more visceral than love of nation. Patriotism is parasitic. Anybody's real homeland is the neighbourhood in which they live – the family, friends, and institutions that provide meaning and identity. Nationalism is successful only insofar as it is able to associate itself with these more basic loyalties. Soldiers do not walk into fire for the fatherland but for the families and communities in which they grew up and which pointed them towards the fatherland in the first place. The sort of altruism that makes for collective sacrifice springs from loyalty to the real group accessed by the imagined community. *Pro patria mori* is soft and beautiful, soothing and fitting, because the sacrifice is really *pro aris et focis*.[47]

By this reading, when we consider the disparate responses of the various communities composing period Canada, we should consider the different ways in which such constituent groups shaped their members for participation in the war. If the Orange Lodge and the local Methodist pastor were more bellicose than the St Jean Baptiste Society and the local *curé*, we might expect that British Canadians would internalize the conflict much more completely than their French Canadian compatriots. If the culture, and affiliations, of British Canadian women caused them to identify more closely with Edith Cavell or to react with more immediate horror to German atrocities in Belgium than their French Canadian sisters, then we might expect that they would seek outlets to make an effective war contribution more vigorously and push their men out the door with greater gusto. If the local Lutheran congregation and the Teutonia club were conflicted, we might expect a lower degree of engagement with the war effort among ethnically German Canadians, particularly among individuals with family still in Germany. It would have been odd, similarly, if the position of Bishop Budka's Uniate congregation had been any less uncertain than it was. It was hearing a very uncertain trumpet. In regard to the First World War, at least, the proto-theory appears to work rather well, particularly when combined with other explanations. Local studies of Newfoundland and Ireland[48] suggest that local, less ultimate loyalties were prime determinants in getting men into khaki. Men were more or less actively patriotic, in effect, as they were more or less active in organizations the patriotism of which was invoked by the particular conditions of the First World War. It is not surprising that Canadian patriotisms were characterized by different world-views, inculcated by organizations with different views of what Canada meant. It should not surprise, therefore, that these produced different levels of engagement in the war and that communal cleavages began to become dangerous as the war impacted differently on communities that felt and participated differently.

Of course, divisions were never perfect. Ambiguous individuals existed. Flexibility in the employment of labels, therefore, was inevitable. In Canada, to a much greater extent than in more coherent nations, identity was already largely a function of self-identification and was accepted as such. Wilfrid Laurier, Emile Nelligan, and Talbot Papineau, for example, are examples of prominent "French" Canadians who straddled the French-English divide. Many Canadians always had to juggle identities, then as now. Through the course of the war, as old enemies became new friends and old friends became new enemies, the issue of self-identification became more urgent. Eventually the government appears, in most cases, to have adopted a simple procedure. Except in cases where legal status had to be taken as definitive – for example, a person of German ancestry born in Germany was simply a "German" and an "Alien Enemy" however they might self-identify – self-identification and acceptance by some coherent group would have to be accepted as proof of identity. And when a questionable case came before court – when a person, for example, claimed to be "British" but was not self-evidently so – then it was up to the judge to decide.[49] What was a Czech, for example? In 1914 a Czech was usually an Austrian national, and therefore an Alien Enemy of doubtful allegiance. In 1917, the same individual remained a suspicious foreigner out on parole. By some magic, however, by 1918, a Czech had become a comrade in arms acceptable for accelerated naturalization as a British subject if certified as suitably "Czech" by the emergent Czechoslovak national council.[50] Even little, parochial Canada was sufficiently sophisticated to appreciate that an Armenian might well be an Ottoman subject but was highly unlikely to be an Ottoman partisan. What was his status? Ask the judge if the issue arose.

A list of Canadian soldiers who volunteered for service with the 117th Battalion CEF, who were accepted in Canada as bone fide British subjects, and who were subsequently sent home from the UK as unacceptable reveals at once how complicated Canadian identity could be and how decisive self-identification could be in the assignment of identity. Private F. Werner of the 138th Battalion was born Swedish of German parents, and naturalized in Vancouver in 1906 at the age of twenty-three. Lance-Corporal C. Shuh was born in 1895 in Freiburg, Germany, to a Scots mother and a German father, though resident in Scotland and Canada from age two. He enlisted in the 117th Battalion voluntarily because he was British. Bombardier R. Schwemann was born in Buenos Aires to a German father and an English mother in 1896, and had lived in England and Hanover before immigrating to Canada in 1913. He enlisted because he thought it was his duty. He had "always considered himself a Britisher." Driver W. Funck was born in Toronto in 1898 to a

Canadian mother and a German father, resident in Canada for thirty-five years. He considered himself a Canadian, and joined because it was his duty. Private Adolph Messerschmidt was born in Kowno, Russia, in 1891 to a Russian father and a Polish mother. He had deserted from the Russian army, fled to the United States, and immigrated to Canada in 1912. He considered himself to be a Canadian. Lance-Corporal L. Bodker was born in Charlottenburg, Germany, in 1894 to a Norwegian father and an English mother. He had lived in Germany until age fifteen when the family moved to London, thereafter moving between London and Berlin. He immigrated to Canada in 1912 and joined at the outbreak of the war, but had been weeded out as undesirable. When the 117th Battalion was formed, he joined up at once because he considered himself a Britisher. Bodker was, however, subsequently arrested in the UK for disloyal utterances.[51] It is striking that it was not until these individuals arrived in Britain that anybody disabused them of the notion that they had the requisite identity credentials to put on the King's uniform.

The most important point, however, is not that a considerable number of such individuals lived in period Canada but that war-induced polarization forced all Canadians to choose. Wherever they might have come from and whoever their parents might have been, the war compelled individuals to declare what they were and to deport themselves accordingly. Those in the foregoing list, for example, decided that they were "British" or "Canadian" and sought service accordingly. Others with better credentials did not make the same choices. In February 1916, a Kitchener German, product of a family which had been in Canada for four generations (and probably, therefore, more exactly a Waterloo County United Empire Loyalist of German extraction), expressed himself in this uncompromising fashion:

> Some of the beggars should be interned. The trouble is that they are proud of their German blood and they do not feel grateful to Canada for treating them so white. They feel all the prouder of their German blood, and claim that it is German cleverness that has won for them these things, through politics, of course. But, of course, its hard to have to read of all these atrocities and know your blood is the same as the so-called Huns. But for that, these pro-Germans would have been shut up by those of German descent long ago.[52]

While he is of German descent, it is obvious that the speaker's tribal affiliation was different and certainly more complex than strict notions of ethnicity or community might suggest it should have been. One of Amy Shaw's more fascinating disclosures takes the form of a list of men who saw service in the Canadian army overseas, but who indicated at attestation membership in one or another "Peace Church." This membership should have precluded participation in the war, while proofing them against operation of conscription. Ernest Wideman, Eby Milton, Nicholas Fast, and Daniel Fretz were volunteers who saw combatant service. They were all killed in action or died of wounds. They were also Canadian Mennonites.[53] How would they have defined themselves?

The existence of different patriotisms ensured that the war would be interpreted and experienced in different ways by members of different categories – that some were born in these categories while others voluntarily affiliated is beside the point. Wartime Canadians violently disagreed on what being Canadian meant, on how Canada fitted into the world, and even on what was and what was not acceptably "Canadian." In the course of the war, compromise and ambiguous positions became untenable. Integrative mechanisms, as elsewhere, were shattered by the requirement to clarify. This dynamic was to prove monstrously divisive as the cost of the war began to tell differently, inviting comparisons and accentuating existing enmities.

3 "A Cleavage in the Population of This Country along Racial Lines": French and New Canada

> If we send our men to the war, as Borden wants[,] they will disappear, and be replaced by whom? [The Crowd:] Blokes and Chinese!
>
> Mayor Martin of Montreal, April 1917[1]

In the next two chapters, we will consider a little more closely some previous generalizations. In this chapter, we will focus more directly on the basic nature of French and New Canada and how they were perceived by British Canadian compatriots in the specific context of the Great War, before turning in the next chapter to British Canada, our principal concern.

French Canada, centred on Quebec and united by language, ethnicity, and religion, had always been prepared to accept alliance with British Canada within a united nation. In the main, French Canadians were ready to accept inclusion in the Empire and the status of British subjects. Indeed, had there been no Confederation, and had an independent Quebec emerged, it might well have sought and gratefully received Dominion status. French Canada, in 1914, was obliged to Britain as an adult child must be to a dutiful and generous step-parent.

Even more, many in French Canada admired Britain, its institutions, and the Empire. The Conquest had saved French Canada from the Revolution. Britain had guaranteed cultural and religious rights. Had royal governors not given French Canadians greater opportunity for advancement and shown more respect to the Church than their French predecessors ever had? It was Laurier, not Borden, who claimed that the highest title a man could have was "British Liberal" and who answered "Ready, aye ready" in 1914. It was Laurier, not Borden, who daydreamed in 1917 that if it had been his lot to be born British then he would have liked to be a Whig of the fine, old tradition.

Relations with British Canada were a little more problematic. While it was "Canadian" and "British," French Canada had probably always thought of itself as a nation with a particular mission on the North American continent. It was to other areas of French and Catholic North America what France once had been. It had learned to accept that fulfilment of this mission did not require that it be a sovereign state. It was wedded to British Canada certainly, but ultimately by necessity rather than by much love. By 1914, French Canada had been critical for some time of British Canada's perceived willingness to accept, without consideration for Canadian interest, whatever London said; its desire to provide whatever London wanted. The more determinedly British Canada insisted on Canada's "Britishness," the more sceptical was the rejoinder from Quebec. Certainly Canada was a member of a family of nations. Certainly Canadians were British subjects, and should take pride in this fact. The obligation Quebec owed to other members of the family (step-siblings and step-parent after all), however, was limited. French Canada was quite plainly inclined to dismiss British Canada's more vigorous attachment to Britain and its tendency to imperialism as a species of immaturity – a sign that British Canadians were immature as Canadians.

What French Canada would not do was spill out its life's blood to meet anything but a direct attack – although if that ever came, *Canadiens* promised, they would resist it savagely as they had in the past.[2] And even if French Canada were utterly convinced that the cause was just and its interest engaged, it might still have attempted to limit its liability in the Great War. In 1914 French Canada was hyper-aware of its demographic vulnerability. It had maintained its place in British North America by high birth rates. French Canada did not intend to disappear, overwhelmed in a sea of English-language culture. By 1916 the war was obviously not going to be over soon, and was productive of horribly long casualty lists. "If we send our men to the war, as Borden wants," Mayor Martin of Montreal asked a large crowd in July 1917, we "will disappear, and be replaced by whom?" "Blokes!" and "Chinese!" the crowd responded.[3] Obviously, victory at this price was no victory at all. French Canada's demographic rivals at home, if less atrocious, were certainly more dangerous than Germany.

Moreover, while French Canadians did not doubt that the Allied cause during the First World War was just, many did not think that it was Canada's cause.[4] While Canada's participation was justified, exceptional departure from "business as usual" was not. Nor was it fair to ask Canada, still building, to shoulder such a heavy burden. Henri Bourassa, the fiery French Canadian journalist and pious Catholic, editor of *Le Devoir* after 1910, had already committed himself to an anti-imperial path during prewar controversies. In the aftermath of the Boer War he came together with like-minded French Canadians who had been opposed to Canadian participation in what they viewed as a war of conquest to found the Nationalist Movement under the chairmanship of the Liberal nationalist Olivar Asselin. The "nationalism," in this case, was as much nativist Canadian nationalism as French Canadian local patriotism – "the interests of the Canada of Confederation should come first for Canadians" rather than "Quebec should separate from Confederation," Mitch Hepburn *en français*. It was essential, the Nationalists believed, for Canada to claim real autonomy within the Empire and for a fully independent Canada to honour the letter and spirit of the British North America Act, which had guaranteed French Canadians their language and their religion.[5] Plank three of the prewar nationalist program was particularly important in the light of wartime controversy. This called for "Canadian military autonomy," by which the authors meant that Canadians should not be sent to participate in any wars outside Canadian territory. Imperial authorities should not be allowed to recruit in Canada. Canada should not contribute to an imperial fleet, and should manage its armed forces with the object of defending Canadian territory, under Canadian command.[6]

Sir Wilfrid Laurier, Canada's first French Canadian prime minister and the Liberal leader in 1914, did not agree with the nationalists' divisive, rabble-rousing methods, though he may have sympathized with their ultimate aims. In imperial questions, however, he saw a whole shoal of rocks on which Canada might well founder if an attempt were made to realize the nationalist platform prematurely. Like it or not, active participation in the Empire was the price that French Canada would have to pay if it were to retain the friendship of British Canada. "If we had refused our imperative duty," he later said of the Boer War, "the most dangerous agitation would have arisen, an agitation which, according to all probability, would have ended in a cleavage in the population of this country upon racial lines. A greater calamity could never take place in Canada."[7] In 1900, the Liberal position was something of a waffle, foretaste of more to come.

By the time of the 1911 election, things had already gone very far. One issue was the fleet – should Canada contribute to an imperial fleet and if so, how? Bourassa and the nationalists were firmly in the Laurier camp, although their objection went considerably further than his. The Liberal position was that a Canadian fleet should be organized, which, under Canadian control and command, could contribute to imperial defence. The Conservative position, floated on the ebullient imperialism that was such a notable feature of Edwardian British Canada, was that Canada should buy ships for a common Royal Navy, although these could be repatriated at some future date to provide the nucleus of a Canadian squadron.[8] The Orange Order defined for many British Canadians the position they were to take again during the First World War when a similar question arose with greater urgency. "A more despicable doctrine," Grand Master Wallace thought,

> has never been propounded by a public man that that Canada should accept the sacrifices of the mother land, and the protection of her Army and Navy to maintain the integrity of the Dominion, and then, like a poltroon, refuse to contribute one dollar or one man to uphold the unity of the empire ...
> So I repeat, the public man who in Canada spreads the notion that a certain section of the people have obligations as British subjects less onerous, less responsible, less far-reaching than those of British birth and blood, is an enemy to his country, a man of perverted ideas, destitute of a pure sense of honour and at heart a traitor.[9]

Another, scarcely less emotive issue was free trade with the United States. The Liberals and the Nationalists were supporters of reciprocity, as indeed were most Canadian farmers. Borden's Conservatives were advocates of imperial preference on the grounds – loudly trumpeted by supporters – that closer economic ties with Britain would ultimately encourage the emergence of a real imperial community.[10] All Canadians were British. Being British entailed support for imperial policy. Effective support would require real contributions and real sacrifices. The aim, ultimately, was a united federal Empire. Any other program was treason. The thing was simple.

In the extremely close "reciprocity" election that followed, British Canada lined up behind the Conservatives and French Canada behind the Liberals and nationalists. With 51 per cent of the poll, Borden collected 134 seats to 87 for the Liberals. The Grits were thrashed in Ontario and the *Bleus* in Quebec. Many prominent English Canadian Liberals, particularly in the West, defected to Borden.[11] The absolutely gushing reception of Borden's imperial program in the British press was fuel on the fire.[12] All of this was a preview of developments after 1914.

Prewar polarity was nothing lessened by a series of provincial political crises, continuing into the war, which always threatened to become national issues. The most important of these was the highly charged "Schools Question" – a sectarian *cause célèbre* before the war, and a canker through the war years. The crux of the problem was that education was in provincial jurisdiction according to the British North America Act. The intention of this provision was to guarantee to the French Canadians control over the language and religion of instruction *inside* Quebec. However, not all French Canadians lived within this jurisdiction. In prewar Canada, Catholic education was generally French-language instruction, and French-language instruction was always Catholic. On the other hand, Ontario and the Western provinces were mainly, and militantly, Protestant in religion and English in language. A majority of Catholics in British Canada – to confound the question further – were not French but Irish Canadians. With the concurrence of Bishop Michael Fallon of London, one of the most vocal leaders of Ontario's Irish Catholic community, the government of Ontario, in April 1912, introduced legislation which made English the only authorized language of instruction in Ontario schools, both secular and Catholic. There would still be French-language teaching, of course, but French would be a subject like any other and not the primary medium of instruction. There would still be Catholic schools, but they would teach the same curriculum as the public schools in English. Other provinces – Manitoba, before the war, and Saskatchewan and Alberta by 1918 – were not far behind in introducing similar legislation.[13] The onset of war did nothing to diminish the inevitable contention.

French Canada was horrified – particularly those French Canadians resident in Ontario, where they had lived for centuries. Bourassa and the nationalists perceived this as an intercommunal attack. Attempts to implement the legislation produced rioting in both Ontario and Quebec. Even a compromise decision of the Judicial Committee of the British Privy Council, in 1916, that Ontario was well within its constitutional rights in establishing a unilingual school system but could do nothing about Catholic education up to grade 10 did not quiet matters. Nor did the personal intervention of Pope Benedict XV have much of an effect; nor did the fact that both provincial parties in Ontario – Conservatives and Liberals – supported the compromise.[14] Nationalists in Quebec led by Bourassa were quick to condemn the *"Boche"* of Ontario.[15] Why, they wanted to know, should French Canadians fight for a nation which did little to protect what were considered in Quebec to be basic, guaranteed, constitutional rights? Could it be, the nationalists wondered, that British Canada was using the war emergency as a pretext for the introduction of measures designed to destroy French Canada? Many feared it was so.

Distrust of British Canada's motives, however, did not necessarily mean disassociation from the Empire's cause in the First World War. While the nationalists might disapprove of Canada's over-vigorous participation in a war in which, by their reading, it had little interest, French Canada as a whole appears to have accepted Canada's entry to the war and the dispatch of the first volunteer contingents in good spirits. In 1914, in some quarters, there was even modest enthusiasm for what was then understood to be an exciting imperial adventure requiring no greater sacrifices than those demanded by the Boer War.[16] In 1915, there was some interest when the idea of a French Canadian brigade was floated. "This measure alone," *La Presse* considered, "will give French Canadians the place and importance which is their right, mobilize their resources, produce enthusiasm and offer a field of endeavour to their officers."[17]

Laurier and the French Canadian Liberals initially concurred. This was Canada's war. A brigade was not a heavy burden, and, they were confident, the volunteers could be found. Henri Bourassa and the Nationalists, on the other hand, were more sceptical. Yes, they reiterated, the cause of Britain and France was just, and they prayed for victory. Canada, however, need make no great sacrifices in what was fundamentally not its war.[18] Elsewhere, talk of a brigade became talk of a division, and there were some attempts to raise the units to make one possible in the early months of 1916.[19] This was a pipe dream. Ultimately French Canada's few volunteers – mainly very young, urban, unattached adventurers[20] – were concentrated into the infantry corps and into those few French-language units they sufficed to maintain. Two battalions was all that French-speaking volunteers could keep going. There were simply not enough for it to be otherwise.

By the time the 1st Canadian Division was destroyed at the Second Battle of Ypres, in April 1915, it had already become clear that Canada was engaged in something rather more serious than just another imperial adventure like the Boer War. In the first year of the war, 1,100 men had joined the 22nd, 1,100 the 41st, and 910 the 69th Battalions. If these units could have been kept up to strength, French Canada might have had its brigade. In 1916, the 105th recruited 250 men, the 117th 40, the 198th 100, the 171st 400, and the 199th only 80, while casualty rolls grew.[21] There would be no division; there could not even be a brigade unless recruiting improved. In the aftermath of the Battle of the Somme, volunteering collapsed. Some new departure would be needed if what was now a very substantial Canadian expeditionary force were to be maintained at anything like full strength. Even so, in November 1916, Quebec's contribution did not look entirely disproportionate. If 150,000 men had gone to the front from Ontario and only 20,000 from Quebec, 108,000 of the Ontarians despatched were British born.[22] A year later, the CEF looked very different, and French Canadians were even less in evidence; nor, of course, was everyone who went from Quebec French Canadian. Quebec's English-language militia units – and there were several – all recruited multiple battalions after all.

By the second half of 1916, viewed as a whole, French Canada withdrew from the war into a policy of limited liability and obstruction of government efforts to both increase the Canadian contribution and ensure that the burden was more equitably distributed across communities. It was charged, and has been often repeated, that French Canadians did not enlist because recruitment was bungled. The appointment of a Methodist minister as Quebec recruiter in 1914 has been indicated as a particular sore point. However, long before recruiting collapsed, the government had remedied this error. In 1916, the man responsible for the recruitment of French Canadians throughout Canada was Arthur Migault, an irrepressible French Canadian patriot.[23] *La Presse* charged, in July 1917, that the problem of French Canadian recruitment existed not because of lack of patriotism but because French Canadians liked fighting. They would not, therefore, enlist in auxiliary corps if they were not fit for service as combatants.[24] Oswald Maynard, editor of *La Presse*, attempted another explanation in Toronto at about the same time. French Canadians, he considered, had experienced no influx of imperialist-minded co-nationals as had British Canada. They had been essentially at peace for 150 years and were no longer a warlike people. They were, moreover, too young a people to have developed any martial traditions of their own.[25] Henri Bourassa was probably closer to the mark. Defending Quebec against the charge that it was not bearing its fair share of the common burden, he wrote, in August 1916, that French Canadian reluctance did not mean lack of patriotism. Rather, as in every other country and at all times, the citizens of the oldest origin are the least disposed to be stampeded into distant ventures of no direct concern to their native land. It also proves that military service is more repugnant to the rural than to the urban population ... British Canada ... contains a considerable proportion of people still in the first period of national incubation ... French Canadians enlist less than British Canadians because they are totally and exclusively Canadian.[26]

Why should Canada suffer holocausts for a Europe which was far away and which had lost most of its powers of attraction in 1789? This was simply, Alderman Pauze of Montreal considered – speaking against subscription to the Canadian patriotic fund – "not our war."[27] When a bill was presented in the Quebec Provincial Assembly to permit municipalities to subscribe to the patriotic fund, Armand Lavergne, another prominent nationalist, moved an amendment permitting subscription to the Ontario School "battle fund" as well. The bill was enacted so amended the following day.[28] Apparently, the Ontario schools question was Quebec's war.

The third Canada, New Canada, asked for tolerance while it went about settling into a land defined by the opportunity it provided. The term "New Canadian" itself was coined at the beginning of the century to categorize all the recent arrivals from exotic locales. A new identifier was necessary not simply because the newcomers were such a diverse group, and no existing term was capable of capturing this variety, but also because other, more accustomed terms were plainly pejorative and too specific. "New Canadians" emerged as a label, Arthur Lower considered, quite simply "because it was not as insulting as 'bohunk' or 'dago' while being more inclusive than either."[29] The term, however, retained many of the connotations of both. It meant "foreigner," in a pejorative sense: the sort of intrusive presences British and French Canadians saw around themselves every day – the "men," as J.S. Woodsworth saw them, "who dig the sewers and get into trouble at police court."[30]

In defence of Woodsworth, it should be added that, while unkind, his description was not necessarily inaccurate. If few were drunken criminals with a penchant for violence and anarchy, New Canadians did tend to work in menial jobs and did disproportionately get into trouble with the law – whether that was because the legal system did not like them, because another community had defined what was illegal, or because immigrants tended to be poor and poor people were more likely to commit crimes. In the years immediately prior to the war the incidence of Canadian criminality appears to have been rapidly increasing with immigration. In 1913, charges of all kinds increased 19.28 per cent and convictions 17.69 per cent.[31] Much of this increase appears to have been driven by the arrival in Canada of hordes of relatively disadvantaged newcomers. New Canadians by 1911 composed 6.2 per cent of the population, and were responsible for 20.84 per cent of all offences.[32] In the ten-year period ending in 1919, Canadian-born persons (78 per cent of the population) were responsible for 59 per cent of all crimes. British-born Canadians (11 per cent) of the population were responsible for 15.5 per cent of all crimes. Foreign-born Canadians (11 per cent of the population, Americans excluded) were responsible for 25.5 per cent of all crimes.[33] The representation of New Canadians among those responsible for crimes of violence was particularly marked. Between 1911 and 1916, for example, twenty-six Canadian-born persons were convicted of murder. In comparison, ten Englishmen, two Scots, three "other British," thirteen Americans, and seventy "other foreign born" persons were convicted of this most heinous offence.[34]

Nor was the stereotype that foreigners were "radicals" entirely without foundation. If New Canadians did not provide all or even the most convinced labour radicals, they were certainly well established as the most obvious socialists. Urban British and French Canadians were treated annually, every May Day, to the frightening sight of thousands of New Canadians "being harangued by demagogic speakers in German, Yiddish, Russian and Galician."[35] Through the war, as labour troubles emerged and as revolution engulfed Russia, perceptions became ever more clouded, fears greatly accentuated, and stereotypes more starkly drawn and confidently asserted. In 1917, J. Castell Hopkins, editor of the *Canadian Annual Review of Public Affairs*, defined Bolshevism as "German socialism in opposition." It was, he thought, the "natural product of the rule of men who were ignorant of all but wild theories immersed in malignant [and] disturbed minds."[36] The audience to which it appealed, most considered, was precisely Macdonald's mass of "foreign ignorance and vice," now overrunning Canada as it had the United States. Plainly the Dominion at war would not be safe unless this internal enemy were restrained.

Disappointment was plainly another factor making for strained relations. Some Canadians had hoped that the war would swing New Canadians behind the government and facilitate their integration into British Canada. Such hopes were imperfectly realized. For example, in 1916, Arthur Meighen trusted that Russia's wartime attempts at reforms would dissipate the legend of Germany as the "liberator of small nations," "and what I think most important from a Canadian point of view,"

> bring closer within range of Canadian life these certain elements of our population that until now have been neglected and under-estimated as a national asset, and lived (if my opinion is correct) under undeserved suspicion regarding their loyalty and integrity.[37]

There were 350,000 Ukrainians (though Meighen did not use the term, since no one was entirely sure what it meant at the time) in Canada – representatives of a people more numerous than the Poles. They should be encouraged to organize, he considered, to oppose the creation by Germany of an independent Poland and autonomous Galicia.[38] In the process, they would be doing valuable war work. In effect, in being better Ukrainians they would be more loyal Canadians. Reawakening Ukrainian nationalism, Meighen believed, was not a threat. Rather, it could be the anteroom to a deeper affiliation, even fellowship between this community and British Canada.

Although it is difficult to generalize, the adherence of most New Canadians to the war effort appears to have remained lukewarm. If this was Canada's war, it was not theirs. Most probably just wanted to be left out of it. How would he feel, Borden was once asked by a member of one of Canada's many minorities – a Kitchener, Ontario, German – about the Canadian war effort if he had five brothers fighting for the fatherland? Probably the same as the questioner, Borden conceded. Many plainly welcomed the war as an opportunity to move into occupations and workplaces previously denied and to earn war-inflated wages. Understandable or not, less than wholehearted support to British Canada at war always rankled, always looked like treason, particularly as wartime impacts were differentially experienced and as British Canada began to become hysterical with fear and grief. "The alien became a problem for the Government," as J.L. Carruthers suggests, "not because he was disloyal – in fact the evidence indicates the contrary [although not as fully as Carruthers believes] – but because many native born Canadians suspected him of being disloyal."[39] Suspected disloyalty, he might have added, was intolerable by 1916.

There were several factors that made New Canadian communities particularly vulnerable to any backlash gestating within the British

Canadian population among which they lived. Immigrant communities had few respected intermediaries – like, for instance, Laurier – capable of explaining their situation. In May 1917, Toronto City Council voted by a majority of seventeen to five to remove the civic franchise from all residents who had not been in Canada for twenty-five years, or who had not served or were not serving, or who did not have a son or daughter in the CEF. Alderman Singer, opposed to the resolution, angrily contended that such a measure was an anachronism. He himself was an Alien Enemy although resident in Canada for thirty years. If the council was worried about disloyalty, he considered, it should consider the case of Quebec and leave foreign-born Torontonians alone. "Do you suppose," he concluded, "that you are going to make them loyal by taking away their votes? I know of no better way by which you could make them disloyal."[40] Council did not relent, but had there been more Singers there might well have been less repression, less animosity derived ultimately from ignorance rooted in isolation.

Furthermore, New Canadians had no geographical concentration sufficient to ensure that they, like French Canadians, were necessarily treated with kid gloves, if only because of a demonstrable ability to protect themselves. If Quebec was a cat that could be expected to respond to a kick with claws and teeth, New Canada was inclined to take it or at least was seldom capable of effectively expressing any resentment – the prickly Vancouver Japanese and the voluble German population of Kitchener, Ontario, perhaps, always excepted.

French Canada, finally, was a unified bloc. New Canada was not. It was a medley of different, divided, and often bickering communities. Profound intracommunal division characterized many of them. Some of them were not truly "communities" at all but collectives of squabbling factions, each determined that it, and it alone, was competent to speak for the essential whole. Some categories that contemporary Canadians have learned to recognize – Ukrainian, Arab, Czech, and until recently "Yugoslav" – were still in the process of sorting out who was and who was not a member. Some included did not always recognize kinship. Some excluded clamoured for entry. Different spokesmen indicated different criteria for membership, while angrily denouncing rivals as frauds. The war added or accentuated divisors. Division was particularly acute following the Russian Revolution – an event followed with great interest, as can be imagined, by many New Canadians. Immigrant communities were already split and squabbling. Divisions had been brought with people from the old country. By 1917, "Red" and "White" factions were emerging quickly in many communities. Who spoke for New Canadians? A babble of voices often more concerned with silencing one another than in expressing any position British Canada could have understood, much less sympathized with.

For example, before the war it was not exactly clear what a "Ukrainian" was, although it was readily apparent that whatever they were, there were a lot of them in Canada. Was a Galician a Ukrainian? Was a Ruthenian? How about somebody from Poznania who was not exactly Polish but was not German either? How about a Jew from Kiev or Odessa? What about people of mixed ethnicity? Did the category "Ukrainian" include Uniates and the Orthodox; those who were primarily nationalist, those who were loyal to the state from which they came, those who yearned for assimilation; how about doctrinaire socialists who were sceptical of all states?[41] Was "Ukrainian" an ethnic, a national, a linguistic, or a cultural descriptor? In 1916, when "Russian" employees of the Grand Trunk denounced some of their number as "Austrians" posing as Russians to get employment (the interlopers were subsequently apprehended and shipped to Montreal for internment),[42] were any of those involved what they said they were? Did any of those involve think of themselves in categories we would recognize today?

By 1918, the Ukrainian national position began to clarify, but the political question returned with redoubled force. "Ukrainian" was now recognized as an ethnic and cultural category encompassing members of most of those groups previously indicated, which, it was hoped, would ultimately produce an amalgamated national identity. What, however, were appropriate politics for a member of this nation? This question remained unclear. How, even if this were established, would suitably Ukrainian politics be accommodated with those of the Dominion? This was less obvious still. The answer of many, perhaps most, Ukrainians took the form of what has been called "proto [Canadian] nationalism." Do not resist registration, the Nationalists and the Uniates advised in common: do not even worry about denaturalization and disenfranchisement. The government of Canada was doing the best job it could, and being as tolerant as it was able. Loyalty would produce normalization. Nothing horrified Ukrainians more, the Ukrainian Executive Council informed the Borden government, than being classified as "Austrian" and "German." Germany and Austria were military autocracies and Ukrainians hated militarism and autocracy. This is why they were in Canada, in the first place. All real Ukrainians desired fuller, not constrained, participation in the war. In exchange for tolerance, the council would direct Ukrainian Canadians into any work identified as furthering the Canadian war effort. If the government needed men for any purpose, it had only to ask. The Ukrainian Executive Council would raise the necessary volunteers.[43] In October 1918, the local Ukrainian associations in Edmonton offered to support the conscription of Ukrainian men for non-combatant service for military pay, as the Great War Veterans' Association (GWVA) had been demanding. In exchange they hoped the government would restore the franchise to those who had previously been granted it.[44] Going further still, shortly after the war, a Ukrainian committee offered to accept a head tax on all men who had not served and to assist in expelling from Canada all "German sympathisers or aliens of a seditious character" in exchange for a return to normalcy.[45] Meanwhile, by 1917, Bishop Budka, leader of the Uniate Galicians – who in 1914 had appealed to his people to support their Kaiser and Fatherland – was demanding that his flock support right manfully the Canadian war effort. He was also giving evidence to the police regarding suspected "Bolsheviks" in the Ukrainian Canadian community. The Red publishers of *Robotchny Narod* he considered to be particularly dangerous.[46] Nor was the position, even, of the "Reds" as well established as it appeared at the time. In February 1918, the Ukrainian Social Democratic Party pleaded with Borden to pay no attention to Budka and other "self styled leaders and ... political manipulators of our own nationality [whose] ... actions are responsible for the misunderstanding existing between the Ukrainians and our English speaking co-citizens." Deal directly, the socialists advised, with the Ukrainian working people. The government would be pleasantly surprised. Ukrainian socialists were not traitors. They did not advocate peace with the Central Powers. They fervently desired an Allied victory in the war. Ukrainians wanted only to work and fight. The best way for the government to ensure effective Ukrainian participation in the war effort, therefore, was simply to recruit them.[47] With what it took to be the abject, lie-down attitude of the proto-Canadians, however, *Robotchny Narod* could not agree.[48]

It is unfortunate that more Great War Canadians did not notice that many New Canadians quite plainly wished to assimilate as quickly and as totally as possible. They were "New": that much was conceded, but some wanted to be Canadian and understood very often that in British Canada this meant assimilating the habits and attitudes, even perhaps the defining characteristics, of the majority. This was a price some – perhaps most – appear to have been willing, wanting to pay. For example, studies of the Catholic German population in Saskatchewan indicate that three-quarters of new arrivals did not subscribe to parochial schools. Fewer still placed much importance on what little German-language instruction was available. German immigrants here generally wished for their children to be educated in English-language secular schools in order to facilitate their rapid transformation into acceptable Canadians according to the definition the majority of their neighbours understood. They did not wish to be Germans so much as Catholic Canadians, albeit with German surnames.[49] The perception of the local Anglican clergy – perhaps acquainted better with the abstaining 75 per cent – was that Anglican mission work would even be welcomed in many German communities on the prairies. Perhaps Anglicanism was viewed by locals as the quickest road to becoming the most acceptable possible Canadians.[50]

Going still further, during the Great War period, "German" was almost as ambiguous a category as "Ukrainian." On the ground, identities were much less clear than most statistics – and even more Great War fears – would suggest. In Western Canada in 1916, 7.8 per cent of the population was of "German" or "Austrian" descent. Nearly all were recent arrivals, as for that matter was almost everybody else. These were Alien Enemies clearly – or so we might think. However, the situation was far more complex than census categories producing comfortably exact percentages might indicate. On the one hand, the actual presence of "Germans" is apt to be understated because American emigrants were listed separately. "American" is not an ethnic descriptor, and incidental evidence suggests that many immigrants listed as "American" were actually ethnic "Germans" or "Austrians." For an appreciable number of these, movement to Canada represented a second emigration: they had first taken leave of Europe and then come north in search of still greener pastures in Canada. On the other hand, many individuals listed as "German" had only tenuous connection with Germany. Half of all recent "German" immigrants to Canada were actually *Volksdeutsch*, Danubian Swabians who arrived in Canada from Russia or Rumania – 18 per cent via the United States. Only 12 per cent of prairie "Germans" arrived in Canada from Germany itself. Most of these, if the indications of desired cultural affiliation apparent for immigrant Catholic Germans are any guide, were exactly the type of German that Bismarck stigmatized as "those who could not wait to shake the dust of the Fatherland off their feet."[51] These followed others from families that had done so long before. If, therefore, a Great War Canadian might have heard a considerable amount of German on the streets of Saskatoon, it is likely that very little of it would have been spoken by recent subjects of Wilhelm II. When considering the state of Great War Canadian "Germanness," it is interesting to reflect on the fact that an American arriving from Milwaukee and brought from Bucharest as a child would have been a more typical a representative of the species than a German fresh off the boat from Hamburg.

During the war, however an individual defined himself, or was defined, military service appears to have encouraged even members of what were otherwise targeted communities to take an extremely patriotic, intolerant attitude towards the less convinced. We have already seen how a Canadian German could denounce the treachery of Huns. The solution to the alien question, Fred Davis, a Manitoba associate of Arthur Meighen, thought, was to apply selective service to all Canadian residents, as was the practice in the United States. If Alien Enemies were engaged in the great crusade, they would return from the experience much more fully Canadian. In his district, those New Canadians who had enlisted in the army and served were coming back from France extremely proud of their war record and scornful of those who had not been to the front.[52] They were real Canadians and had the rank, ribbons, and wound stripes to prove it. The rest were a pack of alien shirkers who had yet to earn the right to reside in the Dominion. In March 1919, a "foreigner" attempted to address what appears to have been a largely Ukrainian audience in Beausejour, Manitoba. He was assailed by "Polander" veterans – probably Galicians – who, having explained what his doctrines meant to the crowd, proceeded to drag him through the streets. The unfortunate socialist was apparently made to kiss the Union flag every fifteen feet, and then put on a train after having been warned never to return.[53] Winnipeg or Vancouver veterans could not have done better and would certainly have approved. Military service, it appears, was the quickest road to affiliation with the ideals of British Canada more generally, even the unlovely ones. It might have been better for Canada, all things considered, had Davis's advice been heeded. It was, however, *post facto* even when tendered.

Some New Canadians, of course, were disliked absolutely, and would have had a rough ride – indeed, were already embarked on a rough ride – regardless of the war. The situation of the Asian population of British Columbia was probably the most difficult of all, regardless of the readily evident, even remarkable tendency of these groups of

New Canadian to support the war. In April 1917, for example, the Privy Council decided that with 10 per cent of British Columbia already Asian and with Asiatics poised to "invade" the prairies, immigration would have to be restricted. The war appears to have played no part in this decision.[54] No perceptible disloyalty in the Asian community made for this verdict except insofar as the war had considerably increased existing xenophobia. Indeed, at the time this decision was reached, the Japanese community in Vancouver was actively agitating for permission to raise a battalion for service in France, and Japan was an allied country. The hope, of course, was that Japanese Canadians would be able to settle in France and Belgium once and for all the question of whether they could ever be proper, loyal citizens of the Dominion. Earlier in the war, Japanese recruits had rioted in Vancouver. They were, it appears, frustrated at not being sent to the front quickly enough. The focus of their rage, in particular, was a newspaper office that had printed an article highlighting and misconstruing the cause of their disaffection, and questioning whether they would make good British soldiers.[55] The Japanese obviously hoped for acceptance through affiliation in a manner that might have been – had they been prepared to consider it – familiar, even welcome, to British Canadians.[56]

By Paula Hastings's showing, perceptions concerning South Asians were a little more complex, but not much different. The Indian Empire was interesting. Indian soldiers got good press during the war, and Canadians developed some fellow feelings for these other "colonials." This did not mean, however, that they were prepare to have them living next door, or were yet ready to imagine that odd beast an "Indo-Canadian."[57] Most Canadians were simply even less comfortable than the government with the idea of Asian Canadians. "Asian Canadian," for most, was an oxymoron. The question was, the staid, Liberal Toronto *Globe* thought, "whether British Columbia is to be yellow, and oriental or white and British?" "This peril," the editor thought, "has increased ten fold since the war."[58] That British Columbia could be part yellow or brown and British was inconceivable. The answer, for many Great War Canadians, was simple: expel Asians or take action, formal or informal, to keep New Canadians of this stripe in their place. Certainly they had no, or at best a modest, part in the great crusade.

The Japanese had company. Other offers to help, from other communities, were likewise rejected. We have already seen offers by several Ukrainian organizations to produce men for whatever purpose the government cared to name. Nor, despite the testimony of Lieutenant-Colonel

Cornwall that Ukrainians were good soldiers – the best in his battalion, "remarkable for their ability to learn English" – were offers to produce more taken up. "I trust," the Ruthenian Committee wrote to Meighen,

> that you will come to the conclusion that we Ruthenians in the Dominion of Canada are able to serve Canadian interests; that we are willing to become better Canadians if you will assist us; and that we realise fully the justice of the allies in the present war.[59]

While Meighen himself was sympathetic, as we have seen, this does not appear to have been a wartime lesson absorbed by much of British Canada. An offer by the Russian Orthodox Church, similarly – and the Russians were alien allies – to recruit among the Orthodox for service with the Canadian army appears to have been refused.[60] On the other hand, an offer by the Serbian government to recruit South Slavs in Canada was taken up with alacrity,[61] as appears to have been the offer of W.G. Edgecomb, the grand master of the Orange Lodge in Manitoba, to raise a mixed Assyrian, French Canadian, and Orange battalion.[62] The fate of this odd conglomeration is not known.

The truth is that most New Canadians, of whatever community, were just not liked, regardless of what they thought or did. In March 1918, Toronto policemen first began to use the new, urban railway (the "radial") rather than the regular steam train to transport Alien Enemies from their Toronto homes to a factory in the west of the city where they worked under police supervision. Women in the streetcar loudly complained to the constables. It was simply unacceptable that aliens should be permitted to ride the radial with decent folk. While the constables understood, there was nothing, they said, that they could do. They had instructions. An altercation followed. The suburban car became the scene, according to a local paper, of "much displeasure." What is remarkable about this passage is that these particular Alien Enemies were being used in a way that British Canada had demanded for more than a year. They were being made to do essential war work under police supervision for a soldier's wage.[63] In the latter war years, it seems, even the presence of aliens was no longer tolerable.

Alien Enemy, Asian immigrant, friendly alien, New Canadian, ethnic American: in the end these categories made not much difference to British Canada at war, and it was British Canada to which the Borden government ultimately answered. Most measures of wartime repression were obviously aimed or were redirected at the local level, at immigrant communities. While, in theory, it was the actual Alien Enemies who were most worrisome, the war accentuated existing nativist sentiment and produced a backlash against all New Canadians. This sort of development is not unusual in countries at war. In the United States, for example, citizens' vigilance committees may have lynched one German at Collville, Illinois, in 1918;[64] they were responsible for the death of many hundreds of Black Americans – not least during the ferocious race riots which rocked St Louis in 1917. This was not fair. It is not excusable. It was, however lamentable, the almost inevitable consequence of the presence of an alien population within a state engaged in a total war.

It is necessary, finally, to remember that not all New Canadians were as quiescent as the majority. For many native Canadians, all the proof necessary of alien treachery was readily available in the newspapers. Much was rumour. Not all appears to have been false. Some individuals do appear to have tried to help the enemy. Reported treachery provided a fillip to British Canadian fears while awakening communal memories of perils past – threats without abetted by disloyalty within.

This is not the way things are now remembered. One historian writes that "the treatment afforded enemy minority groups had little or no relationship to their supposed threat to Canada or to their behaviour during the war but was instead the product of prewar nativism legitimized by an atmosphere charged with patriotism."[65] Other historians and commentators who follow this line are too numerous to be usefully catalogued. This is simply the party line. It is not correct. That there was nativism "charged with patriotism" cannot be gainsaid, although it would be kind to remember that the circumstances were exceptional as, for example, Donald Avery does.[66] That there was no "supposed threat" is where the error lies. Real threat there was, although perhaps not as much as Great War Canadians feared, and mostly from residents of the United States. Some attacks took place. Reported threats were many. Apprehended threats were legion. That it was supposed on good authority that foreign enemies had Canadian confederates is obvious.

Some American Germans, in particular, conspired through the middle war years (1915–16) to strike at the British enemy in Canada. In June 1915, for example, there was a rash of bombings in and about what is now Windsor, Ontario. Bombs exploded in the Peabody plant in Walkerville and at an establishment contracted to make British military clothing. Bombs were discovered at the armoury and near the Gramm Motor Truck Company. Forty sticks of dynamite were discovered near the Ford plant, with thirty-six more coming to light at the Invincible

Machine Company.[67] American police ultimately arrested two men, William Lefler and Albert Carl Kaltschmidt – Detroit-area Germans – for these attacks. American authorities refused to extradite either, though Lefler was sentenced in American court to ten years' imprisonment for his crimes.[68] In March 1916, another local German, Charles Respa ("The Dynamiter of Detroit"), was indicted in Sandwich, Ontario (now Windsor), tried and found guilty of attempted sabotage, and sentenced to life imprisonment. It seems he had conspired to blow up local railways. Detroit-area Germans, local papers suggested, had responded with threats to Chief Justice Glenholme Falconbridge of Ontario who had heard the case.[69] A local woman, Mrs Abraham Slabotsky, was arrested at the same time as a spy. Apparently she had been aiding Alien Enemies to gain employment in local munitions plans and helping them to obtain illegal papers.[70]

In December 1917, after the US declaration of war, Kaltschmidt finally went on trial in Detroit. He had been, it transpired, the mastermind of another conspiracy – to blow up segments of the CPR near Nipigon, Ontario. This cabal also planned, it seems, to destroy the Windsor armoury, the rail tunnels under the Detroit and St Clair rivers, and various local munitions plants.[71] His co-conspirators cooperated with the police. They claimed that they had been involved only because they feared the vengeance of the German government if they did not follow Kaltschmidt's orders.[72] On 21 December, Kaltschmidt admitted his guilt. He had plotted sabotage in both Canada and the United States to aid his fatherland. As a former Prussian cavalry officer he could do nothing else, especially given all the "slander and vilification heaped upon Germany" during the war. He was sentenced to four years in prison. His accomplices received sentences of two to three years.[73] In March 1918, once again, five men were arrested by American authorities, suspected of manufacturing bombs in Detroit with which to blow up Canadian factories.[74]

Earlier, another American German, Fredrich Busse, apprehended attempting to blow up the Welland Canal, testified that Franz von Papen, the German military attaché, was attempting to created German and Irish paramilitaries in the United States and Canada for local action. He himself, he claimed, had been recruited by Horst von der Goltz to do this job.[75] Later, as part of the same campaign (the German General Staff having apparently decided that the destruction of the CPR would be a useful act of war), von Papen appears to have recruited Werner von Horne, a reserve officer, to organize the attempt. A bomb, in this case, actually exploded under the rail bridge at Vanceboro, Maine, but failed to sever the track. Von Horne, unlike Kaltschmidt, was ultimately extradited and imprisoned in Canada.[76] In March 1916, the German consul in San Francisco was indicted for planning to smuggle bomb-making materials into Canada for attacks on the CPR.[77] A later attempt to organize German army reservists, continent-wide, for action against Canada appears to have achieved no greater success. One coup – blowing up the power station at Niagara Falls – miscarried when the chosen bomber, George Fuchs (an alcoholic), told all to New York state police.[78] Later, two Chicago men, Heinrich Orthmann and Peter Baches, were imprisoned for conspiring to blow up the same target, following trial in American courts.[79] In 1916, an explosion had, in fact, occurred at an electro-chemical plant in Niagara. The manager had expressed himself as being utterly convinced that the explosion was the work of "outside agencies."[80] Perhaps it was. Niagara Falls, like the CPR and the Windsor armoury, appears to have been a focus of German intrigue.

Another real (and widely reported) but unrelated Windsor conspiracy appears to have developed among the local "Russian" population, and to have centred on one John Perhuda of Ford City. In June 1918 Perhuda was arrested by the Dominion Police on a charge of "inciting alien residents of the Border cities to resist registration." While making the arrest, the police also discovered a cache of disguises, pictures of railway bridges, and "two small bombs." A full-scale offensive against local New Canadians, organized by the very energetic patriot Justice Leggett, followed. As part of this offensive, Chief of Police Wills ordered four hundred suspected followers of Perhuda apprehended and searched. Was he, the local paper wondered, a German agent, or perhaps an IWW organizer? He identified himself as a "Son of Freedom" (a Doukhobor). To the authorities in Windsor, this sounded suspiciously socialist and radical.[81] It appears that the four hundred suspected collaborators were in fact escorted to police headquarters and there searched. One hundred were found to be in contravention of the MSA for failing to carry the necessary paperwork indicating their exemption from the operation of the Act. Thirty-eight of these were dispatched to nearby London, Ontario, for army in-clearance.[82] Perhuda appears to have been teaching that registration was the first step towards rounding New Canadians up for the army.[83] If this were not the purpose of the thing, he appears to have taught, then registered New Canadians "would be forced to work on their farms without pay ... [T]he Government intended to confiscate all their money."[84] At least one of Pehuda's confederates,

Andrew Bobanko, was subsequently arrested and tried for sedition. He had been advising members of his union to strike against the "bloody militarism of Canada," in defiance of local authorities he characterized as "parasites."[85]

Hapless the *Bundists* might have been. Ill intentioned, however, they were. That most of the saboteurs were not freelance terrorists but German agents was subsequently confirmed when von Papen was expelled from the United States and British intelligence searched his luggage, including his cheque book, which confirmed that payments had been made to most of the saboteurs apprehended.[86] While not the work of New Canadians – although local confederates were suspected, particularly in the Windsor bombings, and it is not certain that some of those involved had not been Canadian residents prior to 1914 – these outrages were enough to transport British Canada back to 1866, the last time good, clean-living, straight-limbed Canadian boys had stood face to face with cross-border treachery. While we might consider period fears or the swiftly developing reaction against potential enemies within excessive, we would do well to consider that attacks did occur and that in 1914 German Americans outnumbered Canadians of all types two to one.[87] The *Bundists* sowed the whirlwind. New Canadians reaped the harvest. Similarly, Perhuda may have been ignorant and alarmist, but he was also frightening and, when placed in context, probably intolerable.

Great War Canadians became edgy. The Canadian press was full of spy stories, as was the British and ultimately the American press. The war began with well-publicized and authoritatively supported reports that an attack on Victoria by German cruisers was imminent.[88] As the *Bundist* bombers began to go on trial, all Alien Enemies fell under suspicion of treachery. When the Parliament buildings burned, in February 1916, it was widely reported and believed that this was the work of saboteurs. On this occasion, as we shall see, a supposed work of sabotage led to severe reprisals against aliens in many parts of Canada. Even Laurier demanded that those guilty be found and brought to justice. Shortly thereafter, a shell factory in Hespeler, Ontario, caught fire. The only explanation that the management could imagine was that this also was sabotage. Suspicious Alien Enemies were arrested. A local man, John Schmidt, was ultimately charged.[89] That same month, Bonaventure Station in Montreal burned. The newspapers hinted darkly that an "enemy hand" appeared to be behind the tragedy, although nobody appears to have been taken into custody.[90] In March 1916, two Kitchener Germans were arrested in Pembroke, Ontario, for no particular reason.

They were there. There was an armaments factory in Pembroke. Connecting the dots was easy.[91] Another Kitchener German, that same day it seems, was engaged in attempting to blow up the barracks of the 118th Battalion. Fortunately, a vigilant sentry frustrated his scheme, although the man was not apprehended, if he existed.[92] On 2 November 1916, the Toronto *Globe* reported a "Dastardly Hun Plot" to deliberately recruit Swiss peasants and induce them to immigrate to Canada so that they could infect Canadian cattle with foot and mouth disease – each of them being armed with a small bottle containing the virus for this purpose. When, that same month, London, Ontario, experienced a rash of fires, it might be that dry conditions were the problem. It might be as well that a "mysterious automobile ... carrying German agents and their sympathizers" had been responsible as part of "a campaign to destroy as much Canadian grain as possible."[93] In September 1917, a man was arrested in Bracebridge, Ontario, for attempted sabotage. He had been found wandering the nearby woods with a head wound and with his right hand blown off. It was obvious to the locals that his plan to blow up a bridge had providentially miscarried. Oddly, the saboteur claimed to be from Winnipeg, and to have miscalculated a charge while prospecting. His claim to be a Scot was set aside in the face of irrefutable evidence. His looks were Balkan. Perhaps the subsequent amputation of his arm allayed some fears.[94] Other Germans, it appears, were using the cover of the Regina hospital to plot the destruction of the Saskatchewan Parliament building.[95]

Next to the destruction of the federal Parliament building, perhaps the most emotive event attributed to the agency of internal enemies was the Halifax harbour disaster in December 1917. The German press celebrated the explosion.[96] Surely this was all the proof that was necessary. The insurance companies, it was reported, could not understand how two ships with experienced pilots aboard could collide in a body of water 250 yards wide. Was it an accident, truly, or sabotage?[97] The suspiciously named John Johannsen, the wheelman of one of the ships involved (the *Imo*), was detained as a suspected German spy on 14 December. He had been acting queer the morning of the explosion. Although he had been at the very epicentre of the explosion, he had survived and was only pretending to be wounded, a nurse reported. Perhaps there was a connection. Halifax lost itself in trying to find one.[98] Shortly thereafter the hidden hand was at work again. A steamer en route for the United Kingdom was forced to turn about and make a run for Halifax. Inexplicably, it had begun to sink in a calm sea. The seacocks, oddly, had been opened. "It was evident," to the Canadian press at least, that "there was an enemy spy aboard, perhaps more than one."[99] In February 1918 a letter arrived at the Foundation shipbuilding company in Victoria, British Columbia. It threatened to blow up industries engaged in war work.[100] An alien, Richard Wilkus, was immediately arrested, although his only proven crime was that he had "failed to report." In his possession, however, were found "documents" which led police to believe that they had a dangerous man on their hands. He remained in detention while ships were searched for "bombs or other destructive engines."[101]

Rumours continued to circulate. When in 1918 the Canada Beds factory in Chesley, Ontario, caught fire, Alien Enemies were quickly blamed. No aspect of the Canadian war effort, it appeared, was too minor for the Kaiser's minions to notice; no hamlet so small that it was immune from attack.[102] It went without saying that, when a package addressed to Joe Zelenskey was opened by censorship authorities and found to contain gunpowder, he could be up to no good.[103] In July 1918 the sinking of the hospital ship *Llandovery Castle* appears to have produced spy mania in Halifax once again. The *Halifax Herald* quickly initiated a campaign to have all local "loafing" aliens interned. They were in the habit, the paper warned, of associating constantly with sailors and soldiers and keeping careful track of maritime movements. "The local spies must go. Halifax," the *Herald* concluded, "must be purged of treachery."[104] When in August 1918 fire ripped through a Montreal neighbourhood causing considerable damage, three men were immediately arrested – one of them an Alien Enemy. Why he should be starting a fire was never much in question.[105] "Harry" Jutting, a twenty-one-year-old native of Germany resident in Windsor, Ontario, was discovered with German literature and maps in his possession and was accordingly taken to be a spy. These things would be translated, the police warned, and appropriate action taken.[106] The next day, "Frank" Jutting was fined $100 with costs for failure to register.[107] Apparently translation had disclosed nothing untoward.

Rumours of other conspiracies came from the most reputable sources. The British director of military intelligence, for example, was worried about Irish-German intrigues against Canada and promised to pass on relevant information directly to the Dominion government.[108] There were, after all, 4,504,360 Irishmen in the United States, many of them with no fond memories, personal or inherited, of the United Kingdom. Even before the war, the British had secret service agents in the United

States keeping tabs on *Clann-na-Gael*. What could be more natural than that it would attempt to strike at Canada as it had once before? Irish republicans had collaborated with Germans to work treachery in Ireland; why not an alliance between Prussianism and the Fenians to bring Canada low? The worst was feared. With the entry of the United States to the war in April 1917, the Canadian press carried daily stories of conspiracies unmasked, traitors uncovered in the United States. No less an authority than Senator George E. Chamberlain, chairman of the Senate's Military Committee, asserted that the American navy was rotten with German spies and that the IWW was nothing less than a German conspiracy.[109] Shortly thereafter, the anarchist leaders Emma Goldman and Alexander Berkman were sentenced to two years in prison and fined $10,000 for opposition to the war and as obvious German confederates.[110]

It is less than accurate, therefore, to say that there were no "supposed" threats. There were real threats, and real attacks, though no actual attack was very effective. Supposed threats were innumerable.

To understand the actions of the Canadian government, however, knowledge of Canadian dissent is not enough. Nor, even, is an appreciation of how much British Canada misconceived and resented French Canadian reluctance, how much it disliked many New Canadians, or how terrified it was of saboteurs and traitors. Quite plainly, the threat was not equivalent to the means often employed to meet it, foot dragging in some elements of national organization for war notwithstanding. A fire hose was employed to put out a match. To understand why, we must understand the position of British Canada at war, the community from which the Borden government came, to which it answered, and which it most feared.

4 "A Life and Death Struggle for Christian Civilization": The Great British Canadian Crusade

We must give more money and accept greater taxation, for the cost of the war is growing greater. We must produce more food though we have fewer men to work, for unless we do, our Allies will starve. We must give more men to the army even though we have not enough men to carry on the country's work, for, unless we give them, the enemy will triumph by sheer weight of numbers. And yet, however impossible the task may appear, we must attempt it, for, as the British Prime Minister has said: **The only alternative now is "to go on or go under."** We would be recreant to all that is noble in British history, to our own brave men at the front, and to the great and just cause which we have made our own, if we falter now at our determination to go on. I say deliberately and with a full sense of the gravity of my words: it is better to go on and die in the struggle for freedom and justice and independence than to go on living and be slaves. For that is the real issue.
        The Right Reverend David Williams, Bishop of Huron, June 1918[1]

The Great War would have presented a challenge for French and New Canada regardless of what was happening in Canada's other community, if only because it raised the questions "What is Canada?" and "How do we fit into it?" in a manner that could not be avoided. Nor could the answers be easily muddled. The way in which the war was interpreted in British Canada, however, ensured that one of the primary tasks of the Canadian government, at home, was to ensure that pre-existing intercommunal dislike and distrust did not metastasize into civil conflict. Steadily through the war, difficult questions produced a dangerous public squabble. By 1916, the bickering was boding well to become a riot. To understand why this was, we must understand the disposition of British Canada: in its own eyes, a long-suffering, much aggrieved plaintiff – the betrayed and vilified Atlas of the nation; an aggressive, intolerant, and often violent assailant, as judged by its communal adversaries.

Even before the war accentuated animosities, British Canada had come to view Canada's other communities with considerable scepticism. British Canada was prepared to accept French Canada provided that it understood what the privilege of being "British" entailed. Pre-war crises had seemed to indicate that French Canada was uncertain, and would have to be guided into the red, white, and blue future. On the other hand, British Canada had not yet come to terms with New Canadians of most varieties and viewed the crowds of foreigners arriving in Canada with a mixture of dislike, disgust, and distrust it did not attempt to hide. They had been let in only because emigration from Britain and the other Dominions was insufficient to permit Canada to be settled quickly enough to keep the Americans out. There was no need to welcome what could not be avoided and did not require encouragement. Few doubted that the assimilation of the New Canadians was necessary. Anybody not with this program had no place in Canada. And though Britain might not be sufficiently strong or resolute to maintain the Empire, this did not mean that it would fail. Canada and the other Dominions would inherit, taking up where failing Britain left off. British Canadians understood that being "Canadian" made them different from other Britons, and they could on occasion make much of this fact. They considered, however, that this difference was less important than the fundamental facts of shared faith, blood, and culture and the common heritages and history that kept the Empire together. Most British Canadians would have concurred with Principal Grant of Queen's University when he said, "We are Canadian, and in order to be Canadian we must be British."[2] Today the statement appears paradoxical. In 1914, for many, it was a simple declaration of irrefutable fact. These perceptions affected profoundly the way this community experienced the Great War and the way in which it interpreted the less fully engaged attitude of other Canadian communities.

The outbreak of war in 1914 had led to intense excitement. The greatest worry of most British Canadians was that Canada would not be ready in time to participate effectively. The year 1915 did not produce doubts but renewed conviction. By the spring, when Canada experienced its first significant casualties, British Canada was engaged in a crusade to save the British empire, Christianity, and – following the great atrocity publicity campaigns[3] – common decency from the German Antichrist. "The last ten months," the Right Reverend David Williams told the synod of the Diocese of Huron in 1915,

> have supplied a sample of Germans ways and civilization. The sack of Louvain, the destruction of Churches, Universities, and Libraries, the murder of old men and women of seventy, the slaughter of innocent children, the rape of young girls, the ruthless devastation of Belgium and Russian Poland by fire and sword take us back over a thousand years before we find a parallel. Not until we arrive at the Huns under Attila or the early Mohammedan hordes under the Caliph Omar and the sack of Alexandria do we meet with such ruthless and fierce devastation. If these are the fruits of German "Kultur," then from all such "Good Lord Deliver us"! Yet can we doubt, if Germany should prove victorious, that the same ruthless methods would be applied to crush the whole world under the iron heel of brute force? This is therefore a world conflict, and all the nations of the world are perforce intensely concerned in it. In short we now see clearly that this is a life and death struggle for Christian civilization.[4]

In 1915 British Canada made the shift from perceiving participation in the war as being fulfilment of a debt of gratitude owed Britain – the price of being "British" – to perceiving it as being full-scale engagement in a worldwide clash of ideals which Canada would have to fight with its fullest powers for itself, alone if necessary. Opposition to the great crusade was not simply wrong but actively evil.[5] Some particularly militant British Canadian patriots even bemoaned the fact that Canada was fighting as a colony rather than an ally, since this provided ready excuse for shirking. They believed that an independent contribution would force Canada to mobilize its full strength for the fight.[6] "If we are merely lending a hand to save our kinsmen and friends in Great Britain," the *Edmonton Bulletin* considered,

> our contribution has ... been a striking testimonial to our neighbourliness and our loyalty ... But if we are fighting ... to preserve our national liberties and our individual lives and rights, the case is somewhat different. On that understanding we are required to put ourselves into the conflict as though we were fighting to protect our homes and country and all that we have to lose.[7]

The principal Protestant denominations – Methodist, Presbyterian, and Anglican[8] – already at the root of British Canadian nationalism facilitated the movement from participation in a brother's war to all-out crusade.[9] The line of the Catholic Church in British Canada was little different. Richard Allen has gone so far as to assert that without the whole-hearted participation of the Canadian churches there could have been no real war effort.[10] He is probably correct. It is a highly significant fact, in this regard, that the Canadian churches were not appalled but confirmed, even exalted, by sacrifice.[11] The worse things got, the more excited they seemed to become, the more directly they related Canada's position in the war to biblical patterns, the more glorious the vision of the postwar paradise they related to their congregations. "Civilisation comes through fire," Edward Harvey Oliver, principal of Presbyterian College Saskatchewan, told his charges in 1916, the cost of the Battle of the Somme then being calculated: "redemption through a cross, life through death. We are learning today what sacrifice means, for the human race is marching to its Calvary."[12] But fear not! This only meant that Canada had been judged and was being purified. The times were desperate, but Canada was Gideon. A sanctified nation would surely emerge out of the war. That the Canada that came out of the war would be cleansed by the struggle none doubted. What this meant depended on the denomination of the observer. For Methodist and Presbyterian social gospellers it meant a new, teetotal, more equitable society[13] – a society that appeared to be actually emerging during the war.[14] For Anglicans the war seemed to promise a renewal, even an increase, of British immigration, more churches, and imperial federation to create a glorious worldwide English-speaking super-state including perhaps the United States.[15] This was a vision surely worth much sacrifice.

Why Canadian churches reacted in a way that would have been considered unbalanced even in the United Kingdom requires some explanation. Part of the reason appears to have been that, finding themselves locked in an increasingly secular, anti-clerical society, the principal Protestant denominations, especially, looked to the war to produce a revival. Indeed, they indicted secular society for having produced the war – an obvious judgment of God. So, at least Major Dixon, Anglican canon and county chaplain, told 1,900 Orangemen in St Paul's Bloor Street, Toronto. "[I]t was because the world had forsaken God and gone after material things that the war was on." "We were steeped to the eyes in materialism before 1914 ... Christianity as practiced in Christian countries has been a sham."[16] The New Jerusalem would arrive through the fires of the Western Front. Only a purified Canada would be worthy to build it. The greater today's pain, the more glorious and certain was tomorrow's reward – so preached the clergy at home and so the chaplains at the front. A significant number of Canada's volunteers, in fact, appear to have shared this faith.[17]

Of all churches, the Anglican Church – third largest Protestant denomination in the Dominion but probably the most culturally and politically influential – was the pace-setter, and to some extent other denominations appear to have been pulled in its wake as it steered full speed, gun decks manned, into the Holy War.[18] Disproportionate Anglican engagement was inevitable. The particular character of the Anglican Church ensured that it would be drawn into the conflict quickly and totally. In Canada, it was not just the Church of England but the church of immigrant English, Welsh, and a considerable number of Irish Protestants – the Church of England and Ireland in Canada. A disproportionate response from this congregation was certain. Canada was, moreover, a new country in which an immigrant, mission church – not established here – had long competed with other denominations for the attention of potential faithful. Prior to the First World War, the feeling was that the Anglican Church should do so by stressing, rather than playing down, those characteristics which made it unique; that the church had a definite role to play in the shaping of a new country and could best fulfil its mission by strengthening and constantly reiterating what it considered to be its particular historical task.[19] It was special because it was overtly British. The maintenance of the British connection and the Anglification of Canada was its ordained work. To view the issue another way would have been to deny what he considered made the Anglican Church special. There was no room for weakness or hesitation.

The Methodist Church in Canada, the largest Protestant denomination in the Dominion, had specialized in mission work in the years prior to the war – attempts to reach the backsliders in the Canadian population, to expand the reach of the Gospel overseas, and to help assimilate immigrants into the emerging Canadian nation defined in suitably earnest, Wesleyan terms.[20] The problem, as J.S. Woodsworth saw it, was not whether the New Canadians would be assimilated. British Canada would assimilate or be assimilated. The latter possibility, of course, was unthinkable.[21] The possibility of an amalgamation, condominium, or fusion was not even considered. In Canadian society, Methodists laboured to produce the attributes of what they thought an ideal society would be like – particularly to eliminate those sources of distraction which they considered "broad and slippery paths leading to perdition": dancing, card playing, music halls and theatres, horse racing, and novel reading, for starters. Through the nineteenth century, the church gradually realized that the state could be a powerful assistance in establishing the New Jerusalem, or at least in keeping pandemonium at bay. Legislation worked much more quickly, it discovered, than attempts at moral renewal. Outlawing the thing was the highway to moral progress. An alliance emerged.[22] In 1914 a mighty obstacle appeared on the progress road: Prussian militarism. It would have to be removed before the journey could continue. The fight was God's. His chosen instrument was the British Empire.[23] Doctor Samuel Chown, rifleman in the Princess of Wales' Own Rifles during the Fenian raids and Methodist national convenor, left no one in doubt of his support for Britain's efforts in the great crusade, as the horrible news from Belgium began to arrive.

> For myself it is enough to know that Christ, as I perceive Him, would not stand with limp hands if a ruthless soldier should attempt to outrage His holy mother as the women of Belgium were violated. To Him all motherhood is sacred; nor would He retreat and give place to the armed burglar, breaking with murderous intent into His home; nor would He witness, without any effort to prevent it, the destruction of the civil and religious liberty which His teaching has enthroned in our British Empire. His manhood is without seam throughout, and I believe Canada is right in this war.[24]

Khaki, he asserted, was now a "sacred colour."[25] The Reverend Doctor Creighton, editor of the *Christian Guardian*, had a son with the 95th Highlanders. He was proud that his son was only one of 252 sons of Methodist clergymen already serving in France by February 1916. Lester Pearson's father, the Reverend Edwin Pearson, advised his Guelph, Ontario, congregation that "the principal reason" that he supported the government was that all his children – all three sons – were at the front.[26] At least one Methodist clergyman carried support for the war effort to its logical conclusion. Reverend E.W. Edwarde actually served as an infantry lieutenant with the CEF, sending against the foe of social and moral progress not simply anathemas but bullets.[27] Chown himself accepted an honorary lieutenant-colonelcy during the war, and as Michael Bliss demonstrates, worked hard to train his own aging body so that if necessary he could ply the sword himself to good effect.

It would have been difficult to find anywhere in the Dominion a Protestant divine prepared to openly disagree; indeed, one who thought much differently. Professor Griffith, in London, Ontario, at a conference of academics and clergyman, used the Bible as his source in declaring that the "aggressor should die by the sword; and Germany was the aggressor."[28] The Reverend George Adams, speaking to a packed house on the third anniversary of the war in Montreal's American Presbyterian Church, recognized only two categories of Canadians: patriots and traitors. It was nothing less than treason, he said, to wear fancy clothes and gad about town, dining in fine restaurants, when allies starved and war work went undone for lack of willing hands.[29] Woodsworth was not the only one who saw a danger in the New Canadians. The Reverend Doctor Peter Strong – the Presbyterian home missions superintendent, and therefore charged with responsibility for missions among New Canadians, which the Presbyterians, like the Methodists, took seriously – saw one too. The trouble was the concentration of these offensive, potentially disloyal peoples in the West. Canada was not waiting to be invaded. It had already been infested, and a considerable "enemy salient" had formed in the West, with its centre in southern Saskatchewan. "We are building a nation in Canada today," he warned, "and one of our difficulties in building these people into it is that they are thus massed together, many alien in thought and ideal and some of them perhaps in sympathy. The Germans say little and are quietly celebrating their gains."[30]

British Canadian Catholics concurred. "Where were you in the Hour of Crisis?" Bishop Fallon of London, leader of the Ontario Irish, demanded of an audience in Chatham, Ontario. If any Catholic failed to do his duty against the hideous evil which had arisen in Germany and which threatened to consume Christendom, he warned, then that miserable recreant had better not come to the bishop's manse looking for "advice or counsel" when the shooting was over.[31] In a field that provided stiff competition, Fallon was tough to beat for expressions of patriotic conviction. In 1910 he had already come to the attention of the militia department for delivering a particularly rousing, patriotic sermon at a church parade for the 7th City of London Fusiliers on the theme of the coming war with Germany (or Japan), during which he lauded the British Empire for carrying the cross against "degenerate" Boers and pagan savages. The minister of militia, Sam Hughes – the notoriously Orange Sam Hughes – was so impressed that he had the sermon printed and circulated throughout the militia.[32] In 1911 Fallon repeated the performance. Speaking at the Canadian Club, with Henri Bourrassa and Mackenzie King in attendance, he stated his "deliberate conviction that Germany intend[ed] to try to take command of the world's affairs."[33] Canada, and the British Empire generally, would be God's instrument in preventing this diabolical outburst. There was a remarkable performance for an Irish Catholic bishop, all in all. In February 1917, he offered one-third of his net income to the patriotic fund, provided that one hundred others with annual incomes exceeding $3,000 did the same.[34]

Other Catholic bishops were equally engaged in the good fight. Archbishops Casey of Vancouver, McNeil of Ontario, and Sinnott of Winnipeg, Bishops Gauthier of Ottawa and Morrison of Antigonish, like Fallon, all followed (indeed, strengthened) the line established by Cardinals Bourne of Westminster and Mercier of Belgium and ultimately taken up by Gibbons of the United States. Germany was apostate – actually, sneeringly evil – and deserved chastisement. This was holy work, a Christian duty; charity in fact. Archbishop Sinnott, drumming for the victory loan of 1917, abjured his flock: "He who willingly and knowingly refuses such aid must be condemned as ungrateful. And recreant in his duty to that country whose protection, prosperity, and liberty he uses and enjoys, and therefore, false to the teachings of our holy religion."[35] Such a viper, it need hardly be added, had better not come slithering up to the archiepiscopal manse looking for postwar unction.

Throughout the war, the causes of the nation and of Christ were so fully conflated in British Canada that members of all denominations gravely scrutinized recruiting figures, which indicated the religious affiliation of soldiers, for fear that members of other communions might be more obviously, militantly engaged in the Holy War. Failure to produce soldiers at least equivalent to a denomination's proportion of the population at large was taken as proof of a lack not only of national but of religious conviction. "For a great crisis," Bishop Williams thought, "reveals not only men, but religious communions as well. If Anglicans have volunteered so much more readily than others, it is because the Anglican Church is the great nursery of loyalty to imperial ideals and national duty."[36] He might have added, by extension, that it therefore obviously did a better job in inculcating Christian principles among the faithful. Methodists and Catholics, worried at their own shirking ways, strove to do better.

It is sometimes thought – and was at the time asserted – that Canada's "British" patriotism during the First World War represented an immature national consciousness. The assertion is not without some merit, but it is only partly correct. It might be that memories *were* greener of a homeland across the sea in British than in French Canada. However, we should recognize as well that period British Canadians wove religion and local and imperial patriotism into a seamless whole and could simply not understand any species of "Canadian" patriotism that did not. "We are fighting for nothing less than our life as a nation," the Reverend Doctor McLeod, a Presbyterian clergyman in Barrie, told men of the second contingent.

> Many people in Canada do not seem to be alive to this fact, and some do not seem willing to be made alive to it, though the life of Canada is as much at stake as the life of Britain. Canadian liberty and security depend now, and have always depended, on Britain. It is a mistaken view of the case to speak of Canada helping Britain in this war. Canada is fighting for her own life and in her own defence. "The Day" the Germans toasted has come, the Day of Destiny for Britain, Canada and Germany. There is no other course for us than to fight. All internal strifes should be swept away in the high tide of patriotic loyalty. The grandest thing in the war is the high, noble and Christian spirit shown by the British nation and army in the conflict.[37]

Not every Canadian clergyman was convinced, of course, nor were all denominations engaged. When, however, religious scruples took the form of criticism, reaction could be swift and ruthless. The Lutherans, of course, could not be expected to much like the thing. They were closely watched, their publications monitored, and on several occasions action was taken.[38] For example, in March 1916, Dominion Police visited a Lutheran pastor, the Reverend Hansen, from Conestoga near Berlin (Kitchener), Ontario. His pro-German treachery, it appears, had grown too great to be borne.[39] He had best relocate or learn patriotism. There were no other choices. We will see more like this. New Light evangelists, as well, speaking to largely immigrant American congregations, could sometimes go too far for Canada's liking. One of them, the Pentecostal evangelist Arthur Watson, expressed himself to his congregation as being of the belief that "men who put on ... Khaki were a disgrace to the country," surely destined for hell as "murderers"; that "the British Parliament was bleeding Canada dry; that King George was just as bad as the Kaiser and did not go any nearer to the battle-front; that people were foolish to enlist." He was immediately arrested, arraigned, found guilty under the WMA – the papers carried the story as "sedition" – and sentenced to a fifty-dollar fine. In fact, Watson appears to have spent ten days in jail. This conviction was upheld on appeal.[40] The pacifist and pacifistic sects were suspect from the beginning, particularly where a foreign origin was obvious. Perhaps Quakers could be tolerated. Christadelphians, Jehovah's Witnesses, and Plymouth Brethren bore watching and correction when necessary. Mennonites and Doukhobors, of course, were very suspicious, even though understood. Mormons, as well, Reverend Doctor Ferguson warned from a Toronto Presbyterian pulpit, were disloyal, even if tolerance of their "veiled polygamy, and attempts to undermine Christianity and Christian institutions" were not a standing provocation to God, dangerous in this time of testing.[41] Members of these denominations, clergymen and otherwise, would have to watch their step and could not count on tolerance for dissent of any kind, however minute, arising from religious conviction.

The transformation of crusading fervour into effective military and political organization was facilitated by interlinking organizations long part, with the principal Protestant churches, of the imperialist complex – the Loyal Orange Lodge (LOL), the militia, and the Imperial Order Daughters of the Empire (IODE), for example. The support of the first was particularly critical not only because the Orange Lodge was, by definition, militantly imperialist and composed of good churchmen but also, quite simply, because one in three adult Protestant Canadian men was a member. The Lodge was particularly powerful in Ontario, New Brunswick, and what was then the Dominion of Newfoundland. Socially it found its primary audience in the skilled working class. The influence of the LOL was much more important in period Canada than might now be imagined, and its actions much less malign, most of the time. However, Orangeism – for most contemporary Canadian academics – remains what Ruth Dudley Edwards notes it has been for their British and Irish counterparts: "a closed, unreadable, and rather distasteful book."[42]

The LOL had arrived in Canada with massive Irish (largely Protestant) immigration in the nineteenth century and flourished. The particular circumstances of Canada, especially Ontario and the Maritimes, provided "ideal conditions"; fertile soil indeed for an ideology based on militant loyalty and Tory social principles, linked inextricably to established Protestantism.[43] The Lodge succeeded not simply because many British Canadians Protestants distrusted Catholics (though they did). In Canada, the sectarianism of the LOL was always subordinate to its militant imperialism in its power to attract adherents. The "garrison mentality" that the Orangemen brought with them from Ireland fitted the Canadian bill perfectly. Canada would be kept loyal against the great, American dissolver. Not for nothing was the highest level of initiation in the Canadian Lodge "Scarlet Marksman," and when a Canadian Orangeman solemnly vowed that he would be citizen of no republic, he did not mean Eire. Canadians who could not be counted on to be loyal would be watched and if necessary prevented from attempting to pull the emerging nation into any other path than that chosen by John Graves Simcoe and the sanctified authors of the British North America Act; that defended by the heroes of 1812, 1837, 1866, and 1885. Canada must be fortified to embrace its destiny – one Dominion under the Union flag, Mariposa *Britannicus et invictus ad mare usque ad marem*, part of a living, glorious, and eternal empire. The LOL and other, often affiliated fraternal organizations, therefore, helped to link members of all of Canada's various "British" communities together into a coherent whole and to yoke it to the British Canadian cause – something, of course, which they had no small part in defining.

In Canada, the LOL had particularly potent ties to both the Anglican and Methodist churches. An evangelical Church of Ireland flavour was powerfully evident in Canadian Anglicanism from the middle nineteenth century, particularly in southwestern Ontario. Much of this part of the country had been settled under the direction of the convinced Tory and very Irish Colonel Thomas Talbot. The moving force behind the establishment of the church locally had been Bishop Benjamin Cronyn, Irish himself, and in the habit of returning to Ireland to recruit clergy.[44] Orangemen were prominent in the prewar Canadian militia, in the trade unions (we have already seen that half of all trade unionists were Orange), and within the ranks of other fraternal organizations – the Oddfellows and the Masonic order most particularly.[45] At least three Canadian prime ministers have been Orangemen – Sir John A. Macdonald, Mackenzie Bowell, and latterly John Diefenbaker. It was usual at the beginning of the twentieth century for Canadian federal governments to contain several Orange ministers. In Borden's government, most particularly, successive ministers of militia – Sam Hughes and then Edward Kemp – were members. Arthur Meighen, the government workhorse, was not an Orangemen, although it was odd that he was not. He was typical of the breed: a quiet, ambitious, humourless man (at least in public life) from an Ulster family; a lifelong teetotaller whose only apparent purposeless recreation was hymn singing around

4.1. Meeting of LOL 2533, Forest Lawn, Alberta, uniformed members in attendance. Picture courtesy of the Glenbow Archives.

a piano played by his wife, at home of course.[46] Meighen was, however, chairman of the Irish Protestant Benevolent Society and remained the darling of the LOL throughout his political career. At lower levels of Canadian politics – the level at which national differences did not have to be accommodated – the participation of Orangemen in politics was more marked, and in 1914 the Lodge was at the height of its influence. In 1915, one-third of the members of the Ontario legislature were actively Orange. In 1914, seven of ten Toronto MPPs were Orange. During the nineteenth century, twenty of twenty-three mayors of Toronto were Orangemen, as was the wartime incumbent, Tommy Church.[47] At the outbreak of war, four of five members of the board of control and two-thirds of city council were brethren.[48] And Toronto, the Belfast of North America, was not unique in the province. If, on 12 July 1914, 15,000 Orangemen marched in Toronto, 7,000 marched in Lindsay, 5,000 in Goderich, 5,000 in tiny Arthur, and 16,000 in St Thomas, the centre of the Talbot Settlement.[49] At a 1914 meeting of the Grand Lodge of Ontario West, 800 delegates attended, representing 700 lodges and 150,000 members. The LOL's newspaper, the *Sentinel*, had tripled its circulation since 1905 and was probably the largest Canadian weekly, with nearly 30,000 subscribers. It arrived faithfully on 81 per cent of Toronto doorsteps by the outbreak of war.[50] The *Sentinel* was simply stating the truth when it exulted that the Lodge was, quite plainly, "the most powerful body of the kind in Canada."[51] Indeed, it was probably then the most powerful political organization to which Canada has ever played host.

For Orangemen, the British Empire was "the fullest expression of Protestant destiny ... the ultimate achievement of world civilisation."[52] The response of the Lodge to war was immediate, and immoderate. Almost every available, able-bodied Orangemen immediately enlisted – "[t]he Loyal Orange Lodge ... virtually transferred itself bodily to Flanders Fields," one historian of the Lodge writes.[53] While aggregate numbers would now be difficult, perhaps impossible, to establish, it appears that 50,000 Orangemen were in the trenches by the Battle of the Somme. Eighty thousand ultimately served. One-third of the first and second contingents appear to have been Orange.[54]

In 1914, the Canadian militia was no longer the social-political power it had been in the first decades after Confederation, but it retained considerable local social cachet – constituting a principal pillar of the hundreds of local systems, the many Mariposas, of which British Canada consisted and which generated the Canadian army. In 1914, it was still not at all unusual for Canadians notable in other spheres of society to hold militia rank, substantive or honorary. Many units, particularly in the West, had only just been raised, generally by local notables commissioned for the task.[55] Several members of the Borden government were members of the militia, including of course Sir Sam Hughes and Major General Sam Mewburn, the minister of militia in the war's last year. The censorship authorities, as well, were dominated by militiamen – undoubtedly one of the reasons why cooperation between civil and military authorities became so quickly so complete in Great War Canada. In many ways, the volunteer army of the first war years represented less a departure from the norm than an intensification of patterns long understood in British Canada. The fact that the wartime army was generated largely from the prewar militia ensured that the Canadian Corps was a little slice of British Canada, retaining connection to the greater whole from which it could never be divorced and by which it would never be disowned. The units which it comprised, moreover, were less formed by national effort, according to a centrally directed plan, than generated by and composed of local enthusiasts serving together – boosters and babbits, flesh of the flesh and blood of the blood of so many Mariposas. The phrase "91st Battalion Canadian Corps" sounded cold, remote, and anonymous. There was nothing cold, remote, or anonymous about the "Elgin's Own," in Elgin County, Ontario.

The Imperial Order Daughters of the Empire (IODE) was founded in 1900 by Mrs Clark Murray, the wife of a McGill university professor. It quickly became the most powerful women's organization in the Dominion. Its stated purposes require no comment. The IODE existed to stimulate patriotism among women and children; create an effective organization in wartime if required; promote the study of imperial questions; care for military dependants; and improve all things "imperial" by female action. How members of this organization were apt to digest the fact of the First World War is obvious. By 1918, the IODE had seven hundred chapters nationwide, and forty thousand members.[56] It was by far the largest and most powerful women's organization in the country. Given the scale of its work, it was probably the most powerful women's organization Canada has ever seen. Like the LOL, it is not much studied today, for much the same reason. The whole-hearted association of the Order with the war effort and its complex linkage to other women's organizations (confessional church groups, political parties, various committees for social amelioration and improvement) ensured that Great War "girl power" was a virtual patriotic monopoly.

It would be fitting to write more on this issue, but this aspect of the war and this facet of early twentieth-century Canadian reality have been too little studied to permit that to be possible.

Different patriotisms and responses to the challenge of war produced necessarily different impacts. While this subject remains a painful one for many Canadians, it is clear that the war was essentially British Canada's crusade, with French Canada and the New Canadians participating much less fully, sometimes cheering on the boys, at other times grumbling at the cost of it all and attempting to distance themselves from sacrifice insofar as possible. Perhaps, even, some members of these communities did rather well out of the affair if they succeeded in individually extricating themselves from participation in a conflict communally viewed as a dangerous option rather than an urgent necessity. It is true that what data remains about the identity of Great War soldiers is not sufficiently complete to establish proportions with absolute precision.[57] While not uncontroversial or unquestioned, period figures indicate something of the degree of difference. We will not dwell on these figures because, for our purpose, gross aggregate comparisons are good enough.

The Canadian army raised and maintained four divisions for service in France, and by 1918 another which never left bases in the United Kingdom. Only one French-language infantry battalion – the 22nd – saw frontline service. By January 1917, figures submitted to the Imperial War Cabinet suggest that 9.6 per cent of all Canadian men were then in uniform; 1.4 per cent of French Canadian men had put on khaki; 6.7 per cent of men of "foreign" (mainly "other European" or "American") extraction had answered the call. Meanwhile, 37.5 per cent of men of "British" origin had rallied to the colours.[58] The *Toronto Telegram* reported in June 1917 that, while Ontario had provided 167,457 recruits, the province of Quebec had only contributed 44,050 – only 7,000 of them French Canadian with the remainder coming from the minority British Canadian population.[59] In March 1917, Canadian figures suggest a total population of about 7,750,000. Just over two million were French Canadians. More than a million of the residual had emigrated from other shores, and were not British subjects. Many of these were Alien Enemies. Something like four million British Canadians, therefore, sustained, with very little help from other communities, an army swollen to almost 500,000 men, while contributing a large share of the 305,000 men urgently needed for munitions work,[60] and otherwise attempting to maintain the war effort at home.

When religion is considered, striking differences in enlistment rates are apparent between denominations, even within British Canada. Most of the first contingent had been Anglican, for the simple reason that the great majority of new immigrants to Canada from Britain were Anglican.[61] In February 1916, however, 47 per cent of all Canadian soldiers were still Anglican, although only one in seven Canadians belonged to that denomination and the British emigrant community had long been tapped. Among troops actually serving in France (176,262), 75,394 were Anglican (45 per cent), 18,164 Methodist (10.3 per cent), 41,029 Presbyterian (23.2 per cent), 26,143 Roman Catholic (14.8 per cent), 8,519 Baptist and Congregationalist (4.8 per cent), 376 Jewish, and 6,637 were members of other denominations and faiths. Even conscription did not much change things, perhaps because Anglican neighbourhoods were more than usually inclined to treat the thing seriously. Throughout the war, Anglicans were, therefore, about twice as likely as Presbyterians, three times as likely as Baptists and Congregationalists, four times as likely as Methodists, and ten times as likely as Catholics to seek service. Anglicans were never less than 41 per cent of the Canadian army. In 1917, if Borden's promise to field 500,000 Canadians had been fulfilled, with every denomination contributing its "fair share," Anglicans would have already filled their quota twice over. Local enlistment rates could be higher still. In 1916, the Bishop of Huron claimed to know of one battalion, passing through London, Ontario, that contained 650 Anglicans, another with 600, and a third recently despatched with 400. All the eligible sons of diocesan clergymen were in service. Eighteen of forty-two students in seminary (currently Huron University College, University of Western Ontario) had gone – three were already dead. In many congregations, every available man had enlisted. One parish had provided, by February 1916, three hundred soldiers.[62] The Diocese of Huron was less peculiar than we might think. Christ Church Cathedral, in Montreal, has more than three hundred names on its First World War honour roll. Methodists might dispute the figures, but it was quite clear to contemporaries that some denominations were doing much more to further the cause of victory than others.[63]

Disproportionate direct participation in the war involved, inevitably, correspondingly heavy sacrifice. By 1916, much of British Canada was feeling the pinch. By 1917, as the casualty rolls grew ever longer, it was becoming hysterical and finding focus, especially in communities disproportionately impacted. "It makes one feel very sad," Lieutenant Roberta Catherine Macadams, soldier representative in the Alberta

SOLDIERS AND NURSES FROM ALBERTA!!

You will have TWO VOTES at the forthcoming Election under the Alberta Military Representation Act.

LOOK FOR No. 14 ON YOUR BALLOT PAPER!

LOOK FOR No. 14 ON YOUR BALLOT PAPER!

Miss ROBERTA CATHERINE MacADAMS,
Lieut, C.A.M.C., Ontario Military Hospital, Orpington, Kent.

SHE WILL WORK NOT ONLY FOR YOUR BEST INTERESTS BUT FOR THOSE OF YOUR WIVES, MOTHERS, SWEETHEARTS, SISTERS AND CHILDREN AFTER THE WAR.

Remember those who have helped you so nobly through the fight.

4.2. Election poster for Roberta Macadams. The message is clear. Picture courtesy of the Glenbow Archives.

Legislative Assembly, considered in April 1918, "to visit the West now. You see the country being cleared of our fine, Anglo-Saxon stock and the aliens left to fatten on war prosperity."[64] Lieutenant Macadams's intolerance should not surprise. Envy is a common vice. The LOL, fully committed and inevitably heavily hit, was always ready with inimical comparisons. In October 1917, Toronto's 101,857 Anglicans contributed $10,031.20 to one of the periodic Red Cross donation drives. The tiny (2,000 member) and less well heeled Salvation Army community had anted up a spectacular $1,393.51. The Metropolitan Methodist Church alone had found $823.00 for the boys overseas. On the other hand, 43,080 Roman Catholics had donated $509.66 for the comfort of the troops. St Michael's Cathedral chipped in five dollars. Similarly, while Protestant and non-denominational colleges at the University of Toronto had lost half their students by 1917, St Michael's College had significantly increased its enrolment. It did not take the LOL long to identify the cause of such striking disparity, its answer predictable.[65] In time of war, with kin being killed and the issue in doubt, tremendous sacrifices made and patriotism deliberately stoked, these sorts of disparity invited comment and quickly produced conflict, particularly in a system in which engagement (or not) in the war effort remained largely voluntary, and in which, in any case, differences between communities were already marked, and politically charged even before the war.

Consider, as well, that in 1914 Canada was (and still is outside the largest cities) predominantly working class in make-up and tone: a beer-quaffing rather than wine-drinking nation. As Arthur Meighen informed a shocked Lord Derby (Lloyd George's war minister) in 1917, there were no "gentlemen of leisure" in Canada – or, in any case, those who amassed the wherewithal to be leisured tended to migrate to more agreeable surroundings. As elsewhere where similar conditions prevail, where in the Canadian working class an individual stood was tremendously important, with the distinction between the "reputable" and the "disreputable" critical to self-respect. "Reputable," "skilled" workers had always tended to be British Canadian, as we have seen. These were now disproportionately at, or going to, the front. Over-enlistment of "British" workers meant the loss of their jobs to members of other communities and the realignment of workplaces to permit more work to be done with fewer, less skilled workers – now of course receiving considerably better pay than had previously been the case. "British" workers in Ontario were the bulk of the unionized population, as we have also seen. These processes impacted most heavily on their interest, and compromised most completely their notion of what was appropriate and equitable. New Canadians and French Canadians, often the obvious beneficiaries of the new dispensation, were quickly targeted for criticism and sometimes for attack. When a Great War British Canadian called a New or French Canadian a "slacker," we can usually take it for granted that "blackleg" and "scab" were included, and "traitor" implied. In Britain, labour "dilution" produced dissent. In Canada, the same process increased intercommunal and wartime polarity.

When British citizens go away to fight," the *Northern Miner* considered, "their places are filled by Austrians and other Alien Enemies ... [this] has great weight with the man underground."[66] "Ordinary workman," H.A. Lovett complained – ignorant foreigners, who "cannot even read or write" – were being paid, by 1917, "more ... than the responsible and educated officials of the mines."[67] Surely this was wrong. Soldiers at the front were making $1.10 a day; perhaps half of what a day labourer would have expected in 1914. Sergeants were only paid $1.60 a day.[68] Even so, part of a soldier's wages was withheld in forced savings. While a single man living in barracks might make a shift at surviving on his pay, this was plainly not enough to support a family. The residual requirement, always too little, was provided to proud families by the patriotic fund as a particularly galling form of charity.[69] By 1916, with a tremendous labour crunch in progress, unskilled labour was being imported to Canada from wherever it could be got – the United States, the Far East, the West Indies – for $3.50 a day. In the West, unskilled farm hands would not work for less than $5.00 a day, by 1917.[70] Even prisoners of war and internees released for work made a soldier's wage.[71] If an internee refused to work he could be imprisoned for six months. This was repression. On the other hand, if a soldier refused to work, he might be shot, and in any case, risked extremely punitive treatment. Such were the exigencies of service. Nor were home front workers, even so favoured, satisfied. Labour unrest in wartime Canada never developed so far as in Britain or most of the other combatant nations. Nonetheless, nearly a million days were lost to industrial action in 1917,[72] while the situation at the front remained desperate. Could more internees and POWs be released for work in the mines, Mark Workman, president of the Dominion Steel Corporation, wondered? Despite the fact that pay had recently been raised by half, Canadian miners were not working. In fact productivity had dropped by 20 per cent. At least internees and POWs were willing to put in an honest day's work.[73] How was any of this "fair"? Anger, even explosive anger, might have been (and was) expected. "There is," Albert Moore, secretary of the General Conference of the Methodist Church of Canada, considered, "a festering sore in Canada, and every day I pray that it may not develop into bloodshed and Civil War."

Signs of polarization are not difficult to find. The position of the Orange Lodge was hardly secret. Horatio Clarence Hocken, mayor of Toronto in 1914, still master of the Grand Lodge Ontario East, and a future Tory MP and national grand master, notoriously opined during the conscription crisis:

> I cannot refrain from giving expression to the resentment that is cherished in the mind of every loyal British citizen in Canada against the people of Quebec, in relation to the war. With our very existence as a free nation at stake, they have exhibited a spirit of disloyalty to the Empire ... Some of their leaders have, since the war began, threatened a rebellion. If we may take the articles in their newspapers, and the speeches of their public men, as a gauge of their sentiments, we must conclude that they have no love for the Empire which has sheltered them and given them their liberties under the folds of its flag ... Within the past month one of their papers has revived the discussion of their ambition to set up a French-Canadian Roman Catholic republic on the banks of the St. Lawrence. That ambition will never be realized. One of the greatest obstacles in its way is the existence of the Orange Association. Fifty thousand of our members are fighting in the defence of France on the fields of Europe. If occasion should arise, 250,000 Orangemen, too old for overseas service, could be enlisted in a month to put down any attempt that might be launched in the Province of Quebec to set up a republic.[74]

"What a glorious opportunity was presented to the French Canadians by this war to prove their loyalty as British subjects," the *Sentinel* considered.

> An opportunity such as this can never recur. The French Canadians have rejected it, and in their rejection have shown themselves to be so violently anti-British that neither their children, nor their children's children will be able to wipe out the stain they have put upon their record in this great crisis.[75]

A former grand master of Quebec, William Galbraith, warned in Brockville that the "pathetic efforts of French speaking Canadians" would not be forgotten. Returning soldiers, he prophesied, would know how to deal with traitors and slackers.[76] The Royal Black Knights of Ireland, a kindred order, had pledged themselves whole-heartedly to "render the Government and the military authorities every assistance in our power in the enforcement of said legislation [the MSA]" should Quebec oppose by any means government efforts to get it to shoulder its share of the cost of Canadian citizenship.[77]

The Great War Veterans' Association (GWVA), a predecessor of the Royal Canadian Legion beginning to emerge by 1916, expressed itself most forcibly upon the nature of the Canada that was to emerge from the war.[78] The government was less disposed to dismiss the GWVA's demands as the vagaries of the war damaged than it was to view the GWVA as the vanguard of the Canadian Corps that must one day come home. This was particularly the case as the organization gained strength through the later war years.[79]

It had, therefore, to be carefully handled to ensure that it remained on the right side of any divide. All types of "socialism," in particular, were to be carefully excluded and the organization kept in safe hands. "The soldiers," Colonel Harold Daly – one time ADC to Hughes, and a prominent Tory bagman subsequently seconded to Meighen's side to help control the veterans – considered, "are having too much to say ... and have an organised campaign to influence the opinion of the soldiers which stretches from the front to their homes in Canada." This movement was making serious headway and was going to have to be watched, alleged grievances redressed before they could be given publicity, a propaganda apparatus constructed and manned by ex-soldiers, and resettlement carefully considered. The trick would be to get the veterans' associations, Daly considered, more interested in combating "socialist tendencies" than making serious trouble for the government.[80]

The government need not have worried over-much, and indeed from December 1917 the militia department was tentatively considering how to capitalize upon the already all too evident predilections of the returned men against apprehended trouble.[81] From the beginning, the GWVA had indicated which way the wind was going to blow. Its line remained essentially the same as that of the LOL for the duration of the war and through the first years of peace. This is hardly surprising, given the nature of the Canadian army (and particularly of the first

4.3. The GWVA, organizing from 1916, was a potent force on the Canadian home front through the latter war years and into 1919. Picture courtesy of the Glenbow Archives.

contingents); still less so when we consider that the principal founders of the movement (Robert Maxwell, Robert Stewart, and David Loughnan) were Ulstermen and Orange. Indeed, at least half of the first-generation leaders of the GWVA were LOL. Even were this not so, in Canada – as in Britain or Australia for that matter – returned men were far more interested in ensuring that the war was waged as vigorously as possible than in changing the basic structure of society; it always being understood, of course, that the sacrifices of veterans should receive adequate recompense.[82]

In Canada, these dynamics ensured that from the beginning the veterans' movement was characterized by virulent British Canadian nativism – virulent even by the standards of the time.

Individual dissenters were simply not to be tolerated. "Resolved that we, the Members of the Great War Veterans of Canada, Quebec Branch" one missive to Borden began,

> strongly protest against the seditious propaganda contained in the articles written by one Henri Bourassa in "Le Devoir," against England and the Allied cause. Articles of such a nature as to corrupt and poison the minds of its readers convey an exaggerated idea of the mentality of the serious classes of the Province of Quebec, to the people of other Provinces; thereby provoking suspicion, discord, and breeding sedition. In virtue of the "War Measures Act," the Government is empowered with all the necessary powers to face such a situation. It should therefore, and it is its DUTY to use this power without delay, to suppress the publication of "Le Devoir" and if necessary bring its Director Henri Bourassa before a tribunal of justice to answer the change of CRIMINAL SEDITION.[83]

A pronounced, even violent, anti-immigrant animus was also evident from the beginning.[84] Grant MacNeil, a prominent leader of Manitoba returned men, wondered how fair it was for Alien Enemies to be taking the jobs of men at the front. The soldier left for the front. He was paid wages insufficient to allow him to maintain a family at home, exposed to the full fury of wartime inflation, and dependent thereafter on occasional handouts. The Alien Enemy took his job and received wartime raises and bonuses. In his heart the wretch wished Canada defeated. There were, MacNeil was willing to admit, "two sides of the much discussed Alien Enemy question – our side and theirs. Our side stretches from Halifax to Victoria; theirs lies on the other side of the Atlantic

Ocean." Of course New Canadians could not be expected to willingly assist in their exclusion from national life. Some were "exceedingly arrogant in their attitudes," and their opposition could be expected. All they would succeed in doing, however, was arouse "the passions of men trained to deal ruthlessly with the prototype at the point of a bayonet."[85] Arthur Hazeldon, another leading member of the organization, warned that "[t]he men who fought for democracy are not going to go hungry while aliens and slackers get all the jobs."[86] Better, the Windsor, Ontario, branch considered, if all slackers and aliens were fired from government employ and returned men appointed in their stead. Best if "all lands held by Alien Enemies should be sold, and the proceeds turned over to the Red Cross society and the GWVA in order to fund substantial pensions for invalid soldiers." Of course it went without saying, almost, that "all subjects of enemy countries, naturalized or otherwise, should be disenfranchised."[87] The demand for land continued. Through 1918 the GWVA insisted that crown lands be made available to soldiers in their home province, preferably near a railroad. Doukhobors and Mennonites should be moved along to make room if necessary.[88]

By January 1918, the position of the GWVA as a whole had clarified. Alien men were to be offered a choice. They could enlist immediately in the CEF; be interned and return to their home country at the end of hostilities; or be industrially conscripted and work in Canada for soldiers' wages. That was all.[89] They "have been laughing at us," and one way or another, were going to be displaced, if not before, then certainly after, the war when the boys came home.[90] Local branches could be more militant still. The Hamilton and Toronto Branches of the GWVA passed resolutions supporting the internment of all foreigners and their employment at forced labour at military rates of pay.[91] In the West, where the GWVA seems to have been particularly extreme, returned men warned New Canadians that they were going to lose their land after the war. They had better, moreover, watch what they said and did for the duration or they would not like what would happen when "the boys came home." The "Fritzies were going to lose their farms." That much was certain. The others would be locked up if they did anything untoward. Some terrified Winnipeg area Ukrainians, it appears, heeding the warning, and expecting that Canadian postwar policy would be driven to this extreme, were by 1918 neither planting crops nor buying in stores, but rather awaiting deportation.[92]

The crux of thing was simple, Hamilton Bruce from the Canadian War Veterans' Association, informed Borden. *Aliens must not be allowed to benefit from the war.* British Canadian boys had left good jobs and were now serving in France. Aliens – often Alien Enemies – had taken their jobs, and were prospering while British Canadians did all the dying. This was totally unfair and unacceptable. If the New Canadians could not, would not, or were not allowed to go to France, then they should be put to work in national industries for military pay, and if they did not like it, be interned. After the war, they would be expelled. This would take the wind out of their sails. Soldiers had voted for the Conservatives. Most came from solid Tory families. If the government felt unable to discipline the New Canadians, then, Bruce concluded, the returned men would understand and "cheerfully accept the burden laid upon us."[93]

Such opinion seems now violent, and extreme. Perhaps it was, but it was, however, shared by many of Bruce's contemporaries. For example, the GWVA agitation to conscript aliens for farm labour and, if necessary, to expropriate their farms was supported by the Victoria League of Patriots, the Montreal Sons of Empire, the Grand Chapter of the Royal Black Knights, the Grand Lodge of the LOL, the Army and Navy Veterans, and the British Imperial Association.[94] Senator George Bradbury thought that Alien Enemies should be disenfranchised for life. Senator George Lynch-Stanton wanted to embargo enemy nations permanently. Mayor Tommy Church of Toronto and prominent Hamiltonian John Godfrey of the National Service League and the "win the war movement" wanted to bar use of the German language in Canada forever.[95] A little later, Mayor Church considered that government inaction regarding aliens was disappointing and provoking.

> Alien Enemies can work in a factory and get from $4 to $6 a day, while British subjects fight for $1.10 a day at the front ... There should be some form of conscription on farms for Alien Enemies ... They can regulate Alien Enemies in other countries but not in Canada. It looks as if the Alien Enemies in the West have more influence than the men in the trenches with the present Government. The Government is afraid of its own shadow in trying to deal with the question. After the war the large cities are going to be a dumping ground for a lot of these people and the municipalities are going to take the matter in hand if the Government has fallen down.[96]

Action followed. The city of Toronto soon began to require employers to furnish names of all alien employees monthly – the obvious first step to action.[97] Within a month the mayor was able to report the satisfying news that no known aliens were working for the city, though, he feared, some of them might still be hiding in the Works department. They would be smoked out and discharged, he promised.[98] Going further still, Alderman Plewman thought it might be a good idea to cancel all business licences owned by aliens on Dominion Day 1918, and drive them permanently out of business.[99] City Council was not ready to go so far, although, following the torpedoing of the *Llandovery Castle*, a hospital ship, it did pass, by a large majority (only Alderman Graham and Controller O'Neill opposed), a motion to deny free hospital treatment, burial orders, and civic relief of all kinds to Alien Enemies.[100] Councilman Crouchman, of Walkerville, Ontario – perhaps reacting to the recent arrest of two local Poles, suspected of being anarchists[101] – thought that it might be a good idea to stop foreigners, particularly Poles and "Austrians," from buying property or owning businesses in decent areas of town. The proposal was introduced and debated in town council. "We have restricted the coloured people," Crouchman said, "and I would far rather have a coloured man living beside me than a Pole."[102] After a deputation of veterans "in deadly earnest" had called on the premier,[103] a mass meeting in Victoria, British Columbia, endorsed a proposal that the provincial legislature conscript all aliens for national civil service before it rose.[104] The Ontario Motor League concurred and thought it might be useful to organize aliens into road gangs, supervised by returned soldiers.[105] Chief Justice Ferguson of Ontario saw no legal obstacle. While it was not possible to conscript foreigners for military service, they could still be drafted for labour service and be deported later.[106] It appeared that there was no end of willing, indeed equally cheerful helpmates prepared to assist the GWVA in shouldering its burden.

While the Canadian government did act to restrict and even to harass resident Alien Enemies in the latter war years, therefore, it did so in the knowledge that the alternative to state action was not tolerance but freelance repression. Cheerfully, British Canada would take upon itself the responsibility for purging the Dominion of the well-hated, vice-ridden, and treacherous foe within. Likewise, by 1917, state action would probably be required to compel French Canadians to do the duty they cravenly, perfidiously shirked – as British Canada saw things anyway. And if the government's scruples prohibited it from doing this work too, then this burden would be cheerfully shouldered as well. In the process, the nation would be prepared and purified for the beautiful tomorrow that would requite its sacrifices in the great crusade in which, by 1916, British Canada was engaged beyond all hope of extraction short of victory.

5 "Down with King Borden and His Boches. Long Live the Jails!": Intercommunal Riot as Social Control, 1916–1917: The Case of Quebec

They tell you to go to France and fight the Kaiser ... Borden is the Canadian Kaiser. If I am to sacrifice my life, brothers, I shall not go to France, but I shall fight it out right here.

H. Leavitt, July 1917[1]

Expressions of polarized opinion were by no means limited to the Orange Lodge or the "win the war" movement, or to British Canada, for that matter. By 1916, violent expression was endemic. Local intercommunal dust-ups were not uncommon. In British Canada, these often took the form of soldier riots directed at the resident New Canadian communities, and against those judged to be generally dissident. Mob violence against French Canadians was virtually unknown, both because of their relative geographical concentration (they were a bumptious majority in Quebec) and because they were not comfortable victims. French Canadians were, on the contrary, the stuff of enthusiastic mobs themselves, in the latter war years often rioting against conscription in particular. They too found victims, an "enemy within." These enemies, however, were typically pro-war French Canadians, or members of the British Canadian minority in Quebec. While intercommunal rioting was hardly new – indeed, the army had been called upon sixty-two times between Confederation and the outbreak of war to suppress riots the police could not handle (Orange-Green fracases were an almost annual affair in Montreal and Toronto in the latter nineteenth century)[2] – the frequency, the scale, and the particularly focused ruthlessness of the riots which racked Canada during the war's latter years and its immediate aftermath represented a departure. It was within this context, emblematic of the polarization that characterized wartime Canada, that the federal election of 1917 occurred. This intercommunal (and in the case of Quebec "intracommunal") violence, of course, was taken by many government luminaries to prefigure what was apt to happen on a much grander scale when the "boys came home" if the government had done nothing very satisfactory in the meantime.

Let us consider the case of Quebec first. In chapter 6, we will turn to events in British Canada. While there was certainly intercommunal violence in Quebec, in general the pattern was the reverse of the pattern we see in British Canada. In Quebec, anti-war French Canadians generally attacked pro-war British Canadians, this violence sometimes reaching substantial proportions before it could be contained.

On 25 August 1916, a Montreal recruiting meeting was broken up by French-speaking men. A lively fight ensued between Irish Rangers (whose meeting it was) and French Canadian "antis" (in this case, "anti-registration; later "anti-conscription"). The antis withdrew. The city police, who appear to have been sympathetic to the antis, intervened to arrest the soldiers, who responded by drawing their bayonets on the police.[3] The government countered a week later with in Order-in-Council making it an offence against the WMA to disturb recruiting meetings.[4] Of course, disturbing recruiting meetings was already a Canadian crime several times over, not least in the Criminal Code and under the Militia Act. Reiterating this fact, through the WMA, would have facilitated prosecution had magistrates in Quebec been so inclined. The civil authorities in Montreal and the provincial government of Quebec were not, and advised the Irish Rangers that they were "over-zealous" in their recruiting. They should, it was considered, only enter neighbourhoods where they would not be provocative. Ultimately they were ordered back to Valcartier. Downtown recruiting meetings would, the city said, henceforth be forbidden.[5] Since, of course, the English-speaking population of Montreal was concentrated in and about downtown, the prohibition in itself was provocative. And a sign of growing local polarity was the fact that the clash appears to have improved, not harmed, the Rangers' recruiting success with British Canadian Montrealers. Local pro-war speakers, in English-speaking neighbourhoods in any case, began to express dismay that the prevalence of French Canadian slacking would ensure that the Canada of the future would be composed, in the main, of the "progeny of the men who stayed at home."[6] Who exactly these were did not have to be spelt out, not in Montreal in 1916. For the moment, the violence in Quebec was not repeated, although intercommunal cleavages were clear.

5.1. Anti-conscription march in Montreal, 1916. Picture courtesy of Library and Archives Canada.

Six months later, however, as the MSA was first nationally debated, the situation in Quebec became extremely volatile. And, by the summer of 1917, as the MSA moved through consecutive readings, first in the House of Commons and then in the Senate, speech began to become immoderate. Tempers began to flare. It was no longer a question of why there should not be conscription, but of what Quebec would do when it was implemented. The motive was no longer public discussion but popular mobilization against the measure.[7] The focus had shifted from attempting to stop the act to opposing its implementation. Political mobilization became civil disobedience; violent words sometimes led to violent acts.

On 26 March 1917, three thousand people turned out in Quebec's St Peter's market hall to hear a series of anti-conscription addresses by local notables – Armand Lavergne (one of the most prominent Nationalist leaders), Alderman Eugene Dussault, and Lucien Cannon. At the meeting there was a "unanimous feeling ... against conscription."[8] Shortly thereafter, a loud, unruly mob scene developed at a recruiting meeting in Montreal, when Captain Eugène Mackay-Papineau, despite constant interruption and hissing, informed the audience that "Quebec had not done its duty."[9]

Two weeks later, on 24 May 1917, mobs in Quebec, chanting "down with conscription" smashed the windows of the pro-government *L'Évènement* and the English-language *Quebec Chronicle*.[10] Rioting turned into a running battle with policemen and soldiers who happened to get in the way of the mob. Three of the latter were hospitalized.[11] On 29 May, Quebec City Council voted an anti-conscription resolution, only two of twenty-one members opposed (George Gibson and Frank Dinan), while a cheering crowd several thousand strong sang "O Canada" and "God Save the King" outside City Hall.[12]

The next day, in Sherbrooke, an army officer who had, apparently, formed the plan of throwing rotten eggs at anti-conscription paraders was apprehended before he was able to put his plan into effect. The crowd, first, forced the man to eat the eggs, and then kicked him about until police were able to rescue him.[13] On 5 July, the town council passed an anti-conscription resolution, despite the total opposition of its English member, Alderman Parker, who subsequently resigned.[14] In September, local mob violence came to focus on the homes of local prominent French Canadian pro-conscriptionists. The home and office of one of them, C.H. Flamand, was assailed with hurled bricks, rocks, and clubs by a mob of four hundred people.[15] In December, a fight between pro- and anti-government mobs, in the town, led to the injury of nine conscriptionists. The "anti" mob had assembled to prevent the minister of marine, C.C. Ballantyne, and the minister of justice, C.J. Doherty, from speaking.[16]

On 15 June, M. Leo Doyon, a Liberal, addressed a large anti-conscription rally in Montreal. For reasons unknown, a scuffle broke out between a party of Boy Scouts – perhaps because they were generally considered at this time an Anglican front organization – and some members of the audience. This was enough to set off the crowd. Doyon soon faced angry shouts of "tuons Borden" – "let's kill Borden." Doyon responded to the anger by promising that Quebec would indeed kill Borden ... politically. He was a militarist, autocrat, and demagogue upon whom the people would have their revenge during the approaching election.[17] Some Quebecers, as events would soon demonstrate, took the enjoinder more literally.

Through June, Quebec orators sharpened their claws on conscription. M. Monsel, a Liberal, speaking in Parc Frontenac in Montreal, wondered how it could be moral to make the poor fight in France and Belgium. While he admitted that French Canada owed a debt to France, which deserved its respect, he also considered that, since Canada was part of the Commonwealth, any military burden would be most properly borne by England.[18] England, another considered, did not really expect Canada to maintain half a million men in the field. Borden's promise had been patently ridiculous. Canada had already spent a fortune on munitions and contributed a large field force. This was enough.[19]

On 8 July, Joseph Demers, MP for Napierville, told a crowd of eight hundred in St Jean d'Iberville that conscription was the product of a "*Boche* Government." But, while Borden might put the measure on the books, he would never enforce it. If Quebecers simply refused to comply, and if Quebec courts made a practice of issuing orders of habeas corpus for resisters, the courts and the prisons would be quickly clogged.[20] The government responded, three days later, by making it an offence punishable by up to five years' imprisonment to counsel anybody to resist the MSA in writing, in conversation, or by public advice, and with a subsequent Order-in-Council which withdrew the right of habeas corpus following a decision by an MSA tribunal.[21] Asked why the government needed such extravagant powers, backed by such ruthless penalties, Meighen typically explained that he did not intend to act on these powers, and would not, unless it proved necessary, but that it was good to have them just in case.[22]

In July, hot words began to produce hotheads. Violence became more common. A new class of agitator began to appear: young men who spoke violently, and who dared the government to do its worst. H. Leavitt, speaking to a working-class audience in Verdun, advised:

> They tell you to go to France and fight the Kaiser ... Borden is the Canadian Kaiser. If I am to sacrifice my life, brothers, I shall not go to France, but I shall fight it out right here.[23]

On 15 July, a Montreal mob attacked Lieutenant-Colonel L.P. Rexford and an unnamed Canadian Highlander – probably a member of Montreal's own Black Watch (Royal Highlanders of Canada). A mass meeting had been convened by Mayor Martin in Fletcher's Field, directly across from the Canadian Grenadier Guards Armoury. Thirty-five thousand Montrealers attended. Colonel Rexford, the Guards' commanding officer, had stopped to listen to a speech by Alphonse Verville, Lib-Lab MP for Maisonneuve, in which he alleged that Canadian and imperial authorities were retaining in the UK Canadian soldiers who had been wounded rather than sending them home. Rexford answered, "That is not true." He and the Highlander, who appears to have been a bystander caught up in the trouble, were rescued from serious injury by the police and by the personal intervention of Mayor Martin. As the car carrying Rexford and the Highlander left the scene, it was stoned. Verville incited the mob to chase the car and catch the soldiers.[24] Later, while police watched, the mob turned truly ugly. Stones were thrown, and windows broken.[25]

That same day, fifteen thousand people attended an anti-conscription meeting in Quebec to hear Armand Lavergne speak. The crowd carried placards reading "Down with King Borden and his *Boches*" and "Long Live the Jails." Lavergne openly advocated resistance to the MSA and defied the government to arrest him.[26]

The next day, a new organization, *Les Constitutionnelles*, made an appearance in Montreal's Lafontaine Park before a crowd of ten to fifteen thousand people. Its leaders were young, their language uncompromising. Elie Lalumière "downed," the *Gazette* reported, "firstly the British Empire, secondly the confederation, and lastly the *Montreal Gazette*, insinuating that this trio should disappear without much delay." A student, following Lalumière, asked what would happen if, following the passage of the MSA, every French Canadian young man called simply forgot how to read, or took a walk ..."[27]

Four days later, Lalumière called for volunteers to oppose conscription by force, if necessary. He had, he told the mob, five hundred men drilling already, under the direction of Yvon Larose, a retired officer of the American army. His army would not seek confrontation. On the other hand, if anybody came to "take us from our homes, we will show them that we can die as free men rather than live as slaves."[28] Unlawful drilling was already an offence in Canada.[29] In September 1917, not coincidentally, the government reiterated by Order-in-Council the prohibition on all training and drilling except under lawful authority. Who, at this juncture, was expected to train and drill outside the established military forces of the Dominion might readily be imagined.[30] The purpose of the reiteration was, of course, to remind, but also to bring the offence under the umbrella of the WMA, in order to facilitate prosecution, once again, and to provide for stiffer punishment than that permitted by the Criminal Code.

Lalumière went further. He promised "something interesting" in the next week. The probable target, judging by the substance of his speech, would be the local garrison commander, General Wilson. His crime?

> I am going to ask Mr. Bicherdike to have General Wilson removed, and if he is not put out, we will settle his account. When Marshal Joffre was here he asked General Wilson something in the most noble of tongues, and he turned around and said "what did he say?" Let him learn French![31]

Perhaps Lalumière had not forgotten that Wilson was also a prominent conscriptionist who had taken to giving interviews to the English-language press in which he indicated all the able-bodied loafers evident in Montreal as evidence that conscription was necessary, in Montreal anyway.[32]

On 1 August, while the MSA was working through the Senate, a Montreal mob several hundred strong, led by the *constitutionnelles*, burned Borden's French Canadian collaborators – Blondin, Sevigny, and Rainville – in effigy on the Champs de Mars. Soon thereafter, seven cases of dynamite and fifteen hundred caps were reported stolen from a construction site. In Valleyfield, meanwhile, John Carrier, an Ontario man, who apparently bore an "astonishing" resemblance to Sevigny, the minister of national revenue, was mobbed by two hundred antis and badly beaten.[33]

On 3 August, the first of the dynamite made an appearance. A "bomb," fabricated from a few sticks and some sawdust, was left on the doorstep of the mayor of Outremont, the brother of Senator Beaubien, who supported the MSA. It appears that the "bomb" was intended for the senator and had been left at the wrong address. This was a warning.[34] Two days later, in case anybody did not get the hint, placards appeared all over Montreal, featuring a skull and crossbones on a red background, titled "À bas les têtes," and containing two lists of names: some of conscription's most notable English and French advocates respectively – Borden, Meighen, Hugh Graham, Smeaton White, and Lougheed in one, Blondin, Sevigny, Rainville, Lesperance, and C.P. Braline in the other.[35]

On 9 August 1917, an attempt was actually made on the life of Hugh Graham, Lord Atholstan, owner of the militantly conscriptionist *Montreal Star*. Early in the morning, a bomb exploded under the sleeping quarters of his Cartierville country house. Although the house was six miles outside Montreal, the explosion was clearly heard in the city.[36] Atholstan's chauffeur was killed. "There could no longer be any doubt," the *Gazette* wrote, "that there was an organisation which would stop at nothing" to stop conscription.[37] Few in Montreal could have been in any doubt "who" that organization was. Fernand Villeneuve, an eighteen-year-old firebrand and a prominent *constitutionnelle*, speaking to a crowd in Montreal that same day, considered that opponents of conscription could simply shoot recruiting officers attempting to enforce the act.[38] In Lafontaine Park, the next day, he deplored recourse to violence; but deplored, as well, that Atholstan had not gone up with the house. "Yes," the crowd is reported as chanting, "and Borden too ..." Other *constitutionnelles*, speaking afterward, vowed to shoot recruiting officers and blow up conscription advocates.[39] A week later, another bomb exploded in Ste Scholastique. This time the object of the attack was Gideon Bigra, a local French Canadian proponent of conscription.[40]

On 29 August 1917, in what appears to have been part of the same campaign, a large anti-conscription mob marched through the streets of Montreal. As it approached the offices of the English-language, pro-conscription *Gazette*, bricks and stones flew. The *Gazette*'s windows were smashed. To underline the fact that they meant business, rioters fired revolvers at the building and into the air.[41] Speakers warned the crowd to collect guns for future action. A collection was taken to purchase arms for Villeneuve's army.[42] The following day, Montreal police – by now also meaning business and having, the *constitutionnelles* alleged, received "hit to hurt" orders from Mayor Martin, along with rifles in case things got too ugly for clubs[43] – broke up a mob of five hundred "antis" before it could start trouble. This, however, did not stop the mob from reassembling and listening to outright, obvious sedition. Robert Parsons, the chief speaker, warned: "if the Government wanted the conscription law to be the spark to start a revolution in Canada, they were going to get it." Villeneuve continued that "if conscription were enforced Premier Borden and the other members of his Government would die."[44] Rioting continued, the following day, with more smashed windows and more baton charges, and ended with four policemen and one protestor in hospital – the police injured by rocks, the protestor shot.[45]

The police, however – as events had demonstrated – were not asleep. They had begun to confiscate arms and dynamite on 9 August, the very day of the first bombings.[46] Elie Lalumière was arrested on 30 August and held in secret detention so that his followers would not be able to launch an assault to free him.[47] He talked freely while in police custody. His arrest changed nothing, he asserted. Many Quebecers thought like him, and he and his friends "had the means to get the rifles and money necessary to defeat conscription."[48] A round-up of *dynomitards* commenced. By 19 September, at least a dozen men had been arrested for participating in what the press considered a conspiracy to stop conscription by murdering prominent Canadians. One *constitutionnelle* – Joseph LeDuc (also known as "Handfield") – committed suicide before he could be arrested.[49] The police, in the course of the raids, reportedly recovered fifty pounds of stolen dynamite.

Atholstan, Lalumière said, was to have been the first. Local English-language newspapers – the *Star*, the *Gazette* – the Mount Royal Club, Robert Borden, and Arthur Meighen were other targets. Another of the *dynomitards* indicated that Sir Joseph Flavelle (Imperial Munitions Board), Sir Donald Mann and Sir William Mackenzie (owners of a transcontinental railway, then in the process of being acquired by the government as insolvent), the Honourable P.H. Blondin, General E.W. Wilson, the Honourable Albert Sevigny, and the offices of *La Presse* and *La Patrie* were all targeted.[50] Those implicated in the conspiracy were initially charged with treason.[51] Since, given the nature of their crime, the death penalty might well have been invoked – these dissenters had done rather more than assist an Alien Enemy to leave the country – the charge was reduced. Canada, wisely, was not in the business of making martyrs; nor, of course, could it be guaranteed that a Quebec jury would convict on this charge. Ultimately the conspirators were tried for attempted murder.[52]

The plot quickly thickened. Elie Lalumière was already known to French Canada, though not as an "anti" firebrand. He had been convicted of election malfeasance in 1913, as a supporter of Louis Coderre, MP for Hochelaga and Borden's secretary of state. On this occasion, Lalumière had received from Coderre one hundred dollars for his efforts. Shortly thereafter, he was released from prison as a "ticket of leave" man – released, that is, on the orders of the minister of justice as a first offender, not apt to be dangerous in the future. Whatever he was, in effect, Lalumière had once been a committed *Bleu* partisan, not above a little skulduggery, who had received favours from the government in exchange.[53] Once Lalumière was arrested, a provincial deputy, Paul Emile Lemarche, immediately denounced the bombing as a clumsy police conspiracy to discredit the nationalists and demanded a provincial inquiry. He got it. Shortly thereafter, another *dynomitard*, Charles "ti-noir" Desjardins, a federal agent, was arrested by provincial police for furnishing the conspirators with arms and money, and for forming part of a gang which planned to rob a bank in Trois Rivières to obtain money for further operations. He was indicted in provincial court, on 21 October, for conspiracy to commit murder.[54]

The trial of the *dynomitards* was not short. This was odd, considering that three key defendants – Charles Tremblay, Joseph Monette, and Lalumière, "the arch-conspirator"[55] – turned King's evidence. Much evidence had to be heard. The case was tangled. What part did Desjardins play in the whole affair? It was he, it appears, who had moved the clique to violence. Which side was he on? Was Lalumière still working for the Conservative Party? Was the Romeo Wisintainer in the dock the Wisintainer who had directed the conspirators to Atholstan's house? Tremblay said it was not.[56] In the end, six of the accused were acquitted – Aurele Goyer, E. Bolduc, J.B. Cyr, A. Chagnon, Wisintainer, and Joseph Paquette. Lalumière and Desjardins remained in prison, and on trial for other charges. Their bail was a colossal $30,000 each. Monette, described as the "leader of the gang" which had dynamited Atholstan's house, was sentenced to life imprisonment for the murder of Atholstan's chauffeur.[57] The whole thing was rather gamey, any way you looked at it. The *dynomitard* incident, however, is probably more illustrative of the polarity the war produced in Canada – a committed *Bleu* and a government agent prominent among the conspirators – than it was the product of any government skulduggery. Also evident was the government's relative forbearance. Men were executed elsewhere for much less.

Shortly after the arrest of the conspirators, Villeneuve, who does not appear to have been implicated, was arrested for sedition – one of the few so charged – and convicted in Quebec during the war. While his supporters were outraged and vowed to continue their campaign, this arrest should have been expected.[58] Other radicals quickly fell afoul of the MSA enabling legislation. Alphonse Bernier and Paul Lafortune, committed anti-conscriptionists, were charged at the end of October with "opposing conscription in public."[59] P.E. Mongeau, Anatole Grenier, and Alfred Côté were arrested around the same time.[60]

Rioting continued, though actual rebellion had been averted, and there was no further recourse to terrorist methods. This notwithstanding, being on the receiving end of a Quebec mob must certainly have been an unpleasant experience. On 26 November 1917, a crowd in Quebec City cornered a Unionist candidate in the "conscription election" then underway. Joseph Barnard, the editor of *Évènement*, tried to speak, but was pelted by the crowd with snowballs and other projectiles. The crowd threatened to hang him, and produced a rope. They charged the platform from which he was speaking, but were prevented from lynching him by the police. Barnard was not safe from assault, however. The mob surrounded him as he attempted to make his way to a police car brought up to help him escape. He was badly beaten before being rescued.[61] Five days later, James Morris, a prominent Unionist in Quebec, was assailed by "antis" who pelted him with rotten eggs and stones, while firing their revolvers into the air.[62]

As elsewhere, opposition to the war tended to become total. In Quebec, other issues tended to amalgamate with conscription as reasons to oppose the government and the war. In British Canada, quite plainly, war accentuated or induced grievances that tended to lead to the demand for more efficient war management rather than to opposition to the war itself. In French Canada, equally plainly, anti-conscriptionist feeling tended to gather to itself all other causes of unrest, pre-existing and accentuated or unique to the war itself. In May 1917, for example, a large meeting held in Montreal to protest the high cost of food developed into several thousand working men parading through the streets under an anti-conscription banner. Fighting developed as soldiers attempted to intervene to snatch the banner. The fracas was "on a scale not known in this city for many years."[63] What had started as a simple protest at wartime food prices escalated into a clash between proponents and opponents of the war effort.

In 1917, one of the most virulent speakers on anti-conscription platforms was the French Canadian Lib-Lab Alphonse Verville, who plainly joined class with national issues. Appearing on a platform with English Canadian trade unionists in June 1917, he was denounced by W.F. Carroll, of South Cape Breton, and Mr MacDonnell, of Toronto, for his opposition to the war and his conflicted priorities. "Verville and his ilk," Carroll and MacDonnell asserted, "degrade labour." What was needed was conscription and greater attention to labour issues, not anti-conscription and greater attention to communal issues, wrongly conceived as having class implications.[64] Verville's policy of opposing conscription on communal grounds and advocating the employment of syndicalist methods – a general strike – to stop it was plainly not appreciated. "Mr. Verville," the editor of the *Montreal Gazette* opined,

> does not advocate a strike. Certainly not. He is as guiltless ... as the man who says "Far be it from me to suggest that yonder house should be burned down but there is the house and over there you will find some oil and matches."[65]

It is clear, in French Canada, that other issues gained importance insofar as they were associated with communal opposition to the war and the way it was being managed. It was not these issues, however, which gave the "anti" campaign its strength. On 8 July 1917, a meeting of two thousand people in Montreal was addressed by a combined slate of nationalist, socialist, and labour speakers in French, English, and Italian. Robert Parsons, adopting a purely socialist critique of the war, only provoked cries from the crowd that it wanted to hear about conscription. Verville and L.N.G. Pagé, with his call for "new Dollards ... to save the French Canadian community from the great danger that menaces it," were more popular with the assembled Reds.[66] A few days later, socialist speakers were heckled by a French Canadian mob for their atheism. They had not come to hear attacks on the Pope and clergy, the speakers were informed, but to listen to an indictment of the war effort and the Conservative government.[67] In October, Alfred Côté had the effrontery to attack Sir Wilfrid Laurier during an anti-conscription rally held in Montreal's St Mary's labour club. Violence erupted. Côté received a slapped face rather than any cheers of approval.[68]

What Quebecers were not, in the great majority, was ready for direct action. They might riot. They might even shoot revolvers in the air. They did not like bombers, or those who shot at people, however hated.

They were plainly not revolutionists. A Catholic, socially conservative consensus was still readily apparent.[69] Perhaps the only thing hated more than conscription in Quebec were those who did not know when they had crossed the line between what was acceptable and what was not. MPs might protest. Priests might absent themselves from recruiting platforms. Mayor Martin might, even, write to the governor general or the Colonial Office.[70] Recruiting cards might be burned. French Canada was, however, a law-abiding and coherent society. For some of the opponents of conscription, indeed, a charge against the government was that it had allowed volunteerism to fail and thus made conscription necessary. If it had acted at the outset with appropriately heavy-handed action against anti-war firebrands, Quebec would have come around before the MSA was needed. If, in effect, it had been prepared to act with American-style vigour against its enemies, it would not now find itself faced with Irish-style dissent.[71] Since, however, the government had made this mistake, it should not now lose a sense of proportion or forget the rules of the game.

When, with the passage of the MSA through the Senate in August, the *constitutionnelles* began to attack the Liberal Party, they lost their audience quickly. At a meeting on 9 August, for example, Elie Lalumière denounced the Liberals as Borden's accomplices and Laurier, in particular, as too spineless to protect his people. Fighting immediately broke out in the crowd and the police were compelled to intervene – this time to protect one species of French Canadian dissenter, the more convinced, from those who continued to honour their old chiefs and who might like incendiary talk but who would not countenance treason within the community.[72] Paul Lafortune received a similar rebuke when, on 17 August, he attempted to rouse the people against the quiescent clergy.[73] Henri Bourassa, more successful and far better remembered, never went so far. While he might assert that the war would only continue to "exhaustion, bankruptcy and national suicide," he was careful to count Borden as far more guilty than Laurier and never opposed the church. These inhibitions represented real constraints on French Canadian politics at the beginning of the century.[74]

The *dynomitards* clinched things. Great War French Canada turned its back on those who did not just theorize about violence but actually were violent, as it did fifty years later on the FLQ. It does not even appear that many of the actual bombers were sure that they themselves liked the movement from violent talk to violence. Most of them turned King's evidence quickly, including the ringleaders. The attempt on

Atholstan, it appears, was less devastating than it might have been because one of the plotters, Joseph Tremblay, not really sure that even a *sale bloke* like Atholstan deserved to die, picked up the dynamite at the last minute and threw it three or four feet away from the house, so the effects of the explosion were muted. Another conspirator, Paul Ranger – much less convincing in his *mea non culpa* – claimed to have joined the *constitutionnelle* club on the understanding that it intended to oppose conscription before it was introduced by constitutional means only. He had been offered a revolver by Desjardins but had turned it down ... or rather given it to a comrade, Paquet. So, in any case, he claimed at his trial.[75]

The day after the attack on Lord Atholston, Quebec papers began to carry occasional notifications from French Canadians bearing the same family name as the most prominent hotheads, informing the community that there was no relation.[76] The *constitutionnelles* had grown used to addressing crowds numbering in the thousands, even the tens of thousands. A meeting the next day drew 150 onlookers.[77] One wonders how many of those who did attend were now looking for the horns under the hair. Napoleon Seguin, MLA, advised French Canadians to keep their children at home. If the violence continued, he thought, the end result would certainly be martial law.[78] Even Paul Lafortune could see the wisdom of that. While he did not apologize for Cartierville, and did wonder that leaders who had called on French Canadians to defend their rights now denounced those who did so as "revolutionaries," he stressed the necessity that anti-conscription activity in Quebec remain non-violent. If it were not, the antis would simply be shot down by the army and beaten up by the police.[79] At least the second half of this prognosis was correct. As we have seen, Mayor Martin sent in the riot squad to restrain violence with greater violence, though an absolute and vocal opponent of conscription himself. Military officials, meanwhile, noticed a much increased willingness on the part of Quebec's civil authorities to cooperate in the implementation of the MSA.[80] Perhaps if the federal government had no business telling proper French Canadian boys that they would have to go to France and Belgium, a few malcontents and loafers could be spared in the interests of peace. In the event, many of those spared appear to have been members of the British Canadian minority, in any case. Writing in *Le Devoir*, the day after the Cartierville attack, Henri Bourassa himself denounced the bombings as senseless, sterile, and criminal. The only result would be that the sectarians in Ontario would be put in a position to say "damned, treacherous, papist

Frogs," with some justice now on their side. When the government had had enough, there would be martial law, civil procedure would be abandoned, and the best weapons in the fight against conscription – lawful weapons – would be lost.[81] "One should be well persuaded of this fact," he informed his readership in *Le Devoir*:

> the day the Government judges that violent acts performed with the assistance of agents provocateurs justify the application of martial law, that will be the total triumph of French Canada's most hateful enemies.[82]

Bourassa was right about one thing anyway. If there had been more recourse to Cartierville tactics, there would certainly have been martial law.

French Canadians were not the only community opposed to the war which sometimes had recourse to violence. Sometimes violence directed against communities or individuals supporting the war could develop outside Quebec where dissenters were sufficiently convinced and concentrated.

In Belmont, Ontario (south of London), a local man, Clark C. Warren, published a letter in the local paper supportive of the government's recent cancellation of exemptions for farmers and "criticizing the latter for their objections." An enraged group of Elgin County farmers paid him a visit, on the evening of 20 May 1918, throwing "stones and clubs at the doors and through the windows" of his house as a way of registering their disagreement.[83] Sometimes violence and threats seem to have produced violence and threats. For the first time in the history of Hamilton, for example, the annual Orange day parade was attacked, in 1917. Crowds of "rowdies" threw rocks and mud, and several shots appear to have been exchanged. A bullet grazed the temple of one Orangeman, Charles Howard, but nobody was seriously hurt.[84] Sometimes local communities, when numerous enough and sufficiently convinced or provoked, could launch limited local counter-offensives against their enemies. In November 1917, in Kitchener, Ontario, local German Canadians went so far as to heckle the prime minister when he tried to speak. "More disagreeable conduct," the Toronto *Globe* considered, "has never been witnessed at any public gathering in the history of Ontario."[85] It appears that the judiciary agreed. Three of the hecklers, Truman Schuller, Otto Lifin, and Albert Nahrgang, were fined for their performance.[86] Reverend C.A. Sykes, a Kitchener cleric, rebuked them from the pulpit. It might be, he thought, necessary to revise the immigration laws to "prevent people of selfish, mean and small dispositions from entering this country." They were no better than the Bolsheviks, he thought, or the "Italian traitors."[87]

In what is now Windsor, Ontario, an attempt by the very pro-war Bishop Fallon to break up what he considered to be the undue influence of nationalist French Canadian priests in parishes they viewed as their "fiefdoms" backfired badly. The problem, as Fallon saw it, was that

> A strong nationalistic element was often evident in their ministry, and this nationalism naturally spilled over into their congregations. [He] decided early in his Episcopal career to confront and demolish the pretensions of these priests and the French Canadian nationalism of their gullible parishioners.[88]

He intended, by his intervention, to mend the split between Irish and French Catholics within his diocese. The school question, and the war situation, as well, were probably not absent from his calculations. He seems to have hoped that confrontation would produce reconciliation. Part of the plan was, apparently, to move Father L.A. Beaudoin from Our Lady of the Lake parish, in Ford City, and replace him with the more pliable Father François Xavier Laurendeau. While Laurendeau was certainly French Canadian, he was viewed by the congregation as a crypto-Irishman. When Fallon attempted to force the issue, in September 1917, a riot ensued which ended with a clash between three thousand Catholics and one hundred policemen,[89] and which ultimately led to a formal request for military assistance by local authorities.[90] There can have been few parochial meetings in history productive of so volatile an outcome. That the plan was executed during the war, when Fallon was such an outspoken imperialist, with conscription looming, and while the Ontario school question unfolded, can only have been highly provocative. That the ensuing riot had much to do with the war cannot be doubted. Indeed, those who suffered property damage during the riot, as was the case elsewhere when riots followed from war-induced or -accentuated causes, applied for compensation to the government. As almost always, they were denied.

In other locales, occasionally, New Canadians could threaten disturbance if some particularly obnoxious local application of wartime practice were not changed. In Timmins, Ontario, in March 1918, for example, Kowitz Olstroski was arrested for making seditious utterances in the

Finland Hall. Magistrate Atkinson, considering this a serious crime, refused bail. Olstroski was, apparently, a popular man. Six hundred of his comrades rushed the jail, bent on getting him out. Atkinson, taken aback, considered again, and granted $2,000 bail, releasing Olstroski forthwith in order to avoid further trouble.[91]

One suspects that sometimes local, intercommunal tensions were at the root of particular incidents remembered as simple crime. For example, in October 1915, the Peace River detachment of the Royal North West Mounted Police (RNWMP) received a call from some concerned citizens. One of their friends, a certain McColley, had not been seen for some time. They suspected that he had been murdered by his neighbour, Otto Buschner, a "German socialist." It appears the two were in the habit of quarrelling, though the neighbours did not say about what. The police investigated and found the McColley farm still smouldering. Still smouldering, as well, was the body of the murdered man. Before they could question him, Buschner – an expert bushman – slipped away into the woods. A chase ensued. Buschner, finally cornered, shot himself through the head with his rifle before he could be questioned.[92] It would be impossible to say now if this were a simple murder, or the result of war-accentuated enmity. In the context of the time, we would do well to admit the possibility that the war might have had something to do with it.

There is not much more to report. New Canada smouldered. French Canada boiled. The government, meanwhile, had something to fear from each. New Canada, however, was too weak, dispersed, and divided to be much of a threat, other than in a few locations, and even then only for small periods of time. There were distinct limits to how far French Canada would go in opposition. French Canadians might march. They might throw rocks and fire revolvers into the newspaper offices. They might take to the woods when called up. Local police might not pursue, and French Canadian magistrates might not prosecute, dissenters with the vigour of their British Canadian colleagues. Quebec juries might not convict. French Canadians would not, however, countenance deliberate political violence, especially if anybody really got hurt. They would listen to sedition. They would not comply with government direction. They were not ready for active treachery. What had developed, however, was a sort of passive insurgency; a local consensus, enforced when necessary by mob action, that the government's writ would only be allowed to run so far, and not at all in some regards. This was the sort of challenge which the government of Canada was unlikely to ignore and was ultimately the rationale behind the much more ruthless conscription regime instituted in 1918, including, especially, the movement to summary procedure and federalization of enforcement. In the meantime, of course, more than enough evidence was available to convince British Canada that "shirker Quebec" refused its imperative duty, and needed to be taken powerfully in hand if the government, as well, showed signs of shirking.

6 "We Cheerfully Accept the Burden Laid upon Us": Intercommunal Riot as Social Control in British Canada, 1916–1917

Khaki ... stands today for service, sacrifice and the great crusade ... We as a nation are going through a baptism of fire that will burn up our low ideals of social and political corruption. Woe to the self-seeker and the grafter, they shall all be cleared out when the men return.
The Venerable Archdeacon Cody, 30 April 1917

get rid of your German and Austrian help remember this is no idle threat you are not the only ones who have been warned ... NO GERMANS IN CALGARY
Men of the 89th Battalion, February 1916

The epicentre of the storm rocking Canada in the middle war years was in British Canada, spectacular demonstrations of the disaffection of Quebecers notwithstanding. Its object was the vulnerable communities of disparate newcomers scattered in its midst. French Canada was relatively immune, although French Canadians were occasionally individually targeted. British Canadians were aware of the unwritten rules of Confederation. They understood that attacks against French Canadians would probably invite reprisal and might well, by further marginalizing the hapless French Canadian federalists, produce a fillip for nationalist extremism. The geographical concentration of French Canadians in Quebec also helped to mute what otherwise might have been a more overtly explosive divide. British Canadians in Quebec were too few to launch much of a local offensive. They played their part in riots as victims rather than perpetrators. In British Canada, New Canadians and suspect individuals were more exposed, safer and more satisfactory victims altogether. In much of British Canada, in the latter war years, the fuel provided by a general sense of grievance could easily be ignited by relatively minor incidents, given charge by the feelings unleashed by the war. What made this species of conflict particularly dangerous in British Canada was that it continually demonstrated the capacity to spiral out of control in the absence of sufficiently credible and effective government attempts to beat it down or buy it off. However, factors prevalent in British Canada ensured that attempts to restrain or subdue were difficult. Here, demonstrations were usually for rather than against the war effort; demands for greater vigour and ruthlessness in prosecution of the war, rather than attacks on government policy (which was, after all, to wage the war vigorously, and ruthlessly). Furthermore, a notable feature of intercommunal violence in British Canada was the prevalence of uniformed participants. This alone would have ensured that government efforts to control intercommunal outbursts in British Canada necessarily focused more on buying than beating.

The fact of soldier rioters is something that requires explanation, if we are to appreciate the nature of this problem, and the shape of wartime society. P. Whitney Lackenbauer, the historian most directly interested in the 1916 riots, provides two. Neither is entirely sufficient, in large measure because he focuses uniquely on the uniformed participants.[1] Although soldiers were certainly often present, and, in some cases, front and centre in riots, they were most often the instruments and not the instigators. Moreover, even in those cases that Lackenbauer considers most closely – Calgary and Kitchener in 1916 – the majority of rioters were not soldiers. If soldiers sometimes started anti-alien riots, they were always applauded and consistently, joyfully assisted by civilian collaborators who on most occasions kept the party going for some time after the imposition of a heavy military hand had returned riotous soldiers to barracks.

Soldiers were, essentially, a catalyst to riot rather than its primary substance. This is key and exactly what we should expect when we keep demographic facts in mind. By the middle of 1916, young, able-bodied British Canadian men were very apt to be in uniform. Most of the pool of effective, potential rioters, in effect, was in khaki. Statistics of prewar crime make clear that in Edwardian Canada the riotous were young and male. Statistics for military participation make another thing obvious: young healthy males, in latter war British Canada, generally wore uniform. In his pioneering work on Great War Toronto, for example, Ian Miller has calculated that, in order to produce the 35,800 men enlisted from Toronto (exclusive of artillery batteries, pioneers, construction battalions, and the Royal Flying Corps) before the passage of the MSA, a minimum of two-thirds of the eligible male population of the city would have had to try to enlist. The remaining one-third (maximum), of course, would include those who had enlisted in corps not included in specifically army categories, those who were obviously physically incapable of military service, those whose duties or employment did not permit them to join, and, of course, those whose civil status prohibited them from direct participation in the war.[2] By October 1917, Miller estimates, 75,000 men, or 86 per cent of eligible Toronto men, must have tried to enlist.[3] Even in April 1916, a door-to-door canvass of the neighbourhood bounded by Queen, Bloor, Yonge, and Sherbourne revealed that every house, with the exception of two or three, had produced at least one soldier. By 1918 the redoubtable Mayor Church began to complain that all the mobilization of opinion against slackers, all the police action against suspected evaders – the sudden sweeps, harassment of the suspicious – were pointless inconveniences. There was no object. The men were gone. Those who remained were not fit, could not be taken, or were not eligible even if they wished to go. The situation elsewhere in Mariposa was not apt to be much different, most times. A residual British Canadian male population composed of the pacifically inclined, the feeble, the stunted, the aged, the very young, the responsibly married, and the essentially skilled was unlikely to produce a very effective mob.

Where there were no soldiers there were few riots. The equation is simple. In southwestern Ontario, for example, the Border Cities (future Windsor) contained a substantial immigrant element. There was also a sizeable French Canadian population given to riot itself. Windsor, more than most communities, had good cause to fear the machinations of hidden enemies. There were actual incidents of sabotage. There were bombs. There were spectacular trials of saboteurs, as we have seen. Battles, during the Fenian invasions, had been fought hereabouts. In Windsor, however, there were also no wartime riots, at least involving denizens of British Canada. Windsor was not a garrison town. However, nearby London was, and it was there that we see rioting.

Similarly, riots seldom occurred where there was not a New Canadian target community. There were garrison communities in the Maritimes, but this region had not seen substantial settlement by newcomers. Soldiers and sailors there might be bigoted and angry. Citizens might have been as vigilant as they were anywhere to deal with the enemy within, but there were few readily available, vulnerable objects on which they might focus. The Maritimes, for the duration, appear to have been largely immune from large-scale intercommunal disturbance, probably because, in most of the region, there was essentially only one community. There were, similarly, not many convictions for war or political offences – no convictions for sedition, for example, in Nova Scotia – and probably for the same reason. Both things were required: soldiers (the catalyst) and New Canadians (the object). Where substantial communities of both existed in close proximity – a garrison town of mixed settlement – violence was common, and sometimes reached substantial and dangerous proportions.

So what? Remember that the majority of wartime rioters were never soldiers at all, but civilians, even if soldiers were sometimes an obvious element. Had they not been, and had civilians not also been involved, few of the major riots would have developed to the proportion or lasted as long as they did. Civilian police had to arrest soldiers in uniform – returned men did not count – before the military police were activated. Civilian police – a civilian occupation group with, as elsewhere, a high enlistment rate and which tended to recruit by preference men with military experience – were always reluctant to act against soldiers, and in some municipalities, the police refused to have anything to do with them. On the other hand, military police or members of a "flying picquet," short of a formal request for assistance, were generally hesitant to act against civilians. While the Criminal Code indemnified soldiers when acting to suppress an honest-to-god riot, even in default of the legal niceties,[4] and while both the Criminal Code and the Militia Act provided for penalties in the event that they did not act with sufficient vigour, determining if an actual riot had occurred and if a particular level of force was appropriate was a matter of law tendered after the fact by a civilian magistrate. If soldiers acted against civilians without proper authorization or with too much enthusiasm, they were liable to face criminal prosecution. Recent experience in Canada and historical experience in Britain left the King's soldiers reluctant to act without the written consent of established authority first, whatever the Criminal Code and Militia Act might suggest.[5] Neither soldiers nor policemen, still further, wanted to visit repression on returned men – seriously wounded veterans by definition. The nature of riotous mobs in British Canada – a mixture of soldiers, civilians, and returned men, often in civilian clothes – was therefore a powerful inhibitor on effective police action.[6]

Even had all of this not been the case, it is likely, by 1916, that there would have been incidents of violence between New Canadians and Great War Canadian soldiers. A volunteer army drawn from a society riven by polar responses to the war, and therefore with great differences in rates of enlistment between communities, must be expected to be informed and impelled by the prejudices of the most patriotic. The way in which volunteers were obtained prior the onset of the MSA virtually ensured that there would be violence. Miller has identified, in Toronto, several "thresholds" – changes of recruiting method calculated to ratchet up the social/cultural pressure on likely recruits.[7] In 1914–15, the armouries simply had to open their doors to fill their quotas. Indeed, many more potential volunteers were turned away than were ever placed in khaki, and the prominence of the British-born in the first contingents of the CEF owed much to the fact that these men were more likely to have had prior military service. Emigrants from the United Kingdom tended to be, disproportionately, young, single men. Battalions in formation had the luxury of turning away those who were not young, fit, single, and experienced. This happy situation did not endure.

Through 1916, local civilian organizations composed of enthusiasts and volunteers were ever more fully co-opted to maintain a steady flow of Canadian volunteers. These, of course, made the propaganda pitch most appropriate to the community they were attempting to convince; and, given that success was measured by numbers, the community which had hitherto produced the goods. In 1916, this meant British Canada – the most fertile recruiting ground – which was subjected to an increasingly shrill Canadian nativist, British imperialist, and religious based appeal. British Canadians would respond to this call. Those who were not British could not go anyway, and therefore did not need to be convinced. In the 1916 recruiting campaign, for example, the Orange Order pulled out all the stops, and from its already depleted ranks found another 5,500 members from Ontario West alone (the Saint Jean Baptiste Society, in comparison, provided three recruits nationally as part of the same campaign).[8] By the end of the year, as the cost of the Somme was calculated, there was an increasing reliance on moral coercion, and sometimes the physical compulsion of "slackers." In effect, the 1916 recruiting drive worked locally by stoking British Canadian prejudice, encouraging intolerance for those not obviously stuck into the great crusade. Such was the method used to ensure British Canada's fullest possible voluntary support for the war effort.[9] Canada used British Canadians. British Canada, in exchange, ultimately demanded an exceptional say in what Canadian society, then in the process of formation, would look like in the future, and fine-tuned their picture of that future in the hysterical atmosphere emerging in the last desperate years of the war. If the government was unwilling to give them this Canada, they sometimes seem to have felt justified in attempting to achieve it for themselves. New Canadians, especially Alien Enemies, had little place in this vision.

Finally, we should note – although this would be impossible to quantify – that the difference between official and local military organization, between state-sponsored and vigilante violence, was by no means as clear to Canadians then as it is now. In Canada, the difference between the regular army, the volunteer militia, and the enthusiastic patriot, hastily assembled doing what he conceived to be the nation's work, was new and not clearly established. In the years before the war, in many Canadian locales, militia units were only just being raised and armouries built – both by voluntary effort. What was the difference between a gathering of patriotic enthusiasts, the Mariposa Light Horse, and the 117th Canadian Mounted Rifles? A date. Just what the difference was between the Dominion Rifle Association and the uniformed militia was uncertain; and in any case, the army supported both. Were not all equally "King's men"? By 1916, all were equally engaged in the great crusade at home and abroad. So it had been in the past. So it still was in 1916.[10]

The end result was a wartime army which was the creature, caricature, and darling of the restricted communities from which it sprang, and which in most local systems can only with difficulty be construed as an entity distinct from Mariposa more generally. Mariposa did not generate soldiers for some army understood as a discrete corporation, fighting some foreign war for somebody else's interest. It generated crusaders for Mariposa militant at home and abroad. It followed that opposition to the war – or any action that might inhibit the maximum effectiveness of Canada in the struggle – was not a disagreement to be tolerated, but an evil to be overthrown. In attacks on the domestic enemy, soldiers were the agent of the society that produced them, and which normally assisted them enthusiastically.

In sum, British Canadian mobs were difficult to either constrain or intimidate, owing to their composition, the convictions that impelled them, and the degree of support they enjoyed. Necessarily, they were

Intercommunal Riot as Social Control in British Canada, 1916–1917 133

cajoled or induced to disperse, generally once they'd achieved something like their purpose. Inducement to go home normally included promises that some level of government would assume the repressive function they appeared to be quite willing and able to accomplish themselves. In appreciating this dynamic, we understand much of what was happening on the home front in the latter years of the Great War. Let us proceed to some illustrations of this pattern.

Calgary, Alberta, in 1914, was a relatively new city, inhabited by citizens who were all of them, virtually by definition, "new," at least to Alberta. There was a substantial European element, 2,608 of whom were "German" (many *Volksdeutsch* from Russia) according to the 1911 census, a relatively large French Canadian community, some Americans, and a British majority, composed of immigrants from the United Kingdom and settlers from Central Canada. As elsewhere in British Canada, this last element reacted to the outbreak of war with alacrity. During the war, 37,000 local men enlisted in the army: at any one time 5,000 to 15,000 soldiers were quartered at the exhibition ground, or at the nearby Sarcee military camp, established in 1915.[11] This was inflammable material. Starting in 1916, a series of blazes occurred. The local pattern appears to have been quite typical throughout Great War British Canada.

In January 1916, news came that two battalions raised locally had suffered severe casualties – more than five hundred men lost.[12] This depressing intelligence was carried on the front page of the local paper and must have produced powerful anxiety, particularly in the restricted communities from which most recruits came. Meanwhile, the usual war news continued: details of the sedition trials of local German immigrants, and the news that the local French Catholic clergy would not contribute to the patriotic fund, for example. In February 1916, news from abroad was not encouraging. Kut-al-Amara was surrounded, and seemed about to fall. Zeppelins were bombing London. The situation in Russia was very bad. The year 1915 had been a terrible one, and Russia was obviously in trouble. At the beginning of February, under the headline "Punish the Murders" – the injunction of Sir Wilfrid Laurier – the burning of the House of Commons was described as self-evident sabotage.[13] A few days later, the paper carried shocking news concerning a supposed *Bundist* plot to invade Canada with thirty-eight thousand armed men.[14] At this juncture, as well, voluntary recruiting of the 1916 pattern ramped up among the residual population of British subjects – by this juncture in the war the only available, receptive audience and therefore the only one targeted. Meanwhile, the local garrison was cooped up for the winter, training largely indoors, and may have been beginning to feel, in common with much of the city's population, "cabin fever."[15] Fear combined with anxiety and grief. Nativist prejudice intensified, and anti-German feeling began to become simple xenophobia. In all of this, Calgary was typical of many British Canadian cities by this point in the war. It was also typical in what followed – a large-scale outburst against New Canadians – one of a series of riots in Canadian garrison cities in the spring of 1916.

The event that sparked the conflagration appears relatively minor in retrospect. In this too Calgary was typical. A week after the Parliament buildings collapsed in flames, and about the same time that *Bundist* plotting was reported, a returned man appears to have been discharged from employment by one of a chain of local restaurants owned by a man (Frank Nagel) with a suspicious name.[16] Nagel had been warned previously, by anonymous post, to toe the line or he would face reprisal. "Beware of the white lunch," one missive began: "get rid of your German and Austrian help remember this is no idle threat you are not the only ones who have been warned." Another, to a local photographer, warned him to take down his signs and cases by 8:00 p.m. Saturday night or "WE WILL." One warning was signed "Men of the 89th," and ended "NO GERMANS IN CALGARY."[17] On 10 February, handwritten notes appeared in the canteen of the Sarcee Camp indicating that White's Restaurant had recently fired British waiters and engaged a German and an Austrian. Nagel informed General Cruickshank, the garrison commander, that he expected trouble.[18]

During the next two days (11–12 February 1916), soldiers from the local garrison rioted, supported by many members of the local community. There were riots at the same time in Berlin (Kitchener), Ontario, Cambellton, New Brunswick, and Winnipeg, Manitoba. On 11 February, five hundred soldiers seem to have been responsible for most of the destruction visited on two of Nagel's restaurants. The soldiers marched in groups to the street in front of the restaurants and there dismissed before beginning their work. Nagel fled the carnage for the safety of the fire department, but was turned away.[19] General Cruickshank, an efficient officer and stern disciplinarian, ordered an investigation and warned that he had the names of the ringleaders. He promised dire punishment.

6.1. Calgary firemen attacking German soldiers hanged in effigy. It is little wonder that Nagel was turned away when he sought shelter here. Picture courtesy of the Glenbow Archives.

The next day, however, 1,500–2,000 soldiers and citizens turned out to wreck the Riverside Hotel, before moving on to other businesses. Why the Riverside? The hotel stood in the middle of the German district, had been founded by Charles Poffenroth, was then owned by Alfred Ebbsworth (like Poffenroth an American immigrant), and was leased to John Rioux, a French Canadian. It appears to have remained in the popular imagination a "German establishment." There were rumours, moreover, that a recent conclave of "foreigners" had met there to celebrate the destruction of Parliament.[20] Kolb's restaurant, Cronn's *rathskeller*, a local brewery, and the Hotel Palliser were threatened, as was the Canadian Bible Society, for distributing Bibles printed in German.[21] The police and Cruickshank's picquets were swept aside "like straw." Confining the troops to barracks and threatening martial law eventually restored order among the soldiers.[22] The local Germans, meanwhile, were terrified and barricaded themselves in their homes.

The *Albertan*, faced with the fact of mass military indiscipline becoming anti-foreign rioting involving both soldiers and civilians, advocated the internment of foreigners as the most "humane and charitable thing to do."[23] The civic fathers in Calgary, obviously scared by what had transpired, immediately discharged all civic employees of Alien Enemy derivation and replaced them, where possible, with returned men.[24] Meanwhile, trials of those deemed most guilty commenced. Thirteen soldiers were ultimately charged as ringleaders. Five were found guilty. Two were discharged from the service.[25] The remainder received fines in civilian court.[26] In potential, as rioters who had been destroying property, they could have been sentenced to life imprisonment.[27] Their punishment, under King's Regulations and Orders, would not have been much less extreme.

In nearby Edmonton, there were no riots, but the garrison commander had taken the precaution of posting substantial armed picquets around businesses at risk. The *Edmonton Bulletin*, a liberal paper, and the McDonald Hotel, suspected of employing "alien labour," were placed under close guard.[28] The *Edmonton Bulletin* appears, in particular, to have been a probable target for destruction. The provocation, in this case, was editorials published on the 9th and 10th of February, unfriendly to the substantial military presence in the town. "The dog is a very useful and estimable animal in his own place," one began,

> and his place is a large one. But the street of a city is not part of that place. Child life in the country would be safer and parental life freed from a good deal of worry if the hides of about three battalions of good-for-nothing mongrels were nailed to the fence.[29]

6.2. The saloon of the Riverside Hotel after the riot. Picture courtesy of the Glenbow Archives.

6.3. Riverside Bar. Picture courtesy of the Glenbow Archives.

Reference appears to have been to the 51st, 63rd, and 66th Battalions, then billeted in the city. In Edmonton, as in Calgary, soldiers and their supporters assembled with mayhem in mind. The police, however, immediately requested help from the garrison. A picquet from the 66th cleared the streets of soldiers and ordered civilians to disperse. The manager of the *Bulletin*, meanwhile, addressed a crowd of angry soldiers assembled in front of his establishment and seems to have convinced them, somehow, that no insult had been intended.[30]

In 1914, Berlin, Ontario (Kitchener after May 1916), was a rapidly growing industrial town with a majority "German" population – partly immigrant, partly long resident; largely Mennonite – sited in the centre of Orange Ontario.[31] Local Germans were powerful enough to block anti-alien measures in a way that would have been inconceivable elsewhere. There was still, in 1916, no alien registrar in Waterloo County. No Alien Enemies had been interned, although immigrants directly from Germany made up approximately 8.2 per cent of the city's population. Berlin had, the *Toronto Star* reported with considerable consternation, seen only two attempted prosecutions for sedition.[32] This made it highly unusual for an Ontario town of this size by this juncture in the war, particularly given its composition. It was widely suspected that Mr Michael Weichel, the local MP, had been working to maintain peacetime normalcy in his riding.[33] Kitchener's Germans, Weichel told Parliament, could be counted on. They were proud to be German, but not proud of German politics or Germany's actions. They would be loyal to the country in which they lived. They were good British subjects.[34] In truth, the attitude of the town's German population was *attentiste* rather than either patriotic or dissident. Local German Canadians were anxious to take the steps necessary to avoid being stigmatized as unpatriotic – by, for example, contributing to the patriotic fund with great enthusiasm[35] – but were not very enthusiastic about actually volunteering for service.

In the early war years, surrounding British Canada appears to have accepted this state of affairs. It was "hard for them," the Toronto *Globe* considered,

> to choose. Blood is thicker than water. The Atlantic has not washed out the patriotism, the hallowed love, the cherished memories, which bind thousands of citizens of Berlin and Waterloo ... to their historic fatherland. For them this call to duty is a call to the cross. But they obey. It is for freedom.[36]

Wilfrid Laurier, leader of the opposition, considered that, while it was true that the Germans were loyal Britishers, "they would not be men if they had not in their hearts a deep feeling of affection for the land of their ancestors. No one would blame them for that. There is nothing so painful as the situation in which mind and heart are driven in opposite directions."[37] Laurier was, perhaps, more understanding because he was quickly to become conflicted himself. Borden agreed, however, with his assessment. Many of the best citizens in Canada were German, Borden thought. There was no reason to believe that any of them might be traitors, or "inspired by the militaristic influences" so apparent in the policies of the fatherland. If the Germans were loyal, they would find tolerance and sympathy.[38]

However, in 1916 this happy state of affairs began to unravel locally and then system wide. In February, Berlin played host to a pro-war speaker, who claimed to have been behind the German lines for some time and to have seen numerous atrocities. The paper, as in Calgary, carried depressing news. As in Calgary, rumours of German plots and the supposed torching of the Parliament buildings were particularly provocative. The attempts of some members of the German community to "to defend Kaiserism" did not produce the intended effect.[39] Meanwhile, the 118th Battalion began to recruit in the city, and in the surrounding county, by the methods inevitable in 1916: virulent appeals to British Canadian patriotism, accompanied by attempts to intimidate dissidents and coerce slackers. Try as it might, however, the 118th could not get more than four hundred volunteers – most of them local men, half of them of German derivation.[40] Its efforts to recruit to full strength stymied by the reluctance of potential volunteers to present themselves, members of the battalion began to "good-humouredly" grab and carry likely looking lads to the recruiting station. When they grabbed a man and his girlfriend, some locals thought they had gone too far. An executive member of the local TLC and an AFL organizer, Fred Ackernecht, certainly seems to have thought so. He led the local TLC in appealing for the removal of the battalion from the city and for the stoppage of the use of civic funds for recruiting purposes.[41] Another local man, Walter Mayer, publicly assured soldiers of the battalion that they were all going to be shot when they arrived at the front. Tried for sedition, he was not imprisoned, but simply bound over to keep the peace.[42] Relations between the town and the battalion soured quickly. While not "anti-German,"

Lieutenant-Colonel Lockheed, commander of the 118th, promised that when he had raised a regimental police detachment and obtained a provost marshal, treachery like Mayer's would no longer be ignored.[43] Not surprisingly, Kitchener had a wartime history of intercommunal violence.[44]

In February, a rumour went that a local German hall continued to display German flags. Ten or fifteen members of the 118th Battalion decided to find out, and raided the hall. Indeed there were flags. They were torn to pieces. A bust of Kaiser Wilhelm I was paraded through the streets and thrown into a pond.[45] Two weeks later, fifty members of the battalion paid a night visit to C.R. Tappert, the pastor of St Matthew's Lutheran Church. The man was captured, frog-marched back to the barracks, and detained. He was, the men claimed, a US citizen, "most indiscreet in his language and attitude towards soldiers." Tappert had, early in the war, been arrested for seditious utterance, but the charges were dropped.[46] It appears that Tappert had been publicly disputing atrocity stories that had appeared in the press and had, more recently, been giving interviews to the *Toronto Star* in which he attempted to explain the position of the local German population.[47] The soldiers of the garrison had placed him on notice. He had until March to leave town or face the consequences. He had not left. It was time for him to experience the consequences. For most Canadians, however, the illegal detention of a pastor was going too far. The police intervened. The man was released. The ringleaders, in this case, were tried by civil authority and received suspended sentences.[48] Even Sam Hughes was shocked at how far the situation had developed in Kitchener. Surely, he thought, German Canadians had given no evidence of disloyalty; indeed, thirty-eight actual Germans had been killed fighting in France, in the Canadian Corps. "It would be better," he thought, "for those who are endeavouring to make a race war out if it to follow their example. This is not a race war but a war of liberty."[49]

Intervention by the minister of militia notwithstanding, trouble continued throughout the year. On 5 May, following an energetic recruiting rally, ten members of the battalion attacked the Arcadian Club and seized a statue of Wilhelm II. Thirty to forty members of the battalion followed this up with a "sharp night raid." The club was demolished. Those responsible were not identified.[50] We will see more incidents in Kitchener apace.

In the Maritimes, where the enemy within was less in evidence, there was violence, but it was sporadic. A restaurant in Perth, New Brunswick, was ransacked on 12 May 1916 after its owner, it appears, had used abusive language to soldiers.[51] In Windsor, Nova Scotia, on 14 November, 150 men of the 239th Railway Construction Battalion assembled to wreck and fire the garage and cars of a German, accused of making anti-British remarks.[52] There was not much more in the Maritimes. Here, New Canadians were few, and we might expect, quickly learned to lie low.

Soldiers were not the sole culprits and were not always necessary, though they were the usual catalyst. Their presence was normally required to produce an explosion. Sometimes, however, critical mass could be reached without them. On 20 April 1916, in Acton, Ontario, hundreds of local townsfolk ransacked the homes of interned aliens, recently transported there for war work in a local tannery. The townspeople, including employees of the tannery at which the aliens were to have been employed, appear simply not to have wanted the internees in their midst.[53] In a similar action, a year later, employment of alien labour in a Nova Scotia car works produced a stoppage of work. British Canadian employees at the Eastern Car Company, in New Glasgow, refused to work until the Alien Enemies in their midst were withdrawn from their workplace and interned. They would not take up tools, they promised, until this was done.[54]

Back in Ontario, soldiers in Kitchener (Berlin, recently renamed) brought in the New Year 1917 with a bang. On 1 January, one hundred men of the 118th Battalion paraded through the town behind the Union flag. The battalion was in a foul mood. It had become apparent that it would not proceed overseas as a formed body. It was too small (238 of its 540 men had recently been rejected as unfit), could not attract recruits, and was already in the process of being broken up. The men had hoped to fight together. We might guess whom they blamed for the failure of their hopes. A local civic election was in progress, with two citizens' leagues – the "British League" (pro-government, and "win the war") and the largely German "Citizens' League" (pro-Liberal, and dissenting) actively campaigning.[55] The Citizens' League had been formed, in 1916, to fight the change of the name of the city from Berlin to Kitchener. When the name change went through anyway, following what was viewed as a "rigged vote," the organization remained in being to turn out the existing council and elect an entirely new, more Germanophile slate.[56] The soldiers, of course – many of them local citizens, half of them German Canadian themselves – were hardly non-partisan. On New Year's Day the battalion was parading, in fact, to demonstrate support for the British League candidate. A person in the crowd, a member it appears of the Citizens' League, attempted to grab the flag from the soldier carrying it. Immediately a riot ensued – rampaging soldiers doing "considerable damage" in particular to the offices of the local Liberal paper, the *News-Record* – an English-language paper owned by Die Deutsche Druck und Verlagsgesellschaft von Berlin (the German Printing and Publishing Company of Berlin). Two councillors-elect were assaulted: Councillors Asmusaen and Bowman – Bowman sustaining a concussion. The situation was not at all helped by the fact that the Citizens' League had considerable success at the polls. Ultimately a 110-man detachment from the 122nd Battalion, stationed in nearby Galt, was brought to Kitchener to restore order.[57] Kitchener was not a happy place.

Toronto also saw significant trouble in the middle and later war years. The demographics of Toronto – 85 per cent "British," 76 per cent Protestant; Irish Catholics and Jews, the most significant minorities, as fully engaged in the war as the Orangemen among whom they lived[58] – did not make it, necessarily, a particularly inflammatory place, but did ensure that it was certain to catch any disease germinating in British Canada. Following disclosures in the Toronto *Globe* regarding the number of foreigners employed in local industry,[59] in April 1917, five hundred soldiers "marched along Yonge Street calling on all men in Khaki to join them in their crusade to wipe out the enemy in their midst." The immediate trigger appears to have been rumours that a returned soldier had been insulted by an "Austrian" employee of Child's Restaurant at Yonge and Richmond.[60] In the end, twenty restaurants were broken into and searched for alien employees. Two men mistaken for Austrians – a Russian and a Swiss – were forcibly detained by the mob and marched to a detective's office. It appears, from the fact that one of the men had "several ugly welts across his face," that the pair had been beaten. In Child's itself, some property damage was experienced – broken dishes and chairs.[61]

The next day, Toronto veterans turned their attention to cleaning up the Russell Motor Company, a large munitions factory. This time they were more successful. Twenty-four Alien Enemy employees were apprehended and subsequently paraded by the veterans through the streets – "a throng of citizens" cheering.[62] Later in the week, despite a "truce," returned men raided the Kemp sheet metal plant and carried away five "Austrian prisoners." To enter the plant, the returned men had scaled a fifteen-foot-high gate, observed by a watchman, who subsequently served as their guide in the workshop.[63]

At the beginning of June, as Toronto mobilized itself to support the fight for conscription, patriot attention focused on those who opposed the measure. When a group of socialists assembled in the Labour Temple to organize themselves, the returned men decided to take a hand. The meeting never properly got under way. The, perhaps, five hundred anti-conscriptionists in attendance – many of them "foreigners," it was asserted – were confronted by a mob of angry veterans. The hall was ransacked, a bugler sounding the charge. The socialists dispersed. Many of them, it appears, were chased through the hall and out into the streets by the returned men, who thereafter marched to City Hall. Throughout this altercation the veterans were cheered by a mob of Toronto's citizens.[64] Toronto's labour movement promised that no future meetings of this nature would be permitted in the Labour Temple; indeed, if the purpose of this meeting had been known, it would not have taken place. The Greater Toronto Labour Party, meanwhile, insured itself by passing conscriptionist resolutions. Toronto police promised, in the future, that anti-conscription meetings involving Alien Enemies would not be permitted, since, during the war, aliens had no right of assembly. In any case, they had been "foolish" in trying to hold the meeting, and had paid the price of folly.[65] When, a week later, the socialists tried to hold a public meeting in the street, Toronto police, perhaps to prevent a repetition, intervened to stop it from taking place. Police swooped in, silenced the speaker, interrogated those in attendance, and left with eighty Alien Enemies in tow. As Miller correctly points out, for an Alien Enemy to attend a "seditious" meeting was, in 1917, sufficient proof of disloyalty for internment to take place or for legal action to proceed by fiat of any magistrate, and not only, we should remember, in Toronto.[66]

On 22 June 1917, an altercation between a "young foreigner" and two returned soldiers created a "small riot." The "foreigner," it appears, made an "insolent reply" to the soldiers, after which they, and a crowd of passers-by, beat the man until police intervened. The man was "severely injured about the face and head."[67] In September 1917, Toronto returned men, hearing that a crowd of Alien Enemies were holding a meeting in Occident Hall, intervened to break it up. What they succeeded in disturbing, however, was a Jewish religious ceremony.[68] Not until 1918 did violence in Toronto reach its apogee. We will consider this shortly.

There were riots in Regina in April 1917. Soldiers do not seem to have been involved in this particular storm, although returned men were much in evidence. The focus of the riot this time was a local German-language paper, *Der Courier*. Under the editorship of the outspoken C.E. Eymann, *Der Courier* had become the most powerful voice upholding the rights of the Canadian German community. Only if the community remained united, Eymann preached, could it save itself from the storm raging outside. This line was, of course, not particularly liked by local British Canadian patriots. Despite the fact that, on occasion, he plainly went too far, Eymann's right to free speech was vigorously protected by Saskatchewan's Liberal government, since the paper was, hardly surprisingly, committedly partisan.[69] In April, a mob of militants and returned men effectively censored Eymann for the duration by destroying the paper's offices.[70] In truth, it is wonderful that *Der Courier* had survived this long. Eymann had welcomed the outbreak of war, and invited readers to prepare to witness German power. By 1917, moreover, the paper had taken to criticizing what it considered to be the insufficient protection afforded German Canadians by the Dominion government – a piece of "Germanism," the censors thought, approaching the limit of what was permissible. In this action the mob was likely only one step ahead of official censorship.[71]

The government's reaction was remarkably restrained, given provocation. A riot by several thousand people, in the streets of Calgary, Winnipeg, or London, Ontario, after all, would be big news now – particularly if property was destroyed, soldiers involved, and immigrant communities targeted for violence. We might expect a still greater reaction in the pint-sized Canada of 1916. After the Calgary riots there was some discussion in Parliament, but not much and all rather half-hearted. This continued to be the case. Questioning in Parliament focused more on the immediate causes – the over-availability, it seemed to the opposition, of alcohol to off-duty soldiers – than what Canada was going to do about a situation plainly getting out of hand in some Canadian cities. Were, Laurier wondered, traitors getting too much drink into the boys in Calgary, and if so, what would the government do? He "was not aware," Borden responded, that alcohol had been involved in the Calgary riots, but would get the minister of militia to look into it.[72] "Should," Laurier asked, "military or civil authorities deal with rioters"? "Civil," Borden considered: this was a law and order issue, and a local responsibility constitutionally. "Military," Laurier responded: the question was indiscipline among serving soldiers.[73] There was little other official reaction. A few questions asked in Parliament, it might be thought, were precious little comfort to the communities in the eye of the storm. The army, for its part, duly investigated those disturbances in which soldiers were involved. The governor-general and the rest of the military hierarchy were, of course, appropriately outraged when a military presence could be established. Some few rioters, as we have seen, were sometimes charged, although generally in civilian courts for civilian infractions. Successful prosecutions for riot, in fact, declined through the war years, and from published statistics it appears probable that many of those convicted were New Canadians, apt in these disturbances to have been on the wrong side of the fist. Occasionally the accused would be paraded, and some soldier would be tried in military court. Penalties imposed, in either venue, however, were invariably considerably less than the law would have permitted. Canadian legal action against those implicated in this sort of excess was plainly muted.

Uncertain how to deal with patriots, Canada nevertheless was compelled to consider the potential consequences of their actions. British Canada – and Canada with it – had a problem. This problem would become more acute as the war entered its crisis period, the issue very much in doubt. As we have seen, there was trouble between Canadian communities even before the possibility of conscription was mooted. Through 1917, as conscription moved ahead on the public agenda, violence in Quebec become endemic. By 1916, already, violence against New Canadians in British Canada could occasionally grow to dangerous levels. Here, attempts later in the war to ratchet up the war effort (of which conscription was part) ensured that British Canada was compelled to shoulder an ever heavier, and probably ever more disproportionate, share of the burden. In a pattern we have identified, the heavier the burden became, the more hysterical was British Canada; the more exalted the war aims it envisioned, the less acceptable to it was any sign of disengagement. What was the solution, previewed in the middle war years? While the government moved to intimidate Quebec, it acted to restrain New Canadians from providing further provocation to British Canada. It did what it thought to be necessary to ensure that the disgruntled in Quebec understood that opposition beyond a certain point would not be tolerated, while it hoped that, by rendering New Canadians as invisible, silent, and obviously quiescent as possible, heavier – albeit unauthorized – sanction might be avoided.

7 "The Politician Who Attempts to Wander About in No Man's Land Must Be Ruthlessly Destroyed": The Election of 1917

> We have committed ourselves as a nation, we have signed the bond, it is for us to discharge the obligation ... 300,000 living men and 20,000 dead are over there, hostages of our good faith. All that remains for us is a choice between fidelity and desertion, between courage and poltroonery, between honour and everlasting shame.
>
> The Hon. Arthur Meighen, June 1917[1]

> The feet of the French Canadians have been set on a wrong path, upon a path whose end is isolation, ignominy and shame.
>
> *Montreal Gazette*, 9 July 1917

> Down in Quebec there was at one time a Blue and a Red party. Now there is only one party, and it is yellow.
>
> Orange *Sentinel*, 6 December 1917

There were, of course, attempts to bridge the gap between, in particular, English and French Canada. The most important of these was the Bonne Entente, designed to put French and British Canadians back on the same side. Violence against New Canadians might be tolerable. Intercommunal or regional squabbling, especially between French and British Canada, all realized, might be suicidal. Leaders of each group, from 1916, did what they could to establish, if not harmony, then a tolerable truce for the duration. The failure of this movement, its subsequent transmogrification into the uncompromising "win the war" movement, and the shape of the ensuing election are particularly revealing of the state of play in 1917.

In June 1916, a group of largely Liberal British Canadian gentlemen, inspired by Lloyd George's ideas on how to deal with the situation in wartime Ireland, met at the Toronto National Club. Their leader was John Milton Godfrey, a prominent lawyer, Liberal, and ardent imperialist. Godfrey was also president of the Canadian National Service League (NSL), founded in April 1916, and many of the gentlemen meeting in Toronto appear to have been members.[2] The group decided that action was necessary to preserve friendly feeling between the French and English communities in Canada, in order to produce an environment in which volunteering would revive.[3]

The involvement of the NSL in an attempt at community outreach might surprise, is important, and requires some explanation. Through 1916, few Canadians of any kind were ready to accept compulsion, or prepared to believe that it could be imposed without a fight, particularly in Quebec.[4] Furthermore, the NSL was aware that while men were needed for the front, exceptional demands were being made on Canadian industry and agriculture, and the manpower requirements of these too would have to be considered. Unrestrained recruiting or knee-jerk conscription would be wasteful and dangerous. It was clear, however, that men had to be obtained from some source. Figures arriving from France suggested a manpower crisis in no distant future. With heavy fighting underway on the Somme, and with voluntary enlistment falling away entirely, it was hard to imagine how the Canadian Corps could be kept up to strength, while the war appeared far from being won.[5] If volunteers could not be found and conscription were excluded, registration had to be made to work. Success seemed to require the cooperation of Quebec, since, as Godfrey realized, by 1916 already British Canada had few men left to give. As well, Godfrey and many leading NSL members were liberals, opposed to compulsion of any kind, and very aware that any question that set British against French Canada would hardly serve partisan interest. Accordingly, any propaganda that the NSL made advocated registration rather than conscription, which it categorized for the moment as inflammatory, foolhardy, and unnecessary.[6] French Canadian cooperation would be enlisted, Godfrey hoped, by establishing a medium through which leading individuals in each community would learn to appreciate members of the other. If the leaders were harnessed in tandem, he hoped, then the communities would follow.[7] The NSL set out to convince; the Bonne Entente was its vehicle.[8]

It should be noted from the outset, however, that if conviction failed, then the position of the Ontario leadership was not reduced Canadian participation in the war in the interest of national unity and intercommunal harmony, but rather the imposition on the government of an all-out "win the war" policy, inspired by Australian example.[9] While the NSL would prefer to convince, it was prepared to constrain, however much it hated the idea. Godfrey set himself the task of organizing both alternatives. In August 1916, therefore, he co-opted the first Bonne Entente committee in Ontario from the NSL,[10] sent feelers out to Quebec,[11] and commenced local organization calculated to establish a total war consensus in Ontario. While prominent French Canadians were contacted, an electoral machine in support of potential Union government and conscription was organized "down to the polling sub-Divisions," with thousands of women organized for door-to-door work.[12] From the perspective of Ontario members, the purpose of the Bonne Entente, therefore – as part of an aggregate movement – was never simply to produce mutual recognition between Canada's constituent communities, but to maximize Canada's participation in the war, by the least disruptive means available. Quebec, having been shown its duty, would do it and render compulsion unnecessary. If this failed to work, alternatives were prepared.

The leaders of French Canada seemed to be in agreement. Provincial committees were quickly established in Ontario and Quebec. Leadership in Quebec was provided by Sir Lomer Gouin, the premier, and Sir Georges Garneau, chairman of the National Battlefield Commission.[13] Representation from the Maritimes and from the West was solicited and despatched in October to Quebec City for the first conference of what was now called the Bonne Entente. A national committee was quickly established with Garneau in the chair and Godfrey acting as vice-chair. National, popular organization followed, with, on the surface, impressive results. The Montreal branch of the Bonne Entente, for example, set itself the task of enrolling more members and raising more money than its Toronto counterpart. It succeeded spectacularly. Ultimately it raised 4.5 million dollars, one million more than Toronto. It did so by organizing itself into ten teams of twenty members each, each determined to enrol as many working men as possible, every new member promising to donate a day's pay every three months to support the aims of the organization. By this method, 106,000 Montreal working men were enrolled (62 per cent French Canadian), and $800,000 raised.[14]

So far so good: it was by no means obvious, however, what concrete purpose organization and money might accomplish. Lloyd George had seemed to suggest that organization was the solution. A series of conferences ensued. Whatever Godfrey might have hoped, these devolved into sightseeing junkets, broken by banquets and speech-making during which delegations tried to explain the war as they saw it to members of other delegations. A joint resolution passed by provincial committees in August 1916 represented the greatest degree of concurrence achieved:

> We, French and English-speaking Canadians, in conference assembled for the promotion of National Unity, having established, by friendly intercourse, a mutual respect and a firm conviction in the innate fair-mindedness of the vast majority of both races, do hereby place ourselves on record as of the unalterable belief that there is not now, nor ever will be in the future, any issue between the two races in Canada which cannot, and of right, should not now be amicably and equitably settled, and in such a manner as to give satisfaction to the majority of all concerned.[15]

Thereafter, Quebec and Ontario delegates talked at one another, hoping to convince without being convinced. Speaking at a banquet in Hamilton, during the second Bonne Entente conference, even the ardent patriot and enthusiastic recruiter Sir Georges Garneau seemed more interested in ensuring that British Canada understood French Canada's reservations concerning the war than in producing voluntary participation in a national "win the war" program originating in British Canada. Some French Canadian members of the Bonne Entente, indeed, appear to have been mainly interested in using the war movement to address the schools question first.[16] Even before the failure of the Bonne Entente was apparent, it was clear that registration was not working and that, if the strength of the CEF were to be renewed, conscription would almost certainly be required. The Bonne Entente perhaps had been a promising venue for national reconciliation short of total war methods. It could never be made over into an unconditional, national, and intercommunal "win the war" movement.

When it became evident that the movement would not result in more effective French Canadian participation in the war, the movement disintegrated. In February 1917, the Ontario Branch reorganized itself entirely in support of the Borden government. At another meeting at the National Club in Hamilton, on 9 February 1917, Godfrey and his Ontario Liberal collaborators crossed the Rubicon. They continued to look for cooperation, but their chosen partners now were British Canadian Conservatives.[17] Union government would be the means, and the method identified was a "win the war" *ralliement* in British Canada behind the war rather than reconciliation with other Canadians.[18] Conscription was very much part of this package. The "win the war" movement was unparalleled both in scope and program as a gauge of British Canadian wartime patriotism.[19] Not all Godfrey's Quebec Bonne Entente colleagues were left behind. One Quebec city delegate, Lieutenant-Colonel L.-G. Desjardins, followed him into "win the war" and later, in *England, Canada and the Great War*, not only attacked the Nationalists but defended virtually the entirety of the imperial war effort, including its consequences at home in Quebec.[20] Insofar as men like Desjardins made this passage, however, they seem to have lost touch with their own community. In reaching out to embrace British Canada, they lost hold of Quebec. Gouin, more typically, continued to support the war effort and to hope for unity but fought against conscription as unnecessary and divisive. Many Quebecers, as we have seen, took to the streets.

Meanwhile, in faraway London, decisions were being taken which made reconciliation impossible. In December 1916, Robert Borden was invited to come to London to attend an Imperial Conference, including an Imperial War Cabinet (IWC), to deliberate on war policy. While in Europe, Borden took the opportunity to visit the soldiers in France, just recovering from the fighting on the Somme, and, in 1917, committed to battle at Arras and subsequently at Ypres. It was clear, however, even before Arras and Ypres, that casualties were so extreme that the strength of the army could no longer be sustained by voluntary methods.[21] Recruiting was collapsing. Through the spring of 1916, voluntary enlistment had remained high – 30,000 men joining in January; 35,000 in March. Even Quebec, some considered, was beginning to come around.[22] By the end of 1916, the Canadian army was lucky to see 5,000 volunteers a month.[23] Local, voluntary organization had done what it could. A third contingent had been recruited. The manpower well, in those communities most disposed to support the war, however, was almost dry. Registration was in the process of failing. Twenty per cent of Canadian men did not even return the cards. When the snow melted and the mud dried, the fighting began anew. The Canadian Corps lost 20,000 men in the month of April 1917 – nearly 14,000 killed and wounded, on one day, 9 April, the day Vimy Ridge fell. Ten thousand men a month were needed to maintain the strength of the Canadian Corps now. Infantry replacements of 7,800 were urgently required.[24] Borden promised the soldiers at the front that Canada would not let them down. "You men," he told soldiers about to storm Vimy,

> are about to enter one of the most serious engagements that ever faced the Canadian Corps. As head of the Government I give you this assurance ... that no man, whether he goes back or whether he remains in Flanders, will have just cause to reproach the Government for having broken faith with the men who won and the men who died.[25]

The new Canadian Corps commander, Sir Arthur Currie, intended to keep Borden to his bond. "I note," Currie wrote in June,

> with special gratification your assurance that the troops in the field can rely upon Canada giving them all necessary support. They have given their blood freely to maintain their nation's honour and now confidently expect that the full fruits of their sacrifice will not be prejudiced. It is an imperative and urgent necessity that steps be taken to ensure that sufficient drafts of officers and men are sent from Canada to keep the Corps at its full strength.[26]

If conscription were not implemented immediately, and if men were not forthcoming quickly, so extreme were casualties that four divisions would become one division by the end of 1918. This, Currie thought, would be not so much dangerous as a grotesque betrayal.[27] It is unlikely that his men took a more enlightened view.

Victory, meanwhile, appeared to be as far away as ever. This much the IWC had made clear to the Dominion premiers. The war, the General Staff informed them, would last for several more years, and might well produce a very inconclusive peace with the possibility of another war following shortly thereafter.[28] This was shocking news, which the Canadian contingent appears to have accepted with alacrity. Canada's leadership was not quickly converted from learned pessimism. Indeed, in 1918, two weeks after the Canadian Corps had broken the German line opposite Amiens, and with what we know now were decisive operations in progress, Arthur Meighen still believed that "there never was anything more obvious in the world than that a strong and determined Eastern policy [was] essential to success in this war."[29] Germany was not on the point of defeat. It would emerge strengthened from the conflict. It would have to be hemmed in before the end of this war if the Second World War that would follow closely were to be anything but a disaster. Nor were short-term prospects favourable. The war had reached a critical stage, and that failure to maintain the Allied armies in the field might well mean defeat in 1918. The Allies could not begin to win the war before 1919. They could, however, lose sooner. An imperial manpower survey, conducted in the winter of 1916/17, identified what seemed to be pools of available manpower, reluctant to enlist.[30] Canada appeared to be one of these. The Canadian army had performed superlatively well in recent actions, and it was continually pressed on Borden, while in Europe, that the strength of the Canadian Corps must be maintained and, if possible, increased. Borden, George Perley (minister of overseas military forces), and Albert Kemp (minister of militia) promised to find another 100,000 men. Borden vowed that Canada would do everything necessary to maintain half a million men at the front.[31] He did not like the idea of conscription. He had promised not to implement the measure. He now believed that it was "militarily necessary." Many historians have concurred with his judgment.[32] Conscription, therefore, was conceived in an environment in which victory in 1918 was not just unlooked for, but the possibility was entirely excluded. A much smaller peace, much later, and won at even greater cost than realized was about the best that was anticipated.

There were profound doubts, however, that Canada could find the men, even with the best of wills. The arithmetic just could not be made to work. Some of Borden's principal advisors did not see how Canada could find half a million men, however imperative the need and great the danger. General Gwatkin, chief of general staff, could not imagine how half a million men could be found, armed, trained, and sustained, even without consideration for what this would mean for the Canadian economy. R.B. Bennett, Borden's parliamentary secretary and director of registration, felt that the promise only made sense if it were supposed that "40 percent of the [eligible British Canadian] population ... was of military age."[33] The governor general, the Duke of Devonshire, also expressed considerable scepticism, and considered that a military effort on this scale might well be far beyond little Canada's strength.[34] If the arithmetic of conscription did not work, how about the mathematics?

Strategic necessity was not Borden's only consideration. As Elizabeth Armstrong writes, conscription for Borden was "not a [simply a] strategic act to win the war, but [also] an ideological commitment to guard Canada's honour."[35] In British Canada, this would have seemed to be common sense. Moreover, Borden was aware that the army as it existed was not reflective of Canada's demographic reality, and he apprehended trouble if steps – even drastic steps – were not taken to redress discrepancies in participation rates. Previously, Borden had worried that even compulsory registration, the anteroom to conscription, might produce "civil war in Quebec."[36] By 1917, however, he had rather more cause to worry about what British Canada would do if baulked. By 1917, it was showing itself more than willing to indicate and take action against purported sources of weakness at home hampering Canadian efforts abroad. In British Canada, Quebec was becoming a focus of hatred, New Canadians of loathing. Voices were raised. They were difficult to ignore. "We can no longer keep silent without disloyalty to Canada," Bishop Williams advised synod in 1917.

> Quebec has practically stood aloof from the war. The French Canadians will not fight for France, their mother country; they will not fight for the British Empire which guarantees to them their freedom. At last they are fighting hard, at least with tongue and pen, against conscription, so as to prevent Canada from exercising her full power in the war. It is not freedom but anarchy when one Province is allowed to balk the policy of the country as a whole – either anarchy, or slavery to the baulking Province. Is the rest of Canada to have its policy in this war dominated by the slacker-Province of Quebec? ... If the influence of Quebec is so great that our public men will not dare to enforce Conscription there, then all I can say is that we are unworthy of our British heritage and unworthy of being entrusted with the powers of self-Government; and that the best thing for us to do is to hand back to Britain our autonomy and ask her to govern us from Downing Street ... I would rather be ruled from Downing Street, or even from Washington than from Quebec ... This is the day of universal service. It must be so in the Church as in the State. It is easy to sit back and to expect some movement or force from outside to come and lift us out of our ruts. The moment has come. The Divine lesson has been writ large before our eyes. What more do we want? The message of the hour to the Church is mobilize, mobilize, mobilize your men and your resources for the conflict with evil and the extension of God's kingdom.[37]

Many British Canadians were now advocating policies more drastic than conscription. The principal Protestant denominations, the LOL with its affiliates, the Toronto *Globe*, and the Montreal Board of Trade now called for full-scale implementation of the Militia Act, which could have provided for a *levée en masse* and for total manpower compulsion.[38] Imposition of conscription, the powerful Archbishop of Quebec,

Monsignor Paul Bruschesi, advised, could only lead to violence in Quebec. While that might be the case, Borden returned, he was much more concerned about the certain violence that would ensue in British Canada if there were no conscription.[39] He was not worried, Borden said, that conscription would prove divisive or that Quebec would boil over in opposition. The country was already divided. Quebec was already boiling over, as was British Canada. At least, with the imposition of conscription, he would not have to worry about the British Canadians ... much. The Military Services Act (MSA) ultimately introduced was the closest thing to a compromise that could be arranged; more than Quebec would voluntarily concede, but less than British Canada appeared disposed to take.[40]

Remember, finally, that it was not clear prior to 11 November 1918 that the war would end in Allied victory. The arrival of the remnants of a defeated Canadian army back home was terrible to contemplate, and Borden was alive to this nightmare. The GWVA, the returning army's vanguard, was already indicating the way the winds were apt to blow. In introducing the MSA to Parliament, later in the year, Borden said:

> God speed the day when the gallant men who are protecting and defending us will return to the land they love so well. Only those who have seen them at the front can realize how much they do love this dear land of Canada. If we do not pass this measure, if we do not provide reinforcements, if we do not keep our plighted faith, with what countenance shall we meet them on their return? ... They went forth splendid in their youth and confidence. They will come back silent, grim, determined men who, not once or twice, but fifty times, have gone over the parapet to seek their rendezvous with death. If what are left of 400,000 such men come back to Canada with fierce resentment and even rage in their hearts, conscious that they have been deserted or betrayed, how shall we meet them when they ask the reason? I am not so much concerned for the day when this Bill becomes law, as for the day when these men return if it is rejected.[41]

While this passage is often cited, its content seldom seems to be digested.

No sooner had the prime minister returned to Canada from England and France than he announced that mandatory national service would be the policy of the government henceforward, the measure introduced as a partisan measure immediately while work went forward to reconstruct the government on a national basis. "It is my duty," Borden announced to the House of Commons, that early proposals will be made on the part of the Government to provide, by compulsory military enlistment on a selective basis, such reinforcements as may be necessary to maintain the Canadian Army today in the field as one of the finest fighting units of the Empire. The number of men required will not be less than 50,000 and will be probably be 100,000.[42]

It was charged that Borden was introducing conscription at the behest of the British government. "No more absolute falsehood," he said "was ever uttered by human lips."[43] The Canadian government deemed it necessary. And while, for the moment, the Tories would carry the ball in Parliament, what he desired, he reassured Canadians, was the creation of a truly national government determined to introduce any policy required to carry the war through to a successful conclusion. Most British Canadians concurred and probably preferred that a national government would make an election unnecessary. If that proved impossible, they hoped that union would follow the election and that a united government would be able to do the right thing. The "win the war" movement had already been beating this drum for several months, and half of Canada appears to have concurred.

The Borden government, which had appeared to be failing, was instantly acclaimed across British Canada. Borden, it appears, was no Asquith after all. Having announced the new course, Borden was immediately swamped with letters and expressions of support. The Orange Lodge had officially supported conscription (and prohibition) since 1916 and heartily commended the change.[44] So did the Women's Christian Temperance Union, which thought, as well, that it was only fair that wealth be conscripted with men.[45] The assembled representatives of the Sons of England and the municipal councils of Montreal, Toronto, Brandon, and Winnipeg signalled their concurrence. Men and money: the government should take both, and as much of each as was needed to see the thing through.[46] From Vancouver, the Women's Liberal Association forwarded copies of their conscriptionist resolutions:

> Resolved – that the Women's Liberal Association endorse the policy of selective conscription of men and further, we pray that wealth, money, resources, labour and service of every man and woman be conscripted, that all may equally do their duty at home as well as overseas in order to win in this terrible war.[47]

The Kitchener and Orillia Boards of Trade demanded the conscription not only of men but of money, as quickly as possible – their criticism essentially that Borden was not going nearly far enough, quickly enough, along a wide enough front.[48]

In the lead-up to the election, British Canadians indulged in a veritable orgy of resolution making – a fad which seems to have spread from the United Kingdom. From Saskatoon, for example, came a resolution, passed unanimously by a mass meeting of fifteen thousand people:

> that, on this the third anniversary of the declaration of a righteous war, this meeting of the Citizens of Saskatoon records its inflexible determination to continue to a victorious end the struggle in maintenance of those ideals of Liberty and Justice which are the common and sacred cause of the Allies.[49]

Nine thousand citizens in Winnipeg resolved that conscription was essential to effective participation in the war.[50] A mass meeting in Toronto insisted that the government introduce conscription, and placed on record its conviction that "certain sections" of the country had not done their duty and that it was time for the government to do whatever had to be done to suppress sedition coast to coast.[51] The GWVA and the Great War Next of Kin Association were adamant. Canada must have conscription, for a start. Thoroughgoing financial and economic controls were projected, including the nationalization of industries critical to the war effort.[52] The GWVA's alien policy we have seen. In the West, Grit veterans announced, in August, that they could no longer support the Liberal Party under Laurier's leadership, but would rather push for a united "win the war Government."[53] The founding, and militant, Winnipeg branch of the GWVA deplored recourse to an election, and promised "to oppose by force ... any attempts by either political party to trifle with questions of national importance." It also demanded a national government, and a win the war policy.[54]

Godfrey's newly created and Ontario-centred "win the war" movement chimed in, demanding conscription of men and wealth, and that aliens – otherwise not available for military service – be conscripted to serve some warlike purpose at home.[55] This was hardly the line of the Bonne Entente. In July 1917, the movement began to attack Laurier directly, and worked to consolidate Ontario Liberals at the side of the government. It was time for Laurier to step down, the organization said. There would be "[n]o money and no men for the war" if Laurier had his way. As the MSA moved through its third reading in the Commons, the organization began an all-out agitation for national, union government.[56]

At a mass meeting in Toronto in August, with Godfrey in the chair and Sir William Hearst, the provincial premier, in attendance, the mayor of Toronto, Tommy Church, concluded a long speech in support of conscription:

> I can only say ... that when conscription is put upon the Statute Books in a few days and enforced by the present Government I hope the Government will have the support of every loyal citizen to enforce that Act. I want to say to the people of Canada this, free speech is one thing and sedition and treason is another thing. Look at the people of the United States. I admire them for the way they are putting down sedition and treason in their own country, and it is an example for us.[57]

With sixty thousand Torontonians already at the front, Church said, if anybody in Canada were still not doing their duty, then they would have to be compelled. Godfrey entirely agreed. "We are gathered together," he said,

> to face as true Canadians a national crisis. In the midst of this world wide conflict a considerable body of our fellow citizens have demanded that we go no further in the fight and that the one effective weapon with which we can fight be not used, and they have insisted on trying this in a general election. The challenge has been accepted, and we are here today to enrol ourselves in the grand army which in this country will have to make battle for human liberties and a free democracy. We will fight the good fight until victory is ours, until we have swept aside all those who would deny Canada's right to maintain her high place in this struggle to save a world.[58]

The real issue was not conscription. It was:

> shall we have a war Government or an anti-war Government in this country? We must not be self delusionists, we must look the facts squarely in the face. The issue is, are we for the war or shall we forget the war? Shall we win the war, or quit the war? Shall we go on to glorious victory, or shall we get out dishonoured? I do not believe in any third party. There has only got to be two parties in this fight, and the time has come for those two parties to line up, and the line up is going to be this, all who are for

the war have got to get on one side and all who are against the war on the other (Applause). The politician who attempts to wander about in no man's land must be ruthlessly destroyed (hear hear).[59]

Union government to introduce conscription: that was the policy. "Some people do not like that word 'conscription,'" he continued: "I do."

> It is a good strong forcible word, and it means exactly what it means. It is the high explosive of war organisation. You cannot get along without it. It is the antithesis of compromise and the time for compromise has gone by (hear, hear). Personally I have no use for the man who states he is in favour of conscription and nevertheless continues to politically associate with those who are against conscription.[60]

Liberal wiffle waffle could no longer be entertained. "Speaking as a Liberal," Godfrey continued, "I must take this position today, that I do not believe the leadership of Sir Wilfrid Laurier can be accepted by anyone who wants to keep Canada effectively in the firing line." He was, he assured his listeners, not against Quebec. Quebec had contributed too much already. What he was against was narrow regionalism, including Quebec's wartime reservations. Too much political hay had been made of regionalism in the past. What was required was a national policy, imposed if necessary on a Quebec that had produced no leader capable of guiding it in the right direction.[61] With "win the war" mass meetings taking place across British Canada, Godfrey now seems to have believed – or so he advised Borden – that if the war effort were pursued with sufficient vigour, party and communal differences would fall away.[62] The salvation of Canada would be a whip for dissent and compulsion for shirkers.

Other British Canadians were inclined to like the idea of communal punishment for itself, whatever this might mean for the country. In November 1917, H.C. Hocken told an audience in Toronto's Orange Hall that

> the [anti-conscription] speech of Sir Lomer Gouin was seditious from first to last. He defied the Federal power, and an example should be made of him. When a man in a responsible position such as his takes a stand like that, what are we to expect from the ignorant and illiterate? No man has ever used more discreditable language than he used in the capital of his province. We Orangemen serve notice upon him that he must obey the law.[63]

Hocken's line was, by and large, British Canada's line taken to a logical extreme. The French Canadians were children led by the seditious, quite possibly the treacherous, however deeply they claimed to love something they called "Canada." French Canadians would have to be shown their duty, and if they did not do it, they would be compelled.

Other British Canadians considered that the Conservatives should use any fillip of power not to introduce policies to reduce communal tensions, but to solve, once and for all, the challenge presented by the New Canadians. The Canadians who had done more than any others to help the government win the war expected the government to use victory to settle some outstanding accounts with their rivals. When the votes were tallied, one prominent government supporter – H.S. Clement of Vancouver – considered that Borden now had all the political power he required to do anything he wished. Clement had, therefore, taken it upon himself to make aliens in his district understand that

> the Government of Canada intends to see to it that they change their attitude very materially and also that they be given to understand that if a country is worth living in it is not only worth fighting for, but its institutions and laws should be appreciated.

The government, he thought, should catalogue all aliens, including those who had been naturalized, and place all information before a military board to see who was useful and who was not. "If we are going to save Canada for the Anglo-Saxon race," he concluded, "now is the time to begin doing it."[64] A sign that Clement suffered from a failing common to period British Canadians – the inability to distinguish between members of other communities – was the list he provided of arrogant foreigners in need of discipline: "Greeks, Italians, Austrians, Swedes, and naturalized Germans." Greece and Italy were Allied nations. Sweden was neutral. Naturalized Germans were Canadians, and therefore British subjects. "Austrians" alone would have been Alien Enemies, although some "Austrians," of course – Czechs, for example – were on the point of being declared wartime allies. Those foreigners, all foreigners of any derivation, who could not learn to love the new Canada would just have to get out.

Canada labour was not much in opposition, as we might expect when we remember who organized Canadian workers tended to be. The Independent Labour Party (ILP) Association of Canada expressed strong support for Borden's plan. "We hereby declare ourselves," the organization informed the prime minister,

> in favour of conscription of wealth and all resources of the Dominion and the entire manhood of Canada. We consider it of the utmost important that this should be, to bring the war to a victorious and successful conclusion.[65]

Of course, the ILP Association was still organizationally attached to the British parent, dominated by British immigrants, and concentrated in Ontario – the centre of the pro-war agitation; British immigrants were among the most vigorous patriots, and skilled labourers among the most vociferous.[66] Some Ontario unions – the Amalgamated Society of Engineers (ASE), for example – were local offspring of British parents. Conflicted the parents might have been, in 1917, regarding the appropriate policy for Britain. They were in no doubt about what Canadians should do. Support conscription, and support union government, was relayed loudly and consistently.

Other working-class organizations were, at least officially, less certain. The trade union movement, as a whole, did not really know what to do. The National Trade and Labour Congress (NTLC) formally expressed itself as being against conscription. A vote taken in Montreal, in January, registered the NTLC as being forty-three to twenty against mandatory military service. The movement, however, was plainly of two minds. J.T. Foster was leader of the pro-conscription opposition, against the anti-conscription president of the movement, Z. Lesperance, a French Canadian delegate of the Shoemakers' Union. As a proud British subject, Lesperance "did not want it said elsewhere that the French-Canadians had failed to respond."[67] William Appleton, the secretary of the General Federation of Trade Unions (GFTU), however, was already on the record as being "irrevocably opposed to any form of compulsory military service." "[T]o Labour," he asserted, "a flag is nothing."[68] In Winnipeg, labourites were advised to "take their [registration] cards to the Labour Temple and burn them." The official policy was to bundle the cards of labour men and return them to Ottawa.[69] Privately, however, the secretary of the Nova Scotia Council, Joseph Steele, had already told Borden that this was all a lot of posturing and hot air: the rank and file knew what was required to support their brothers overseas.[70] Ontario labour leaders sent similar assurances. The popular Sam Gompers, moreover, was on hand from the United States to ensure that AFL affiliates played up and supported the "win the war" Unionists – a significant factor, of course, since AFL supremacy in the NTLC had long been established.[71] Gompers, incidentally, played a similar role in the UK – touring from time to time to pull organized labour behind the war. In January 1918, he was back in Canada touring Canadian clubs. The government arranged for him the exceptional honour of speaking to both houses of Parliament. Copies of his speech were printed and distributed to every labour organization in Canada.[72] In the end, it was the NTLC that shattered, rather than the government – the less militant, more pro-war AFL dominated Ontario-based sections, carrying national resolutions not to resist conscription and to do what was necessary to help the government at this time of crisis. The more militant Westerners decamped.[73] It should be stressed again that, despite the amount of historical attention they have received, anti-war labour radicals, indeed labour radicals of any variety, were a minority of a minority in Great War Canada.

The problem of Canada in the war was increasingly becoming the problem of Canada as perceived by British Canada at war. Subsequent suggestions that the government organize something like the Bonne Entente itself fell on deaf ears.[74] The thing had been tried, and already failed. "The people of Canada," the *Montreal Gazette* fretted in July 1917,

> are being divided politically into two camps; those who are for winning the war at all costs and those who are not, and there is nothing more regrettable than that the two camps have been formed on racial lines.[75]

That this was so was self-evident. That this was regrettable, many at the time would have been prepared to dispute. Godfrey, his brief effort at voluntary unity a failure, was one of them. He now considered that the way to national unity now lay through universal, pan-communal, and compulsory participation in the war effort.

The impetus for a national, union government appears to have come mainly, at this point, from within Liberal ranks, from leaders like Godfrey. British Canadian Liberals suspected that they could probably throw out Borden in a general election, but desired rather an end to partisan politics and a policy of *ralliement* behind the war effort, which would allow them a hand at the tiller. In British Canada, the Grits as much as the Tories wanted victory in the war. Like the Tories, they were prepared to pay almost any price for it. While they doubted that Borden had the capacity to imagine or introduce real "win the war" policies, like Borden they feared an election for the dangerous and divisive passions it might unleash. They worried, as well, that if an election were fought at this juncture in the war, with the Tories solidly conscriptionist and the Liberals anti or uncertain, their party might well be annihilated in British Canada, perhaps forever.

Prominent British Canadian Liberals began to defect. Twenty-six Liberal MPs now voted to defeat Laurier's proposed amendments to the MSA as it began to move through the House of Commons, and sang the national anthem as vigorously as their one-time Tory opponents when it passed third reading.[76] Most of these rebels were consolidated, in July, into an independent pro-war caucus that sat with the government.[77] Prominent regional Liberals followed, including Arthur Sifton, the premier of Alberta (the brother of Sir Clifford Sifton, who had made the passage to the Tories during similar prewar controversies), J.A. Calder, president of the Executive Council and the minister of railroads and of highways in Saskatchewan, N.W. Rowell, the Liberal leader of the opposition in Ontario, and T.A. Crerar, president of the Grain Growers' grain company and one of Laurier's most trusted provincial lieutenants. All of these men found seats in the new Cabinet, introduced in November.[78] The newly elected Liberal premier of Manitoba, T.C. Norris, expressed himself as entirely in favour of conscription and as being of the belief that opponents of the measure should be interned or jailed for the duration. "[W]e find some set against National Registration," Norris said.

> [T]hey are going up against statesmen of the nation who have decided that the right thing is to fight. We have gentlemen in Canada who think they know better. These people should have been interned a year ago. I believe that the men who oppose the Government's request at such a time as this should be put into jail or some other place.[79]

Rowell, similarly, had earlier informed the people of Woodstock, Ontario, that at the present time all politics could be reduced to one question about Canada's men at the front – "whether we are going to back them up or whether we are going to forsake them."[80] As early as 1914, as leader of the Ontario opposition, he had demanded that Canada do as much as possible to ensure victory in a war that pitted the hateful Germanic ideal against British liberty.[81] In 1917, the *Brantford Courier*, a Liberal paper, agreed whole-heartedly that Rowell was on the right track. "The only objectors," it thought, "will be the slackers, who will now be forced to do what their small-souled patriotism failed to teach them" or accept the consequences.[82] Dr Michael Clarke, Liberal MP for Red Deer, Alberta, told a meeting of Liberals in Toronto's Massey Hall that any talk of a referendum on conscription (widely advocated in Quebec and by Laurier's Liberal residual) was treacherous nonsense.

> There are people [Laurier] who tell us that there ought to be a referendum. Well, that means that behind the backs of the men in the trenches, the red-blooded men who saw their duty and went, you are going to ask those who have not gone voluntarily if they would be good enough to step into a ballot box and vote on whether they should go to the front or stay at home. And while you are doing that the boys at the front are being decimated ... It is a poor game, gathering ballot boxes when Haig and his men are gathering Huns. It is no question for long parliamentary palaver. Action should be taken, and I have made up my mind to support the Government of the day ...[83]

A Union War Committee emerged, pledged to remain in being until after demobilization specifically to implement the MSA, conduct the war, and deal with any emergency that might follow.[84]

The powerful national Liberal machine quickly began to disintegrate. The allegiance of the English-language Liberal press frayed away to nothing. Laurier, the *Orillia Times* editorialized on 21 June 1917, "seems to overlook the fact" that his political stonewalling of conscription cost time – and "that time is essential in winning the war."

> Liberals can best show their loyalty to Canada by supporting every enactment that will further the Empire's cause and strengthen the hands of Canadians, who are fighting the Nation's battles in Europe, and the present duty is to uphold conscription.[85]

How could the grand old man play politics when Canadians were dying, the cause for which they gave their lives palpably failing? A month later, the Liberal press in Ontario defected to the government lock, stock, and barrel. Meeting together, Grit editors decided that they were for conscription, determined to see Canada properly organized for total war, convinced that the Liberals needed to play their part, and of the opinion that the Borden government did not have sufficient talent to see the war through to a successful conclusion and needed Liberal assistance.[86] Liberal funding likewise dried up, with business aligning itself almost entirely behind the Unionists. This in itself, Laurier considered, would have been sufficient to produce a Liberal rout in the election that followed.[87]

Attempts by the Liberals to produce a compromise platform, which would restore party unity – first in Toronto (to consolidate rebel Ontario, excluding Rowell, who had already gone too far) and then in Winnipeg – failed to produce real consensus. Indeed, the GWVA was quick to denounce all such partisan activity. The "so-called win the war resolution," moved by the Liberal Party at its Winnipeg conference, it thought, was nothing more than "a mockery and an insult to Canadians at the front." The delegates who had produced it were simply "traitors to the country."[88]

All expressions of support notwithstanding, Borden did not want an election. The war was at too critical a stage for an election to be anything but dangerous and divisive – a pointless distraction from the business of winning the war. "It was my strong desire," Borden remembered, "to bring about a union of all parties for the purpose of preventing such discussion [i.e., a debate on conscription] as strife was apprehended."[89] In Borden's opinion, Canada was already too polarized to permit it to indulge in a dispute that would inevitably become a test of strength between French and British Canada, with any election reduced to a communal roll call and a referendum on the war.

Borden was right. Any election in 1917 would be dangerous, and divisive. If, for example, the press in British Canada was consolidated behind the government, *Le Devoir* was pushed into even greater opposition. "[S]ince when," Bourassa wondered,

> have our Parliamentarians had the power without consulting us to embark on an undertaking of which we shall not soon see the end, and of which we must pay all expenses? Mr. Borden's promise of 500,000 men he will pay – with our young men.[90]

The fact that Borden's announcement of a conscription policy had been followed, within a week, by anti-conscription rioting in Montreal and elsewhere showed the way the wind was blowing. Moreover, if loyal declarations were arriving from Brandon and Saskatoon, St Canut,[91] Verdieres,[92] Maisonneuve, Hull, Ste Dorothée, St Joseph d'Alma, Ste Anne des Plaine, St Hyacinthe and Terrebonne, Sherbrooke, Montreal, and Quebec had passed official protests against conscription.[93] Public protests took place at Charlesbourg,[94] Richelieu, St Mathias,[95] Mont Laurier, Saint Simeon, Saint Justin, Nicolet, and elsewhere.[96] La Tuque,

Joliette, Lamorale, Montebello, Sainte Therese, Deschenilles, St Bruno, and Lac Stalleau followed a week later.[97] By the middle of April, Quebec was plastered from end to end with posters denouncing conscription. No one seems to have known who put them up.[98] If the Sons of England and the Orange Lodge were jubilant and aggressive in support of the measure, the St Jean-Baptiste and Garneau Taschereau societies were openly hostile. Borden was a hypocrite. He had promised there would be no conscription. He had broken that promise. He said now that government manpower polices would not be used against the French Canadians or the working class. This also was a lie. How could conscription be used in any other way?[99] New leagues formed when the old ones would not go far enough. The "Ligue patriotiques des intérêt canadiens" called upon French Canadians to unite to save their distressed fatherland from this new enemy.[100] The *constitutionnelles*, of course, we have seen. They obviously went rather further than calling for the unity of the French Canadian community. But even Quebec's Young Liberals were not much more moderate.[101] On 21 May 1917, for example, the Montreal Young Men's Liberal Association expressed itself as being opposed to conscription at a mass meeting at St Ann's. "Borden is taking your sons," Mr Charles Query asserted, "and sending them away to be killed."[102] *Le Devoir* was correct in characterizing this all as an "avalanche of protest."[103]

Borden's principal collaborators shared his belief that an election would be dangerous. Joseph Flavelle, the chairman of the Imperial Munitions Board, advised:

> I am of the opinion that if a general election on party lines is held shortly it will mean setting the heather on fire, English versus French, with long years of bitterness to follow. I am of the opinion if the liberal party is returned to power, with or without having Laurier for leader they will owe their election to the French Canadians who refused to fight, and to German and Austrian voters who will undoubtedly vote against the Government. I am of the opinion that when a Government so elected undertook to determine in conference the future relations of this country we should have strife.[104]

Much better, he thought, for there to be no election, and for an all-party Union government to function until the end of the war.[105] Borden's new Liberal colleagues agreed. The problem was that Laurier would simply not cooperate. Whatever he had been in his youth, he was now probably less a French Canadian nationalist than a doctrinaire liberal and a Canadian patriot who knew well how far his own community could be drawn. "I am a Liberal of the old school of England," he told Parliament in April 1918. "I would have been a Whig if I had been in England."[106] In this respect, Laurier was probably as close to John Morley as to Henri Bourassa. Laurier did not doubt that the Empire's cause was just, or that Canada belonged at Britain's side.[107] As a Liberal, Laurier indicated, he could not enter any Union government because he was opposed to conscription on ideological grounds, and conscription was the only rationale for the formation of the union. Moreover, Laurier was opposed to conscription – "the apple of discord" – he said, because of its certain effects on Canadian unity.

> It is a denial of those principles of democracy which we hold dear and sacred. I oppose this Bill because it has in it the seeds of discord and disunion; because it is an obstacle and a bar to that union of heart and soul without which it is impossible to hope that this Confederation will attain the aims and ends that were in view when Confederation was effected. Sir, all my life I have fought coercion; all my life I have promoted union; and the inspiration which led me to that course shall be my guide at all times, so long as there is a breath left in my body.[108]

Union would not eliminate division but by silencing one party in the dispute, pushing opponents of the war into more dangerous forms altogether, if only out of the desire to have their case heard. This was not only dangerous but undemocratic and certain to have permanent effects on the way in which Canada's constituent communities regarded one another. Whatever else it might accomplish, conscription would drive an enduring wedge between the regions while giving the extremists in Quebec the upper hand locally. Laurier was, quite simply, convinced that conscription would be a national disaster. What price Belgium if Canada were destroyed? What price victory if, in the process, liberty were impaired?[109]

There were other reasons. There appears to have been an element of pique in Laurier's refusal to accept union. Borden appears to have been clumsy in the way in which he chose to introduce the issue. According to Laurier, Borden had asked him for an extension of Parliament, which he had granted, not foreseeing that Borden would use the extension to introduce conscription as a partisan measure, inviting Laurier only thereafter to enter a national government. "As in the play of children," he claimed, "they asked me: close your eyes and open your mouth and swallow. I refused."[110] More important, there did not initially appear to be any pressing reason for Laurier to cooperate. Defections nothwithstanding, the Liberals appeared to have the upper hand. In the spring of 1917, it was likely that Laurier would win any election that took place. If wartime polarization had consolidated most of British Canada behind a "win the war" platform, it had placed the other constituent communities of the Dominion even more firmly on the side of "Canada first." British Canada, even amalgamated, was only half the country. British Canadians plainly doubted whether Borden had the stuff to see the war through. In 1916, Borden himself was being denounced even from within his own party as a "well meaning incompetent" presiding over a policy of drift.[111] Laurier's position was clear. Even Liberal disharmony was not necessarily a bad thing. If Liberal conscriptionists had not ultimately accepted union, the result would have been a three-way contest in most English Canadian ridings, with Liberal and Tory conscriptionists splitting the "patriotic" vote. Many such contests would probably have gone to one or another Liberal contestant on a minority poll. Even when elected, conscriptionist Liberals thereafter would have been compelled to choose whether to sit with party, with comrades of conscience on the issue of conscription, or as independents.[112] The government had, moreover, recently faced some nasty scandals, involving prominent ministers. Sir Sam Hughes, the minister of militia until November 1916, was, notoriously, Borden's cross. The Liberals had taken good care to make sure that the causes of his resignation and subsequent disgruntlement were well known.[113] More particularly, the government was in trouble at this juncture because of what appeared to be some very dirty business involving no less a luminary than Sir Joseph Flavelle, the chairman of the Imperial Munitions Board and Canada's leading Methodist layman. He was reputed not only to have monopolized war contracts for his friends and political allies but to have made a 300 per cent profit on some of those he assigned to himself. Flavelle was, moreover, no friend of organized labour, which had learned during the war to return his distrust with loathing.[114] While Flavelle was ultimately cleared of profiteering, much muck stuck, and this was a type of scandal the Borden government could simply not afford. Remember, again, that the motor of the war was working-class British Canada. It seemed that while the boys died, the rich were so many vampires battening on their blood. "I can truly say," one intimate informed Borden, "that I never before met with such widespread *rage* over any other scandal."[115] Orange Ontario could vote Grit, and had before. Profiteering was precisely the sort of charge which might be expected to set the most patriotic of British Canadians at the government's throat rather than at its feet. Why should Laurier cooperate if the price were not right? Why should he buttress what he might replace, if Borden were so ill advised as to take the thing to the polls? Surely "no conscription" would be a small price to pay for a united nation, and a Liberal government?

If such was Laurier's calculus, provincial auguries were favourable. In wartime provincial elections, Canadian voters had uniformly voted Liberal – Manitoba in 1915, British Columbia in 1916, New Brunswick in 1917; Quebec and Nova Scotia, already Liberal, returned even stronger Liberal majorities during the war. Some of the turnarounds had been spectacular. In 1914, the Liberals held no seats in British Columbia. In the 1916 provincial election, they gained thirty-seven seats in a forty-seven-seat legislature.[116] Two of these elections were particularly significant for the procedure adopted, and for the results achieved. While soldiers were allowed to vote, in Alberta and Saskatchewan, wartime election provisions directed their votes not into territorial districts, but towards specially established soldiers' seats. These seats the Tories had won hands down, but in the process, the soldier vote was concentrated and removed from geographical contests in which it might have made a decisive difference. Meanwhile, the naturalization of immigrants had continued apace – denaturalization rulings of imperial and Canadian courts notwithstanding – and the 1917 provincial election campaigns were waged by the Liberals on national issues. The provincial Liberals would, voters were assured, encourage the federal party to bring on reciprocity with the Americans (always popular with farmers) and help keep conscription out of the statute books by helping to bring Laurier to power. The Liberals swept both provinces.[117]

If Laurier believed that a Liberal victory was possible, he had company. Robert Brown and Ramsay Cook, for example, consider that one of the reasons why Borden pleaded with Laurier so earnestly to join a Union government was that he feared defeat and believed that a Liberal government brought in at this stage in the war would be a catastrophe.[118] French Canadians could easily align themselves with British Canadian farmers, angered by war impacts, attracted by reciprocity, and already exercised about rural depopulation, transport and milling monopolies, and the cost of mechanization. New Canadians might be brought on side. Conscriptionist Liberals could beat the Tories with wartime scandals in order to distinguish themselves from the opposition, thus splitting the "win the war" vote. George Perley, the Canadian representative in London, was advised that given the political landscape the government might well face defeat in any election while these dynamics remained in play.[119] The canny Joseph Flavelle feared it was so. J.W. Dafoe, a Manitoba Liberal rapidly becoming a Borden collaborator, considered Conservative defeat inevitable in the approaching election "unless some new factor enters the contest and gives them a good battle cry."[120]

In the summer of 1917, Borden was obviously faced with a problem. Canada needed conscription. There could be no conscription without an election. This election he might lose. Loss of an election would produce a Laurier government, dedicated to waging the war by what half of Canada would view as half measures. The position of this government would be impossible from the beginning. French and New Canada might rejoice. British Canada, already seething with discontent, would explode. The postwar consequences were too terrible to contemplate. What if the Allies lost, and four hundred thousand Canadian soldiers came home "with rage in their hearts"? How could a government elected, in large measure, by anti-war constituencies control Canada at war? Such a situation might precipitate a rebellion in British Canada, even civil war.[121] Would Canada go the way of Ireland? Ludicrous situations were not difficult to imagine: soldiers mutinying after having been called out to protect New Canadian dissenters marching in support of the government of Canada as it attempted to distance itself from the war from patriot members of the same community that had produced the soldiers. All of this, of course, excludes the issue of personal interest and conscience. Borden had promised Canada's soldiers that he would back them to the hilt. He intended to do so. Meighen, probably the second most important man in the government by this time, the man responsible as attorney general and later minister of the interior for the orchestration of Canada's war against dissent and by the end of the war the Tory heir apparent, was equally determined and had a personal stake in the issue. His brother Ed was an NCO in the Machine Gun Platoon of the 102nd Battalion CEF – the best in the battalion, according to his commanding officer.[122] Volume 6 of the Meighen papers is full of correspondence from his brother, sometimes marvelling that he was still alive.[123] Meighen felt the pull of the front himself. In 1915, he had been powerfully tempted to go overseas as quartermaster of the Canadian

Grenadier Guards (87th Battalion CEF), then in the process of formation, and had sought permission to withdraw from politics to take up arms. Borden had convinced him, however, that he had more important duties at home.[124] Meighen's loyalties were not in doubt. If leading Tories were driven to act, they were willingly driven. What else could they have done, all considered?

The answer, less edifying than the motives that produced it, was "gerrymander." Some alterations to voting practice had already been introduced. Aliens recently resident in Canada had been effectively disenfranchised, for national elections anyway, in 1914. This was less a Canadian initiative than it was a requirement if the common imperial citizenship produced by the Imperial Naturalization Policy in January 1914 was not to be jeopardized. With the Electoral Disabilities (Naval and Military Service) Removal Act, 1914, soldiers and sailors gained the right to vote in Canadian elections.[125] By 1915 legislation, their vote would apply in federal elections, not in soldier seats but in the last electoral district in which they were resident.[126] In the spring of 1917, Meighen was putting the final touches on further alterations, should an election be called.[127] In the summer, Meighen's legislation was introduced, and passed. The Military Voters Act, 1917, enfranchised all soldiers, regardless of how long they had lived in Canada, and made special provisions for the application of the military vote. Soldiers, unlike other voters, did not live in a particular district and had not necessarily voted anywhere before. If a soldier had voted in a district four months prior to enlistment, he would be counted there. If he had not, then his vote would be applied to his district of residence; and otherwise, he was free to vote in whichever riding he chose, indicating only that he was "for" or "against" the government. If he did not indicate a riding, then the vote could be applied at the discretion of the returning officer.[128] As early as October 1916, Meighen proposed that it might be an idea to disenfranchise the anti-government foreign vote and give the vote to "patriotic women."[129] This is exactly what the War Times Election Act (1917) did. All immigrants who had arrived in Canada since 1902 were stricken from federal voters' lists. Exception was made, however, for the members of the families of serving soldiers. All members of the immediate family of soldiers, including grandparents, were permitted to vote, even where some other item of wartime electoral legislation might have disqualified them. All women over the age of twenty-one who had sons, husbands, or brothers in uniform, or who were serving overseas themselves, were given the vote.[130] Disenfranchisement of men who had not turned in their registration cards was considered, though not introduced. Conscientious objectors and members of pacifist religious sects (Mennonites, Hutterites, etc.), however, lost the vote.[131] Dr Margaret Gordon, president of the Canadian Suffrage Association, and no friend of the Conservatives, considered that "[i]t would have been more direct and at the same time honest if the bill simply stated that all who did not pledge themselves to vote conservative should be disenfranchised."[132] Her observation, while waspish, was not without merit outside Quebec. Most women so enfranchised do not seem to have minded that a female franchise had been granted for a purpose and not simply because it was right. In the main this appears to have been because they agreed with the purpose.[133]

In the ensuing election, Laurier's Liberals faced a united front of Conservatives, conscriptionist Liberals, and labour candidates running as "Unionists" on a joint ticket in all but a few ridings. Laurier, therefore, faced a unified "win the war" vote where division might have given him victory.[134] The Union platform was constructed to appeal to the prejudices of those portions of the electorate that had already expressed themselves in favour of a more vigorous war effort. The first plank in the government's policy was conscription of manpower. Conscription of wealth, the elimination of profiteering and waste, the annihilation of the patronage system, provision for soldiers and their dependants, and the delineation of a new Canada that would emerge from the war followed. Rapid movement to imperial federation, even, appeared to be Union policy.[135] Laurier, Borden said, promised that there would be no conscription before the people had an opportunity to vote on the issue in a referendum. If Laurier had his way, Borden asserted, there would be no men for the army. The Canadian Corps would wilt. Canada, if not its allies, would be effectively out of the war. The imperial cause might fail, and it would be in some measure Canada's fault. The thing was too shamful to contemplate.[136] When conscription was introduced to Parliament in the summer, once again, twenty-six Liberals broke with Laurier to vote with the government. When the bill passed its second reading, 118 for and 55 opposed, the House of Commons, Liberal and Conservative, broke into spontaneous applause, followed by a chorus of the national anthem. Government supporters in and out of the House, Liberal and Conservative, believed that they had saved the country. CANADA, NOW AND FOREVER, ONE AND INDIVISIBLE, the *Toronto Telegram* exulted:

Canada is in the British Empire to stay.

Quebec is in Canada to stay.

The British Empire is not going to be disrupted.

Confederation is not going to be smashed.[137]

Faced with what might have been the destruction of his fractured party, Laurier permitted Liberals to join the government and run on a Unionist platform in the forthcoming election. Three possibilities were envisioned: Liberals could run on the basis of "no union, no conscription" (Laurier's own position), "no union, but conscription," or sit with the government as independents (union and conscription). There was no possibility of restoring party discipline and fighting an election on traditional partisan lines. Laurier believed that, 1917 being what it was, to oppose the government on conscription absolutely without permitting divergence from the party line would lead to the permanent extinction of his party in British Canada. Union and conscription both, however, were transient issues. The most important thing was to accept the near certainty of defeat in this election and make provision for the future: "we must remember that we will be playing the game against them with loaded dice," Laurier informed one collaborator.[138] Whatever the outcome, the party would have to be maintained in being with as many Liberals as possible in Parliament, wherever they chose to sit for the moment. The Liberals would thereafter, and with a clean conscience, be well placed to take control of the ultimate, unhappy peace. Borden, fearing the polarizing effect that must ensue if the Liberal Party were reduced to a Quebec rump, was satisfied with this compromise.

The willingness of Liberals in British Canada to cooperate by remaining Liberals while supporting conscription and the Union should not necessarily be taken to suggest lack of polarity, or that thinking on these issues remained muddied, or that everyone agreed with Laurier that both issues would be transitory. For example, Brigadier General Victor Odlum, a BC Liberal, Boer War veteran, and Great War hero (then commanding 11th Brigade), wrote to H.H. Stevens that he believed that it was Laurier's intention to passively resist conscription and then to oppose the measure and the government on the grounds that other measures had not been sufficiently tried. If this were his game, Odlum promised, then he would break with Laurier, but not with the Liberal Party. To go this far, he considered, would be to allow exclusive use of the label "Liberal" and of party funds and machinery to the dissenting Laurier French Canadian group.[139]

While the party endured, Liberal divisions could be rancorous. J.W. Dafoe, the truest of True Grits, Laurier's personal friend, and the editor of the strongly Liberal *Manitoba Free Press*, had supported recourse to war from the beginning. By 1917, he had two sons at the front. Faced with what he considered to be irrefutable evidence that only conscription would allow the Canadian Corps to be maintained at strength, he came first to deplore what he considered to be the petty, partisan spirit which animated the Liberal Party and made conscription an electoral issue, and finally to break with the party altogether and support the Borden government. "I think" he informed Laurier,

> that public opinion is very strongly in favour of the formation of a National Government and the adoption of whatever policy is necessary to secure such reinforcements for our troops at the front as will prevent the gradual disappearance of our armies by wastage.[140]

Partisan considerations must not be allowed to jeopardize the war effort. This would be treachery to the men at the front. Shortly thereafter, Dafoe, now a Borden supporter, wrote to his one-time friend and long-time collaborator Thomas Côté, a Laurier man, on New Year's Day, 1918. "You can do precisely as you please," he informed him, "and we shall do whatever is necessary." The emergency, he believed, was too grave for party feeling or friendship to jeopardize the requirements of victory.[141] Laurier, the previously Liberal *Montreal Gazette* editorialized, had never

> ardently favoured Canada's participation in the defence of the Empire ... [O]n the contrary he has regarded the greatest struggle for civilization and democracy in which the world has ever engaged with an eye singularly to party advantage.[142]

A vote for Laurier, the *Mail and Empire* considered, in an election day editorial, was a vote for "Bourassa; a vote against the men at the front, the British connection and Empire; a vote for Germany, the Kaiser, Hindenburg, von Tirpitz and the sinking of the Lusitania."[143] "It is really too bad," the newly enfranchised Lucy Maud Montgomery – author of

7.1. Unionist poster from the 1917 election. The message is obvious and typical of the most highly charged election in Canadian history. Picture courtesy of the Glenbow Archives.

Anne of Green Gables – thought, "that I should have to cast my first vote against Wilfrid Laurier, whom at one time I thought little lower than the angels ... But he is an old man now and he has outlived his glory and betrayed his country."[144]

Laurier might privily protest, but did not actively combat the many, and poisonous, attacks to which he was subjected in the latter war years. To do so, he and what was now his "faction" rather than his "party" considered, would only further polarize Canada and might well lead to "the set of things that has happened in both Ireland and Russia."[145] Nor was legal remedy available. Suit for slander was neither realistic nor desirable. "I have very much fear," he informed H.H. Hartley, that

> we could not obtain a verdict from a jury. Of course, we might go out of the province of Ontario ... For obvious reasons [however] I would not prosecute in Quebec, and everywhere else we would be met by a flood of recrimination, as a plea of justification, that the chances of a [favourable] verdict would be very slim indeed.[146]

With passage of the new electoral legislation and Union, a Borden victory was inevitable. Nevertheless, critical constituencies were carefully managed. Collaborators were identified in Quebec so that at least the appearance that the Union was a national government could be maintained. Expressions of support for government candidates were arranged from sources, it was felt, that French Canadian opinion would respect – prominent churchmen and notables from the French Republic and Belgium particularly.[147] Major General F.L. Lessard, the most respected French Canadian soldier, prewar commander of the 2nd Division Area and wartime inspector of troops, was sent on a speaking tour with local clergy at his side, following his earlier criticism that, while prominent episcopal authorities might express pro-government opinions, lower clergy had been notably lacking in expressions of loyalty.[148] *La Presse* and *La Patrie* remained sound and committed to the government. *La Patrie* announced that it favoured conscription in May 1917. *La Presse* reminded readers that it was George Etienne Cartier, as minister of militia, who had introduced the principle of conscription in the Militia Act of 1868 and Laurier himself who had subsequently strengthened the principle in 1907.[149] Meanwhile, there were allegations, at least, that money was provided for the Bourrassa nationalists with the hope of splitting the anti-conscription vote, and perhaps tarring Laurier with the nationalist brush.[150] All of these things notwithstanding, the Union had no hope of winning in Quebec. How could it when the French Canadians in the Cabinet – Blondin and Patenaude – accepted the requirement for conscription, promised to support it, but resolutely maintained that they would be destroyed politically, and that the Conservative Party would be ruined in Quebec for a generation?[151] Already electors in their ridings were calling upon them to honour promises previously made to do everything in their power to ensure that there was no conscription.[152] The government did hope, however, to confuse the issue in Quebec for the duration.

Management of the Canadian electorate, even so refined, continued. Canadian soldiers were important. They, male and female, had the vote, as did their relatives of both genders. They would, it was hoped, vote overwhelmingly for conscription, not only of course because they came in great disproportion from communities which supported a "win the war" policy, but because they had a vested interest in doing so. Major General S.B. "Sam" Steele, commander of the Canadian troops at Shorncliffe, considered that soldiers wanted the vote and were taking a keen interest in the election from the beginning. Their aim was precisely to vote Tory to force on conscription, which for soldiers represented not just a more vigorous war policy, but a more equitable distribution of the burden – even an increased chance of survival.[153]

Even so, soldier support for the government was not left to chance. Propaganda, orchestrated in Europe by Lord Beaverbrook, was intense and entirely one-sided. Quickly, the perception appears to have developed that a Union victory would mean three months' home leave for first contingent men.[154] What the minister of militia actually said was that home leave for men with three years at the front would be impossible, "until sufficient reinforcements are actually available." This was freely interpreted as confirmation that chances of "getting home on furlough [would] be vastly improved by the success of the Military Services Act," which of course was dependent upon a Borden victory.[155] If the government did not precisely promise home leave, its military supporters did put up posters at the front, reading:

> A vote against the Government means
> You are here for life
> A vote for the Government means
> Another man is coming to take your place.[156]

When, in September 1918, the issue of home leave was taken up by a Conservative backbencher, Mr William F. Nickle, Borden denied that such a promise had ever been made. Even if it had, he considered, it was not possible to bring Canadian soldiers home while the war continued.[157] Perhaps the government did not say it, but soldiers had certainly been encouraged to believe that there were only three ways out of the trenches: victory, a debilitating wound or death, or a vote for Borden.

Furthermore, on 29 November 1917, the Borden government announced a 20 per cent increase of the grants allowed to soldiers' wives. "This," the government claimed,

> is in accordance with the policy which has been followed by the union Government and is another evidence of its desire to advance the welfare of the soldier and their dependants in every way consistent with sound national policy.[158]

Other more coercive tactics might have been employed locally to secure the critical military vote. "Dear Friend," a soldier supporter of Laurier began a letter, on 5 December 1917,

> A soldier dare not express himself as against the Union Government, while the whole army organisation is used for the Government. It is common knowledge that anyone in the Army in England speaking for or voting for the opposition will be sent to France ... the pressure has been so strong that I was beginning to think that possibly I was a traitor.[159]

In the end, the soldier vote was so fully consolidated behind the government that the Liberal opposition had trouble finding willing scrutinizers in most units. Evidence suggests that on some occasions, pro-government soldiers took on this job as a lark, Liberal organizers accepting their assistance as the best available.

In the Union program, announced in November 1917, conscription exemptions were projected for families with men already at the front, men essential at home, and farmers.[160] Farmers were an important constituency, particularly in the Canadian West, which had already given evidence of disgruntlement, both general and war induced. Clifford Sifton warned that the government would face trouble if it did not exempt both farmers and their sons. It was simply too much to expect that they would swallow nationalization of the grain trade, including expropriation of crops (from September 1917), and conscription of their remaining sons, whatever they might think about the importance of winning the war. In 1917, farming was still largely unmechanized, and a farmer's sons were his capital and pension. One elderly Manitoba farmer, in March 1918, appears to have been driven to insanity and suicide by the combined impact of the nationalization of his crop and the mandatory enlistment of his sons following the withdrawal of this exemption. "Larou" was last seen, we are told, "out in the country ... a raving maniac."[161] Another man, James Bright of Innerkip, Ontario, was fined $10 and costs in August 1918 for attempting to influence his son, Homer, not to register. Mr Bright worked a large farm and drove a milk cart. He needed his son, though not, apparently, as badly as the nation. Homer was taken as a defaulter. His father might well have lost both farm and business.[162]

While exemptions worked against the grain of the government's war policy, they were a tactical concession essential if British Canada were to remain united in the election.[163] Besides, they could always be cancelled after victory in the election (and were).[164] Exemptions, combined with local management, appear to have worked. Hugh Clark, from Meighen's Manitoba riding, for example, informed him in January 1918 that opposition to the government had not been much in evidence during the election. Most of the grumblers, even, had supported the government. Farmers with sons already in service, in particular, were playing up marvellously and silencing the voice of "agitators."[165]

Even organized labour was courted for the first and last time in wartime Canada, a sign of how desperate things seemed. In June, Borden met with the heads of the most important international (i.e., AFL "Gompers") unions – bypassing the NTLC altogether, along with Western (there were no representatives of unions west of Ontario at the meeting) and Maritime workers – to read them the government's labour war policy and to promise worker representation on the War Trade Board, Canada Registration Board, Labour Appeals Board, Soldiers' Vocational Training Board, and Canadian Railway Board. Meanwhile, a safe man acceptable to Ontario labour – Gideon Robertson (vice president of the Order of Railway Telegraphers, a government advisor, Meighen collaborator, and previously a Canadian representative of labour in the British mission in Washington)[166] – took position as minister of labour in July.[167] If labour could not be entirely consolidated, therefore, it could at least be split, and the cooperation of the more powerful segment secured.

The election itself took place amidst frantic appeals from British Canadian pulpits for solidarity behind the Union government and its "win the war" platform.[168] Archbishop Matheson, the Anglican primate of Canada, went so far as to endorse both conscription and Union government before the national synod in June 1917.[169] This was powerful support. That same day, the Methodists came out officially for conscription and Borden.[170] Not to be left behind, a week later on 10 June 1917, the Presbyterian General Assembly passed a resolution "express[ing] its approval of the efforts being made to rouse sluggards among the youth of Canada to a sense of duty and to make these available to the armies of Canada."[171] In Mariposa, no one ever much doubted, or for long, what the churches thought.

When the vote was tallied in December, the Unionists had a majority with 151 seats, and Laurier's opposition was reduced to 82 seats. The Liberals had won all 62 seats in Quebec, 10 of 28 in the Maritime provinces, 8 of 82 in Ontario, and 2 of 57 in the West. The wonder is not that the Liberals were so heavily defeated but that they won as many seats as they did, considering the circumstances of 1917. Government attempts to manage Quebec had obviously failed miserably. Bourassa had swung behind Laurier, and the election provincially had been waged nakedly on the issue of conscription. Blondin and Patenaude had been proved right. Outside Quebec, however, three-quarters of the electorate had supported the government.[172] Attempts to manage the farmers' vote had proved successful, although the Grits retained some presence in Missinaba County, if little in Mariposa. Organized labour provided overwhelming support for the Unionists. Labour in British Canada had demonstrated quite simply, the Ukrainian paper *Danylo Lobay* considered, a lamentable lack of class consciousness.[173] In the end, the NTLC's attempt to run independent "Lib-Lab" candidates had failed, even though Ontario Lib-Labs had run on a "win the war" platform. All twenty-seven had been defeated.[174] All the Western Lib-Labs lost their deposits.[175] The army had played up marvellously. In the event, 92.89 per cent of all Canadian soldiers in France supported the government, as did 80 per cent of soldiers in Canada. Their womenfolk appear to have done their bit – from a Tory perspective – as well.[176]

While Borden's victory looks like, and is often taken to be, a decisive vindication of the government's "win the war" policy, the Unionists had only gained a plurality of one hundred thousand civilian votes nationally. Laurier had taken 45 per cent of the popular vote.[177] Meanwhile, three hundred thousand new voters had been enfranchised because it was nearly certain that they would vote "win the war," and a similar number disenfranchised because they probably would not. While these measures tended to reinforce existing partisan strength in most ridings[178] – and therefore the number of seats lost and won might not have been as powerfully affected as might be thought – in some cases, gerrymandering made all the difference. Without the provisions of the Military Voters Act alone, the Liberals would have won at least seventeen more seats, and constituted an effective challenge to Tory dominance in Nova Scotia, PEI (the Liberals would have swept it), and Alberta. In the Maritimes, as a whole, Laurier would have carried eighteen of twenty-eight seats.[179] The impact of the Wartime Electors Act is less easily quantified, and might well have had a greater effect on the outcome, since the great majority of these excluded votes would have been registered in ridings otherwise won by the Tories (outside Quebec) and sometimes with less of a margin than might be supposed. The inclusion of the disenfranchised vote would not, that is, have magnified success but might have reversed some contests. In Waterloo North, for example, the incumbent, Weichel, ran a close third between a National Liberal and a Tory who split the pro-war vote. Had the substantial immigrant German population retained the vote, this previously popular MP might well have been returned handsomely because it is doubtful that his voters would have preferred any alternative. Without Meighen's gerrymandering, therefore, the election would have been a much more nearly run thing than the proportion of seats won might suggest. The government might even have been defeated.

At least, the Liberals consoled themselves on the morrow of defeat, the election had helped avert a revolution by giving the "antis" a chance to blow off steam.[180] Laurier reassured himself, as well, that war dictatorship had been averted and the form if not the substance of the constitution preserved. It was worth having an election just to have an election, even if there was no hope of victory, in order to establish the fact that one was still possible. "I knew from the first," Laurier confessed,

> that with the "War Time Elections Act" it would have been folly to expect a victory, but the fight had to be made if constitutional Government was to be carried on at all.[181]

Not all were convinced that the contest had accomplished even this. "The election," O.D. Skelton wrote, leaves us in a most deplorable condition, with the country split absolutely on racial lines. It will take a generation to build up what the fanatics have destroyed in a few months. What is likely to be the outcome in Quebec if the Government proceeds to enforce conscription there? Will the people accept the verdict of the election as final?[182]

It was, however, precisely for a revolution in practice, at least, that many of the government's supporters looked. And in any case the election served its primary purpose. "Win the war" was government policy now. Conscription was introduced and ever more vigorously enforced. The size of the Canadian Corps was maintained through 1918, and would have been maintained through 1919 or 1920 if it had come to that.[183] Of course, this came at a price. Canada was split as never before or since. Both proponents and opponents of the war had been forced to declare themselves, the communal basis of each position was now obvious, and the violence potential in each position had been previewed. In December 1917, the war still had another year to run; the war emergency was not over until June 1920. Trouble on the home front got much worse before it began to abate.

8 "Absolute Masters of All Authority": Intercommunal Violence, 1918

As to our duty. The first line of defence is held in France and Flanders; the second line of defence is here. Will those in the second line desert and betray the first? If such an outcome were possible it would be to the everlasting disgrace of the Canadian people.

The Hon. Robert Laird Borden, April 1918[1]

If we are going to save Canada for the Anglo Saxon race now is the time to begin doing it ... Wherever I went in my district our own blood and kin bitterly complained that these aliens were openly opposing the Government and supporting the Laurier Liberals. Whenever they were in large numbers they were intensely arrogant ... you will understand how we feel ... they will either have to change their attitude or they will have to get out.

H.S. Clement, December 1917[2]

In the immediate aftermath of the election of 1917, with the introduction of conscription and the gradual emergence of a more fully repressive system at home, Canada seemed to quiet down. It was an illusion. The apparent absence of widespread disturbance for a few months after the election probably had more to do with the nature of the Canadian climate than anything else. When the cold abated, trouble returned with redoubled force.

The most famous example of what could happen in Quebec occurred on Easter weekend 1918, shortly after the government unilaterally assumed the power to amend MSA exemptions while taking the first steps to federalize enforcement. Some historians have seen this as nothing less than incipient rebellion – Quebec's first and failed attempt. While this is probably too much to claim for what happened, it was a particularly nasty passage, indicative of what way the winds were apt to blow if the government failed to appropriately manage the situation in the province.

In April 1918, a Quebec City man, Mercier, was detained by Dominion Police during one of the sweeps they were then commencing across the country to apprehend MSA resisters and deserters. He had no papers and was escorted home to find them. Had no papers been produced, he would have been moved quickly to the barracks for processing into the army at this stage in the war. Mercier, however, was one of the lucky few still in possession of a valid exemption. When the papers were produced, the police released him. Most times, most places, nothing more would have happened. Nobody would have noticed.

However, in Quebec in April 1918, a crowd of several thousand angry French Canadians began to collect almost immediately. This time they did not intend to restrict their activities to listening to firebrands and moved quickly to action. The Dominion Police station was burned to the ground. The police, plainly at a loss how to respond, appealed to the army for help and were advised that, short of a formal request from somebody competent to make such a request, law enforcement was a civil and provincial matter. While the buildings burned might be federal property, it was up to the city and the province to maintain order. The mayor was frightened by the direction things had taken but was not ready to ask for help and refused to have the Riot Act read. The mob, finding itself without effective opposition, now turned to the offices of the *Quebec Chronicle* (English-language and pro-government) and *Évènement* (French-language but pro-government). They were sacked and looted. The following day, the mob attacked and burned the office of the Quebec City MSA registrar while the city police watched. Riots and demonstrations continued throughout the city despite an appeal for calm from Archbishop Begin.

That same day, Easter Saturday, soldiers began to arrive from Ontario. The civic authorities, plainly incapable of maintaining order and faced with a riot spiralling out of control, requested military assistance. French Canadian rioters soon confronted British Canadian soldiers, and the inevitable happened. The rioters appear to have been the first to fire. Quebec rioters had long been in the habit of bringing revolvers to disturbances, as we have seen. This time they did not just fire them into the air or at buildings. The soldiers, however, had more effective weapons than a few old revolvers and returned the fire with gusto. Cavalry charges followed. Five soldiers were wounded. Four rioters were killed and fifty wounded.[3] Habeas corpus was suspended in the city while the search proceeded for the ringleaders.[4]

Several incidents of wartime repressive practice followed the Easter riots almost immediately. The consolidated censorship regulations of 1918 were, in part, a consequence of this rioting in that irresponsible local press reportage of the action of MSA agents was indicated at the time as a principal cause of unrest.[5] Local papers had criticized federal police and the registrars without restraint. The resultant mob, likewise, had demonstrated little restraint when dealing with these targets. In the future, inhibiting the circulation of violent opinion would hopefully discourage violent acts. The press was going to have to be more vigorously controlled, and was. An Order-in-Council legalizing the activities of government servants in restraining the riots in Quebec and another promising more of the same if disturbances continued were almost certainly provoked by the opening moves of a Quebec Grand Jury called to indict the over-vigorous enforcement of the MSA by the Dominion Police as the ultimate cause of the trouble.[6]

Orders-in-Council were all very good. They could not, however, fix what was basically wrong in Quebec. French Canada had been dragooned into compulsory participation in the war against its will and was resentful. British Canada was not disposed to admit expression of this grievance except as evidence of some species of illegal activity. Most of the middle ground – the dialogue that would have filled the intervening space between these positions – had become impossible. In Quebec, for the duration of the war, intercommunal strife and anti-government violence was always potential. Subsequent rioting, however, did not again reach the proportions of that at Easter. The government, of course, had shown how far it was willing to go. So had the rioters.

However, local, less immediately confrontational violence became endemic. In June 1918, angered by what they viewed as oppressive application of the hated MSA, Quebec City rioters looted the office of Deputy Registrar J.A.L. Rodrigue, a consistent local focus of trouble. Registration cards were seized and destroyed in a large bonfire in the street. Reports of similar riots came in from across the province. At St Francis the rioters even appear to have tried to blow up the MSA registrar's office with dynamite, but were prevented by the failure of the fuse to function.[7] On Dominion Day 1918, farmers angry at Borden and the "Unionist liars" seized cards and wrecked registration offices throughout Beauce and Montmagny counties. Registration cards again were burned in the streets. At St Ludger and St Godeon, greater respect was shown to the operation of the law. The cards were stolen and more discreetly destroyed at an undisclosed location.[8] There were in 1918 more attempts on the lives of French Canadian conscriptionists: Mayor Pouliot of Sainte Croix was one target; Notary Paré, registrar of Nicolet County, was another. Neither was hurt, although local defaulters paraded openly, defying the registration authorities to do their worst.[9] In Quebec, even postmen came in for occasional, casual attack. It was, after all, their responsibility to deliver the hated registration cards and conscription notices, the receipt of which signalled induction into the army. They were widely accused of being over-zealous in their job performance, in that, no doubt, they did their job at all.[10]

Sometimes local violence had an overtly intercommunal flavour. In August 1918, in Montreal, an English-speaking corporal accosted a French Canadian man and demanded that he produce his papers, as was his right under recent regulation. When the papers were not produced, the corporal attempted to place this supposed defaulter in custody. In British Canada such an event would have passed without much notice; indeed, it was a daily occurrence in many locales. A short notice in the paper that one or another evader had been apprehended and handed over to the army for in-clearance would have followed. That summer, in Montreal, a substantial riot ensued. The corporal was knocked to the ground, and a general mêlée commenced. Three hundred heavily armed city policemen, accompanied by military police, thereafter conducted an impromptu slacker raid in St Henri and St Paul – two working-class French Canadian Montreal neighbourhoods – in reprisal.[11]

Meanwhile, in some areas of the country, it became a downright dangerous business to hunt evaders. In some places, something like a very low level insurgency began to develop. Exchanges of gunfire between police and evaders in and around Sudbury, Ontario, were not unusual. The Gatineau district in Quebec as well was a place in which clashes between the Dominion or military police and gangs of evaders sometimes occurred, with victory not always going to the authorities. In July 1918 the Toronto *Globe* complained that police in this region were being subjected to a veritable reign of terror. Armed men had held up some. Others had been pulled from automobiles that were then destroyed.

Most were subjected perpetually to personal violence and intimidation.[12] Shortly thereafter, a gang of Gatineau area defaulters mistook two Queen's University students, M.C. Fleming and A.R. Garrett, hiking in the Lac Frontière region, for military police because both were wearing khaki clothing. The students came under brisk small arms fire. Fleming ultimately suffered a wound to the leg.[13] Indian reservations were places as well in which it was sometimes not advisable to go in the search for defaulters. Federal civil servant Duncan Campbell Scott advised the Department of Militia to keep police off the Caughnawaga Reserve, a Mohawk reservation near Montreal. Violence could be safely anticipated if the warning were ignored.[14] Scott should have known what he was talking about. While normally remembered now as a poet and short story writer, he had worked all of his life in the Department of Indian Affairs and was particularly well acquainted with, and friendly to, Native issues.

By the spring of 1918, in the aftermath of the riots in Quebec City, British Canada appears to have accepted that its differences with Quebec had gone just about as far as they could without inflicting serious damage on the nation. Besides, the government had made it clear that regionally based polarity would not be tolerated and had amended its censorship policy accordingly. Anti-imperial nativist, interregional, or French-English intercommunal attacks in the press would now be dealt with as just another species of sedition and punished accordingly. The official line was that the attitude in Quebec was changing – evidence that Quebec courts would not indict on war-related crimes, reports of riots, violence, massive MSA evasion, and continued sedition notwithstanding. The province was accepting the MSA graciously and would henceforward play a full part in the war, whatever manpower figures might still suggest. It was forbidden to challenge the official line publicly. "There is the best of reasons for believing," Borden informed the press in May,

> that a remarkable change of sentiment is beginning to develop in the province of Quebec in respect of the attitude of that Province towards the war. The recent drastic change in the Military Services Act has been received by the French-Canadian population in good spirit [remember: this is one month after the Easter riots and with attacks on registrars and the system of registration underway].
>
> In the national interest the members of the Government make the most earnest appeal to all the English press that the utmost moderation

in statement and comment may be exercised and that whenever possible appreciation should be expressed. It must be remembered that the French-speaking population is exceedingly sensitive and that the fine spirit which is now being developed might be checked or discouraged by comment or criticism which would be regarded much less seriously in other Provinces.[15]

British Canada did not love Quebec in 1917. It did recognize, however, that there was very little more that could be done which would not prove almost immediately fatal to Confederation. It also recognized, of course, that the official line was mandatory in law. New Canadians and supposed radicals, however, did not require such careful treatment. Here there was neither tolerance nor, it seemed, a requirement for forbearance. Insofar as it attempted to moderate tensions here, the government focused, in the main, on removing provocation rather than seeking to restrain the excesses of British Canadian patriots.

By 1918 worker disaffection was growing across the country, as sometimes very heavy war demands strained society. While Canadian workers had been quiescent through the first years of the war, by 1918 they were less so, particularly in the West. Some were becoming downright bumptious. Labour unity, moreover, had fractured at the beginning of the year, and the more militant West was no longer restrained by considerations of solidarity with its pro-war Ontario brother. As some of the government's servants immediately saw, however, the labour trouble of 1918 resulted more from distress than unrest – "distress," of course, confounded with the usual communal grievances, perceptions, and prejudices. Canadian workers less wanted than needed relief. The government, assuming an ever more commanding authority in the economy, continued to ignore them in a way that Lloyd George would have found incomprehensible and perhaps unconscionable. What is surprising is that labour troubles did not develop more dangerously than they did. The communal differences separating different sorts of labour and different sorts of critique undoubtedly served to prevent the adoption of any common line while setting different working-class communities at one another's throats. No common program and no possibility of solidarity, of course, made any effective challenge from this direction unlikely, though unrest could still be locally dangerous.

While British Columbia workers logged more strike days and were given to making public threats – for example, that there would be trouble if police were not withdrawn from working-class neighbourhoods and immunity given to local MSA evaders[16] – the centre of Canadian labour radicalism was Winnipeg. Labour unrest had reached dangerous levels here in 1917. A major strike of construction workers in June 1917 had ended with the arrest of twenty-three foreign strikers and the internment of those who were defined as Alien Enemies.[17] The next year was worse. In May of 1918, as MSA exemptions were cancelled, and as slacker hunts were ratcheted up, there was almost a general strike when city workers walked off the job – water workers and operators, firemen, railway workers, carriers, and teamsters ultimately going out. One thousand workers remained on strike for a week.[18] The situation was quickly becoming impossible, a worried Winnipeg Board of Trade informed Borden, due to the "situation created by [the] unpatriotic action of professional troublemakers."[19]

The nub of the problem in Winnipeg appears to have been that a town which had grown marvellously fast and increasingly diverse in the generation before the war[20] continued to be owned and operated, politically and economically, by British Canadians from Ontario. It cannot have helped that much of the British Canadian emigration to Manitoba had been organized as a patriotic duty by Ontario Orangemen determined to keep the Americans out, to ensure that the West was won for the Union flag, and that a properly British imprint was placed on the frontier from the beginning. Communal differences in Winnipeg were, therefore, particularly obvious and provoking. Voting in municipal elections, for example, was restricted to male residents of the city who were British subjects and who paid property tax in excess of $100 or annual rent over $200. Residents could vote in every ward in which this qualification was met. The end result was a situation in which, in 1906, of 100,000 residents, only 7,784 were enfranchised for civic elections. Some of these men voted in several wards. We might imagine that the clarification of wartime voters' lists, following the denaturalization of aliens, distorted the Winnipeg political framework even more than was already the case. The Board of Trade bore a marvellous resemblance to the city government.[21] In neither manifestation were the Winnipeg elite much friendly to New Canadians, viewing them by turns as another inert input for production or as a revolution waiting to happen.

In Winnipeg – as always in Canada at this time – communal divisions reinforced class divisions. Those who had arrived most recently tended to be New Canadians, clustered in squalid shantytowns on Winnipeg's north side, sprung up in the prewar boom years. The hope of many of these slum dwellers was that they might be able to assemble the stake that would permit them to homestead. Theirs was a grinding existence at the best of times. Many, however, had moved into more comfortable employment during the war as better jobs were vacated. As job-minded soldiers began to trickle back, through 1917, as prices rose through the roof in the last terrible years of the war, and even more as the end of the war obviously approached in the late autumn of 1918, hopes of improvement faded.[22] Unhappy prewar realities, it seemed, were about to return. British Canadian employers and civic authorities in Winnipeg – as throughout Canada – were quick to fire the war employed to make space for returned men. With victory in sight, production was reduced. When production and workforces were scaled back, employers demonstrated much more loyalty to "their own" than to the regrettably but temporarily essential.[23] War workers became the end-war and then postwar unemployed. Meanwhile, the local veterans, organized in a particularly militant branch of the GWVA, began to agitate for the absolute removal of New Canadians altogether. These cries were taken up with alacrity by other organizations. Might it be that exploitation might become expulsion? There were sound grounds, particularly in Winnipeg, for believing that this might be so. The situation in Winnipeg – the polarity between British and New Canadians, the general effects of the war and how these were differentially experienced and interpreted by ethno-classes – may have been extreme, but not exceptional. Winnipeg cultural-social dynamics were a particularly acute manifestation of the central problem of British Canada in the war.

Other communities experienced similar unrest, for similar reasons. In May 1918, five thousand British Columbia shipyard employees of the Imperial Munitions Board went out on strike.[24] For Joseph Flavelle, the situation was plain. British Columbian workers were traitors – "dangerous men ... activated by pro-German motives."[25] Flavelle – as responsible as anyone was for the operation of Canada's war economy – apprehended trouble among the local boilermakers and loggers as well, and had already instituted surveillance of the disaffected.[26] Whoever was causing the trouble, however, many people in British Canada thought that they knew the ultimate culprits: New Canadians. The *Vancouver Sun* was probably not far off the mark in asserting that the manifest, local popular fear inspired by the BC strikes had more to do with loathing of foreigners than anything else.[27] The strikers were Bolsheviks. British Canadians knew that. How did they know so? Strikers were foreigners. Perhaps a few deluded souls might be duped into helping, but surely a foreign hand was behind this treachery. And was it not self-evident in any case that foreigners were Bolsheviks? Industrial action was Bolshevik activity that signalled the presence of foreigners, just as surely as the presence of foreigners indicated a Bolsheviki hidden hand. What more proof was required? The consequence of this particular tautology was inevitable. One enterprising BC firm began to sell riot insurance.[28] BC began to steel itself for the wave of WMA prosecutions to come, this "spike" probably more pointless than the rest, if the object were to forestall radicalism rather than to calm local patriots.

Whatever British Canada might have thought, however, influential agitators and revolutionary organizations were not readily apparent to those charged with rooting them out. Not at least in 1918. Once again, Canada's wartime strikers generally just wanted a voice and amelioration of their local grievances. Rebellion was not normally part of their program. Not all of them were New Canadian; indeed the most prominent leaders were British subjects. All of this was apparent to the Dominion Police, if not to British Canada. The more the police looked for the much-feared IWW agitator, for example, the less often he appeared – indeed he disappeared. The social democrats – the closest thing Canada had to Bolsheviks – were a trace element and frankly did not appear very dangerous. Their ability to "pull" outside of those restricted, vulnerable communities that had spawned them was non-existent. There was, federal police thought, "nothing to fear from these people. They are too small, and unknown." Some modest penetration should do the trick, and allow the police to monitor the progress and plans of what was, they considered, too minor a threat to worry about.[29] In Canada's largest and most turbulent city, Montreal, police and military authorities were plainly not worried about any threat from the Left. Social democrats elsewhere were usually "Austrian," "Russian," or "German." Here they tended to be Jews – enough of them were, in any case, that it was axiomatic among many French Canadians that socialism was a "Jewish disease." Socialists were therefore incapable of producing, or capitalizing on, mass disaffection – all too readily apparent in 1918. The only trouble apprehended was that violent confrontation would almost certainly occur if the socialists attempted to stage a 1918 May Day parade. Of course this confrontation was of little concern to the wartime government. It would not involve soldiers and marchers, but marchers and angry French Canadian Catholics. Better, the mayor of Montreal considered, to forbid any procession in the interests of peace.[30]

The situation in Quebec City was similar. A secret military-police meeting held after the Easter riots to establish if they had been socialist-inspired indicated that there was absolutely no evidence of any socialist involvement whatsoever.[31] The thing was laughable. Certainly local socialists were active. As in Montreal, however, socialists were Jews and other New Canadians. In a predominantly French Canadian milieu they were easily identifiable and monitored. During the war the socialists had managed, it was conceded, to put out one or two anti-conscription posters, but the police had promptly torn these down. Even if they had stayed up, it was unlikely that they would have had much of an effect. Popular opinion was impervious to anything the socialists might attempt. Although there might be sporadic disturbances, there was unlikely to be any more substantial trouble. The population was resigned to the MSA. Easter had been frightening. Systemic trouble now came mainly from a "certain class of lawyers ... not so much interested in getting a man exempted as they are in getting his money," and a "virulent press" which seized on "and magnified out of all proportions" any supposed provocation.[32] Of course, recent censorship regulations were designed to take care of this last. Any labour trouble in Quebec City or in the province in general could be dealt with "promptly and effectively." There was "absolutely no reason to be apprehensive."[33]

Still, the very idea of the IWW was worrisome. Its members were difficult to distinguish from the rank and file British Canadian worker. Hysterical American intelligence, arriving through 1917, considered them not only to be very powerful but to be little less than a pro-German, crypto-Bolshevik conspiracy willing, indeed anxious, to betray the Allied war effort. Canadian politicians, if not always police authorities, caught the panic. They exhorted the police to look harder. Try as they might, the police continued to be unable to find any evidence that the IWW had much strength north of the border. "I consider them a very dangerous, socialistic and perhaps murderous lot," the commissioner of police informed the minster of justice, in March 1918,

> and that a little money properly spent now in learning their anticipated movements will save the Country thousands of dollars. If we can establish that they have any headquarters in Canada, I think it should be raided with a view to obtaining more information concerning them; that all their literature should be seized; and, if possible, their principals sent to Penitentiary.[34]

8.1. While the IWW was not much in evidence in Canada, the Canadian government feared it as a Bolshevik conspiracy, anxious to turn impressionable New Canadians to its evil purpose. Poster courtesy of the Glenbow Archives.

The IWW was obviously getting ready to establish a foothold in Ontario and was behind union organization province-wide. On the other hand, the commissioner also considered that a few exemplary prosecutions for, say, seditious utterance would "pretty well crimp their operations."[35] Accordingly, the IWW (along with a fairly lengthy list of other suspicious, radical organizations) was proscribed under the authority of the WMA. Suspected operatives were arrested when they could be caught, and IWW literature was absolutely censored. Even if revolutionary intent were apprehended, police penetration hardly ever revealed anything very substantial; nor did the proposed cure suggest that the police considered that there was much of substance to find. An IWW presence in Canada was feared. In 1918, an effective IWW apparatus probably did not exist.

There was, in any case, little evidence that one did; much that one did not. In March 1918, for example, an appeal arrived in Ottawa from the Temiskaming Mine Managers' Association. One Frank Simpson, they charged – an IWW operative from Toronto – was responsible for mine disturbances up around the Porcupine River. The police promised to have their man in Timmins look into it.[36] A month later, the police had successfully infiltrated two agents into the local miners' organization. Reports were also solicited and received from special agents employed by the Hollinger Consolidated Gold Mines. They were closely analysed.[37] In the end, intelligence revealed that two "Russian" men – F. Coralenko (from Toronto) and F. Conosevitch (already in custody and awaiting trial for seditious utterance) – had been obtaining subversive literature, some of it IWW-inspired, from comrades in the United States (Adolph Schnabel in New York and A. Sviga in Detroit). In total, five packages of books and literature had been received.[38] Coralenko was arrested. The police already had Conosevitch. Two men, one of them already in prison, might be considered a slender infrastructure on which to build a revolution, although the police did take the threat seriously enough to round up "several hundred aliens" – Conosevitch's suspected confederates – whom they had been keeping under surveillance. In the process, several defaulters and Alien Enemies who had failed to register were taken into custody.[39]

Shortly thereafter, apprehended IWW-inspired unrest in Fort William led, once again, to police investigation. This time the chief commissioner of Dominion Police, A.P. Sherwood, went out for a look himself. The railway companies, the shipbuilders, the grain storage managers were all upset about IWW agitators, he found, and seemed "to feel more than know, that there is trouble for them in the way of strikes in the near future." This trouble, they considered, was apt to originate within the Finnish community – a hotbed, apparently, of Red radicalism. Investigation revealed, however, that local union organizers were all "British" and not IWW at all. George Armstrong, the Canadian business manager for the Carpenters' Union – "a socialist and a great talker" – was wont to make anti-conscription speeches when it was safe to do so; also, there was "one McCutcheon," a labour organizer who had arrived in Fort William via Winnipeg in 1914. These men had no contact with the Finnish community, whatever its politics may have been. They were big-mouths, not Lenins or Heywoods. Talk of rebellion was nonsense.[40] Police found no trace of the IWW at the lakehead at all.

In May 1918, the police conducted something of a national survey to ascertain the reach of worrisome, subversive organizations. From British Columbia came the news that both city and provincial police concurred that the IWW was an unknown quantity in fractious Vancouver. The Saskatchewan Provincial Police pronounced the province free of IWW supporters, "with the exception of an individual member who happens to stray across the border" from time to time. Alberta Provincial Police considered that while the IWW had demonstrated prewar strength, it had not been heard from in some time. Perhaps some individuals continued to support it secretly, but the IWW had no headquarters or effective organizations in the province. Two letters intercepted from Mr J. Wood, of the Ukrainian Social Democratic Party (USDP), indicated that he, at any rate, had been attempting to apply for membership in the IWW directly to Heywood. Conosevitch, awaiting trial in Timmins, had, of course, collected clippings regarding IWW activities and appeared interested. Chief Commissioner Sherwood conceded that there might be some connection between the "Farmers' Non-Partisan League" and the IWW. A.C. Townely, the president of the League, and its secretary, Joseph Gilbert, had been arrested in the US, for example, a year previously for attempting to impede the draft.[41] The Farmers' Non-Partisan League, moreover, had carried a resolution recently assailing the American government for a police raid on the IWW Spokane headquarters earlier in the year, "thereby showing its sympathy with this body." Perhaps they were wobblies. There were also forty locals of the USDP in Canada, but this organization had to date demonstrated no desire for "general malicious destruction." However, it should be and would be watched.[42] "In answer to your memo of yesterday," Sherwood concluded a missive a month later,

> regarding above matter [IWW and suspicious, kindred organizations], I may say that through the active cooperation of the Police organisations throughout the Country, together with the services of several private detective organisations, thorough and exhaustive investigations have been made, and no trace can be found of any activity on the part of the I.W.W. in this Country.

That the IWW or its friends were responsible for the 1918 strikes was a myth. Its supposed involvement in recent accidents – fires in Vancouver and Niagara Falls – was nonsense. Yes, there was some forbidden literature. Talkers, of course, have always been present, and some small organizations of pinkish hue had set up shop in Canada. Nothing, however, indicated that "they exist for any sinister purpose, but rather for the improvement of their conditions as workers and toward the securing of better pay." Only one IWW attempt to get a foothold in Canada had been located – in Sault Ste Marie – and the single worker implicated was being given "appropriate attention."[43]

What police authorities might have noted more formally, had they not taken it for granted, was that communal division in Canada virtually ensured that no matter how bad things got at home – how inimical to the interest of workers – there could be no coherent class response whether originating from trade union or political sources. Most of Canada's existing trade unionists not already at the front would sooner have starved than harm the war effort or associate themselves with what they perceived to be attempts by foreigners to foment revolution. Canada's few, effective working-class radicals were mainly British or American immigrants – particularly influential in the bumptious coal-mining towns of British Columbia.[44] They had and desired little contact with New Canadians. Political organizations unique to New Canadian communities – the USDP or Montreal's socialists, for example – by no means consolidated the entire membership of the communities from which they emerged (as we have seen, Ukrainian nationalists were actively hostile to Ukrainian socialists) and had no influence in British or French Canada whatsoever. Indeed, the fact that socialist organizations could be rather accurately characterized as "foreign" ensured that they would achieve no broader constituency. It cannot be said too emphatically: no effective challenge to the war could ever have come from this quarter.

The Canadian government, however, seems to have convinced itself – whatever the quality and quantity of the evidence put before it – that Bolshevism was a real threat, a bacillus to which New Canadians were particularly susceptible.[45] As indicated already, this perception derived from a combination of existing distrust, reaction to events unfolding in Russia, and intelligence received from the UK and the US then in the throes of their own first Red scares. The government shared its fear with many influential members of the French and British Canadian communities. While it employed repressive measures, tried and true or unique to the war, and sometimes with a heavy hand, the government ultimately depended upon the soundness of Canada's charter communities to provide the antidote to this contagion. "[I]f the extremists should really start any trouble," Major Jukes of Military Intelligence in British Columbia considered, "their only allies would be the aliens." The returned soldiers, on the other hand, could be counted upon to show the same vigour they had in France in clearing up the situation at home.[46] Major Jukes was right about one thing. Whoever might be causing trouble in Canada, the veterans were going to prove a mighty ally against perceived social-political dissent. The way in which events were headed was already apparent in the spring of 1918.

In February 1918, the GWVA and the British Columbia Federation of Labour (BCFL) sat down to discuss their future: how to ensure that the interests of returned men were accommodated.[47] The GWVA wanted its members absorbed back into the economy as painlessly and quickly as possible. The BCFL wanted no trouble with soldiers. The first fruit of the understanding was that the GWVA and the BCFL jointly demanded the expulsion of Asian workers from the railway and fruit companies and vowed to resist "under any conditions" further attempts to import cheap Asian labour.[48] The federal government almost immediately promised that there would be no further importation of Chinese labour until the supply of White labour gave out.[49] There were no surprises here.

When, however, the death of Ginger Goodwin – a prominent labour leader in British Columbia, killed during a shoot-out with police attempting to detain him as an MSA resister – led the Vancouver Trade and Labour Council (VTLC) to call for a one-day strike by four thousand streetcar workers in protest, the veterans were no longer willing to proceed with labour. Indeed, Mayor Gale of Vancouver warned the

Council that if striking workers would not man the streetcars, angry citizens and returned men certainly would, and that these patriots would probably not content themselves with simple scabbing.[50] On the afternoon of 2 August 1918, hundreds of veterans reacted to strikes in Vancouver by destroying the Labour Temple, and, having failed to throw him out of the window, dragged Victor Midgley, the secretary of the VTLC, into the street, where he was forced to kiss the Union Jack. In the offices the men found documents that they claimed proved that the Metal Trades Council had been the moving force behind the strike.[51] Afterwards the veterans demanded that radical leaders – Ernest Winch, Jack Kavanagh, George Thomas, Bill Pritchard, Harry Cottrell, Joseph Naylor, and Victor Midgley – leave British Columbia for the duration of the war. The intimidated VTLC agreed to put the proposal to a vote.[52] The executive, frightened, decided to resign prior to the vote and asked the union leadership to select a new slate.[53] Shortly thereafter, Naylor at least was arrested for action contrary to the MSA.[54] This procedure was easier, as local lawyers realized, than trying him for sedition.[55]

Published local and official opinion was strongly supportive of the returned men. Reverend Lashley of the Vancouver Methodist Church praised the conduct of the veterans in the recent disturbances and called upon union members to play up and expel the vipers from their midst.[56] The local GWVA, as well, passed a resolution calling upon the government to use its full powers to punish strikers.[57] The federal minister of labour, T.W. Crothers, meanwhile, was "hounded" to invoke existing mechanisms – the Lemieux Act (1906) as reinforced by wartime regulation – to punish those responsible for the strikes. While he was not willing to go so far and insisted that both sides would have to be more accommodating, he was careful to stress that "the Government would not hesitate to use its ample powers to suppress seditious attempts to stir up unnecessary disputes."[58]

There was more trouble of the same sort in Toronto, which in 1918 saw its worst rioting. That February, unknown assailants attacked Charles Thompson, a returned man. They beat him and threw vitriol into his face, leaving him temporarily blind. His attackers were, he believed, New Canadians whom he had "recently reprimanded for insulting a girl."[59] The GWVA responded in predictable fashion. At a meeting in April, veterans called upon the city and county government to "deal with the alien question." If it failed to do so, they warned, then the veterans could always – as one enraged man shouted at city council – "go down to Yonge Street and clean them up themselves," as indeed they had shown a willingness to do in 1917.[60]

The following day at least some veterans acted. Twenty or thirty returned men paid a night visit to Fred Spade, an alien. They dragged him to the front steps of his house and "made him kiss a large Union flag which one of the veterans held. A large tin of grease was poured over him and an attempt was made by the ex-soldiers to feather him." The trouble arose, Spade thought, from a letter that he had allegedly written to the GWVA. Other than this, he could see no reason why the soldiers apparently hated him so much. Yes, he was of German derivation, but he had been born in the United States. His nephew was serving in the American navy, and a boy "he raised from infancy" was then serving overseas with the Canadian Forces.[61] The York County executive of the GWVA admitted that the Spade incident had been a mistake and was going too far. It had been led to believe that Spade had insulted the wife of a soldier. It appeared this was incorrect. A resolution against mob rule followed this "deplorable" incident.[62]

In August, however, while Vancouver veterans were sacking the Labour Temple, and with the Canadian Corps poised to begin its "hundred days," Toronto returned men were responding to rumours that Greek waiters at the White City Café on Yonge Street had attacked a disabled veteran, Albert Cludray. This rumour came at a most inopportune time. The GWVA was holding a Dominion-wide meeting in Toronto with two hundred delegates from across the country in town and excitement running high – particularly due to a looming fracture as Winnipeg, Ottawa, and Toronto delegations struggled for control of the movement and its agenda.[63] Two months earlier, Toronto had come close to experiencing a general strike, as workmen responded to the same issues troubling their brothers in Winnipeg, Vancouver, and elsewhere. In July, news arrived that thirteen locals had gone down with the *Llandovery Castle*. Remembrance ceremonies followed mid-month. Meanwhile, of course, the last, terrible German offensives in France came within an ace of securing victory for the Fatherland.[64] Bad news spawned hard deeds, as was often the case in wartime British Canada.

While Toronto was not a garrison town, there was a substantial military presence in the city. From time to time, troops passing through or units in the process of formation would be quartered on the Exhibition grounds. In addition, Military District Number Two (Toronto) catered to no less than one-third of all Canadian wounded despatched home. At any time, 900 wounded men would be undergoing treatment in the city, although the number could sometimes be much higher. By March 1918, there were 3,733 beds in the city.[65] With the exception of those patients with communicable diseases, those too injured to move, and the venereals, most of the wounded had been moved out to private homes in the spring-summer of 1918 to make way for an influx of patients stricken by the influenza epidemic then raging. Discipline now was almost impossible to maintain, particularly because of the "indulgent attitude of the public and press towards these men, and also due to the fact that a supply of intoxicating liquor was easily got."[66] It appears that Torontonians were in the habit of fortifying the seriously wounded by standing them drinks serially. More generally, returned men were apt to be present in Toronto in exceptional number and proportion for the simple reason that much of the Canadian army had been recruited locally. Anaemic Toronto, which would probably have had difficulty raising the mass for a decent riot in 1916, had some of its darlings back by 1918. A foreigner, it seemed, had insulted one of them. The subsequent riots, the district commander considered, were entirely motivated by "the ALIEN QUESTION, concerning which certain civilians and some returned soldiers appear to hold strong views." They were "encouraged thereto by utterances of certain public men and a portion of the press."[67]

Soldiers and their civilian benefactors responded to the assault on Cludray by looting and destroying some Greek restaurants (ten, twelve, or fourteen depending on the source) and dragging the owners into the streets to kiss the flag, while police did nothing and spectators cheered.[68] One restaurant, found to be in the habit of employing veterans, was spared.[69] The original rioters were two hundred men in uniform, all of them, the provost marshal noted, "patients receiving treatment," egged on by civilians who would "deny them nothing."[70] Indeed, far from denying them anything, the perhaps three hundred civilians who participated on the first day of the disturbance mobilized themselves not only to assist the work of destruction but also to drive the wounded men about the city from location to location, from focus of destruction to focus of destruction.[71] The soldiers were, the Toronto *Globe* wrote,

> absolute masters of all authority[. They] defied the police and the military, and utterly tore to pieces the interiors of a dozen restaurants and stores, leaving wreckage in their path like unto the devastation they saw themselves after their advance in France following a great artillery battle.[72]

The next night, the rioting began again, and this time the rioters clashed with police and the violence began to spiral out of control. Almost all of those involved were civilians this time, with some few returned men in evidence. One of those injured in the scuffle was Lieutenant-Colonel A.T. Hunter, a prominent GWVA leader who does not appear to have been actually involved in the rioting.[73] The arrest of two returned men, Ernest Haggart and Arthur Draymond, by city police was particularly provocative. Police escorted the two men to the Dundas Street station, which came immediately under heavy attack.

> Here a regular pitched battle was fought, blood was spilt, some persons were knocked unconscious, and had to be taken to hospital. Two similar attempts were made later in the evening to break into the station, but without success.[74]

Mayor Church was so alarmed by the turn events were taking that he – unlike the mayor of Quebec shortly before – arrived personally at the local district headquarters armed with a formal request that the military do whatever was required to restore order. What he suggested was application of the "riot act."[75] Indeed, the army made preparation to read the Riot Act, should circumstances warrant. Reliable troops from the local garrison were assembled. Each detachment would be accompanied by a civil magistrate empowered to say the necessary words.[76]

For two more nights riots continued, although the GWVA made it clear that it disapproved of what was now happening. W.P. Purney, the president of the GWVA, stated that he was "disgusted" with the behaviour of some returned men. He was particularly upset, he continued, by "the idea some returned men have"

> that they can take constituted authority by the throat and do as they like, regardless of the law, and regardless of their own people. The sooner they get that idea out of their heads the more readily will the right-thinking people of Canada be prepared to award them their just dues ... The convention will place itself out of sympathy with such actions ... The objects that the unrestrained men were so desirous of accomplishing can be so much more easily gained by lawful methods.[77]

From France, Arthur Currie took time out from preparing for his great attack at Amiens to appeal to the returned men among the rioters to remember the ideals they'd recently been fighting for in Europe.

Perhaps the ideals that had sent them to France were not those that Currie supposed.

Tempers, however, continued to boil. Angered by what they charged had been inappropriate use of force by the police against wounded men and women, five thousand men assembled in Queen's Park. On this occasion only the deployment of five hundred soldiers, brought into the city specifically for this purpose, restored order.[78] Some of these soldiers were COTC candidates trucked in from training and armed with rifles and ten rounds each, precisely because they would be dependable if firing proved necessary. Fortunately it was not.[79] Things quieted down.

Hardy surprisingly, in Ottawa, the adjutant general (responsible for military discipline) was livid and ordered that those responsible suffer promptly and heavily.[80] Ultimately nine soldiers were arrested for the Toronto riots: two were day patients, five were actual inmates of the College Street military hospital, one was a warden at a casualty depot, and one was a recovered casualty – a member of the 4th Battalion awaiting discharge. This time some of those found guilty went to prison. Four were convicted and sentenced to terms of between four and six months' detention with hard labour. Those still in hospital do not appear to have gone to detention barracks.[81]

One of the oddest but most revealing facets of the August 1918 riots in Toronto was the attempt to blame them on what had been, after all, the first targets. Mayor Church claimed that the riotous crowd had been composed of young "foreigners, socialists, and idlers."[82] The GOC of No. 2 District warned officers commanding units that slackness in enforcing discipline would not be tolerated.

> Alien Enemies will take every advantage of the returned soldier to sow the seeds of discord and do damage to civil property. Soldiers who may have grievances are reminded that these Alien Enemies will use them as their tools on every possible occasion and continue damage beyond all reason wherever the soldiers have been the instigators. Soldiers are therefore requested to beware of Alien Enemies and not to become involved in any manner in unlawful assemblies.[83]

As in Vancouver, in Toronto violence was blamed on those who passively provided provocation rather than on the violent and provoked.

In the future, military authorities warned, wounded men would not have it so easy. They would be brought under stricter discipline. All absentees would be noted with their time of return. If there was trouble, these men would be paraded for police inspection, and proceedings instituted if any positive identifications were made.[84] Nor, by September, in the aftermath of the Quebec City and Toronto riots, was it any longer necessary for regional GOCs to refer requests for assistance to the civil power in Ottawa. By Order-in-Council they received the power to turn out troops on their own authority to quell riots.[85] There would be no repetition. This at least was the hope.

Shortly thereafter, a meeting of trade unionists at the Toronto Labour Temple on Church Street was broken up by a group of soldiers and returned men who had counter-organized themselves at the Armoury before marching through the streets announcing their intention to "beat up the Reds and pacifists." No one intervened. No one this time appears to have much protested. Indeed bystanders applauded the action.[86] A short while later, a "well organised gang of several hundred" broke up another meeting of trade unionists in nearby Guelph, Ontario. Tim Buck, later secretary of the Communist Party of Canada, was plucked from the resulting mêlée, "seized and carried bodily to the nearby bridge and thrown over the parapet into the river Speed."[87] In Halifax, Nova Scotia, and Lindsay, Ontario, meanwhile, rioting veterans smashed Chinese businesses.[88]

What the returned men wanted, what British Canada wanted, was more vigorous action – really, repressive action – against New Canadians and other perceived opponents of the war. The GWVA might have been against clashes with the police. It did not disapprove of operations against New Canadians or malcontents, particularly when these were undertaken by the government. Its position was the same as a year previous. It would step in, but only to do necessary work the government had first shirked. Repressive action quickly followed. One of the primary reasons for the much stricter regime instituted through 1918 – tighter censorship, stricter federal enforcement of the MSA, and more stringent enforcement of ARRs – was quite simply that, if the government did not take at least half measures, British Canada was very apt to institute a full-blown policy of repression with or without government authority. Vancouver and Toronto had shown the direction in which events seemed to be tending.

Why, the GWVA wanted to know, did the government tolerate publication of a foreign-language press at all? Surely the German press, at least, should be prohibited, the national organization thought.[89] Why stop there, the truculent Winnipeg branch wondered? If the government did not take action against all papers published in the languages of enemy countries, then, for its part, the GWVA would not be held "accountable for actions of returned soldiers who threaten to smash up these German publishing houses."[90] It is probably not coincidental that severe government regulation of foreign-language publication followed immediately.[91] Tolerance was simply not in the cards.

Why did it tolerate subversive organizations? If the government were not willing to undertake the necessary work of suppression, then would not British Canadians have to act as in Vancouver and Toronto? Pre-emptive police action quickly followed. Suspicious organizations were catalogued and outlawed. In May 1918, further, federal police raided the headquarters of the USDP in Ottawa. Sixteen "Austrians" were arrested and sent to internment camps. The organization's printing office, on Clarke Street, was ransacked for May Day circulars and ordered "seized" by the secretary of state.[92] Further afield, in September 1918, police action was directed at socialist party and labour offices in Vancouver. In October, the Toronto offices of the USDP, the Socialist Party of North America, and the offices of the national organizations of the Ukrainians, Finns, Russians, and Austrians were raided. Prosecution followed for the leaders of the USDP[93] – most of whom, at least, would have been no strangers to the police. The Toronto city police had searched the USDP ("the Ukrainian branch of the IWW," they considered, a little confused) a year previous, taking eighty New Canadians into custody.[94] And so it went.

There were some places the government simply would not go; indeed, would not permit anybody to go. Throughout the latter war years, the government was careful to attempt to maintain contact with critical intermediary bodies – those bodies which by their nature provided bridges between Canada's communities. One of these was the Liberal Party, which, of course, was maintained in being in the latter war years largely by the formal acceptance of the fiction by both Laurier and Borden that British Canadian Liberals remained effectively Liberal. Another such organization was the Catholic Church, which the government carefully courted throughout the war. Yes, the church could deliver votes and volunteers. This was not the only function it could perform. In Canada the dangerous effects of communal division could be considerably ameliorated if members of combatant communities shared membership in something. Such an organization, by its nature, inhibited the development of polarity by confusing identity answers. Even more valuable was the organization if it was capable of aligning itself on issues of common interest with others of different persuasion. The Catholic Church was a very important "defuser," strained but not broken by the war. If French Canadians felt excluded as "French," how did they feel as Catholics? The church itself, moreover, needed to adjudicate between equally strident Irish and French constituencies. The ambiguous answer it was apt to give on most divisive questions did not generally conduce to polar oppositions. Further, whatever Rome might have suggested was appropriate, the Catholic Church in Canada had a long and fruitful history of combining, on occasion, with other faiths on issues of common interest. For example, during the highly inflammatory Manitoba Schools Question, the Anglican Church – dissatisfied with the quality of religious education provided in provincial schools, and possessed of considerable authority (if not power) in British Canada as the effective founder of the "Protestant" school system – tended to align itself with Catholics against members of other Protestant denominations determined to institute the one-language, secular Ontario system.[95] On this issue, some British Protestants and French Catholics found common ground. Similarly in Ontario, the divisive School Question could never perfectly amplify wartime polarity, though Quebec was manifestly highly provoked, in part because it did not have to account for local ambiguity. In Ontario, in a rather useful fashion, this question helped to diffuse wartime polarity by producing a political constellation altogether different from that encouraged by the war. Education did set French against English Canadians (what language would be spoken in the schools, and when?), and Catholics against Protestants (what religious instruction, if any, would be provided in the schools and by whom?), but it ended by producing not two, but three squabbling parties. Franco-Ontarians insisted on maintaining schools that were Catholic and French-language. Protestant English speakers, on the other hand, wanted a unified school system in which the language of instruction would be English and religious instruction would be interdenominational. Still again, in Ontario the powerful Irish Catholic lobby led by Bishop Fallon emphatically wanted Catholic schools but was absolutely opposed to education in French. Indeed, if the choice were between non-denominational English and Catholic French education, then the Ontario Irish were powerfully tempted to send their children to school with their English-speaking Protestant neighbours.[96] The federal government, in both cases, assumed its customary (and comfortable) role of helping local authorities and religious confessions arrive at an acceptable compromise – sympathetic to all and enemy of none.

In 1917, if Borden could no longer appeal to French Canadians as fellow British subjects, then it was doubly vital that he maintain contact with them as Catholics. If, as a community, French Canadians were anything but satisfied with his government, then the Roman Catholic Church was still sound (if sometimes locally unenthusiastic), and in the end all but a few Quebec hotheads would quail at the possibility of direct action in defiance of ecclesiastical authority. It is certainly revealing, in this regard, that a loyal Catholic and son of Ireland, C.J. Doherty, the minister of justice, was assigned the thankless task of carrying the MSA through Parliament and introducing the necessary enabling and repressive legislation. Doherty was important to the government, both as a devout Catholic and as an Irishman in the loyalist "D'Arcy McGee" tradition. In the latter war years, there was some fear in Ottawa that Canada's large Irish Catholic population might not remain as steadfast behind the war as it had been hitherto, given events in Ireland. They might even, some considered, join their French Canadian co-religionists in dissent. A perceived association of Irish Catholic and French Canadian MPs in the fight against conscription was particularly worrisome for the government.[97] In Australia, at just this time, the alignment of Roman Catholics against conscription was held to have produced successive defeats for Premier Hughes in referenda on the issue. If the Catholics were to be kept "on-side" it was equally vital that Orange Ontario, which had already made the wartime equation that "French Canadians are traitors," not continue the series that "Catholics are traitors." The "alliance monstrueuse"[98] that had developed between Ontario's Orangemen and Irish Catholics, in the Ontario schools question, was something to be preserved at all costs so far as the federal government was concerned. This is why the issue of the Guelph Noviate of June 1918 produced such evident angst in Ottawa and why what should have been a minor distraction came to implicate so much of the time of very busy, powerful men.

The story is quickly told. On 7 June 1918, following a local agitation originating in Hamilton and carried on largely by the Protestant ministerial association, army officers raided the Jesuit Noviate in Guelph, Ontario, looking for MSA evaders. Eighteen or nineteen were thought to be on the premises. The commandant of Military District Number One had heard that the Jesuits were hiding men eligible under the MSA and he believed that Jesuit noviates had not been included in the class of people excluded from operation of the MSA as clergy. When his inquiries had gone unanswered, officers were despatched to Guelph. Doors were kicked open. Monks and novices were paraded and examined. Arrests were made. Things thereafter unravelled swiftly.

Investigation followed and evidence was gathered. Action was ultimately taken, but not against the Jesuits. The minister of justice, Doherty, almost immediately instituted proceedings against several of those involved in launching the raids. The charges, he considered, had been unfounded and malicious. The officers executing the warrants had exceeded their authority. Doherty, however, was hardly the man to deal with this issue. He was the most prominent Catholic in a government that contained few others – a matter of substantial criticism the previous year.[99] It did not make matters easier that his son Marcus was at the time of the raid a Jesuit novice in Guelph, having previously been judged "unfit for military service." Sam Hughes – only recently excluded from the government – took up the cry in Parliament.[100] No less a luminary than the minister of justice, it appeared, was harbouring slackers – indeed, had spawned one. The Orange Lodge commenced a letter-writing campaign.[101] How, the Congregational Union of Canada wanted to know, was it fair that Congregationalists had given everyone from their own theological college while Jesuit institutions were allowed to function, business as usual?[102] The Ministerial Association in faraway Edmonton had similar questions.[103] A chastened Doherty withdrew into the background. It is a sign of the importance the government attached to the affair, however, that Arthur Meighen – absolutely Protestant, as Irish as Doherty and credibly Orange – was assigned to deal personally with this question.[104] If Meighen judged that the thing was wrong, then it was wrong. Case closed, so far as the LOL was concerned. The government succeeded in defusing what might have produced a considerable ruckus.

In the end, the Irish Catholics were not alienated. The government had given ample demonstration that it knew the difference between novices and slackers, and that it was not afraid to stand up to one faction of its supporters on a question of principle. British Canada, for the duration, was prevented from splintering into ethnic, or Protestant and Catholic, factions. French Canadian did not become wider Catholic disaffection. Everyone worked to calm things down. French versus British, Protestant versus Catcholic: these were old games, and the government knew the rules and played a good hand. Trouble between British and New Canada, on the other hand, steadily increased in scale and frequency through 1918. Even the end of the war in Europe, in November, made little difference to events at home in this respect.

9 1919: The War at Home Continues: When the Boys Came Home

But the Conservative elements of the country, I do not mean conservative in any party sense, are thoroughly behind any Government that will enforce law and order; but they insist that revolution shall be declared unlawful and that the laws should be enforced.

Unless the Government deals with the revolutionary phases of the propaganda, I am convinced that the conservative elements of the country will unite in a widespread political campaign against the Government that will unite the property owning elements of the country in a program declaring in favour of the enforcement of law and the maintenance of order.

C.H. Cahan, director of public safety, January 1919[1]

Feeling intense against all Alien Enemies ... Consider whether stipulations necessary in peace treaty to permit as under legislation to deport after conclusion of peace Canadian residents of enemy nationality who have been here many years ... Public opinion will force legislation ... There is great danger of outbreak against Alien Enemies in many parts of Canada and the feeling growing daily.

Sir Thomas White to Sir Robert Borden, February 1919[2]

On 11 November 1918 the shooting ended in on the Western Front. Although some Canadian soldiers were involved in the ill-fated intervention in Russia and more were slated to go, Canada's heart was not in the thing and they were withdrawn as soon as practicable. A relaxation at home might have been expected. The war, from Canada's perspective, was over, though fighting continued on other fronts, and while peace was being negotiated the war emergency remained. In 1919, however, an immediate return to normalcy was simply not possible. The various communities making up Canada were not ready for that yet. The war at home continued – the year 1919 constituting, effectively, part of a latter war continuum. And, as in 1917 and 1918, the government remained convinced that only vigorous state action would suffice to maintain public order. Not until 1920 did something like prewar normalcy return.

That said, there was some relaxation of wartime practice where the maintenance of the wartime regime could no longer be justified. Interning people because of what they were (rather than what they might do) was expensive and could no longer be easily defended. Some of the 2,500 aliens still in camps were released immediately. In April 1919, however, there were still 2,119 detained aliens, and 847 in September. Local justices could still order Alien Enemies detained at discretion, if "advisable in the public interest." In the ten months following the Armistice, there were 91 new detentions.[3] Not everybody released returned to a Canadian home. The consensus was that "a great many [of the hard cases] will [have to] be deported to their own homes as undesirables."[4] Ultimately, it seems that 302 "Austrians" and as many as 1,600 Germans (including those brought from the West Indies) were deported, and some detained until 1920 until that could be arranged.[5] The last convicted saboteur was not released until 1924.[6] Those who had fled Canada to avoid persecution were, it seems, seldom allowed to return. The wartime self-exiled became the permanently undesirable.[7]

The hunt for MSA defaulters and evaders slowed and then ceased, although initial reports that they would be pardoned and face no punishment were quickly and strenuously denied.[8] Perhaps a period of disenfranchisement, the government thought, might be a just punishment for unrepentant slackers coming in from the cold.[9] Meanwhile, MSA evaders, taking advantage of the amnesty provided for men who did report for duty (and of the fact that the war was over), poured in for service – two thousand in the two weeks following the Armistice.[10] Prosecutions under the Militia Act continued through 1919 for the obdurate, although a prison sentence was rare. A fifty-dollar fine was the usual cost of a return to normal life. This, of course, is the reason for the postwar spike in Militia Act convictions registered in Quebec.

However, for some defaulters and those who had abetted them, there would be no forgiveness. Finlay Stonehouse, a Bracebridge native who had shot a civilian attempting to aid the Dominion Police in apprehending him, was jailed for ten years in December.[11] Fred Whissel, a Sudbury native, received a four-year sentence in the same month for shooting at and wounding a police officer attempting to arrest him for MSA evasion.[12] The authorities were no more forgiving of some of those implicated in assisting resisters during the war. A Quebec ring which had specialized in providing false exemption papers to MSA resisters was identified two weeks after the Armistice. Its members were quickly arrested.[13] Canada's few conscientious objectors, similarly, were not easily forgiven. In May 1919 there were still thirty-four of them imprisoned.[14] Most appear to have served their sentences.

Otherwise, after the Armistice, the repressive powers of the government continued to grow, not shrink, while most of the mechanism created under the authority of the WMA remained in place until 1920. The reason was simple. The Canadian government apprehended profound unrest in the aftermath of war. It was advised, and believed, that social, political, and intercommunal antagonisms, accentuated by the war, would continue to agitate and divide Canadians for some time. The most potentially explosive of the intercommunal divides remained that between British Canada, about to be reinforced by an army of returned men the vanguard of which had already demonstrated its proclivities, and New Canadian communities, already established in the popular mind as nests of traitors and subversives. "As one who has worked night and day to elect you," Meighen was warned by D.A. Ross, a Manitoba MPP and a constant correspondent,

> I wish to say with all the force I can command; unless you wake up the Government to act and act promptly in connection with the seditious propaganda that is going on all over the country you are going to see bloodshed here within two or three months. I am continually told by the returned soldiers that they do not propose to allow this state of affairs to exist any longer.

He had toured his riding. There had been subversive meetings, and open talk of revolution in the spring of 1919. He had reported this treachery to the proper authorities. Nothing had been done. The boys were trickling home now. Soon there would be a flood. Quite plainly, they were not going to tolerate any slackness on the government's part.[15] "You tell [the Government] to *act damned quick*," a delegation or returned men from St Clements had advised him, "or there will be mighty serious trouble one of these days as these aliens are more saucy and independent to-day than they ever were."[16] Later, Borden remembered 1919 as a strange time indeed.

> In Canada, as elsewhere, the conditions of business and employment were abnormal. Equally abnormal was the state of mind of the people in general, or at least of the great majority of them. There was a distinctive lack of the usual balance; the agitator, sometimes sincere, sometimes merely malevolent, self-seeking and designing, found quick response to insidious propaganda. In some cities there were deliberate attempts to overthrow the existing organization of the Government and to supersede it by crude, fantastic methods founded upon absurd conceptions of what had been accomplished in Russia. It became necessary in some communities to repress revolutionary methods with a stern hand and from this I did not shrink.

It is odd that Borden did not mention patriot pressure, ensuring that his hand was firm if only so that it was not supplanted. In many ways the year following the war was the inevitable postlude to the war itself, during which wartime dynamics burned themselves out, with the government doing what it could to moderate the process.

In January 1919, C.H. Cahan was appointed director of public safety and charged with the coordination of measures for internal security.[17] Cahan had been corresponding with Borden for some time. He was a native Nova Scotian and an old friend. He was primarily of interest to the government, however, as a man who claimed to have extensive knowledge of the American system for dealing with dissent by voluntary methods. It did not hurt that he also claimed to be a friend of Lord Milner and to have worked for several years in the United States for the British Secret Service.[18]

Cahan had come to the attention of the government as a man who knew what to do earlier in 1918, at a time when it was still by no means certain that the war would be won. In May, Borden had written to Cahan looking for advice. Cabinet considered, Borden disclosed, that some organization was going to have to be created to deal with New Canadian dissenters, and with malcontents generally. It feared that German agents might be inspiring recent outbursts of opposition. Perhaps they would seek to capitalize on these as they had in Ireland. Borden wondered if there was something worthwhile to be learned from the American example. Citizens' vigilance committees, unofficially controlled by the Department of Justice, appeared to be working wonders there.[19]

Maybe something like these could provide the "stern hand, when dealing with challenges to the state" that Borden had always advocated.[20] Cahan began his response by reviewing the situation in Canada. While his assessment of the threat faced by Canada would become ever more urgent until his resignation in July 1919, his thinking on how to meet the challenge remained constant. His analysis was highly astute and revealing not only in the light of postwar but of Canada's wartime practice.

Cahan did not think an American solution would be appropriate. Canada was too different. Neither Cahan nor any other responsible agency believed that rebellion in Canada would arise from within suspected communities. "I am convinced," he wrote in July 1918,

> that German and Austrian subjects, and other aliens, resident in Canada, have very generally refrained from committing any acts in contravention of the orders and regulations made under the provisions of the War Measures Act, and the other Acts, Orders-in-Council and proclamations made for regulating the conduct of such Alien Enemies while resident in Canada.[21]

It was a fact, he later considered, that "there [is] no evidence that during four years of war any registered Alien Enemy resident in Canada has attempted to commit or has committed a single outrage upon persons or property in Canada."[22] It was possible that some American residents had been conspiring against Canada before the entry of the US to the war. They had, however, been frustrated and now faced prosecution at home. It was certain that some East Indians in BC had affiliated with their brethren in San Francisco and wanted to cause problems in India, but "their efforts have been thwarted and rendered futile." There were rumours of espionage among the resident German population, but no proof. There was mental unrest among the Slavs – the Russians, Ukrainians, Ruthenians – due to socialist and church propaganda, but nothing substantive. So what actual threat would the committees seek to root out? And it was not just absence of a threat. Immigrants no longer had any associations that vigilance committees could monitor. Wartime regulation had already seen to that. There was, in Canada, no geographic concentration of disgruntled Germans, no German associations, no anti-patriotic Irish leagues, no *Sein Finn*, no Fenians, no Southside Boston. The American committees, Cahan considered, were essentially informers' leagues that infiltrated and tracked the actions of defined, existing, potentially effective dissenting groups. Without any of this sort of activity in the Dominion, what would informers do? If the government encouraged Canadians to form vigilance committees, then those in Quebec, deprived of Alien Enemy activities to report on, would direct their energies against "alleged Protestant aggression, the restricted use of the French language in Ontario Schools and other matters of local controversy." Meanwhile, Ontario committees would immediately "degenerate into forums for discussing the alleged Roman Catholic aggression, Papal neutrality, the disinclination of French Canadians to comply with the Military Services Act, and other like subjects of political and religious controversy."[23] Citizens' committees, in effect, would be poison rather than an antidote. They would facilitate the expression of intercommunal hostilities and the dissent arising from them, rather than constituting any useful mechanism for the control of an actual threat. Canada would certainly find volunteers if it wanted them. Their work, however, would be dangerous to the state. American-style vigilante solutions would be simply inappropriate and dangerous. In Canada, the nature of dissent meant that an effective response must come from the government and take the form of police action.

Cahan continued that causes of unrest in Canada were numerous. There were industrial issues which could sometimes result in strikes, general dislike of continuing conscription, and criticism about the treatment of soldiers, taxes, and other facets of war management. "In travelling from one end of the country to the other," he confessed, "one hears everywhere manifestations of such discontent." The reason was simple: the "enthusiasm of the Canadian people in respect of the war is rapidly diminishing and ... the dominant moral purpose of the people to sacrifice everything to ensure the successful prosecution of the war is sadly weakening." Much sacrifice had left little stomach for more of the same. The Canadian workman, fed up with rumours of rampant profiteering, was now "frankly contending for his share of the alleged profits and his patriotism is obscured while he serves his own selfish personal purposes."[24] Those who had lost family members did not want remaining sons to enlist. Returning soldiers expected much, and had received little. Farmers were anxious about their crops, hated expropriation, did not know how they could continue without labourers and horses, and were generally disgruntled from overwork and downright angry about the cancellation of exemptions. "I am convinced," Cahan concluded,

> that the unrest now prevalent in Canada is due to the weakening of the moral purpose of the people to prosecute the war to a successful end; to

the fact that the people are becoming more clearly conscious of the bloody sacrifices and irritating burdens entailed by carrying on the war; and to the growing belief that the Union Government in failing to deal efficiently with the financial, industrial, and economic problems growing out of the war, and which are, perhaps, incapable of early, satisfactory solution.[25]

Cahan considered that all Canadians were war weary, and that no group of Canadians, cultural, religious, ethnic, or otherwise, was actively treacherous. None of this meant that the situation was "safe." On the contrary, registration of aliens should continue and be extended to include Russians, Ukrainians, and Finns. Miners appeared to be the target audience for the subversive attention of both the IWW and the Social Democratic Party. Apparently, he thought, these were operating in Canada in tandem and in receipt of assistance both from revolutionary Russia[26] and Germany.[27] The thing to do, Cahan thought, was to employ

> the most stringent measures to curtail the import, publication, and distribution of such doctrines – at least until the termination of the present war; and to prohibit, during the same period, the oral advocacy of such doctrines at public or private meetings.[28]

The IWW, the SDP, the USDP, the Ukrainian Revolutionary Group, the Russian Revolutionary Group, and any other organization with similar doctrines should simply be declared illegal. Membership in such organizations, or advocacy of their doctrines in any form, should be an offence punishable by imprisonment. No newspapers, pamphlets, or other publications in any language other than English and French should be permitted without licence. Officers should be granted the necessary powers to enforce these regulations. "In other words," Cahan wrote,

> drastic regulation should be drawn up under the War Measures Act for the purpose of preventing foreign propagandists from advocating and organising revolution in Canada, and especially, by the use of propaganda expressed in foreign languages, which are only read and understood by aliens resident in Canada who, at least during the war, must be kept under strict supervision and control.[29]

The government accepted Cahan's advice as tendered, and implemented his suggested measures in the last months of the war. These organizations were proscribed, when not already forbidden. In addition, censorship was ratcheted up one final notch.

Very shortly after the conclusion of peace, some elements of wartime practice were grafted into the Criminal Code as methods of restraining sedition in peacetime. War regulations in restraint of expression gave way to Section 98 of the Criminal Code, which aimed to make permanent the most important and useful of the wartime innovations. While often considered to be a knee-jerk and ill-considered reaction to the Winnipeg General Strike, this legislation was in preparation for weeks before the strike took place, though enactment was considerably facilitated by what was widely assumed to be attempted revolution in Winnipeg.[30] "Unlawful associations" – already seditious conspiracies by definition – were held to be any organizations that advocated change in Canada, politically, socially, and economically, by force or threats of force. One can well imagine that the short list of such organizations was very like the list proscribed by Order-in-Council during the war.[31] Membership in such an organization was established by attendance at its meetings, speaking in favour of its program, distributing its literature, contributing funds to it, wearing its badges and insignia, or just about anything else that might be found suspicious. Once the Crown had established that a malefactor had done any of these things, the onus, as under wartime regulation, was on the accused to disprove membership. When a magistrate determined that a seditious organization was setting up shop in his jurisdiction, he could issue a warrant that authorized police to seize its property, arrest its membership, and confiscate its literature, as indeed he could have done during the war. Purported membership in a seditious organization could now lead, in theory, to imprisonment for twenty years.[32] Publication, possession, or distribution of seditious books and literature – any literature advocating the same sort of policy, or produced by an unlawful association – carried the same penalty,[33] as did seditious speech.[34] Even providing facilities to an unlawful organization could lead to a five-year stay in jail and a five-thousand-dollar fine.[35] As always, the government was assuming greater powers than it required. These laws, while sometimes used in the postwar period, do not appear ever to have been employed with the fullest possible vigour provided. The wheel had come full circle, however. War regulation had been informed by peacetime notions as to what constituted unacceptable expression. Now how peacetime criminality was defined and prosecuted was being influenced by wartime practice.

In order to enforce the new regulations, new machinery was required. The government, Cahan advised, required a branch of the Department of Justice to enforce federal law (the MSA, alien registration, censorship, workplace controls). Dependence on local or provincial forces would allow too much to slip through the cracks and mean a policy of continued tolerance of regional discrepancies. The differences between the vigour with which wartime regulations were enforced in Ontario and points west, for example, and in Quebec was obvious and provocative. This organization would include not only special secret police but prosecutors to prepare federal cases. The government should, moreover, be prepared to maintain this organization after the war during the inevitable period of dislocation that would follow. "[I]f we are to preserve a united Canadian Nation, we will not, for a long time, be in a position to revert to the old policy of laissez faire, and leave the haphazard enforcement of federal laws to Provincial and Municipal authorities." He would be willing to accept, Cahan closed, leadership of such a branch temporarily should the call come.[36] The call from the Cabinet came immediately. Cahan took office, in October 1918, as director of public safety, "with a view to perfecting an organisation that would enable your Government to control, if not extirpate, the enemy and revolutionary propaganda now being carried on throughout Canada."[37] He assumed the full magnitude of his powers three months later.

Having taken office, however – and now having the interests of a burgeoning bureaucracy to defend – Cahan appeared to believe that he had previously understated the danger considerably. The greatest threat to Canada, he now considered, was not so easily dealt with. As in 1914, the most aggressively political were British Canadians – often recent arrivals from the United States or the United Kingdom – and simple repression might be dangerous here. These provided the leadership of the IWW, the strike leaders, and much of the leadership of the radical labour parties. The newspaper *Red Flag* – in Cahan's view "the chief exponents of German propaganda throughout Canada ... [dedicated to] undermin[ing], without restraint, the very foundation of our social, industrial and political system"[38] – appears to have been structured, from its foundation in January 1917, upon an ILP base and to have worked closely with Ramsay MacDonald, the notable British anti-war dissenter. The SDP – setting aside the previous police assessment that this group was essentially a tiny collection of cranks – was now denounced by Cahan as the party of Red Revolution, advocating submission to German might, subversion of constitutional Government, robbery of personal property, and the accomplishment of its avowed aim of sabotage and general strike.[39]

At its numerous meetings, "treason and sedition are openly advocated."[40] It would have to be suppressed as a "matter of self preservation."[41]

Not everyone in the government agreed with Cahan, although much of what he proposed was instituted. N.W. Rowell, a political heavyweight, thought that there was no existing threat that "justifies us in suppressing a recognised political labour party." A "policy of repression"

> is not only contrary to the public interests, but will alienate from the Government the support of the progressive elements of the community who, while out of sympathy with the programme of the Social Democratic Party, still insist on freedom of speech on social and economic questions.[42]

In any case, the *Ottawa Citizen* had recently defended the party – publishing a list of prominent social democrats in other countries. It was no new agitation: there had been an SDP in Canada for ten years. Previous Orders-in-Council, drafted by Senator Robertson, Ottawa's pocket labour man, had contained the expressed reservation that they did not apply to the SDP. Moreover, the war was almost over and tolerance was advisable.[43] When the organization was, in the end, suppressed (while he was away in the West), Rowell was very angry. A labour delegation had come to see him, he warned, and they were most unhappy at this turn of events. Many prominent trade unionists were members of the SDP. Taken as a group, trade unionists had played up marvellously well during the war, as we might well imagine, when we remember who they were. They should enjoy the same rights as any other Canadians. The wording of the restrictive Order had been so broad that it could be employed against any organization, Rowell considered, whether or not it was revolutionary or unpatriotic. The result, he prophesied, would be great unrest and resentment in Canadian labour.[44]

Cahan responded in a manner which must have struck a chord with the government, so consistent was his analysis with its worst fears, and this again is highly germane both to what had gone before and to what followed. There was another danger. Failure to take such measures against the disgruntled would be viewed in British Canada as permission to take matters into its own hands. Rowell could complain as he wished. Perhaps he was even right. The government could be as tolerant as it wanted, and congratulate itself on its forbearance. However, in default of a sufficiently vigorous government lead, British Canada would simply do the work for itself, as it had demonstrated an alarming willingness through 1918 to do. "I am afraid," Cahan wrote in January 1919,

> that the Government really hears only one voice, that of the English-speaking agitators; for English brains are directing this movement in Vancouver, Calgary, Winnipeg, Toronto, and Montreal; and they make their views known by procuring resolutions to be passed at public meetings all over the country. But the Conservative elements of the country, I do not mean conservative in any party sense, are thoroughly behind any Government that will enforce law and order; but they insist that revolution shall be declared unlawful and that the laws should be enforced.
>
> Unless the Government deals with the revolutionary phases of the propaganda, I am convinced that the conservative elements of the country will unite in a widespread political campaign against the Government, that will unite the property owning elements of the country in a program declaring in favour of the enforcement of law and the maintenance of order.[45]

Other leading lights of the state machine enthusiastically endorsed Cahan's conclusions, although they seem to have missed his ultimate argument that the government would have to increase repression if only to restrain "conservative elements." They also missed his rather astute assessment that the greatest actual dissenting threat, in 1918, was largely internal to British Canada. The chief censor, Colonel F.E. Chambers, "entirely agreed with the conclusions of Mr. Cahan." Censorship, he felt, should be maintained at least at until the negotiation of a peace.[46] "I am afraid," he informed his British opposite number, Brigadier Cockerill,

> that we are going to have rather a bad time in trying to handle Bolshevist propaganda and other material calculated to cause unrest during the period of reconstruction. One of the great difficulties we have to contend with arises from our unabsorbed elements, the alien mind whether German, Ukrainian, Yiddish, Scandinavian, Finnish etc., failing to grasp the significance of legislation, laws being regarded as something specially

devised to be broken or evaded provided sufficient pressure or misrepresentation can be brought into play.[47]

The acting chief commissioner of Dominion Police, A.J. Cawdron, appealed to the government to maintain its repressive apparatus as a method of allowing the police to deal with dangerous individuals at least until "Bolshevikism and radicalism [were] under proper subjection."[48] From Ottawa, the chief of General Staff, Major General Gwatkin, expressed himself as of the opinion that, while repression was no longer necessary to facilitate and safeguard military operations,

> there is a sense that the war is not over. The operations to assist the Russians to thrust out the murderous ruffians who with the aid of mercenary troops, under the name of Bolshevism are destroying Russia, continue. We have evidence in this Department that propaganda exists in favour of Bolshevism in this country, and that it is dangerous to social order. This, it is considered, should be kept in control, and a judicious press censorship allied, not to discourage ordinary political discussion, but to prevent inflaming of social hatred, still is needed.[49]

In May 1919, Borden told Cahan that while much of the apparatus would remain, the government was going to have to moderate its actions, since controls that could not be amply justified might force even moderate men to extremes.[50] Cahan's forebodings were soon justified. In British Canada, the war was not yet over.

With the end of the fighting overseas, the militia began to put its house in order against apprehended internal disorder. Commanders checked and rechecked the security of ammunition and weapons to ensure that functional military firearms could not be obtained by a mob.[51] The Canadian Corps was going to demobilize. That was obvious. A socially and politically reliable militia was the next order of business. Serious trouble was expected, but the army thought it had the answer. Major-General Ashton informed the General Officer Commanding No. 2 (Toronto) District in January 1919 that the postwar militia would have to take care at all levels to fill out its establishments with good men and set up reliable regimental reserves of returned men who were not willing to serve in the militia but who would answer a call *in extremis*. There should be no shortage of these, Ashton thought; particularly in the eventuality that they were required to contain a social-political challenge to existing Canadian society. Training should focus less on military skills than on developing *esprit de corps* and unit cohesion. Bayonet fighting, musketry, and machine-gun training were the ticket. At all costs the disaffected should be ruthlessly weeded out.[52] No district commander should have been blindsided by much of this. Ashton had sent out similar instruction two years previous, although it is doubtful that effective preparation had been possible then, as these instructions had come labelled "absolutely confidential," not to be discussed with anybody, even other officers or critical subordinates.[53]

Following Cahan's admonitions, the wartime police organization, directed to keeping tabs on Alien Enemies and apprehending MSA resisters, was dispersed, and a new one immediately created. Until 1919, the West was the responsibility of the RNWMP. East of the Lakehead was the responsibility of the Dominion Police. However, in November 1919, both organizations were amalgamated into the new Royal Canadian Mounted Police (RCMP).[54] The Secret Service Branch of the RNWMP had been formed earlier, in January 1919, and was subsequently rolled over into the RCMP Special Branch. The "mounties" were specifically designed to counter the "activities of agitators and [combat] the spreading of Bolsheviki and I.W.W. propaganda."[55] Soon the Special Branch had thirty-five secret agents and thirty detectives active in the most dangerous centres of disaffection: Winnipeg, Edmonton, Calgary, Vancouver, and Victoria.[56] Other police organizations were also engaged in the domestic spy game. When places were identified into which the police could not lawfully, or effectively, intrude, they hired experts. The Dominion Police, the superintendents of provincial police and of city forces, the Immigration Department, and the CPR Department of Investigation were all agreed that it was desirable, where available, to hire private operatives "with the inside track" to penetrate dangerous organizations, locate their headquarters, and identify their leadership.[57] Some of these operatives appear to have been of the traditional "Pinkerton man" variety – indeed, actual Pinkerton men had been on the payroll for some time, patrolling US cities for signs of cross-border conspiracy.[58] Others were drawn from the target communities themselves. The revived gendarmerie informed local authorities that they were ready to provide force should any disturbance get out of hand.

The Militia Department, now strengthened and given an internal role against apprehended rebellion, conducted surveillance as well. The Immigration Department likewise had a highly effective secret apparatus, particularly in Vancouver.[59] Even manufacturers spied on their workers and on the communities in which they were sited. Many, like the government, hired detectives. In any case, from 1918, when any employer believed that conditions warranted it, special agents could be placed in their establishments. Meanwhile, at the front, surveillance of potentially disaffected soldiers was instituted and a mechanism created by which intelligence could be collated and shared. "Every man born an alien or of alien stock now in camp," the army directed, "should be listed and carefully investigated": "[t]he importance of this [could] not be overestimated."[60] Intelligence from all these sources was widely shared. Detective Wallace, a policeman of great seniority, experienced in undercover work, was recruited from the Toronto police department to operate a newly created national surveillance desk full time.[61] The entire police apparatus operated under Cahan's general supervision until his resignation.[62]

Surviving evidence suggests that many of the new special agents were members of target communities themselves. Many appear to have served in the Canadian army. Some expressed profoundly anti-socialist sentiments. Sergeant William Perelstoos of the 85th Battery CEF, working with No. 3 Casualty Clearing Company in Kingston, for example, called upon the RNWMP comptroller in April 1919 to elicit his assistance in getting employment as a special constable so that he could help combat Bolshevism in British Columbia.[63] The soldier in question was a Russian from Moscow, who spoke both Russian and German. He had graduated before the war from New York's Columbia University as a construction engineer. During his interview with the comptroller, Perelstroos demonstrated extreme loathing of Bolshevism. It appears that Lenin's men had liquidated his mother's family.[64] Another volunteer was a demobilized signaller. Although his father was French, his mother was Rumanian and he had been born in Rumania. Until 1918 he had lived in the United States, at which time he had enlisted in the CEF. He spoke fluent Russian, Ukrainian, German, Polish, Russian, Yiddish, and French. Could he enlist as a constable, he wondered? Was there secret anti-Bolshevik work that needed doing? Enlist him for a year, the comptroller advised, and see if he's any good ...[65] One of the most successful RNWMP secret agents was Detective Constable F.W. Zaneth (Zanetti). He was the scion of a family that had immigrated to Saskatchewan before the war. Disguised as Harry Blask, Zaneth successfully masqueraded as an American IWW organizer and infiltrated several significant labour organizations, including the Socialist Party and the IWW-inspired One Big Union (OBU) movement.[66] Another effective agent was Robert Gosden. His credentials as a potential revolutionary were excellent. He actually had been an IWW organizer and was a known OBU activist. He had, moreover, been an anti-conscription agitator who had served time as an MSA evader. Sometime in 1918 he appears to have been taken on the police payroll. For five dollars a day he worked as a labour spy reporting to RNWMP Lethbridge headquarters. Gosden was good at what he did – good enough to fool other policemen. He appears in police records both as a trusted agent and dangerous radical.[67]

If there were Canadian revolutionaries, they never had a chance. Already, by December 1918, police penetration of the local labour movement was sufficiently complete for the government to be receiving stenographed records of meetings of the Vancouver branch of the Socialist Party.[68] Many other radical organizations were infiltrated, with secret agents taking up positions of authority. The courts were disposed to support this activity. When infiltration of Vancouver radical organizations led to the arrest of fourteen leaders of the Russian Workers Union, it responded with a charge of perjury, since the evidence upon which successful prosecution depended had been obtained by undercover agents who had taken certain oaths before information had been disclosed to them. The courts, however, determined that nothing untoward had been done.[69]

All the sound and fury, at least officially, was directed towards defeating a perceived Bolshevik menace. There was, however, no Communist Party in Canada at this time, although through 1919 there were furtive attempts to found one. These efforts proved abortive due to police pressure and, it needs be added, to the lack of substantial interest in the bulk of the target audience. The first attempt in February 1919 simply led to the arrest of the emergent leadership – John Boychuk, Tom Bell, Mrs Florence Custance, and Mr and Mrs Everhardt – two of whom (Boychuk and Bell) were sentenced to prison under provision of the WMA, and one of whom (Mr Everhardt) was deported to Germany to become a member of the central committee there.[70] Ultimately, in the absence of any Canadian organization, the American Party was held to represent Canada at the Third International. Not until June 1921 was the first, secret meeting of the Communist Party held in a barn on Fred Farley's farm, near Guelph, Ontario.[71] Thereafter, the Canadian Party played in the conspiratorial minor leagues until 1929, when its leadership was once again rounded up altogether, and once again tried and convicted for sedition. The Party's problems were particularly acute because it had been thoroughly penetrated by both the RCMP and the Toronto

Metropolitan Police from the beginning. Indeed, as became apparent at the 1929 trial, one of the Party's leading lights, J. Leopold – a member since 1919 and the representative to a Moscow Comintern conference in 1924 – was an RCMP agent.[72]

While Canadian authorities were obviously unnerved by the prospect of Canadian "Bolsheviks," without ever obtaining much evidence that many existed, we should remember that 1919 was the year of a great Red Scare throughout the English-speaking world. Ottawa's response was far more subdued than that of London or Washington, the sources of the most hair-raising revelations. With frightening information arriving daily, with the Americans especially apprehending imminent Red rebellion, and with the leading members of the government in Europe, it seemed impossible that Canada could be immune. Moreover, new police organization and more thoroughgoing surveillance meant more, scarier, and thicker files altogether distributed more widely for the edification of concerned ministers.[73] It seems likely that greater access to information simply provided greater cause for fear.

In 1919, as during the war, it was difficult for Canadians to separate politics from community. As in 1918, fear of Bolshevism inflamed intercommunal hostility, as existing and endemic suspicion of communities viewed as apt to play host to this disease became acute. "Feelings intense against all Alien Enemies," Sir Thomas White, Borden's minister of finance and acting prime minister, cabled the absent PM:

> Consider whether stipulations necessary in peace treaty to permit as under legislation to deport after conclusion of peace Canadian residents of enemy nationality who have been here many years. Public opinion will force legislation ... There is great danger of outbreak against Alien Enemies in many part of Canada and the feeling growing daily.[74]

As was by now usual, action followed, if only so that the government could stay ahead of the impromptu activities of its most convinced supporters, although repression was never as thorough as White believed would ultimately be necessary. Most aliens were harassed, not deported. Deportation, after all, would have undone twenty years of patient effort just beginning to pay off in 1914. Although it was sometimes proposed – for example, by the Toronto Local Council of Women[75] – actual mass expulsion of undesirables was rejected as too expensive, given the scale of the "problem" in Canada.[76]

Alien Restriction Regulations (ARRs) remained in force through 1919, and in some particulars and places became even more restrictive than they had been during the war itself. By Order-in-Council, from February 1919, aliens deemed to be causing trouble could now be interned on the authority of a county judge. A writ was signed: the alien was interned. For those incarcerated there was no recourse – no right of appeal or counsel unless the judge permitted it.[77] In April 1919, the Immigration Act was amended to permit the government to arrest and deport anybody, naturalized or not, engaged in anarchistic or revolutionary activities – war powers, once again, consolidated into the permanent legal framework. Grounds for deportation now included advocating the overthrow of the government or "constituted law and authority" in Canada, a province, or any other constituent part of the Empire; creating or attempting to create riot or disorder by word or deed; belonging, or being thought to belong by common repute, to any secret society employing coercion or threats to control any portion of the Canadian population; and, broadly speaking, belonging to any seditious organization as defined by the government. Calling for the assassination of an official of any government was added to the list. This provision was aimed at Indian and Chinese nationalists.[78] In the case of an alien, membership at any time in any seditious or criminal organization since 1910 would be taken to be evidence of continued association, failing the production of evidence to the contrary. In the course of the Winnipeg General Strike, the Act was hurriedly amended once again to permit the expulsion of British malcontents as well. Now only the Canadian-born were safe ... from expulsion anyway.[79] Ultimately two hundred known "anarchists and revolutionaries" – these in addition, of course, to the interned incorrigible Alien Enemies – were deported under the revised ordinance. In total, about nineteen hundred New Canadians were shipped out, for one reason or another.[80]

Better still, the government thought, if more of the same were prevented from arriving in the first place. In June 1919, immigration regulations were revised in order to prohibit immigration by members of communities deemed "undesirable"

> owing to their particular customs, habits, modes of living and methods of holding property and because of their probable inability to become readily assimilated or to assume duties and responsibilities of Canadian citizenship within a reasonable time.[81]

The measure appears to have been aimed initially at the Hutterites. The Hutterites, of course, were not Bolsheviks, but they dressed strangely, refused to fight, owned land in common, and spoke some odd form of German. They were thoroughly disliked as a consequence. Germans, Ukrainians, Russians, and Finns were other categories of foreigners who might also be usefully denied entry to the Dominion, and they were for a time.

Some consideration, meanwhile, was given in Saskatchewan to restoring the franchise to those who had lost it under the Wartime Elections Act, but the proposal was defeated by what bode well to become massive, violent counteraction if the government were perceived to be insufficiently restrictive. If the provincial legislature had attempted this, James Calder – minister of immigration, and former provincial cabinet minister – warned, it would find itself surrounded in the Parliament buildings "by an army of many thousands in a very few days."[82] Continuation of some sort of exceptional repressive regime for aliens appears to have been considered as late as 1922.[83]

In fairness to the government of Canada, the Ukrainians at least did have their defenders. The minister of immigration was one. There had been serious riots throughout the West, Calder complained to Meighen in February 1919. "[T]he result is that today in Western Canada there are literally thousands of homes of which the members are sitting up at nights discussing their future in anxiety if not in terror." Particularly offensive in their actions were the veterans who, returning home, threatened confiscation of land. This would be a disaster. What would the Dominion do if land were not planted or if labour were withdrawn? The government, he protested

> ought to show towards them the same scrupulous care and generosity as is incumbent upon trustees. It would be not only a source of national disgrace, but an economic calamity of the first order, if the temporary passions aroused by the war are allowed to send out of Canada a body of men and women who might become the most efficient and creditable members of our community and whose economic services cannot be dispensed with without serious consequences.

To argue, as White had, that expulsion might be necessary to prevent violence was to put the cart before the horse, Calder thought. The government would have to stop the anti-foreign agitation and educate the general population to be more tolerant if a calamity were to be avoided.[84] However, many wartime tensions took some time to dissipate, and probably would have lingered whatever education might have been provided.

The end of the war witnessed the worst rioting by Canadian soldiers overseas. There had been riots in Canada before deployment. Some soldiers had been involved in wartime affrays in the United Kingdom, and in France. With the war over, delayed demobilization sparked further incidents. The most famous occurred in January 1919 when rioting broke out among soldiers billeted at Kinmel Park in Wales, protesting delayed sailing times for return to Canada.[85] The army in England and the British courts were much less tolerant of indiscipline among Canadian soldiers than authorities back home. Justified or not, continuing violence encouraged imperial authorities to place this particular problem, as quickly as possible, back in the Dominion's hands. Violent men, a critical and wasting asset two months before, were no longer essential or in short supply. Canada's soldiers began to arrive home quickly thereafter.

The bulk of the soldiers arrived in the summer of 1919. The effects of the sudden end of the war and demobilization were as unevenly experienced across the country as the rest of the war had been. Communities that had contributed more soldiers, of course, experienced greater disruption as returned men attempted to pick up their lives, often in the process displacing those who had been living them meanwhile, sometimes forcibly. In smaller Quebec communities – ethnically homogenous, relatively disengaged from the war – the end of the conflict was the end of a bad dream. There were, of course, residual grievances, but there was no postwar disorder. In places like Calgary, heavily implicated in the war effort, ethnically diverse, and required to find places for fifteen thousand returned men,[86] the end of fighting in Europe oftentimes meant the intensification of trouble at home.

In Calgary and other Mariposas, the end of the war, the readjustment of workplaces that followed, and the presence of large numbers of returned men at loose ends – "looking for much and getting little" – might have produced a revolution. Some historians claim that it did. The great story of 1919, however, was less what happened than what did not. After a short period of unrest and social-political turbulence, confined to a few predictable localities, peace returned. This was less because causes for unrest disappeared than because returned men, disgruntled though they might have been, massively affiliated themselves with the authorities against perceived internal dissidents and

9.1. The boys come home. GWVA parade in Manitoba, June 1919. Picture courtesy of the Manitoba Archives.

thus expedited the process by which they were reabsorbed into civilian life. This produced less violence than it might have because those who were most angry and inclined to violence tended to blame less dangerous, more vulnerable scapegoats than "the government," "the rich," or "society in general," while the preponderance of force rested so completely on one side of the contention. James Eayrs is entirely correct in observing:

> Hostile as he [the returned man] might be toward big business, bossism and the officer class, his resentment of what were loosely described as "aliens" was far fiercer ... Whatever appeal Bolshevism might have had for the veterans was lost because of their hatred for those "aliens" ... suspected of being Bolshevik.[87]

The situation in Canada was not unique. G.L. Kristianson has argued that the obvious and virulent anti-Bolshevism of the Australian Returned Servicemen's League was part of its attempt to maintain and enhance the status of veterans within society. Most members were working men. They needed all the assistance they could get in readjusting to civilian life, within a disrupted economy. Returned men would get a better hearing, Australian veterans believed, if they were respectable, which in the context of the times meant "on the Government side of whichever barricades went up."[88] One must remember what British Canada was. It is likely that Canadian soldiers – predominantly the products of the earnest British Canadian working class – were motivated by the same consideration. Indeed they may have been incapable of any other sort of reaction to the social turbulence sometimes awaiting them at home in 1919. "If you are respectable, you will be respected" was a lesson well learned by members of the social groups that had produced the volunteers making up the great bulk of the Canadian Corps after 1914. The end result was that if there was an attempted revolution in 1919, it was a khaki not a red revolution. It was an attempt to turn the clock back to the halcyon days of the Canada of 1896 rather than to wind the hands forward. In the Canada of 1919, effective violence – violence that produced an appreciable effect – was almost entirely a prerogative of patriots, not dissenters.

The most serious disturbance in Canada, in the immediate aftermath of war, of course, was the Winnipeg General Strike. It was the most dangerous postwar clash between the authorities and those who looked for a basic change in Canadian society, led in the main by individuals who had been wartime dissenters.[89] We have already seen that Winnipeg was, by composition, one of the more war-inflammable cities in Canada – a centre of wartime strikes and riots. It is often asserted that Winnipeg veterans supported the general strike, and it is true that the allegiances of local veterans were not as easily stereotyped as elsewhere.[90] Indeed, before the strike began, the local GWVA supported the Jewish Revolutionary Socialists and the Women's Labour League in calling for a united front to defeat craft unionism and "combat united capital."[91] It is evidence of the social polarity characterizing Winnipeg that the position of local veterans was this uncertain, and that such an improbable combination was possible. Even in Winnipeg, however, it would be wrong to speak of an alliance between veterans and home front malcontents. During the strike itself, while some returned men were notable strikers, the veterans' movement generally quickly swung behind the forces of law and order. Veterans may not have been opposed to strikes in theory and they loathed "profiteers."[92] War-accentuated xenophobia, however, remained a powerful force. Most Winnipeg veterans plainly comprehended the 1919 strikes not as an attempt to produce a new order but as an attempted revolution by radical foreigners. It might be that profiteers opposed the strikers, but they were British profiteers to be dealt with when the time was right by British patriots. At present, alien Bolsheviks remained the first order of business. "The alien," declared F.W. Law of the GWVA in May 1919, "has been one of our first objects you might say, since the return of the men ... We are opposed to the alien and will be opposed to him until such time as he gets out of the country."[93]

The line veterans were inclined to take was indicated shortly after the first returned man arrived home, and has been established. Veterans were capable of acting on their own and needed no alliances, especially with slackers and foreigners. The purpose of the authorities was to maintain order. The purpose of the returned men was not restricted to this goal. They were quite willing to take extra-legal direct action in a way the authorities plainly found disconcerting against what they believed to be the ultimate source of disorder at home and the principal obstacle to their own re-establishment – the New Canadians in their midst. The returned soldiers' aim was to force their way back into the Canadian economy while restoring the Canadian society they had left, where possible improving it by correcting earlier mistakes – recent immigration policy, for example.

Even before the Winnipeg General Strike got underway, earlier incidents indicated which way the veterans were apt to go. On 26 January

1919, for example, a party of 1,500–2,000 Winnipeg GWVA men assembled in City Square to pre-empt a scheduled meeting of socialists, convened to commemorate the recently murdered Karl Leibknecht and Rosa Luxembourg. Those socialists apprehended in the neighbourhood were dragged into the square, "roughly handled," and made to kiss the Union flag.[94] The party then split into raiding columns that moved about the city destroying socialist establishments and businesses owned by New Canadians. Targets receiving special treatment were the Edelweiss Brewery, owned by a naturalized German, and the dry-goods store of the prominent local Jewish socialist Sam Blumenberg.[95] The next day, the veterans appear to have determined to visit all substantial employers in the city and cleanse them of New Canadian employees. These businesses were to be "raided and wrecked and the aliens employed thereat beaten up and chased out of town."[96] A column of ex-soldiers was, in fact, intercepted on the march. It intended to proceed to Swift's packing plant to throw out foreigners and put "white men" into employment there. City and Mounted Police refused to oppose the marchers. The raid was only prevented and the men dispersed when the mayor and Brigadier General H.D.B. Ketchen, the garrison commander, promised that if the men went home their demands would be met.[97] The return of order can only have been small comfort to the New Canadians subsequently discharged wholesale to satisfy the requirements of the veterans, although the employers were probably relieved.

While unrest escalated in Winnipeg through the spring, it became steadily apparent that a politically motivated strike could not be the government's only concern. The returned men continued to operate according to their own agenda, which was increasingly compounded with the reactionary policies of Winnipeg elites. In March 1919, the RNWMP informed the government that there were rumours that an American-style Citizens' Protective Association ("the Alien Enemy Investigation Board of Manitoba" – subsequently retitled the "Committee of 1000") was being formed in Winnipeg in order to organize "direct action" against leading socialists and foreigners.[98] The RNWMP was disconcerted and did not know what to do. While the organization was plainly "loyal," how could the existence of such a board be squared with previous Orders-in-Council promising tolerance of New Canadians for good behaviour? Should not this be construed as some sort of illegal conspiracy, in any case?[99] The federal government was appalled upon receiving this intelligence, and Meighen – the most prominent MP from Manitoba – warned his local supporters that this sort of vigilante

9.2. Winnipeg veterans attending an anti-Bolshevik, anti-alien rally. Picture courtesy of the Manitoba Archives.

activity was less forbidden than unnecessary. The government could still be counted upon to enforce the law. It had not lost its understanding of mathematics. "We have," he wrote,

> recently modified the restrictive laws that had been in effect by reason of war conditions but in doing so, we have been careful not to relax farther than the present semi-peace conditions require. I have not much of a belief myself in the efficiency of forbidding the preaching of political doctrines however foolish those doctrines may be. Any attempt however to stir up people to the use of force or to incite revolution is, of course, forbidden and will continue to be forbidden.[100]

Despite Meighen's assurances, the Winnipeg elite would not stand down. Since the government had not seen fit to heed his warnings, D.A. Ross warned, even in Meighen's own riding the English-speaking population was about to take matters into its own hands. The "returned soldiers are back and they are going to see that such a state of affairs [as prevailed in Winnipeg] is not continued." Ultimately they would also have their revenge on the government for its weakness. "I never thought," Ross continued,

> when working so hard that we would have such a spineless Government. I thought that we would have a Government that would do things, but instead of that we seem to have one which protects the disloyal and the Alien Enemies among us.

The Union government, he concluded, was finished. It would not elect a single man in Manitoba in the next election.[101]

On 15 May, local trade unions voted to strike in order to gain union recognition and wage raises. Very quickly, thirty-five thousand workers were in the streets. The initial intention was to stick to strictly non-violent means. The strikers well knew – as had wartime dissenters in Quebec – that, the mood in Canada being what it was, any serious trouble that could be set to their account would be. A crack-down would almost inevitably follow. As might be expected, however, even large-scale striking was too much for the Citizens' Vigilance Committee. Was not a general strike something like a revolution, in intention anyway? And were not the strikers, J.W. Dafoe (the Liberal editor of the *Manitoba Free Press*) thought – arriving at the same conclusion as the citizens of most of British Canada a year earlier – just a collection of "alien scum"?[102] The strike was obviously "engineered by the Reds." Most assuredly, the *Winnipeg Citizen* thought, this was no mere protest, but a revolution aiming at the establishment of Bolshevism in Canada.[103] If the strikers did not wish violence, that did not mean that there would not be any.

Whatever was intended, the local district commander, Brigadier Ketchen, believed that there were no grounds for concern. He informed the adjutant general the day the strike began that he would be capable of dealing with any eventuality. Local unrest, he thought, was unlikely to amount to much, unless a "bad outbreak" was produced by the dangerous, but defined, "element of socialist and bolsheviki tendencies" behind all the trouble.[104] And even so, he was confident of his ability to manage any possible threat. Certainly, the Permanent Force did not have much strength in the city (51 officers and 605 men were in barracks, many of them conscripts awaiting demobilization). It was true, as well, that the city police force would almost certainly go out on strike. It was unlikely, further, that the 22 RNWMP constables in town would be able to provide much security, especially as they were fully occupied registering aliens. There was no cause for dismay. Cooperation with the GWVA had done the trick. Its leaders had been to see Ketchen and had promised, with the army and navy veterans, to place at his disposal "any number" of returned soldiers required "for the purposes of maintaining the peace."[105] Veterans had filled out the ranks of the local active militia: 326 officers and 4,295 soldiers had been taken on strength. These men were reliable, with the possible exception of the 106th Winnipeg Light Infantry recruited on the troublesome north side (and not, in the event, called upon to produce volunteers for anti-strike action). Ketchen had at his disposal, as well, two full battalions of returned men informally organized by Lieutenant-Colonel H.F. Riley, ready to answer any call for "special service" should this be required. There was nothing to worry about, the garrison commander thought, whatever the strikers might attempt ultimately.[106]

Ketchen's confidence was well founded. During the strike, the militia provided daily support ranging from 54 officers and 409 soldiers to 74 officers and 1,039 men, with two companies of Riley's storm troopers always on stand-by. This was in addition to police preparations that included the employment of large numbers of returned men as auxiliaries.[107] When the strike broke out, the citizens' protective association and many of the returned men were drawn into still more auxiliary units operating with the militia, the police, and the RNWMP.[108] When the city police did indeed go out on strike, and were promptly discharged, the auxiliaries became the special police, who notoriously clashed repeatedly with strikers. Some thousands of veterans, ultimately, confronted thousands of disgruntled strikers. The different social and ethnic derivation of each was readily apparent to contemporaries.

On 21 June 1919, the *Manitoba Veteran* informed soldiers aligned against the strike that the movement as a whole was with them. J.O. Newton, vice president of the Winnipeg GWVA, advised that the strike was obviously the product of foreign, Bolshevik agitators in the pay of German agents, attempting to turn military defeat into an economic victory. It was mortifying to think that any man "who had fought for liberty and freedom overseas" would now link himself to a strike being conducted by and for aliens.[109] "All the returned soldiers I have interviewed," C.E. Crawford, chairman of the Strathclair Branch of the GWVA, informed readers, "are heartily in sympathy with the stand of the GWVA. We are keeping an eye on the foreigners in this district and will surely notify you if they show signs of organising in any way."[110]

Ultimately the Winnipeg General Strike collapsed in the face of effective police action, much of it involving returned soldiers. The most important strike leaders were arrested on 17 June – Robert Russell, William Ivens, John Queen, A.A. Heaps, R.E. Bray, and George Armstrong. Bolsheviks they were not, nor were they New Canadians. Armstrong was a native Canadian. The remainder had emigrated from the United Kingdom. R.J. Johns and William Pritchard, two other strike leaders, were arrested in Montreal and Calgary. Both of these men were Britons. All eight were charged with seditious conspiracy in that they had conspired to overthrow the state.[111] Shortly thereafter, Fred Dixon, the author of the strike bulletin, was arrested for seditious libel, as was ultimately J.S. Woodsworth.[112] On 21 June, the mayor of Winnipeg caused the Riot Act to be read to disperse an illegal march led by returned soldiers, gathered together to demand an explanation for the arrests from the minister of labour, Gideon Robertson, then in the city. When the marchers did not disperse they were confronted by mounted policemen and rank on rank of special police. A wild mêlée ensued in which dozens were wounded and two strikers were killed. Thirty-one strikers (all New Canadians) were arrested. That day is remembered in the history of the strike as "Bloody Sunday."[113] The strike collapsed three days later.[114] Shortly thereafter, the legislation amending the sedition provisions of the Criminal Code jetted through

9.3. Winnipeg special policemen. Picture courtesy of Glenbow Archives.

a thoroughly aroused Parliament: the first reading was on 27 June, the second reading on Dominion Day, and the third reading passed through Senate and was signed and sealed the next day.[115] Amendments to the Immigration Act moved even more quickly. Introduced on 6 June, day twenty-six of the strike, these passed all three readings in the House of Commons in twenty minutes, then flew through the Senate and received royal assent on the same day.[116]

The prosecutor for the ensuing trials, A.J. Andrews, was a celebrated local lawyer, ex-mayor, and personal friend of Arthur Meighen, then minister of the interior and the acting minister of justice. Andrews, who had also been a prominent member of the citizens' committee, was subsequently appointed "special agent" in Winnipeg by the Ministry of Justice, and as such he had planned the arrests.[117] A disinterested officer of the courts he was not. The presiding judge, Mr Justice Metcalfe of the Manitoba Court of King's Bench, was hardly unbiased and at the ensuing trial worked hard to ensure conviction.[118] All the accused were arraigned in November and denied bail. Russell was tried first, with the other accused held over until January 1920. Russell was selected to stand trial first primarily because of the quantity and quality of the subversive literature found in his possession. This made his conviction a simple matter, particularly given Chief Justice Perdue's decision, consistent with wartime regulation, that the fact that Russell owned this material would be taken to establish *prima facie* that "he knows their contents and has acted on them."[119] This material could be read into the record. Surely the members of the jury were the "sole judges" as to whether the accused had intended to produce a disturbance, but, Metcalfe charged, "speaking to you as the judge, if I were on the jury, there is much in that matter that I would find no difficulty in concluding was seditious." The charge quite plainly was "based on the premise that Russell's guilt was unquestionable." It was seditious on point of law. The only thing left for the jury to decide, really, was whether or not Russell had actually owned and therefore advocated the treachery under consideration.[120] The jury decided that he had. The rest followed naturally. Once Russell had been convicted, the conviction of the remainder on evidence held to imply conspiracy was an easy matter.

Seven of the eight strike leaders were subsequently found guilty. The ensuing appeals failed. The strike had been, Justice Cameron of the Manitoba Appeals Court found, "a bold attempt to usurp the powers of the duly constituted authorities and to force the public into submission through financial loss, starvation, want and by every possible means an autocratic junta deems advisable." Chief Justice Perdue concurred:

> What took place before the strike shews that the accused and his associate "Reds" aimed at ... revolution. The overthrow of the existing form of government in Canada and the introduction of a Socialist or Soviet rule in its place. This was to be accomplished by general strikes, force and terror and, if necessary by bloodshed.[121]

The defendants who were not Canadian citizens were deported under provision of the revised Immigration Act.[122] So ended the supposed revolution of 1919 in Winnipeg.

British Columbia as well was obviously severely disturbed after the war. In the spring, the situation appeared actually dangerous. The federal Cabinet appears to have considered revolution probable. "Council very much concerned over situation in British Columbia," Borden (then in Europe) was informed in April 1919.

> Bolshevism has made much progress among workers and soldiers there. We cannot get troops absolutely dependable in emergency and it will take a long time to establish old militia organisation. Plans are being laid for revolutionary movement which if temporarily successful would immediately bring about serious disturbances in Calgary and Winnipeg where Socialism is rampant. We think most desirable British Government should bring a Cruiser from China station to Victoria or Vancouver. The presence of such a ship and crew would have steadying influence. Situation is undoubtedly serious and getting out of hand by reason of propaganda from Seattle and workers and soldiers.[123]

The situation was so serious, Commissioner Perry of the Mounted Police warned, that the government might ultimately have to reconquer British Columbia.[124] Perry should have taken a page from Ketchen's book. The government need not have worried. Once again, veterans were the antidote.

Through 1918, as we have seen, and again in January 1919, veterans raided New Canadian and socialist establishments in Vancouver. So thorough was the damage inflicted by returned soldiers on the local socialist apparatus in Vancouver that effective socialist organization became impossible. In fact, it ceased to exist. Local leaders were reduced to requesting that no further literature be sent to them – particularly the newspaper *Red Flag*, which was indeed a red flag – since it only invited violent reaction. Also, since local socialists were without any place to meet and were unable to organize, distribution of propaganda was no longer possible.[125] This did not stop the government, however, from once again running to put itself in front, leading the troops where they wanted to go. The late war spike in WMA prosecutions in BC has already been noted and followed from this dynamic.

Meanwhile, police agents reported in March from Fernie that any talk of revolution in the British Columbia coal fields was simply nonsense because the rank and file miners were just not interested, and were, in any case, paralysed by fears of police reprisal should anything happen. Any inflammatory talk was simply an attempt to keep the foreign miners discontented and would disappear when normal conditions returned. Why? "Undoubtedly," one police agent considered,

> the ulterior motive behind this is, to have the miners ready to back up these leaders by creating trouble in the case of any eventuality, such as interference by the Great War Veterans etc., which might otherwise cause those same leaders to lose their soft and easy jobs.[126]

If that were indeed the intention, it failed. The returned men, operating with the owners, were more than up to any challenge in the BC coal fields.

In April 1919, throughout the region, mine owners combined with the GWVA to employ "mob rule and vigilante violence" to clear radicals out of the area. There had been previous incidents of this sort of activity. In 1915, for example, Fernie miners struck to force mine operators to purge the mines of foreign labour, as had miners throughout the Western coal district.[127] Now the returned men kicked out British radicals as well. In 1919, Joseph Naylor – an OBU organizer and convicted MSA resister, prominent on the veterans' list of radicals to be expelled from British Columbia – was chased out of Trail by a crowd of returned men. He later appears in police files attempting to get the OBU going in Cumberland, on Vancouver Island. He was run out of this town as well. In Cranbrook, Alexander Mackenzie, another labour radical, was mobbed. An attempt to organize a loggers' union – a perennial OBU focus – was broken up in May by veterans while police stood by, even when the vigilantes proceeded to wreck the hotel in which the loggers' meeting was taking place. The police watched as well while the veterans seized the union's receipt book and initiations funds and gave the OBU organizer two minutes to get out of town. George Stirling, an organizer for the Federated Labour Party, was ordered out of Nakesup and Silverton as an "undesirable." Tommy Roberts, the Silverton Miners' Union leader and an OBU supporter, was also chased out of town three times by rampaging veterans.[128]

A similar pattern is evident in other Mariposas. The Winnipeg General Strike produced sympathy strikes across the West, in Vancouver, Edmonton, Calgary, Saskatoon, and Brandon. By June, sixty thousand workers nationwide had taken to the streets.[129] Like Winnipeg, most of these places witnessed the alliance of returned men and local authorities to restore their version of order; indeed to wage a counter-offensive. Hamilton, Toronto, Calgary, Drumheller, Winnipeg, Port Arthur, Sudbury, and Halifax were all centres in which GWVA men assailed alien workers and what were thought to be their political parties.[130] In Kitchener, Ontario, rumours that some local Germans might be scheming to change the city's name back to Berlin produced a predictable response. William Daum Euler, a local MP and reportedly the ringleader, was dragged through the streets by returned men to Victoria Hall. He was publicly beaten when he refused to sing the national anthem and kiss the flag.[131] Arnop Bitzer, a city councillor, was similarly dragged from his house and thrown in a nearby lake. Other prominent local German Canadians were threatened.[132] Kitchener remained and remains Kitchener. Meanwhile, the RCMP responded with a nationwide series of raids, striking across the country at socialist organizations. By the end of the month, police action had bagged the most important labour leaders. They were tried in December for sedition. The Crown argued that the 1919 strikes were part of a grand revolutionary plan, directed to overthrowing the government. Local prosecution of dissenters continued apace, while the war emergency continued, as we have seen. Red revolution – if such had ever been anybody's intention – was stillborn.

Gradually, as the sense of emergency abated and the new decade arrived, the situation returned to something like prewar "normal." Dissidents remained discontented but restrained (and constrained when not). Patriots were disgruntled but prepared to accept that a tolerable first step towards re-establishment on their terms had been taken. The government withdrew from emergency powers as the times permitted. In December 1919, Ottawa announced that, with the war and postwar emergencies survived and with the signature of the peace at hand – the Treaty of Versailles was signed 11 January 1920 – all but a few wartime restrictions would be lifted. Only those few still necessary to the maintenance of public order would be retained, and, except where wartime departures had been grafted into legislated peacetime practice, all emergency powers would end at the end of the next parliamentary session, on 1 July 1920.[133] Prewar patterns began to re-emerge, even in those communities in which they had been forcibly re-established after the war. Canada returned to "normal," although animosities persisted, with perhaps better reason.

If wartime Canada had taken the first step towards the patriotic New Jerusalem, it did not take another. While the government had tapped British Canada's particular patriotism to wage the war, and had used the returned men to maintain order afterwards, its gratitude was neither freely given, long lasting, nor marked. The wartime patriots had prophesied a Union flag-draped red, white, and blue future. The government had promised no less. If only British Canada had the will to endure, this would be the sure reward. But, by 1920, it was becoming clear that this vision had been a delusion, and never an actual government policy. Canadian veterans, similarly, had hoped to have some significant say in the definition of postwar realities. They never became the powerful, permanent force in political life that, for example, their comrades in Australia were.

Part of the reason that the veterans' movement, in particular, never reached potential was that the government operated, through 1919, to ensure that it did not. The Borden government may have used the veterans. It may even have simulated concurrence with their program for a time. It was not friendly to any challenge to lawfully constituted authority and did not take kindly to anybody or any organization that contested its monopoly on the use of force. Better, it was thought, that veterans not join the postwar militia after all, despite their obvious and superior military credentials. Their hard-drinking, lawless, two-fisted ways would only repel the reliable, good citizens that the militia needed. Better even if the GWVA just went away. It was composed, Clifford Sifton considered, of the sort of useless drifters and grifters originating from the UK whom Canada had never really wanted and did not need now.[134] The veterans were going to be disappointed. In Canada, the fractured, demoralized veterans' movement gradually became just the Royal Canadian Legion. Best of all, the army advised, if the postwar army and militia included a powerful French Canadian component. Whatever they had done and not done during the war, French Canadians were not active in causing trouble afterward. Perhaps they did not much like going to Europe to fight Germans. Perhaps occasionally they had even been combative at home. They were, however, noticeably absent in fights with the police in 1919. A regular French Canadian infantry battalion, backed by a revived French Canadian militia, was added to the order of battle. These troops, the army's director of organization, Colonel J. Sutherland "Buster" Brown, considered, would be highly useful in maintaining order in other parts of Canada.[135] It is difficult to imagine that anybody in British Canada, in 1918, would have predicted this outcome.

There was, as well, a political price to pay for wartime shifts and excesses. Results in postwar provincial elections were not favourable to the government. In 1919, faced with a choice of "Liberal" or "Conservative," many British Canadians chose "neither." Certainly the Liberals had not played their part in the great crusade, but unquestionably, as well, the Conservatives had manipulated, deceived, and exploited their friends and supporters as well as their opponents. Farmers, of all varieties, seemed most inclined to punish the Tories. They did not quickly forgive the 1918 exemption betrayal. In postwar elections, "The United Farmers" thrust a third political force into what traditionally had been binary contests, the party actually forming governments in Ontario in 1919, in Alberta in 1921, and in Manitoba in 1922. Moreover, by the time of the first postwar national election, in December 1921, the Liberals had put their house in order. The Liberal leadership race divided the party exactly on the issue of who had and who had not stood with Laurier in 1917, with the Laurier loyalists (or more particularly Mackenzie King) winning the nomination. Meanwhile, Meighen's Tories, despite all the evidence to the contrary, continued to operate on the presumption that much of the wartime program could still be sold to postwar Canada. By 1921, however, wartime electoral innovations were gone. Prewar allegiances were re-emerging, wartime solidarities dissolving, and intercommunal cooperation reawakening quickly. One should remember, further, that Arthur Meighen was held personally responsible for many repressive wartime departures as solicitor general, then as minister of the interior, and as the chair and then as a member of the Censorship Committee. He was the man most closely associated in Canadian minds with the WMA, the MSA, the Wartime Elections Act, the Military Voters Act, the postwar crackdown on labour radicalism, and so on. He was too divisive a figure altogether to be very successful in the postwar world. To make things worse, for Conservatives and Unionists, Meighen had always made the Liberals feel like "a class of not very bright pupils."[136] He made many Canadians of all communities feel the same way. During the war, perhaps, when Canada wanted strong, decisive leadership, feeling "not very bright" was permissible if the correct decisions were made and appropriate action taken. Postwar was a time for Mackenzie Kings, men who could unite by obfuscation rather than polarize with clarity. The indispensable man during the war, Meighen was not much use to his party in postwar Canada.

From a Tory perspective, the 1921 federal election was a debacle. The Liberals won the most seats nationally and carried Quebec handsomely, with remarkable strength in Ontario and the Maritimes. The real news, however, was the collapse of the wartime coalition between Conservatives and conscriptionist Liberals. Unionist Liberals either returned to the Grit fold, or more generally, in the West and British Canadian rural ridings, moved into more full-blooded opposition, following Borden's minister of agriculture, Tommy Crerar, into the new Progressive Party. In 1921, this new party swept the West, taking all but two seats in Manitoba, Saskatchewan, and Alberta, and picked up nearly a third of the seats in Ontario. In the end, the Conservatives ran third nationally.[137] Toryism truly never recovered thereafter. The Conservative Party re-emerged, and occasionally demonstrated strength, even from time to time forming a government. It was no longer, however, Borden's party, which, it seemed, had become an unexpected casualty of the war. The affiliation of New Canadians and French Canada with the federal Liberal Party for most of the remainder of the twentieth century was one of the most basic political facts in postwar Canadian national life.

The problem of the Conservative Party was essentially the problem of British Canada. British Canada may have dominated Canada during the war. It was demographically too weak to maintain political control during the peace, when votes trumped fists most times. It needed allies from other communities. It did not find them, since the possibility of cooperation had been sacrificed to a vision of a future Canada that did not materialize. Even had that not been the case, the purposefulness and awesome cohesion that had won wartime battles and allowed British Canada to dominate the home front during the war did not last. Intracommunal divisions re-emerged, as the results of postwar provincial and federal elections eloquently testify. The patriotic social-political *ralliement* which had characterized the war period was co-opted in its elements or simply faded away. Happily, nowhere did wartime patriotic political mobilization go feral, as similar phenomena did in parts of

Europe or in the United States, where wartime vigilantism metastasized quickly into fascism or the invisible empire of the revived Ku Klux Klan.

There were greater realities. The increased immigration from the United Kingdom that British Canada's leaders had promised during the war never happened. Perhaps those who might have come had died in the war. Immigration patterns shifted. It was New Canada which grew by leaps and bounds, ever more diverse. New Canada was absorbed, and it absorbed in turn. The possibility of imperial federation (the great, emotive vision of 1917) faded, and the Commonwealth emerged instead. It revealed itself very quickly to be a feeble and uninspiring successor. The New Jerusalem imagined and promised during the war was plainly not going to descend anytime soon, however heroic some immediately postwar attempts to winch it down might have been. Organizations that had promised a postwar, Union-flag-draped paradise faded with the promise. Some, the Orange Order for example, almost failed entirely. The type of militant Canadian patriotism they had worked to inculcate – a very British Canadian garrison, watchful and armed against threats, active within a living and powerful Empire – foundered with them. Little by little and then with a rush British Canada became simply anglophone – a linguistic reality encompassing members of many communities, most of them not ethnically British at all, some not Christian, more still not Protestant. In the end, British Canada had destroyed itself by its activities in the Great War.

In the first postwar decades there was an effort to memorialize – even mythologize – the war as a great, heroic, and necessary national endeavour.[138] This process ultimately involved forgetting a few inconvenient facts and rough passages at home, particularly as a unified Canadian nationalism began to emerge. Different mythologies, quite simply, require different myths. "British Canada's great crusade to save Christian civilization" became "Canada's baptism by fire." Soldiers, most of whom rejected violently the notion of Canada as a mosaic of communities, were ultimately conceived as paragons of this ideal. Eventually most details about the war were just forgotten, the good with the bad – awkward reminders of other times, and another Canada.

Conclusion

When detriments and benefits resulting from the use of that [emergency] power are balanced one against the other, it appears that the course of action adopted by the Borden Government was both necessary and beneficial to the system it threatened most.[1]

In Britain, a considerable degree of tolerance of wartime dissent was possible because dissenters were dispersed and a minority everywhere. Regulation specific to the war was about all that was necessary to ensure that they never mobilized an effective movement. In the United States, the Great War never reached the levels of totality (and therefore never produced the same level of polarization) that it did in the other English-speaking democracies. No truly exceptionally repressive measures were necessary. In addition, an inhibited constitutional framework made the imposition of a regulatory regime difficult. American emergency measures speak more to passing hysteria than requirement. Both America and Britain concluded that it was best if repression occurred mainly out of doors and was left to enthusiastic volunteers who could thereafter be repudiated. In Canada, the situation was much more difficult. Canada did fight a total war. Patriots were not a self-evident and confident majority, but in general were members of a set of communities embattled abroad, embattled at home, and increasingly frantic. The government had to tread a fine line, urgently.

Maximizing the effectiveness of the Canadian war effort remained the single most important goal throughout. This meant, as elsewhere, that methods of managing dissent were not optional, and had to be those best calculated to answer the challenge of the particular type of anti-war dissent emerging in Canada. In Canada, dissent was powerful but also geographically and communally concentrated. Canadians were hot or cold – increasingly, as the war went on, "for" and totally engaged in the great crusade, or disinterested or even opposed and disassociated. The major factor determining whether a particular Canadian was "for" or "against" the war was communal identity; albeit that even in 1914 identity was very often a matter of choice, not birth. What was not really a choice by 1916 was the requirement that a Canadian decide who he was and then where he stood, usually in that order.

The generalization British Canada "for," French Canada "against," and New Canada necessarily disengaged from the war, except insofar as its labour could be exploited, is far more true than might be imagined today. This was the critical characteristic of Canada's Great War dissent, and thereafter the decisive consideration in making for the particular characteristics of the repressive regime that emerged.

The heartland of British Canada extended from Ontario west to the Rockies. British Columbia and the Maritimes shared many of the characteristics of this heartland. In 1914, Regina or Brandon was very like Guelph or St Thomas, quite plainly, in most respects. In the course of the previous half-century, British Canada had become more self-consciously British and "imperial" than it had been at Confederation. Canadian politics in the decade before the war amply attests to this fact. Here, from 1915, the Great War was accepted as nothing less than a crusade. British Canada was by any measure the motor of the Canadian war effort. The reaction to the onset of war in French Canada, centred on Quebec, was more nuanced. French Canadians certainly appreciated the justice of the Allied cause and were prepared to do what was prudent, but they were always able to distinguish between Allied and Canadian interest. In aggregate, their engagement was always less complete and, for British Canada, unsatisfactory. New Canada was constituted by members of an enormous variety of other communities understood then as not native to the country. Most had arrived relatively recently. Many were Alien Enemies. It would be impossible to generalize concerning the reaction of New Canadians to the war, so various was this grouping. Some seem to have believed that the war might provide an opportunity to make a more secure place by obvious, open affiliation with the great cause. Some members of other communities appear to have been disengaged altogether. Some, hardly surprisingly, sympathized more with the cause of the land of their birth than their nation of temporary residence. British and French Canada, however, did not clearly see this diversity. Especially in British Canada, as the war progressed, all New Canadians were increasingly lumped together as part of a problem ripe for solution. It is not surprising that, as the war reached levels of greater totality and as its impacts were differentially experienced, significant intercommunal squabbling emerged. British Canada had inadvertently, but obviously, passed the point of no return by 1916. It grew increasingly frenzied, demanding that an all-out effort be made and that members of other communities do their duty. French Canada, always tentatively engaged, steadily withdrew into dissent. It was sufficiently confident, concentrated, and powerful that it was not only difficult to compel, but difficult, in fact, to restrain from launching counter-attacks. New Canada, diverse, dispersed, and socially vulnerable, provided provocation and individual targets. The Borden government, like all wartime governments, had to do what was necessary to maximize effectiveness in the war, and part of this involved the management of dissent. Like all others, as well, it had to satisfy patriots that it was doing what needed to be done. Alas, the mathematics of this equation were terribly difficult. Management of dissent was never easy, and each measure was the product of a complicated calculation.

There was no obviously correct or easy answer. More coercive policies might well have permanently estranged some communities from the emerging nation. This would have been fatal to the maturation of the country, particularly if French Canada were encouraged to turn its back on Canada generally. On the other hand, more tolerant policies, or attempts to regulate the thing away, would almost certainly have produced de facto local environments in which supporters of the war did what they conceived to be necessary regardless of what the government might have preferred. Throughout the Great War, in many locales British Canadian patriots demonstrated considerable willingness to force compliance on less convinced members of other communities. A policy of toleration therefore was apt to misfire very badly as British Canada took up what it considered to be the government's proper work. The "slacker" or "alien" communities it would certainly target, however, were not vulnerable minorities, peripheral to the nation as in the United States or Britain. Vigilante action would be, quite plainly, the precursor to profound civil disturbance with powerful implications for the future, as Cahan, for one, realized. Borden's nightmare, of course, was a Laurier victory in the election of 1917 – a contest fought directly on the most provocative item of war management, conscription – an eventuality which, Borden was certain, would produce something like civil war either during the Great War or after it when "the boys came home."[2] Borden was probably right to be afraid.

In Great War Canada, management of dissent meant, therefore, not only containing dissent in the interest of maximizing the war effort as it did for Lloyd George or Woodrow Wilson. It also meant taking sufficiently open repressive action against perceived dissidents to satisfy the war's militant supporters that they would not have to assume this responsibility for themselves. Lloyd George could tolerate, use, and even encourage patriot violence against dissenters in Britain. In the United States, the demonstrated willingness of "patriots" to employ vigilante methods against opponents allowed the government of the Republic to pretend that nothing untoward was happening – nothing done to violate the constitution permanently. In both Britain and the United States, where this was insufficient, regulation could fill the gaps. The Borden government, on the other hand, was required to be more openly ruthless in some sectors of national life than the emergency probably warranted if domestic peace and Canada's future as a nation were to be safeguarded. Aroused patriots, while certainly noisily present and occasionally active, could not be permitted to do this work. Regulation, plainly, would not be an adequate preventative. The management of dissent had to be painfully negotiated item by item, line by line, day by day, Mariposa by Mariposa. Some forms of obvious repression, however, were not an option. Similarly, the minimum level of repression necessary would not be established by perception of what was actually required to restrain a threat, but what was necessary to minimize disruption at home. The target audience, very often, were patriots to be satisfied rather than dissidents to be compelled.

Some of this work the government did enthusiastically and with a heavy hand; some tentatively and with a heavy heart. As has been demonstrated, Canada was particularly disposed to effectively criminalize anti-war expression, in large measure in an effort to reduce perceived provocation. Here Canadian practice was uniquely extreme among kindred countries. Canada's provision for wartime censorship, especially, was much like its arrangements for dealing with peacetime sedition. Both were unusually ruthless. Censorship was, of course, only part of a complex system because most elements of Canadian war management accounted for the probability that they would face opposition and were designed with this in mind. Aliens, it is obvious, could not always be expected to demonstrate loyalty or even to just lie low, and they were most mercilessly regulated when most freely expressive of their misgivings. The government simply did not need British Canadians to become more excited, or to fixate more firmly on any internal enemy. Nor, for that matter, did Ottawa need them to provoke other groups, for example by giving free rein to nativist tendencies which might well set New Canadians scurrying, thus undermining decades of patient government policy. Best therefore if British Canadians keep quiet too. By 1918, similarly, if the government appears to have concluded that dissidents in Quebec had best shut up about conscription, then it had also arrived at the notion that it would be a good idea for Canadians generally to keep their thoughts about Quebec (and one another) to themselves. In Great War Canada, if you did not have something nice to say about the war or another species of Canadian, then it was truly wise to keep quiet altogether. In enforced silence, perhaps, sufficient consensus might be preserved to see the war through.

The government of Canada also adopted an unusually punitive conscription regime, albeit introduced late and never truly effective on a national level. Nonetheless, conscription in Canada was more thoroughgoing and allowed fewer boltholes for opponents than that produced by the "total war" Lloyd George government in Britain. Canadian conscription was introduced, moreover, despite manifest evidence provided to the party then forming the government that the permanent alienation of Quebec and of rural Canada would probably follow. Let us set aside for a moment the fact that Borden appears to have judged that the Canadian Corps needed the men absolutely, as surely it did irrespective of what some of the folks at home might think, and that the government was probably disposed from the outset to do whatever was necessary to ensure compliance with the law. As we have seen, a relatively ruthless conscription regime was intended not only to get men or compel cooperation but also to convince British Canada that the government was acting appropriately, understood the importance of the issue, and did not need help in dealing with traitors, malcontents, and weak sisters during the war or afterward. Moreover, the government always had to account for the fact that many British Canadians considered the conflict, in part, as a trial of strength not simply with foreign enemies but also with French Canada and as a settling of accounts with New Canadians. "Victory" had domestic and foreign implications, and "victory" on the home front for the patriot constituency critical to the war had to be defined in suitably red, white, and blue terms. The use of compulsion to show French Canadians their duty as Britons while spreading the demographic burden of the war and perhaps the ultimate expulsion of New Canadians as dangerous – even repulsive – competitors were what much of British Canada truly desired. Rigorous conscription, censorship, and rather restrictive local regimes for Alien Enemies were what British Canada was offered, the minimum that it was prepared to accept and a portion of what it had announced itself cheerfully able to get with or without official sanction.

War management in Canada may not have been elegant, and it was certainly not edifying. It was, however, one of the many compromises required of the emerging country; inevitable if the war were to be seen through without profound wartime disruption on the home front. It is difficult to see how things could have been otherwise, Canada being what it then was.

It is probably worthwhile, however, to finish by examining more directly some of the patterns demonstrated here. While it is true that the government of Canada sometimes intended to act in a repressive manner, it is also true that it was generally dependent on local actors to give form to intention. The nature of Confederation ensured that while the federal government might make laws, it was largely up to the provinces and local authorities to enforce them. Since the war was interpreted so differently by different communities, very dissimilar local regimes emerged. British Canada, as defined here, quite plainly waged a more vigorous total war and produced a more ruthless Great War home front practice than that which existed in Quebec, or, to some extent, in the Maritimes and British Columbia. In British Canada, a failure to openly affiliate with a war effort envisioned as a great communal crusade could lead to drastic consequences both in and out of court; indeed much of the reason that the courts acted so vigorously in British Canada was to provide open, obvious demonstration that vigilante methods were not necessary. As during previous times of national stress and division, such as the crises of 1812, 1837, 1866, and 1885, it was hoped that it would be accepted as pointless to beat a dissident who was on his way to jail anyway. Besides, a legitimate trial was much more satisfying. Dissenters of all sorts here – and communal enemies most particularly – were repressed with gusto, and with evidence of great satisfaction. In Quebec, on the other hand, few local or provincial authorities were willing to take any coercive action relative to a wartime offence until murder had actually been done or rebellion was apprehended. The inconsistencies in wartime realties, in retrospect, are marvellous. In Ontario, a beating and prison awaited a man who failed to signal openly his support for the war effort. In Quebec, violent crowds paraded through the streets, inviting a response that seldom came. In British Canada, an MSA resister might well be chased through the streets by patriot mobs, inducted into the army whatever the nature of his objection, and despatched to Europe for detention as an incorrigibly disobedient soldier. On the other hand, the action of the MSA in Quebec cannot now be safely reconstructed. Most of the necessary records were destroyed exactly to ensure that this would be the case. It would be safe to say, however, that the MSA can have claimed few victims in Quebec from any community and that crime statistics testify eloquently that mandatory service appears to have meant, for most Quebec resisters, little more than a few months in the woods after the appeals mechanism had been exhausted, followed by a postwar fine of fifty dollars to clear the books. Indeed, the man most apt to be chased through the streets by an outraged mob was probably a federal policeman or soldier attempting to enforce the MSA. For most of the war, because law enforcement was a provincial and local responsibility, the federal government's intention was often effectively voided. It appears that British Canada drove the Borden government to adopt "win the war" policies, making mandatory the engagement of other less engaged communities. By 1916, these policies appear to have rendered still more rigorous a wartime regime in British Canada already remarkably stringent in most respects. Elsewhere, federal intention had little actual effect before the war ended, though this situation probably would have changed if the war had continued into 1919, given the federalization of law enforcement for some types of war crime. It is true that by 1916 in some locales Alien Enemies had a very difficult time of it, and that all aliens in Great War British Canada were best advised to keep their thoughts on the war to themselves. It is also true that the Canadian government orchestrated the campaign against Alien Enemies with no relish, and that Canadian practice here was neither relatively harsh nor entirely incomprehensible given other imperatives: there were real threats; not all decisions were Canada's to make; greater formal tolerance might have invited greater real repression.

Some significant issues of chronology should also be noted, before we make an end. The late war spike in government repression of all kinds is remarkable, as is the fact that, in most respects but the levying of force and the fighting, the war at home continued for the duration of the war emergency. For the Great War, 1914–20 was the home front reality, and discussion which prematurely turns to the "postwar" risks making significant errors. It does not seem likely that wartime Canada actually experienced a crime wave starting in the latter months of 1916, even though the early war consensus – in Canada as elsewhere – collapsed in the aftermath of the Battle of the Somme, as Mariposa became aware what total war meant. There had always been dissenters and dissidents, and perhaps they were more inclined to express their misgivings in 1916, but an increase in anti-war activity or in the number of activists cannot alone account for the spike in formal repressive action. This much is obvious from what we have seen concerning the geographical distribution of "war crimes." It seems certain that more war crimes were registered in the latter war years because more things were criminalized in an attempt to constrain dissent, increasingly obnoxious to British Canada, and that laws made were being enforced with greater vigour. An increase in convictions, therefore, signifies amplified polarity rather than increased criminality. British Canada itself could not criminalize opposition to the war. For this, it looked to its agent, the Borden government. In default of a suitable government lead, however, it demonstrated through the latter war years a disquieting tendency to take matters into its own hands. Rightly or wrongly, from conviction and because it felt that it had no choice, therefore, the government repressed to avoid a situation in which it became a spectator watching passively while one community disciplined its rivals.

While we might be tempted to blame the government for its failure to enjoin or even enforce tolerance, it would, once again, be kind to remember that this was the Great War and the Borden government had few choices. While we might be disposed to condemn the intolerance of Great War British Canada, in particular, it would also be kind to remember that the burden of the Great War was not equitably shared, and that while British Canada was certainly inspired in part by prejudice and intolerance, not all of its motives were reprehensible, all of its fears groundless, or all its adversaries entirely innocent of similarly base motives. We might also consider that, whatever we might think of it, the cause for which British Canada fought appeared then to be both more critical and more fragile than is easily recognized today, the great crusade having become the mutilated peace, probable defeat giving way to actual victory, and the Dominion transmogrified into modern Canada. The cost of Great War victories is rather more easily borne by Canadians today than in 1917; the often unhappy consequences of victory more accurately assessed now than what seemed then to be the likely and bitter fruits of potential defeat.

Conclusion 253

The hysteria which gripped British Canada in the aftermath of the Battle of the Somme – increasing monthly with the bad news of the latter war years – and the siege mentality which appears to have been its principal symptom are ultimately responsible for much that occurred during the war and also for the continuance of wartime patterns after the shooting in France stopped. Appendix C seeks to juxtapose some of the more important developments on the home front against the context of the war overseas. When we consider the nature (the exceptional lethality, for example) and supposed implication of some of these events overseas, a loss of equanimity in a particularly engaged community is understandable. A feature of British Canada's hysteria was the way in which fighting front and home front issues amalgamated to the point where it was difficult for British Canadian crusaders to differentiate between the actual enemy without and the perceived enemy within, between fighting front and home front, crusaders abroad and crusaders at home. Enemy became quickly Alien Enemy, faded ultimately into New Canadian, and then into "foreigner." All must be dealt with necessarily if a purified Canada worthy of victory were to emerge from the testing. Through the latter war years, popular war aims were redefined and expanded. Victory in the crusade against Germany was now to be accompanied by the subordination – perhaps the expulsion – of the Alien Enemy resident within. French Canada, meanwhile, would be shown its duty and dragged if necessary into the red, white, and blue future. British Canada would also be purified. The holocaust at the front demanded no less. Dissidents would be expelled or re-educated when possible, quarantined when necessary. The thing would be glorious. It was also a chimera. Attempts to achieve the great vision were not without consequence during the war emergency, or after.

A principal actor in the latter war drama, unfolding both at the front and at home, was the Canadian army, hardly present here at all. The army had grown too large for British Canada alone to maintain. It played too important a part in a failing Allied war effort, while being too consequential altogether to be easily abandoned or neglected. It loomed glorious and terrifying in government calculations as in the perceptions of Great War Canadians. The fact that this army – massive relative to little Canada, and especially relative to its British Canadian primary parent – would one day come home was never forgotten. The boys would come home, and if there had been fiddling at home, there would be trouble. That was self-evident. The thought of a defeated army, coming home to a British Canada defeated itself in the contest at home – as for example, by a Laurier election victory – was terrible to contemplate, and a major factor in latter war decision making. Even a victorious army would not be easily demobilized and re-established. Considerable dislocation could be safely apprehended, and those portions of the population apt to be most seriously discommoded by re-establishment were easily imagined. In the end, the thing more or less settled itself along the lines previewed after 1916. The government gave British Canada some of what it had the communal power and will to take anyway. The members of the Canadian Corps, returning home, seemed generally to have re-established themselves in something like the lives they had left, with the active collaboration of British Canada, regardless of the consequences for those persons who had been living those lives for the duration. Whatever the political effects of the war might have been, the local social consequences were minimal. Communal action ensured that, at least at the local level, the Mariposa of 1920 looked in most respects very like the Mariposa of 1914. In some Mariposas considerable violence was involved, as, for example, in Western mining towns, in Vancouver, and in Winnipeg. Such violence, however, is best understood as it was conceived in the last years of the war emergency: as a restoration, as a khaki counter-revolution rather than anything else.

Perhaps the most astute criticism of Robert Borden's wartime leadership comes from his biographer Robert Brown. Certainly the prime minister was successful in mobilizing Canada's war potential. By this measure, Borden was a great leader. "Where his limitations were most evident," Brown continues,

> he turned to others to fill the gap. But a people so aroused can be dangerous to restrain and channel their enthusiasms, check the abuses of patriotism, the slander of minorities, the harassment of aliens and the exploitation of politically and economically powerless groups within society. In this second function Borden was less successful. In part it was a matter of timing, for the exercise of this second, restraining role became most important when the war crisis was at its worst ...[3]

In Brown's view, in effect, Borden allowed himself to be driven – to become the prisoner of one community frenetically energized by the war. If the criticism is fair, it is difficult to see how the thing could have played out otherwise, Canada being what it was "when the war crisis was at its worst."

Appendix A: Opinion and Punishment

Examples

- In 1915, Oscar Felton was convicted of Criminal Code sedition ("saying seditious words") for observing in an Okotoks, Alberta, barroom that he "would like to see the Germans come across the channel and wipe England off the map." His defence – that nobody he was speaking to was a British subject and therefore he could not be seducing them from their loyalty – was set aside. Resident aliens, the Alberta courts decided, owed their sovereign temporary loyalty in exchange for his protection.[1] The judgment in this case was the more far reaching in that the chief justice of the Alberta Supreme Court considered that the proof of Felton's seditious intent lay not in what he said – what he had enjoined anybody to do or think – but in the reaction which he must have known would follow. "In the present day of the great war," he considered,

    > When all our people are in a state of nervous tension, and intense feeling against the enemy due to the struggle in which we are engaged, words which, in ordinary times, would have no outward effect in creating disorder, cannot be used now without much greater danger, and such words as those in question would likewise not be likely to be used now unless with some intent to stir up trouble.[2]

    An interesting gloss, certainly, on the meaning of "intent." By this reading, it was now up to a judge and jury to determine if a particular expression of opinion was intended, by its nature, to produce

a "breach of the peace" not by what was advocated but because of violence with which the audience could be expected to respond.[3]
- In October 1915, an immigrant Englishman, Robert Wright, disrupted a Vancouver recruiting meeting with the claim that Canadian men should not enlist, since Britain was treating its prisoners of war as badly as was Germany. He was tried for sedition and sentenced to three months' imprisonment.[4]
- In 1916, Theophilus Nandzik, a Roman Catholic priest of German origin, resident in Saskatchewan and naturalized in 1911, was indicted for sedition. Corporal LePage, a parishioner and a new member of the 214th CEF, complained to RNWMP Constable Healey that the reverend was in the habit of advising members of his congregation not to enlist. It would be better, Nandzik had told a schoolteacher, if Canada had a German ruler. Statements were taken from other parishioners, and Privates Braconnier and LaRiviere confirmed LePage's story. Nandzik was arrested for seditious utterance.[5]
- In January 1916, John Reid, a Canadian socialist, made numerous seditious utterances while speaking before a meeting in Calgary. A police officer was in attendance. Canadians, Reid asserted, had no country. British soldiers cut the fingers from German dead. This was a capitalists' war of no interest to workmen. The presiding magistrate thought otherwise. Reid was sentenced to fifteen months' imprisonment, with hard labour, on each of three charges for sedition – nearly four years' hard labour, in total.[6]
- In 1916, George Cohen – who claimed to have been a German officer – was convicted of sedition for expressing publicly the same sort of sentiment.[7] His crime was the more interesting in that his seditious utterance had taken the form of an outburst heard by one other person, with whom he was not acquainted. This man was not a British subject. The Alberta courts, however, found that the facts of the case were sufficient to ensure conviction, if the jury were satisfied that Cohen's intent was seditious – perhaps his words might have weakened the loyalty of the listener; perhaps they would be repeated. Cohen went to jail.[8]
- Two Alberta farmers of German extraction were sentenced in the winter of 1916 to, respectively, fifteen months' imprisonment, and three months' imprisonment with a $2,000 fine, for saying that they hoped the Fatherland would be victorious.
- C. Clausen, on 3 August 1916, was charged with sedition for making several unwise statements in the presence of a plain-clothes

mounted policeman. He would shoot all Englishmen if he could. The more who died the better. Every ship carrying Canadians to England should sink. The Germans had been right to shoot Edith Cavell and to sink the *Lusitania*. If King George V were present, he, Clausen, would kill him with his own hands. He got no further. He had said enough, and was arrested. At his subsequent trial, Chief Justice Harvey of Alberta sentenced him to a $500 fine or one year in prison. Clausen's father, T. Clausen, had been fined for sedition a year previously for asserting, in the Windsor Hotel Barroom in Red River, that Germany was right and that the *Lusitania* had been fair game. Out of respect for his grey hairs, Mr Justice Simmons had sentenced him to a $50 fine, or fifty days with hard labour if he did not have the money.[9]

- W. Black, of North Battleford, was let off less easily, though again the presiding magistrate tempered the requirements of justice with respect for the aged and infirm. This man, the police report tells us, had used "disgraceful, infamous and indecent" language about the Canadian war effort, "particularly about the soldiers." Judge Newlands found him guilty, but let him off with a warning – one month's hard labour.[10]
- In 1916, J.L. Justus, a German American resident in Saskatchewan, was accused of making seditious statements. Constable Keene, operating undercover, observed Justus in an Elbow pool room. Among other things, Justus held Lord Kitchener up to ridicule and offered a bet at 2:1 odds that the Germans would take Verdun. At his subsequent trial, in Moose Jaw, Judge Ouseley, not amused, fined him $500 for seditious utterance (alas, he also would have lost his bet, had there been any takers).[11]
- A Regina native, Sam Farrer, was in the habit of talking wide. A plain-clothes policeman decided to see how wide. Farrer asserted to his audience in a pool room that England had never waged a just war; that Germany was justified; that England was mean and cowardly; that he would like to go to the US to volunteer for the German secret service; that he never sang "God Save the King" but "God Damn the King." He was immediately taken into custody. His sentence is not recorded, though we might suspect that the judge did not let him off lightly.[12]
- The unfortunately named William Kaiser came before a Guelph, Ontario, magistrate for saying that he would like to see the Union Jack torn in pieces, and that he would walk to Berlin in British

blood up to his knees to shake the Kaiser's hand. Kaiser was fined $19 – an oddly lenient sentence; perhaps the judge let him off easy since, as he was a hack driver, $19 must have been, in 1916, a lot of money.[13] Or, perhaps, the deal was the same as that struck with the "Russian," Albert Reices of Montreal. Reices was found guilty of sedition, in May 1918, for using disloyal language in referring to the royal family and stating that "if conscripted he would break up half the Battalion." He was fined $12 and court costs. He also asked leave to enlist in the CEF.[14]

- Alexander Stewart, a Walkerton, Ontario, farmer, pled guilty to sedition on 11 April 1917 – a crime, in the view of Chief Justice Sir Glenholme Falconbridge, presiding, "differ[ing] from treason only in that no overt act had been committed." Stewart's treachery consisted of expressing to the complainant, Mr Roland (unfortunately for Stewart, a man with two sons at the front), that "soldiers [were] a lot of bums and loafers." He would not permit, he vowed, any of his sons to enlist to fight for Britain.[15] Chief Justice Falconbridge was disposed to be merciful. Stewart was released on a bail of $2,000 plus costs.[16]
- Another Walkerton man, Moses Filsinger, the reeve of Carrick township, who, unfortunately for him, appears to have spoken with a heavy German accent, repeated to some Mildmay, Ontario, friends rumours what he had heard at an Ottawa farmers' convention. The Borden government, it appears, was shipping "women overseas for the men to use," and selling them in England "for $8 a piece, like little pigs." Seditious libel indeed – so, at least, considered the Reverend R. Perdue Walker. The justice system concurred.[17] Filsinger's bail was set at $500.[18]
- In September 1917, a naturalized American Swede, Alex Auer, was visiting some friends in Toronto. They appear to have called him a "German." He, meanwhile, was reading about conscription in the newspaper, and getting ever angrier. He responded by suggesting that real patriots should bomb all papers that wrote such garbage. He also suggested that if he were conscripted, he would consider himself a conquered enemy, and shoot the first and highest-ranking English officer he saw. Apprised that the highest officer was the King, he did not change his line. Although two witnesses said that Auer had not said any such thing, two were adamant that he had. The presiding magistrate initially thought that one year on a prison farm would teach Auer how to manage his anger. After a word from

the Crown attorney, however, the punishment was changed to two years' hard labour, perhaps to teach Auer patriotism.[19]
- On 11 July 1918, in Simcoe, Ontario, John Stuart was fined $25 and costs for "uttering statements detrimental to the national interest" (i.e., seditious libel). Stuart's crime was that he had "remarked lightly" to a returned man, George Wingrove, that personal interest, not patriotism, had taken him into the army. His consideration in enlisting, Stuart charged, was finding an easy way of getting the public to support his family. Justices of the peace throughout the country had received orders from the Ministry of Justice, the Toronto *Globe* reported, to take action against all "criticisms derogatory to the cause."[20]
- On 30 July 1918, Ashton Van Volkenburg, a Hamilton, Ontario, man working in a St Catharines munitions plant, was fined $100 plus costs in Magistrate's Court for saying that "he would like to see the company that would put him in khaki, [and] that he could shoot here as well as in France." Magistrate Campbell, in his summation, allowed that while the words were spoken in anger and did not promise or threaten anything, they "were akin to words which would be used by Bolshevik agents who were in the city, and that a dismissal of the charge would be an encouragement to those agents."[21]
- A Belleville, Ontario, farmer, Charles Hawkes, was found guilty of seditious utterance in March 1918. The crime, apparently, followed from a chance meeting between Mr Hawkes and one of his young workers with a soldier of the 248th Battalion. The soldier was attempting to get the young man to enlist. Words were exchanged. A writ was issued. Also arriving on the judge's bench, however, was a petition for clemency signed by every resident taxpayer of Candos township. Evidently Hawkes was a popular man. This did not save him.[22]
- In 1918, J.M. Lewis, a railway clerk *suspected* of being a Bolshevik, received a $2,000 fine and was sentenced to three years' imprisonment for distributing prohibited literature.[23] He was therefore, several times over, seditious by definition. In Britain for this crime he would have received a much smaller fine and been spared jail.[24]

Appendix B: "War Crimes" in Canada during the First World War

Table B.1. "War crimes" by province

PROVINCE →			PEI	NS	NB	PQ	ON	MN	SK	AL	BC	Total
CHARGE ↓												
1912												
Treason	# charged											0
Sedition	# charged											0
Militia Act	# convicted					8	4		2	3	7	24
	Disposal	Fine				8	4		1	2	4	19
		Committed							1	1		2
		Deferred									3	3
1913												
Treason	# charged											0
Sedition	# charged											0
Militia Act	# convicted						7	1	1		4	13
	Disposal	Fine					4	1	1		2	8
		Deferred					3				2	5
1914												
Treason	# charged						1					1
	# convicted						0					0

CHARGE ↓							
Sedition							
# charged					1		1
# convicted					1		1
Disposal Other					1		1
Militia Act							
# convicted			19			5	27
Disposal Fine			16			4	22
Committed			2		1		2
Deferred			1		1		3
1915							
Treason							
# charged			18		8		29
# convicted			9		5		15
Disposal Fine					1		1
< 1 year			3		3		6
> 1 year			1			1	1
2–5 years			1			1	1
5+ years			2				2
Other			2		1		4
Deferred							
Sedition							
# charged	2		2	6	7	4	14
# convicted			1	5	4	2	7
Disposal Fine				1			3
<1year					1		3
Other					1		1
Militia Act							
# convicted	3	14	41	4	1	2	74
Disposal Fine	1	3	37	3	1		48
Committed		6	2	1		1	11
Deferred	2	5	2			1	15
1916							
Treason							
# charged	1		8				8
# convicted			4				4
Disposal Other	1		4				4

(Continued)

Table B.1. (Continued)

CHARGE ↓	PROVINCE →		PEI	NS	NB	PQ	ON	MN	SK	AL	BC	Total
Sedition	# charged				1		5	1	12	25	5	50
	# convicted				1		2	1	6	18	3	31
	Disposal	Fine										10
		< 1 year										5
		> 1 year										5
		2–5 years										2
		Other										9
WMA	# charged					2	159	2	4	2		169
	# convicted					2	147	2	3	2		156
	Disposal	Fine										136
		< 1 year										8
		> 1 year										3
		2–5 years										1
		Life										1 ?
		Other										7
Militia Act	# convicted			31	20	161	395					725
	Disposal	Fine			7	7	36					50
		Committed		26	13	127	273					439
		Deferred		5		27	86					118
1917												
Treason	# charged			2	1					1		3
	# convicted			0	0					1		1
	Disposal	Other								1		1
Sedition	# charged						5	4	5	5	2	29
	# convicted						4	2	2	5	2	15
	Disposal	Fine					3	1				4
		< 1 year						1	1			2
		Other					1		1			2

CHARGE ↓											
WMA	# charged		2		16	3	2	7	4		34
	# convicted		2		16	3	0	7	3		31
	Disposal	Fine	1		14	2		7	3		27
		< 1 year			1	1					2
		Other	1		1						2
Militia Act	# charged		33	22	144	385	74	38	28	41	765
	# convicted		3	11	15	45	12	10	7	2	105
	Disposal	Fine	10	10	89	238	28	19	14	27	435
		Committed	20	1	40	102	34	9	7	12	225
		Deferred									
Alien Rest.	# charged					1,430	140	677	308	48	2,601
	# convicted				1	1,336	139	661	291	40	2,467
	Disposal	Fine				38		6	13	6	64
		Committed			1	56	1	7	1	2	70
		Deferred									
1918 Treason	# charged				1	3					4
	# convicted				1	3					4
	Disposal	< 1 year			1						1
		Other				3					3
Sedition	# charged			1	1	13	5	7		12	39
	# convicted			0	1	6	5	2		7	21
	Disposal	Fine			1	4	3			3	11
		< 1 year				1	1	1	1	1	4
		> 1 year					1			1	2
		Other				1		1		2	4

(*Continued*)

Table B.1. (Continued)

PROVINCE →			PEI	NS	NB	PQ	ON	MN	SK	AL	BC	Total
CHARGE ↓												
WMA	# charged			1	3		8	3	1		1	17
	# convicted			1	3		7	2	1		1	15
	Disposal	Fine		1	3		2		1			7
		< 1 year					3					3
		2–5 years						1			1	2
		5+ years					1	1				2
		Other					1					1
Militia Act	# convicted			66	6	23	1,894	252	509	383	578	3,711
	Disposal	Fine		14	2	7	888	86	422	237	219	1,873
		Committed		21	2	7	390	31	27	100	95	673
		Deferred		31	4	9	616	135	60	46	23	924
Alien Rest.	# convicted			15	1		1,466	58	792	377	122	2,832
	Disposal	Fine		11			1,414	58	784	387 ?	111	
		Committed		3	1		27		4	100 ?	8	
		Deferred		1			25		4	85 ?	3	
WMA (SP)	# convicted		1	15	17	85	1,086	77	297	241	755	2,582
	Disposal	Fine	1	11	13	67	908	58	269	179	418	1,924
		Committed		3	4	6	28	1	7	54	79	182
		Deferred		1		12	150	18	21	8	258	468
1919												
Treason	# charged					1						0
Sedition	# charged					0	5	4	13	4	10	37
	# convicted						2	1	9	2	5	19
	Disposal	Fine					1	1	7			9
		< 1 year							1			1
		> 1 year									1	1
		2–5 years										1
		Other					1		1			1
WMA	# charged									2	4	7
												0

CHARGE ↓										
Militia Act	# convicted	4	56	34	2,626	1,469	130	272	117	166	4,875
	Disposal Fine	2	30	32	2,354	1,062	89	233	99	89	3,990
	Committed	2	7		88	165	11	1	9	34	317
	Deferred		19	2	184	242	30	38	9	7	568
Alien Rest.	# charged		2			643	119	145	104	59	1,072
	# convicted Disposal Fine		1			618	119	142	101	51	1,032
	Committed					3		2	3	5	13
	Deferred		1			22		1		3	27
WMA (SP)	# convicted		33	13	12	592	39	226	142	150	1,207
	Disposal Fine	11	19	11	11	408	24	210	108	117	908
	Committed		2	1	1	29	6	7	8	7	60
	Deferred	2	12	2		155	9	9	26	26	239

1 Includes 2 from the Yukon Territory.

Table B.2. Total "war crimes" Canada

	Treason	Sedition	Militia Act	WMA	Alien R	WMA SP	Total
1912	0	0	19	0	0	0	19
1913	0	0	13	0	0	0	13
1914	0	1	27	0	0	0	28
1915	15	7	74	0	0	0	96
1916	4	31	725	156	0	0	916
1917	1	15	765	31	2,467	0	3,279
1918	4	21	3,713	15	2,832	2,582	9,167
1919	0	19	3,990	0	1,072	1,207	6,288
Total	24	94	9,326	202	6,371	3,789	19,806

Table B.3. Total "war crimes" by province

	PEI	NS	NB	PQ	ON	MN	SK	AL	BC	Total
1912	0	0	0	8	4	0	2	3	4	21
1913	0	0	0	0	7	1	1	0	2	11
1914	0	0	0	0	16	1	1	2	4	24
1915	0	2	14	14	60	6	9	6	4	115
1916	0	32	21	163	548	37	41	51	24	917
1917	0	35	22	161	1,822	216	724	345	921	4,246
1918	1	104	27	110	4,462	389	1,604	857	1,452	9,006
1919	15	91	58	2,639	2,706	289	663	365	380	7,206

Appendix C: Great War Timeline

Table C.1. Great War Timeline

Date	Censorship	Aliens	Manpower	Canadian event	External event
August **1914**	Militarization of telegraphs and cables, under direction LCol C.F. Hamilton. Postal censorship instituted, under direction Dr R.M. Coulter.	Declarations of tolerance from the federal government and provincial courts. Alien Enemies defined as those subjects of enemy states who have provided an indication of hostility. Internment of Alien Enemies begins, especially army reservists. Internees to be treated in accordance with the Geneva Convention. Most quickly paroled.		Passage of the War Measures Act. Government assumes effectively total power.	Outbreak of war.
September		Alien Enemies prohibited ownership of firearms and explosives.			
October					1st Contingent arrives in Britain.
November		*Re: Chamyrk*: Alien Enemies, even if naturalized, have no right to habeas corpus. Judgment confirmed in *R. v. Beranek*, *Re: Cimonian*, *Re: Gusetu*, and *Re: Herzefeld*.			

(Continued)

Table C.1. (Continued)

Date	Censorship	Aliens	Manpower	Canadian event	External event
December					1st Battle of Ypres. BEF destroyed.
January **1915**		Denaturalization and loss of legal rights by Alien Enemies, following decision of British courts.			2nd Division begins to arrive in England.
February					
March					
April		Joseph Snyder found guilty of "attempted treason" for trying to assist the flight of Alien Enemies. This finding was overturned on appeal.			2nd Battle of Ypres. 1st Canadian Division destroyed. Battle of Festubert.
May		Alien Enemies warned that celebration of the *Lusitania* sinking would constitute a demonstration of hostility.			
June	E.J. Chambers appointed "chief censor," to coordinate other efforts, and with special responsibility for published materials.	Acquittal of Emile and Uedwig Nerlich on a charge of conspiracy for attempting to assist the flight of a German army reservist.			
July		Alteration of Criminal Code provision for treason to include assisting Alien Enemies to leave the country. Twenty-four Canadians convicted in the course of the war.			

August		
September		Canadian Corps formed under command Gen Alderson. 3rd Division commences organization in France.
October		
November		
December	Kitchener court finds that Alien Enemies have "no rights whatsoever" for the duration. Not all Canadian courts concur.	
January **1916**		
February		
March		Battle of St Eloi.
April	Police ordered to enforce the Lemieux Act when faced with workplace dissent. Elements of Lemieux Act introduced by Order-in-Council and enforceable under WMA.	
May		LGen Byng becomes commander of the Canadian Corps. Battle of Mount Sorrel.

(*Continued*)

Table C.1. (Continued)

Date	Censorship	Aliens	Manpower	Canadian event	External event
June	Censorship committee established under the direction of Arthur Meighen. J.A. Fortier responsible for translation bureau.				
July			Canadian National Services League begins to agitate for national registration.		First Battle of the Somme begins.
August				Bonne Entente forms provincial committees	4th Division arrives in France. Canadians committed to the Somme.
September		Alien Enemy transients become subject to internment.	Canadian recruiting collapses. Compulsory registration fails.		
October				First national meeting of the Bonne Entente.	

November	Unconditional censorship of all Hearst publications. Communications with Hearst addresses severed.		Battle of the Somme burns out.
December			German peace note rejected. Unrestricted submarine warfare initiated. Lloyd George government takes power. Borden invited to attend an "Imperial War Cabinet" in Britain.
January **1917**	Publication of the consolidated censorship regulations.	Second national meeting of the Bonne Entente. Borden promises another 100,000 men for the Canada Corps, and to maintain 500,000 men in the field for the duration.	Borden in Britain and France.

(Continued)

Table C.1. (Continued)

Date	Censorship	Aliens	Manpower	Canadian event	External event
February		Chief commissioner for police authorized to prohibit Alien Enemies from living in any place, if he considers residence to be prejudicial to public safety.		Ontario Bonne Entente reorganized in support of conscription and in support of the Borden government. Bonne Entente restyled "win the war."	
March	Ness trial. John Ness imprisoned for 30 days, for "utterances against recruiting." He had failed to raise his hand at a recruiting event to signal his approval of the war.				First Russian Revolution.
April			Canada Corps loses 20,000 men in one month. 10,000 men a month needed to maintain the strength of the army. Borden returns from Europe and announces a conscriptionist policy.		First Battle of Arras (capture of Vimy Ridge, Lens, Hill 70). Entry of the United States to the war.

May	Mail between Canada and foreign addresses, exclusive of the US, becomes an imperial responsibility.	Conscription introduced to Parliament. Passports of Canadian men cancelled.	Mutinies in the French army.
June		Arrival of first military objectors in Britain, followed by their detention. Conscription endorsed by the most important Protestant denominations.	LGen Sir Arthur Currie becomes commander of the Canadian Corps. Third Battle of Ypres begins.
July	Canada refuses to censor mail with US addressees.	First large strike (construction workers) in Winnipeg. MSA passes third reading in the House of Commons.	Board of Wheat Supervisors created. Food controller appointed. Canadian grain crop expropriated and distributed centrally. Liberal Party effectively defunct as a national institution, following the defection of much of its British Canadian membership.

(Continued)

Table C.1. (Continued)

Date	Censorship	Aliens	Manpower	Canadian event	External event
August	C.J. Doherty, minister of justice, becomes chairman of the Censorship Board. Declared an offence to send anything out of Canada except through the mail.				
September	Seizure of *Sault Ste Marie Express*.				
October				Military Voters Act, 1917, passed Wartime Elections Act, 1917, passed. Union War Committee formed from splinter conscriptionist Liberals and Conservatives.	Canadian Corps committed to the Third Battle of Ypres.
November				National "Union" government formed.	Passchendaele village captured. Second Russian "October" or Bolshevik Revolution.

December		Ontario courts (following British precedent) find that open opposition to conscription is a crime.	1917 Conscription Election produces Unionist victory.	Italian army nearly collapses, following the disaster at Caporetto.
January **1918**	Suppression of newspapers characterized by Quebec nationalism or anti-imperial "nativist feeling" at the behest of the army.		Unity of the labour movement shatters. Sam Gompers in Canada.	
February	Efforts to destroy Jehovah's Witnesses commence.	"Slacker hunts" commence in major cities. Manpower survey ordered for all Canadian residents, male and female, over age sixteen.	First attempts to organize an apparatus for domestic propaganda (to counteract anticipated Bolshevik-inspired propaganda), with N.W. Rowell as director of public information.	
March	Five more papers suppressed for "nativist" agitation.	Canada-US "Slacker Treaty" comes into effect.	Crown assumes powers to requisition anything, in furtherance of the war effort. War Trade Board convened.	German final offensive commences on the old Somme Front. British V Army destroyed.

(Continued)

Table C.1. (Continued)

Date	Censorship	Aliens	Manpower	Canadian event	External event
April	Prohibition of publications in enemy languages without a licence from the solicitor general. Censorship prohibits almost any expression of opinion, liable to impact of the prosecution of the war, critical of elements of war management, or apt to produce disharmony at home. Censors warned to watch for "fanatical" political materials, particularly for IWW activity. Henri Bourassa withdraws from political agitation.		Cancellation of 70,000 MSA exemptions. Federalization of enforcement. Local military authorities permitted to take whatever steps are necessary to suppress disturbances arising out of the MSA, including suspension of civil procedure. Anti-idling regulation introduced by Order-in-Council. First conscientious objector (David Cooke, Jehovah's Witness) exhausts appeals process and is jailed.	Easter riots in Quebec City.	Germans attack in Flanders.

May	Publication of new censorship regulations. All media, existing and potential, now examined.		Opposition to the operation of the MSA in Quebec chronic. Worrisome strikes commence in the West. Almost a general strike in Winnipeg. Shipyard strikes throughout BC. Provincial authorities warned to start enforcing Canadian law relative to industrial relations.	Germans almost produce collapse of France.
June	All aliens required to register with police and compelled to carry a registration card at all times. Chief commissioner for police authorized to prohibit Alien Enemies from speaking in any public place, writing, or belonging to any organization, if deemed dangerous.	Transfer to the Dominion Police to the Militia Department to ensure unified enforcement of the MSA.		Germans attack the French. Second Battle of the Marne.

(Continued)

Table C.1. (Continued)

Date	Censorship	Aliens	Manpower	Canadian event	External event
July		Alien Enemy employees in Sydney, NS, warned that if they strike they will be interned.	Habeas Corpus Act declared suspended in consideration of MSA resisters by Order-in-Council and judgment of the Supreme Court.	Government announces "War Labour Policy": eight-hour day conceded, right to organize granted, unions legalized, living wage and equal pay accepted. All existing contracts extended until the end of the war. Strikes and lockouts prohibited.	
August		Railroad and shipping officials permitted to refuse transit to Alien Enemies, at discretion.		Death of Ginger Goodwin leads to large strikes in BC, suppressed by returned men. "Coal controller" appointed. Government directors of operations appointed for other critical industries. All authorized to militarize operation of, particularly, industries in unstable regions, if required.	The "Hundred Days" begin, with BEF attacking at Amiens on 8 August.

September	Offence to possess in any way materials published in an enemy language, without French or English translation provided. All civilian magistrates empowered to order search and seizure. Temperance agitation censored. Establishment of the "reverse onus" in consideration of censorship prosecutions, perfects connection to criminal sedition.	Native Indians become subject to operation of the MSA.	War Trade Board authorized to set quotas for critical production, particularly steel. Authorized also to expropriate any asset or premises. Commissioner of Dominion Police charged with enforcing statutes relative to industrial relations when, in his opinion, this was necessary. "Special officers" appointed throughout Canada to monitor labour unrest.
October	Michael Charitinoff, editor of *Rabotchy Norod*, sentenced to three years' imprisonment with fine for breach of censorship. Isaac Bainbridge arraigned for seditious libel. *Canadian Forward* seized for publication of materials in violation of censor. Jehovah's Witnesses, IWW, most socialist	Federal police directed to enforce anti-idling provisions.	Minister of justice authorized to control the movements of hostile labour agitators (socialists and IWW predominantly). C.H. Cahan charged with coordinating public safety.

(*Continued*)

Table C.1. (Continued)

Date	Censorship	Aliens	Manpower	Canadian event	External event
	organizations and publishers, anarchist organizations and publishers, and Chinese Nationalists unconditionally censored. Possession of materials held to constitute membership, seditious intention, and conspiracy.				
November				Any person inciting or participating in a strike subject to fine or imprisonment, and deemed to have enlisted.	Armistice on the Western Front.
December	William Barron tried and ultimately convicted of sedition despite the fact that his "anti-war statement" had been made after the end of hostilities.				
January 1919				C.H. Cahan becomes minister of public safety. Government begins propaganda efforts to establish a suitably anti-Bolshevik popular line.	Kimmel Park riot leads to expedited passage home for Canadian soldiers. Decision made *not* to send Canadians to Russia.

February			Guidelines for postwar militia make it clear that political and social reliability is most important. Secret Service Branch of RNWMP formed. In Winnipeg, raids by returned veterans on establishments employing New Canadians commence. First attempt to form a Canadian Communist Party broken up by police. Action by returned men in BC crushes radical movement.
February		Any judge can intern any alien.	
March			
April		Immigration Act amended to permit the expulsion of troublemakers, regardless of citizenship status.	
May	Section 98 of the revised Criminal Code imports into peacetime law the most important wartime provisions for restraint of expression.		34 Conscientious objectors still in prison. Winnipeg General Strike

(Continued)

Table C.1. (Continued)

Date	Censorship	Aliens	Manpower	Canadian event	External event
June	Raids, across the country, net most important labour radicals.	Immigration Act amended to permit prohibition of entry to targeted groups: Germans, Ukrainians, Russians, Finns, Hutterites.		Winnipeg General Strike collapses. Ringleaders arrested and tried. Sympathy strikes crushed by returned men, nationwide.	
July					
August					
September		847 incorrigibles still detained, pending ultimate expulsion.		Cahan resigns	
October					
November				RNWMP and Dominion Police unify as RCMP.	
December	Sedition trials for those held responsible for 1919 strikes.				
January **1920**					Treaty of Versailles signed. War emergency ends.

Notes

Introduction: Trouble in Mariposa

1 LAC Laurier Papers, vol. 715, reel C915, item 198584, King to Laurier, 21 November 1917.
2 I have written elsewhere about the British government's attempts to pre-empt, co-opt, and defeat the challenge of dissent in *Managing Domestic Dissent in First World War Britain* (London: Frank Cass, 2000).
3 We might think that an "Alien Enemy" would be anybody born in an enemy country or owing allegiance to an enemy government, or even somebody even who, in time of war, was found nationally obnoxious. Then as now this would be the commonly accepted definition, and the term will be used so here except where a closer definition is necessary. Legally, however, it was rather hard to be classified as an "Alien Enemy." The Canadian legal presumption was that residence implied loyalty. All residents of an enemy country were enemies *de jure*. For resident aliens, wherever born, a definite act of hostility was required to establish actual "enemy" identity; while a simple declaration of loyalty – "seeking the King's protection" – was sufficient to establish an alien as "friendly." There were Alien Enemies, in effect, and then there were actually hostile Alien Enemies. It should be noted, as well, that British subjects living in enemy nations were, from the perspective of the Common Law, Alien Enemies too.
4 Indeed, many British immigrants were intentionally directed to Canada by British organizations – the churches, the army, and fraternal, improving, and charitable societies – confident that these individuals would be welcomed, precisely because so many others drawn from the same pool had successfully preceded them across the Atlantic. It was

not unusual, for example, for immigrant farm labourers to arrive with testimonials from clergymen addressed to members of the flock who had made the voyage earlier, or for Irish Protestants to arrive with letters from the Loyal Orange Lodge testifying to their soundness, intended, of course, for delivery into the hands of a Canadian Orangeman.

5 Herbert Marx, in a comparison of emergency regulation in Britain, the United States, and Canada, observes this communality: "During wartime, people will put up with a myriad of restrictions that they would normally find unbearable. Most often, however, the ordinary citizen does not feel any acute pinch on his civil liberties – and few will criticize a curtailment of rights in wartime. The tendency is also to generally press for harsher and severer punishment of the wrong-doer." Herbert Marx, "The Emergency Power and Civil Liberties in Canada," *McGill Law Journal* 16 (1970): 73.

1. "They Exceed in Stringency Anything We Know Here"

1 LAC MG 30 C11, vol. 1, Report of Proceedings of the Convention of the "Win the War" Association, Held in the Arena, Toronto on Thursday and Friday, 2 and 3 August 1917. See also Ian Miller, *Our Glory and Our Grief: Torontonians and the Great War* (Toronto: University of Toronto Press, 2002), 140–1.

2 For a reminder that police statistics require refinement see Taylor Howard, "Forging the Job: A Crisis of 'Modernization' or Redundancy for the Police in England and Wales, 1900–39," *British Journal of Criminology* 39.1 (1999): 113–35; and "Rationing Crime: The Political Economy of Crime Statistics since the 1850s," *Economic History Review* 50.3 (August 1999): 569–90. There is a tendency especially, as well, to suggest that high crime figures indicate high criminality. Might they not, on the other hand, indicate an effective police force, and a vigorous judiciary? Canadian published criminal statistics, moreover, contain some obvious errors – places in which the math simply does not work – and, while aggregate numbers are available in the absence of court records, it is impossible to ascertain exactly what a particular malefactor was convicted for rather than the statute he was convicted under.

3 All figures derive from Canadian Sessional Papers, which in the period under consideration contained annual summaries of crime statistics, covering the previous judicial year (September–September).

4 There is a large and not always helpful literature concerning Canada's wartime treatment of Alien Enemies. Best are James R. Carruthers, "The

Great War and Canada's Alien Enemy Policy," *Queen's Law Journal* 4.1 (Summer 1978); and Donald Avery, *Dangerous Foreigners: European Immigrant Workers and Labour Radicalism in Canada 1896–1932* (Toronto: McClelland and Stewart, 1979).

5 David Carter, *Behind Canadian Barbed Wire: Alien, Refugee and Prisoner of War Camps in Canada, 1914–1946* (Calgary: Tumbleweed Press, 1980), 22.

6 In September 1918, there were 2,087 Alien Enemies interned. See Carruthers, "The Great War and Canada's Alien Enemy Policy," 74.

7 Ibid., 44. Curtis Cole, citing Sir William Otter's Report, has 3,138 enemy army reservists in Canada in 1914. Cole, "The War Measures Act, 1914: Aspects of the Emergency Limitation of Freedom of Speech and Personal Liberties in Canada, 1914–1919," MA thesis, University of Western Ontario, 1980, 70.

8 Carruthers, "The Great War and Canada's Alien Enemy Policy," 74. Otter suspected that Canada's cities were using the camps as a form of free "out of doors" relief. Cole, "The War Measures Act, 1914" 70.

9 J. Castell Hopkins, *The Canadian Annual Review of Public Affairs 1918* (Ottawa: Canadian Annual Review, 1919), 581.

10 *Re: Chamryk*, W.L.R., 14 November 1914, and *R. v. Beranek* (1915), 24 C.C.C. 252 (Ont. H.C.). See also Carruthers, "The Great War and Canada's Alien Enemy Policy," 83, and Patricia Peppin, "Emergency Legislation and Rights in Canada: The War Measures Act and Civil Liberties," *Queen's Law Journal* 18.1 (Spring 1993): 147.

11 Amy Shaw, *Crisis of Conscience: Conscientious Objection in Canada during the First World War* (Vancouver: University of British Columbia Press, 2009).

12 Desmond Morton, *When Your Number's Up* (Toronto: Random House, 1993), 68. For the operation of conscription in general, see Elizabeth Armstrong, *The Crisis of Quebec, 1914–1918* (1937; Montreal: McGill-Queen's University Press, 1974); *Conscription 1917*, ed. Ramsay Cook, Craig Brown, and Carl Berger (Toronto: University of Toronto Press, 1969); J. Granatstein and J.M. Hitsman, *Broken Promises: A History of Conscription in Canada* (Toronto: Oxford University Press, 1977); and A. Williams, "Conscription, 1917: A Brief for the Defence," *Canadian Historical Review* 27.4 (December 1956).

13 Military Services Act, 7–8 George V, assented 29 August 1917, Statutes of Canada.

14 For the federalization of enforcement, see PC 1305, 5 June 1918. For cancellation of exemptions, see LAC MG 26, H, Borden Papers, reel C4331, item 53570, 12 April 1918. See also item 53573, Newton to Borden,

286 Notes to pages 15–17

13 April 1918, and item 53574, Hume Cronyn to Borden, 13 April 1918, for background to the Order-in-Council. The Order-in-Council cancelling exemptions can be found at PC 919, 20 April 1918. See also Cole, "The War Measures Act, 1914," 94–5. See any period newspaper for "slacker hunts," "slacker sweeps," and the action of police and courts generally in enforcing the.
15 PC 1725, June 1917, appoints directors of coal operations in mining regions of British Columbia and Alberta. PC 2835, 6 October 1917, appoints a director of elevator operations in Fort William and Port Arthur. PC 1940, 5 August 1918, appoints a new controller with considerable powers over critical coal mines in the Canadian West.
16 PC 2299, 19 September 1918.
17 PC 2532, 17 October 1918.
18 PC 2786, 13 November 1918.
19 PC 2525, 11 October 1918. Repealed 19 November 1918 (PC 2461).
20 See B. Millman, *Managing Domestic Dissent in First World War Britain* (London: Frank Cass, 2000), especially chapter 7.
21 The Industrial Disputes Investigation Act (1907), popularly remembered as the Lemieux Act, made striking effectively illegal.
22 Canadian Great War censorship has not been well written. Jeffrey Keshen has done the best work, in *Propaganda and Censorship during Canada's Great War* (Edmonton: University of Alberta Press, 1996), in "All the News That Was Fit to Print: Ernest J. Chambers and Information Control in Canada, 1914–1919," *Canadian Historical Review* 73:3 (1992): 313–43; and in "The Great War Soldier as Nation Builder in Canada and Australia," in *Canada and the Great* War, ed. Briton C. Busch (Montreal and Kingston: McGill-Queen's University Press, 2003), 3–26, but his definition of "censorship" is too narrow to be of much use. Essentially, he focuses solely on state regulation designed to restrict expression of unacceptable opinion. Censorship, however, more broadly is the method by which the government seeks to silence opposition and therefore dominate public debate. Regulation is only one method which it might employ.
23 Some examples. For the Sault Saint Marie *Express*, see LAC RG 6, E, Records of the Chief Censor, Chambers to Cockerill, 30 September 1917. See also Cole, "The War Measures Act, 1914," 26. For Canadian *Forward*, see LAC MG 26, H, Borden Papers, reel C4334, item 56698, Public Safety Branch, 21 October 1918; and item 56703, Cahan to Doherty, 22 October 1918.
24 Case of John Ness. Toronto *Globe*, 17 March 1917, 8
25 Case of William Barron. Joseph Boudreau, "Western Canada's Alien Enemies in World War One,"*Alberta Historical Review* 12.1 (1964): 6. *R. v.*

Barron (1919), 12 Sask. L.R. 66 [1919] 1 W.W.R. 262, 30 C.C.C. 326, 44 D.L.R. 332 (C.A.); and *R. v. Barron*, 44 D.L.R. 332, 30 C.C.C. 326, 12 S.L.R. 66, [1919] 1 W.W.R. 262.

26 Case of Oscar Felton, *R. v. Felton*, 28 D.L.R. 372, 9 A.L.R. 238, 25 Can. Cr. Cas. 207, 33 W.L.R. 157, 9 W.W.R. 819. For Felton, see also Peter MacKinnon, "Conspiracy and Sedition as Canadian Political Crimes," *McGill Law Journal* 23 (1977): 625–6.

27 Case of J.M. Lewis. LAC RG 18, A2, Office of the Comptroller RCMP, letter book, comptroller to commissioner, 27 February 1919.

28 LAC RG 6, E, Records of the Chief Censor, under-secretary of state [Thomas Malvey] draft of the Consolidated Regulation, April 1917. Cable, radiotelegraphy, telegraph, telephone, written material, movies, photos, theatrical or musical performances, paintings, and "talking machine records" were all censored. The very broad scope of media indicated was exceptional among combatant nations. The 1917 regulations were further expanded in 1918, by which time a judicial system had developed by which most malefactors could be dealt with locally by competent authorities, directed to consider the censor's world as definitive on the question of whether something was permissible or not. Cole, "The War Measures Act, 1914," 126.

29 The books of the British temperance advocate Arthur Mee – *The Fiddlers* and *Defeat? The Betrayal of Britain* – were censored absolutely in Canada although passed by censor in Britain. When a Canadian, the Reverend Ben Spence, quoted Mee in an open letter to Lloyd George, he was arrested for breach of censorship. When Captain G.T. Bailey, a Canadian Corps medical officer, testified to the truth of some of the assertions contained in Spence's letter, he was arrested in court and ultimately sentenced to three months' imprisonment. J. Castell Hopkins, *The Canadian Annual Review of Public Affairs 1918* (Ottawa: Canadian Annual Review, 1919), 576.

30 For example, LAC RG 6, E, Records of the Chief Censor, Gwatkin to Chambers, 27 March 1918.

31 The 1918 attempts to break up the Jehovah's Witnesses (largely as anti-conscription advocates, but also as anti-British) are particularly enlightening. Once all literature produced by Witnesses' publishing houses was proscribed, the arrest of individual Witnesses would follow, since they now possessed prohibited literature. Arrest of leaders would produce lists of ordinary members (mailing lists, etc.) who could then be rounded up. If literature were not actually found, then in any case association with those already convicted could be taken to imply

conspiracy. Precedents were created very useful, for example, to the trial of the leaders of the 1919 Winnipeg General Strike.

32 By 1918, all Canadian magistrates were judged competent to determine if material found in an accused's possession were actionable, according to guidelines provided by the chief censor and contained in Orders-in-Council. Meanwhile, Canadian courts had already ruled that material specifically prohibited by Order-in-Council was legally objectionable by definition. If the chief censor said the thing was wrong, then it was wrong: "it matters not what it contains." Cole, "The War Measures Act, 1914," 126. Possessing prohibited material was the offence – rather than attempting to publicize or publish it – because this was held to indicate by definition the intention of propagandizing the treachery contained. In September 1918, by Order-in-Council, the "reverse onus" existing by precedent in sedition cases was applied to WMA censorship prosecutions (PC 2381, 25 September 1918). Essentially, once seditious intent could be inferred from content or context – even if this only meant that some prohibited literature had been found in somebody's possession – it was up to the accused to establish that they had not harboured any malignant intent. Association with a person held to be guilty of sedition could be taken as evidence of conspiracy. No other system went so far.

33 See, for example, *R. v. Oma* (1915), 8 Sask L.R. 395, 9 W.W.R. 584, 25 C.C.C. 73, 25 D.L.R. 670 (C.A.); *R. v. Shaefer* (1918), 28 Que. K.B. 35, 31 C.C.C. 22, leave to appeal to S.C.C. refused (1919), 58 S.C.R. 43, 45 D.L.R. 492); and *R. v. Snyder* (1915), 34. O.L.R. 318, 24 C.C.C. 101, 25 D.L.P. 1 (C.A.).

34 Legal writers have been fairly interested in the issue of sedition in Canada. Most, however, distinctly underestimate the relative frequency of such trials. For the most part, this is because they search for recorded trials and, where records do not exist, take this as evidence that no trials took place.

35 "Political Trial, in this sense, means simply that the Government is taking action to protect itself against perceived threats." MacKinnon, "Conspiracy and Sedition as Canadian Political Crimes," 622.

36 In 1916, for example, in Renfrew, Ontario, there were fifty-five WMA convictions, and in the same year, in the judicial district of Parry Sound, eighty. There were, in that same year, three in Saskatchewan, and two each in Quebec, Manitoba, and Alberta. The relative vigour with which the law was applied locally is obvious. Sessional Papers, vol. 52 (Session 1917), no. 9, "Criminal Statistics 1916."

37 How a sentence for life imprisonment was possible under the WMA is unknown, although an Essex County court is recorded as having called

for it. Sessional Papers, vol. 52 (Session 1917), no. 9, "Criminal Statistics 1916."

38 Amy Shaw, *Crisis of Conscience: Conscientious Objection in Canada during the First World War* (Vancouver: University of British Columbia Press, 2009), 150.

39 LAC RG 13, vol. 1370, Report of the Aliens Committee, 1 July 1917.

40 See HMSO, *Criminal Statistics England and Wales*, particularly the useful summary in *Criminal Statistics England and Wales, 1919* (London: HMSO, 1920), 6. Scottish and Irish statistics are catalogued separately.

41 For the extraordinary leniency shown John MacLean, "the icon" of the British revolutionary movement, see Robert Shiels, "The Criminal Trials of John MacLean," *Juridical Review* 5, part 1 (2001): 20. Bertrand Russell and E.D. Morel, officers of the dissenting General Staff, similarly, were astounded and embittered when HMG, at a desperate time in the war, went so far as to actually prosecute them for breach of postal censorship. See Millman, *Managing Domestic Dissent*, 188–9. In Canada they would have been in jail earlier and longer. Their literature would have been suppressed. Their organization would have been proscribed.

42 Paul Murphy, *World War One and the Origins of Civil Liberties in the United States* (New York: Norton, 1979); Zechariah Chafee, *Free Speech in the United States* (Cambridge, MA: Harvard University Press, 1920); and Robert Murray, *Red Scare: A Study in National Hysteria* (Minneapolis: University of Minnesota Press, 1955).

43 Geoffrey Stone, "Judge Learned Hand and the Espionage Act of 1917: A Mystery Unravelled," *University of Chicago Law Review* 70 (2003): 343n34. For examples of American vigilante action on the home front during the First World War, see Christopher Capozzola, "The Only Badge Necessary Is Your Patriotic Fervor: Vigilance, Patriotism and the Law in World War One America," *Journal of American History* 88.4 (2002): 1354–82; Robert Cherny, "Patterns of Toleration and Discrimination in San Francisco: The Civil War to World War One," *California History* 73.2 1994): 130–141; John Edwards, "Playing the Patriot Game: The Story of the American Defence Society 1915–1932," *Studies in History and Society* 1.1 (1976): 54–72; James Fowler, "Creating an Atmosphere of Suppression, 1914–1917," *Chronicles of Oklahoma* 59.2 (1981): 202–23; Matthew Good, "Obey the Law and Keep Your Mouth Shut: German Americans in Grand Rapids during World War One," *Michigan History* 78.2 (1994): 18–23; John Linquist, "The Jerome Deportations of 1917," *Arizona and the West* 11.3 (1969): 233–46; Seymour Lipset, "The Anatomy of the Klan," *Commentary* 40.4 (1965): 74–83; Hugh Lovin, "World War Vigilantes in Idaho, 1917–1918," *Idaho*

Yesterdays 18.3 (1978): 2–11; and Carlos Schwantes, "Making the World Unsafe for Democracy: Vigilantes, Grangers, and the Wala Wala Outrage of June, 1918," *Montana* 31.1 (1981): 18–29.
44 *Manchester Guardian*, April 1918, and subsequently republished widely in the Canadian press.
45 House of Commons Debates, vol. 133 (1918), 2513. Lemieux may have been particularly appalled by Canadian censorship, since, in his youth – prior to a legal education and his entry to politics – he had had been a journalist by trade, variously at *La Presse*, *Le Monde*, and *La Patrie*. William F. Swindler, "Wartime News Control in Canada," *Public Opinion Quarterly* 6.3 (Autumn 1942): 444–9.
46 For example, S.W. Horrall, "The Royal North West Mounted Police and Labour Unrest in Western Canada, 1919," *Canadian Historical Review* 61.2 (1980): 171–86.
47 See, for some recent contributions, Edward Bloustein, "Criminal Attempts and the 'Clear and Present Danger' Theory of the First Amendment," *Cornell Law Review* 74 (1988–9): 1118–50; and Stone, "Judge Learned Hand and the Espionage Act of 1917."
48 For example and for background, Carruthers, "The Great War and Canada's Alien Enemy Policy," 43–110; MacKinnon, "Conspiracy and Sedition as Canadian Political Crimes," 622–43; Kenneth McNaught, "Political Trials and the Canadian Political Tradition," *University of Toronto Law Journal* 24 (1974): 149–69; Herbert Marx, "The Emergency Power and Civil Liberties in Canada," *McGill Law Journal* 16 (1970): 39–91; Peppin, "Emergency Legislation and Rights in Canada"; David Smith, "Emergency Government in Canada," *Canadian Historical Review* 50.4 (December 1969): 435–48; and Barry Wright, "Sedition in Upper Canada: Contested Legality," *Labour* 29 (Spring 1992). For the Winnipeg General Strike and its legal aftermath, see Desmond Brown, "The Craftsmanship of Bias: Sedition and the Winnipeg General Strike," *Manitoba Law Journal* 14.1 (1984): 1–33; Barry Cahill, "Howe (1835), Dixon (1920) and McLachlan (1923): Comparative Perspectives on the Legal History of Sedition," *University of New Brunswick Law Journal* 45 (1996): 281–330; Leslie Katz, "Some Legal Consequences of the Winnipeg General Strike of 1919," *Manitoba Law Journal* 4.4 (1970): 39–52; J.B. Mackenzie, "Section 98, Criminal Code and Freedom of Expression in Canada," *Queen's Law Journal* 1.4 (November 1972): 469–83. An honourable exception is Keshen in "All the News That Was Fit to Print," who tends to the belief that the chief censor, in any case, did a rather good job.

49 Great Britain, General Statistics Office, *Annual Abstract of Statistics 1903–1919* (London: HMSO), 1919. Aggregate figure includes convictions in all the UK's judicial districts, England-Wales, Scotland, and Ireland.
50 Sessional Papers, vol. 50 (Session 1915), no. 12.
51 Henry Kissinger, *A World Restored* (Boston: Hougton Mifflin, 1957), 192.
52 Pennie Reddie, "The Crimes of Treason and Sedition in Canada,"*Laurentian University Review* 11.1 (November 1978): 17. See McNaught for the argument that Canadian courts have generally been buttresses of order rather than agents of change: "Canadian courts were seldom used to organise movements for social and economic power and control; they have, however, very often been used in an attempt to suppress such movements" ("Political Trials and the Canadian Political Tradition," 149).
53 Ibid., 149–69.
54 Marx, "The Emergency Power and Civil Liberties in Canada," 42.

2. "Because They Are Totally and Exclusively Canadian"

1 LAC RG 6, E, F.E. Chambers to Cockerill, 30 September 1917.
2 Gerhard Fischer, "Fighting the War at Home: The Campaign against Alien Enemies in Australia during the First World War," in *Minorities in Wartime: National and Racial Groupings in Europe, North America and Australia during Two World Wars*, ed. Panikos Panayi (Oxford: Berg, 1993), 270.
3 Donald Avery, *Dangerous Foreigners: European Immigrant Workers and Labour Radicalism in Canada 1896–1932* (Toronto: McClelland and Stewart, 1979), 38–89.
4 John Porter, *The Vertical Mosaic: An Analysis of Social Class and Power in Canada* (Toronto: University of Toronto Press, 1965).
5 Wallace Clements, *The Canadian Corporate Elite* (Toronto: McClelland and Stewart, 1975).
6 Fredrick Armstrong, "Ethnicity and the Formation of the Ontario Establishment," in *Ethnic Canada: Identities and Inequalities*, ed. Leo Driedger (Toronto: Copp, Clark Pitman, 1987), 242–55.
7 For example, Mark McGowan, "Sharing the Burden of Empire: Toronto's Catholics and the Great War 1914–1918," in *Catholics at the "Gathering Place": Historical Essays on the Archdiocese of Toronto 1841–1991* (Toronto: Dundurn Press, 1993), 177–207.
8 Frederick Armstrong, "Ethnicity in the Formation of the Family Compact: A Case Study in the Growth of the Canadian Establishment," in *Ethnicity,*

Power and Politics in Canada, ed. Jorgen Dahlie and Tissa Fernando (Toronto: Methuen, 1981), 32.
9 McGowan, "Sharing the Burden of Empire," 244.
10 Ross McCormack, "Cloth Caps and Jobs: The Ethnicity of English Immigrants in Canada 1900–1914," in *Ethnicity, Power and Politics in Canada*, ed. Dahlie and Fernando, 38–52. Actual paupers often did not receive a favourable welcome in the Dominion, and the government worked to discourage charitable societies from using Canada as a dumping ground. See, for example, Desmond Glynn, "Exporting Outcast London: Assisted Immigration to Canada, 1886–1914," *Histoire Sociale* 15.29 (1982): 208–238.
11 McCormack, "Cloth Caps and Jobs," 38–52.
12 Robert Rutherdale, *Hometown Horizons: Local Responses to Canada's Great War* (Vancouver: University of British Columbia Press, 2004), 30.
13 John Hagan, "Finding and Defining Discrimination," in *Ethnic Canada*, ed. Driedger, 337–43. For "democratic racism," see Francis Henry and Carol Tator, "The Ideology of Racism. Democratic Racism," *Canadian Ethnic Studies* 26.2 (1994): 1–14.
14 Frederick Armstrong, "Ethnicity in the Formation of the Family Compact," 32.
15 Craig Heron and Myer Siemiatycki, "The Great War, the State, and Working Class Canada," in *The Workers Revolt in Canada*, ed. Craig Heron (Toronto: University of Toronto Press, 1998), 7–8. For an interesting discussion of divisions in the prewar Canadian labour movement, from a participant, see Tim Buck, *Canada and the Russian Revolution: The Impact of the World's First Socialist Revolution on Labour and Politics in Canada* (Toronto: Progress Books, 1967), 1–64.
16 David Bright, "We Are All Kin: Reconsidering Labour and Class in Calgary, 1919," *Labour* 29 (Spring 1992).
17 Robert Brown and Ramsay Cook, *Canada 1896–1921: A Nation Transformed* (Toronto: McClelland and Stewart, 1974), 94–101.
18 Martin Robin, *Radical Politics and Canadian Labour, 1880–1* (Industrial Relations Centre, Queen's University, 1968), 13.
19 Ibid., 8–10.
20 Desmond Morton and Terry Copp, *Working People* (Ottawa: Deneau, 1981), 115.
21 *Toronto Star*, 18 August 1916.
22 Cecil Houston and William Smyth, *The Sash Canada Wore* (Toronto: University of Toronto Press, 1980), 95–6; and P.S. Pennefather, *The Orange and the Black* (Toronto: T.H. Best, 1984), 116. For trade unionism in general,

see Brown and Cook, *Canada 1896–1921*, 109–24. See also Donald Avery, "Canadian Immigration Policy and the Alien Question 1896–1919: The Anglo-Canadian Perspective," PhD thesis, University of Western Ontario, 1973, chapter 8.
23 By 1912, there were, it is claimed, ten thousand IWW members in British Columbia and few anywhere else in Canada. Robin, *Radical Politics and Canadian Labour, 1880–1930*, 150–7. During the war, the IWW appears to have grown in strength, though this is difficult to establish, and it seems to have been partly a function of the movement of American workers into Canada from 1916. In 1917, with the entry of the United States to the war, "wobblies" were said to be flocking to Canada to avoid the draft. Avery, *Dangerous Foreigners*, 73; LAC MG 26, H, Borden Papers, reel C4334, item 56588, Mountain Lumber Manufacturers' Association to Borden, 11 February 1918; and item 56593, D.H. Robertson to the Privy Council, 20 February 1918. It should be added, however, that none of this was readily apparent to police observers always on the lookout for radicals of this stripe.
24 Bruno Bettelheim and Morris Janowitz, *Social Change and Prejudice* (New York: Free Press of Glencoe, 1964).
25 Toronto *Globe*, 8 August 1918.
26 Brown and Cook, *Canada 1896–1921*, 240 and 309; and M.C. Urquhart, ed., *Historical Statistics of Canada* (Toronto: Macmillan, 1965).
27 Robin, *Radical Politics and Canadian Labour, 1880–1930*, 154.
28 Peter Krawchuk, *The Ukrainian Socialist Movement in Canada, 1907–1918* (Toronto: Progress Books, 1979), 2.
29 Buck, *Canada and the Russian Revolution*, 18.
30 Ivan Avakumovic, *The Communist Party in Canada: A History* (Toronto: University of Toronto Press, 1975), 119–20.
31 Brown and Cook, *Canada 1896–1921*, 251.
32 See, for example, correspondence in LAC MG 26, H, reel 4238.
33 *Le Devoir*, 30 May 1917, 2.
34 *Le Devoir*, 2 July 1917, 6.
35 Brown and Cook, *Canada 1896–1921*, 2–3.
36 Figures from ibid., 68, 98–9.
37 Urquhart, ed., *Historical Statistics*.
38 Avery, "Canadian Immigration Policy and the Alien Question 1896–1919," 101.
39 Urquhart, ed., *Historical Statistics*.
40 A. Gordon Darroch and Wilfrid G. Marston, "Patterns of Urban Ethnicity," in *Ethnic Canada*, ed. Driedger, 83–5.
41 Ibid., 82–110.

42 See Brown and Cook, *Canada 1896–1921*, 50–63.
43 Ibid., 136.
44 See, for example, Carl Berger, *The Sense of Power: Studies in the Ideas of Canadian Imperialism, 1867–1914* (Toronto: University of Toronto Press, 1970).
45 Avery, "Canadian Immigration Policy and the Alien Question 1896–1919," 306.
46 Ibid., 106.
47 Paul C. Stern, "Why Do People Sacrifice for Their Nations?" in *Perspectives on Nationalism and War*, ed. J.L. Comoroff and Paul C. Stern (Amsterdam: Gordon Breach Publishing, 1995), 100–14. Robert Rutherdale arrived at a similar understanding in his examination of the Great War home fronts of Guelph, Lethbridge, and Trois Rivières: "How local populations in Canada came to respond to the war stemmed from how they used local sites to activate a coherent sense of what seemed to be happening overseas or elsewhere, often well beyond immediate references of locale – the sights, sounds, feelings, and meanings that local, war-related experiences generated in the midst of a significant period of historical change. The war, in other words, often unfolded as a story that had to be told and retold, through sermons, parades, speeches, editorials, gossip and a host of local events that broadcast in very ordinary terms what many understood, quite correctly, was an extraordinary period in history. The printed news, posters, rituals or snatches of conversation used to fashion specific reactions were both produced and embedded in the local spaces that people used to broadcast them" (*Hometown Horizons*, 2–3).
48 For Newfoundland, see Jason Churchill, "Of Baymen and Townies – Towards a Reassessment of the Newfoundland Conscription Crisis," in *Canadian Military History since the Seventeenth Century: Proceedings of the CMH Conference, Ottawa 5–9 May 2000* (CMHC, 2000), 167–172. For Ireland, see David Fitzpatrick. "The Logic of Collective Sacrifice: Ireland and the British Army, 1914–1918," *Historical Journal* 38.4 (1995): 1017–30.
49 *R. v. Oma* (Sask.) W.L.R., 1915, 958.
50 LAC MG 26, H, Borden Papers, reel C4371, item 89040, Long to the governor general, 4 November 1918.
51 LAC RG 13, vol. 1369, J.J. Williams, under-secretary of state for the Home Office to Colonial Office, 6 November 1916.
52 *Toronto Star*, 10 February 1916, 2.
53 Amy Shaw, *Crisis of Conscience: Conscientious Objection in Canada during the First World War* (Vancouver: University of British Columbia Press, 2009), table 2.

3. "A Cleavage in the Population of This Country along Racial Lines"

1 *Montreal Gazette*, 16 July 1917, 4.
2 A.I. Silver, *The French Canadian Ideal of Confederation, 1864–1900* (Toronto: University of Toronto Press, 1982), 218–26. See also Jean Paul Bernard, *Les idéologies québécoises de 19e siècle* (Montreal: Boréal Express, 1973); and Fernand Dumont, *Idéologies au Canada français* (Quebec: PUL, 1971).
3 *Montreal Gazette*, 16 July 1917, 4.
4 Robert Brown and Ramsay Cook, *Canada 1896–1921: A Nation Transformed* (Toronto: McClelland and Stewart, 1974), 240.
5 Ibid., 137.
6 Henri Bourassa "Nationalism and the Parties," *Le Devoir*, 14 May–6 June 1913.
7 Brown and Cook, *Canada 1896–1921*, 41.
8 Borden's position was designed to help Britain meet the seeming requirements of the moment – the naval race with Germany – and followed from British desires. "Whatever may be the decision of Canada," the Colonial Office informed the governor general, "at the present juncture, Great Britain will not in any circumstance fail in her duty to the Overseas Dominions of the Crown. // She has before now successfully made head alone and unaided against the most formidable combinations and she has not lost her capacity by a wise policy and strenuous exertions to watch over and preserve the vital interests of her Empire. // The Prime Minister of the Dominion having enquired in what form any immediate aid that Canada might give would be most effective, we have no hesitation in answering that such aid should include the provision of a certain number of the largest and strongest ships of war which science can build and money supply." LAC MG 26, H, Borden Papers, reel 4200, Colonial Office to governor general forwarding memorandum prepared by the Board of Admiralty, November 1912. In the Naval Aid Act, the Canadian government voted seven million pounds (thirty-five million Canadian dollars) to buy three dreadnoughts for the Royal Navy.
9 *London Daily Free Press*, 1 June 1900.
10 See, for example, LAC MG 26, H, Borden Papers, reel 4199, J.S. Williams (*Toronto News*) to F.S. Oliver, 15 December 1911.
11 The vote in the 1911 was very close: 666,074 to 623,554. Brown and Cook, *Canada 1896–1921*, 185. The Sifton brothers were the most prominent Liberal defectors.
12 *The Times, Morning Post, Telegraph, Standard, Advertiser, Graphic, Express, Daily Mirror* ("This ... indicates a new era in the history of the British

Empire"), *Westminster Gazette, Globe, Pall Mall Gazette, Evening News,* and *Evening Standard* all gave the Canadian election considerable attention and fulsomely welcomed Borden's victory.

13 Brown and Cook, *Canada 1896–1921*, 254–62. For Fallon's position, see Michael Power, "The Mitred Warrior: Bishop Michael Francis Fallon," *Catholic Insight* 8.3 (April 2000): 18–26; John Farrell, "Michael Francis Fallon, Bishop of London, Ontario, Canada: The Man and His Controversies," *Canadian Catholic Historical Association Study Sessions* (1968); and Michael Fitzpatrick, "The Role of Bishop Michael Fallon, and the Conflict between the French Canadian Catholics and Irish Catholics in the Ontario Bilingual Schools Question," MA thesis, University of Western Ontario, 1969.

14 *Robert Laird Borden: His Memoirs* (Toronto: Macmillan, 1938), 2:588.

15 For example, H. Bourassa, *Le Devoir*, 12 July 1917, 3, subsequently published as H. Bourassa, *Win the War and Lose Canada* (Montreal: Le Devoir, 1917). See also Arthur Hawkes, *Canadian Nationalism and the War* (Montreal, 1916).

16 See, for example, Mason Wade, *The French Canadians, 1760–1945* (Toronto: Macmillan, 1955), vol. 2; and Brown and Cook, *Canada 1896–1921*, 264.

17 Pierre Vennat, *Les "Poilus" québécois de 1914–1918: Histoires des militaires canadiens-français de la Première Guerre mondiale* (Montreal: Meridian, 1999), 1:231.

18 Gerard Filteau, *Le Québec, le Canada et la Guerre 1914–1918* (Montreal: Les Messageries Prologue, 1977), p. 23.

19 Ibid., 324.

20 Jean Pierre Gagnon, *Le 22e Battalion* (Quebec: Les Presses de l'Université Laval, 1986), 331–64. The van-doos were 87.2 per cent single, 95.6 per cent Catholic, 95 per cent Canadian born (with most of the remainder – 3.4 per cent – being US-born *Canadiens*); 51.8 per cent were recruited in Montreal with much of the remainder coming from other urban areas. Most of the volunteers were, by occupation, labourers. Sixteen- to twenty-one-year-olds predominated among the rank and file.

21 Vennat, *Les "Poilus" québécois de 1914–1918*, 1:24–5.

22 Ibid., 2:31. These figures do not tell us, of course, what proportion of the volunteers from Quebec were British Canadians – several English-language battalions having been formed already, primarily in Montreal.

23 Ibid., 1:324.

24 *La Presse*, 19 July 1917.

25 Vennat, *Les "Poilus" québécois de 1914–1918*, 1:62–3.

26 Toronto *Globe*, 11 August 1916, 4.

27 Toronto *Globe*, 18 January 1916, 10.
28 Brown and Cook, *Canada 1896–1921*, 261.
29 Arthur Lower, *Canadians in the Making* (Toronto: Longmans, Green and Co., 1958), 372.
30 J.S. Woodsworth, *Strangers within Our Gates; or, Coming Canadians* (Toronto: Methodist Church Missionary Society of Canada, 1909), 5.
31 Sessional Papers, vol. 50 (Session 1915), no. 12, "Criminal Statistics 1913–1914."
32 New Canadians were not responsible for the entire crime wave, of course, and other statistics might suggest that the lowly social position of immigrants had more to do with criminality than either predisposition or prejudice. Crime statistics for the "other British," residents of British descent not born in Canada, were also high. These constituted 11.06 per cent of the population and were responsible for 18.81 per cent of all crime. Anglicans, the predominant denomination among immigrants from the United Kingdom, while 14.47 per cent of the population, were responsible for 15.6 per cent of all crime, compared to the much more Canadian Methodists, 14.98 per cent of the population and responsible for 8.93 per cent of crime, and Presbyterians, 15.48 per cent of the population and responsible for 9.3 per cent of crime (ibid.).
33 Sessional Papers, vol. 56 (Session 1920), no. 10d, "Criminal Statistics 1919."
34 Sessional Papers, vol. 52 (Session 1917), no. 9, "Criminal Statistics 1916."
35 Brown and Cook, *Canada 1896–1921*, 325.
36 J. Castell Hopkins, *The Canadian Annual Review of Public Affairs 1918* (Ottawa: Canadian Annual Review, 1919), 42.
37 LAC MG 21, I, vol. 1, reel C3214, Arthur Meighen to R.B. Bennett, 24 November 1916.
38 Ibid.
39 J.L. Carruthers, "The Great War and Canada's Alien Enemy Policy," *Queen's Law Journal* 4.1 (Summer 1978): 47–8.
40 Toronto *Globe*, 1 May 1917, 9.
41 See, for example, Peter Krawchuk, *The Ukrainian Socialist Movement in Canada, 1907–1918* (Toronto: Progress Books, 1979).
42 *London Free Press*, 3 March 1916, 5.
43 LAC MG 26, H, Borden Papers, reel C4331, item 53438, Resolution of the Ukrainian Executive Council of Canada, 22 February 1918.
44 LAC MG 26, I, Meighen Papers, vol. 1, pp. 234–8. A "memorialist" writing to Borden, proposing this solution, estimated that of half a million Ukrainians in Canada, perhaps 35,000 were "for" Austria. Was

it not in any case curious, he thought, that the Ukrainians were being harshly dealt with when they were doing more than "certain races in Canada" which had enjoyed British citizenship for more than a century? (243). While the local MP, H.A. MacKie, was supportive of this idea, most of his Western colleagues were not, and the offer was not taken up

45 LAC MG 26, I, vol. 1, reel C3214, minister of immigration to Meighen, 24 February 1919.
46 Donald Avery, *Dangerous Foreigners: European Immigrant Workers and Labour Radicalism in Canada 1896–1932* (Toronto: McClelland and Stewart, 1979), 75.
47 LAC MG 26, H, reel C4331, item 53427, Ukrainian Social Democratic Party to Borden, 17 February 1918.
48 John Thompson, "The Alien Enemy and the Canadian General Election of 1917," in *Loyalties in Conflict: Ukrainians in Canada during the Great War*, ed. Frances Swyripa and John Thompson (Edmonton: University of Alberta Press, 1983), 27–33.
49 Clinton White, "Pre–World War One Saskatchewan German Catholic Thought concerning the Perpetuation of Their Language and Religion," *Canadian Ethnic Studies* 26.2 (1994): 15–45.
50 Trevor Powell, "The Church of England and the 'Foreigner' in the Diocese of Qu'Appelle and Saskatchewan," *Journal of the Canadian Church Historical Society* 28.1 (April 1986): 31–43. The bishops, however, discouraged mission work among the New Canadians. The Anglicans had their hands full providing for all the immigration from the United Kingdom. Many German Canadians were already Anglican. In part this was because Protestant Germans – Lutherans – immigrating into a country in which, during the nineteenth century, the Lutheran Church was not well established attended Anglican services as the next best thing.
51 Joseph Boudreau, "Western Canada's Alien Enemies in World War One," *Alberta Historical Review* 12.1 (1964): 1–2. See also Heinz Lehmann, *The German Canadians 1750–1937: Immigration, Settlement and Culture* (St John's: Jesperson Press, 1986); and K.M. McLaughlin, *The Germans in Canada* (Ottawa: CHA, 1985).
52 LAC MG 26, I, Meighen Papers, vol. 1, p. 239, Fred Davis to Meighen, 9 October 1918.
53 LAC MG 26, I, vol. 1, reel C3214, Ross to Robertson to Meighen, 24 March 1919; Richardson to Meighen, 28 March 1919; Ross to Meighen, 16 April 1919.
54 LAC MG 26, H, Borden Papers, item 35522, Blount for Council to Borden, 23 April 1917.

55 *London Advertiser*, 20 March 1916, 6.
56 LAC MG 11, CO 616, deputy minister of militia to Yashuski Yamazaki, president of the Canadian Japanese Association, Vancouver, 21 April 1916. Although British authorities wanted Canadian Japanese battalions, they did not get them. This was not because the government was opposed to the idea, but because there simply were not enough Japanese Canadians to sustain entire units.
57 Paula Hastings, "Fellow British Subjects of Colonial Others? Race, Empire and Ambivalence in Canadian Representations of India in the Early Twentieth Century," *American Review of Canadian Studies* 38.1 (January 2008).
58 Toronto *Globe*, 25 October 1917, 8.
59 LAC MG 26, I, vol. 1, reel C3214, item 225, Ruthenian Committee to Meighen.
60 Toronto *Globe*, 12 February 1917, 12.
61 LAC MG 11, CO 616, item 18954, Foreign Office to Colonial Office, 14 April 1916.
62 Toronto *Globe*, 7 January 1916, 9. Reference may have been to the "Manitoba Beavers," the 183rd Battalion. If so, the battalion appears to have thrown its net more broadly still. At least two members of the battalion (Hymie Bell and Alex Cordin) were Jews. Francis Dyule, Riccardo Diprofio, and Frank Ferrer were Catholics. Nikita Drach's religion was "Russian," and William Charne was apparently "Polish" by denomination. Sam Hughes announced, at various times, that an Indian (*Manitoba Free Press*, 20 December), Metis, Japanese Canadian, Black, Irish (*Toronto Star*, 3 January 1916, Toronto *Globe*, 4 January 1916), and Scandinavian unit would be raised (*Winnipeg Evening Tribune*, 1 February 1916). Thanks to Richard Holt for this reference.
63 Toronto *Globe*, 7 March 1918.
64 Panikos Panayi, *Minorities in Wartime National and Racial Groupings in Europe, North America and Australia during Two World Wars* (Oxford: Berg, 1993), 15.
65 Thompson, "The Alien Enemy and the Canadian General Election of 1917," 26.
66 Donald Avery, "Ethnic and Class Tension in Canada, 1918–1920," in *Ukrainians in Canada during the Great War*, ed. Swyripa and Thompson, 79.
67 Graeme Mount, *Canada's Enemies* (Toronto: Dundurn Press, 1993), 28–30.
68 Ibid., 30.
69 *London Free Press*, 19 March 1916. See also Grant Grams, "Karl Respa and German Espionage in Canada during World War One," *Journal of Military and Strategic Studies* 8.1 (Fall 2005).

70 *London Free Press*, 10 March 1916.
71 *Windsor Record*, 20 December 1917, 9.
72 *Windsor Record*, 18 December 1917, 6.
73 *Windsor Record*, 22 December 1917, 1.
74 Toronto *Globe*, 1 March 1918.
75 Avery, "Ethnic and Class Tension in Canada, 1918–1920," 31.
76 Mount, *Canada's Enemies*, 32.
77 LAC MG 11, CO 616, Consul General A. Carnegie Ross to Cecil A. Spring Rice, 7 March 1916.
78 Mount, *Canada's Enemies*, 32.
79 *Montreal Gazette*, 10–11 July 1917.
80 *London Free Press*, 8 March 1916.
81 Toronto *Globe*, 19 June 1918.
82 *Windsor Record*, 19 June 1918.
83 *Windsor Record*, 17 June 1918.
84 Toronto *Globe*, 20 June 1918.
85 Toronto *Globe*, 6 July 1918, 3.
86 Mount, *Canada's Enemies*, 32.
87 There were fifteen million German Americans in 1914.
88 Jeffrey Keshen, "All the News That Was Fit to Print: Ernest J. Chambers and Information Control in Canada, 1914–1919," *Canadian Historical Review* 73:3 (1992): 319.
89 *Calgary Herald*, 7 February 1916.
90 For example, *London Free Press*, 1 March 1916.
91 *London Advertiser*, 14 March 1916, 1.
92 *London Advertiser*, 14 March 1916, 4.
93 Keshen, "All the News That Was Fit to Print," 320.
94 Toronto *Globe*, 25 September 1917, 2.
95 Toronto *Globe*, 2 October 1917, 5.
96 Toronto *Globe*, 14 January 1918.
97 Toronto Globe, 15 December 1917.
98 Toronto *Globe*, 14 December 1917. Two months later, Commander Wyatt, chief examination officer of the port, was arrested, as were Captain Lamodec and Pilot Frank Mackay of the munitions steamer *Mont Blanc*. These men alone, owing to their negligence, the Drysdale Commission found, were wholly responsible for the disaster. Toronto *Globe*, 5 and 6 February 1918.
99 Toronto *Globe*, 29 January 1918.
100 *Vancouver Sun*, 6 February 1918.
101 Toronto *Globe*, 6 February 1918.

102 Toronto *Globe*, 27 April 1918.
103 Toronto *Globe*, 23 July 1918.
104 Toronto *Globe*, 6 July 1918, 18.
105 *Vancouver Sun*, 6 August 1918.
106 Toronto *Globe*, 11 September 1918.
107 *Toronto Star*, 12 September 1918, 5.
108 LAC MG 11, CO 616, War Office to Colonial Office, item 1806, M.I.1, 15 March 1916.
109 *Montreal Gazette*, 4 July 1917.
110 *Montreal Gazette*, 10 July 1917.

4. "A Life and Death Struggle for Christian Civilization"

1 *Journal of the Synod of the Church of England of the Diocese of Huron, 61st Session* (London, ON: A. Talbot, 1918), 45.
2 Robert Brown and Ramsay Cook, *Canada 1896–1921: A Nation Transformed* (Toronto: McClelland and Stewart, 1974), 27–43.
3 The years 1914–15 saw a number of events which gave the Allies a permanent propaganda advantage. Notable atrocities included the sinking of the *Lusitania*, the shooting of Edith Cavell, the "rape" of Belgium and subsequently the Armenian massacres revealed in the two *Bryce Reports*, the Battle of Ypres with the first use of gas, and the purported crucifixion of a Canadian soldier.
4 *Journal of the Synod of the Church of England of the Diocese of Huron, 58th Session* (London, ON: Advertiser, 1915), 39. Bishop Williams was born in a Cardiganshire village in 1859, the son of a cobbler. After earning a DD at Oxford and ordination in 1886, he immigrated to Canada in 1888 to take up a position at Huron College, London, Ontario. In 1904, he was elected bishop. In 1926, he was installed as primate of Ontario. Spencer Ervin, *The Political and Ecclesiastical History of the Anglican Church of Canada* (Ambler, PA.: Trinity Press, 1967), 88. See also Robert Willis, "David Williams 1859–1904: The Background of a Bishop," MA thesis, University of Western Ontario, 1957.
5 R. Matthew Bray, "'Fighting as an Ally': The English Canadian Patriotic Response to the Great War," *Canadian Historical Review* 61.2 (1980): 145.
6 Ibid., 141–68.
7 Ibid., 153.
8 These three were so dominant in 1914 that it is possible to generalize from their experience alone. Of 3,999,081 British Canadians, in 1921, there were 1,116,071 Presbyterians, 1,079,993 Methodists, and 1,043,017

Anglicans. If the French Canadians (2,061,719) are excluded from the Catholic total (2,833,041), to allow for Irish and Scots Catholics, the story is just about told. The only substantial "other" Protestant denomination was the Baptists – about a quarter of the strength of the others, concentrated in the Maritimes, particularly in Bible Belt New Brunswick. M.C. Urquhart, ed., *Historical Statistics of Canada* (Toronto: Macmillan, 1965).

9 For the role of the churches in creating English Canadian nationalism see Neil Smith, "Nationalism and the Canadian Churches," *Canadian Journal of Theology* 9 (1963): 112–25.
10 Richard Allen, *The Social Passion: Religion and Social Reform in Canada, 1914–1928* (Toronto: University of Toronto Press, 1973), 72.
11 Michael Gauvreau, "War, Culture, and the Problem of Religious Uncertainty: Methodist and Presbyterian Colleges, 1914–1930," *Journal of the Canadian Church Historical Society* 29.1 (April 1987): 16.
12 Ibid., 14.
13 J.M. Bliss, "The Methodist Church and World War I," in *Conscription 1917*, ed. Ramsay Cook, Craig Brown, and Carl Berger (Toronto: University of Toronto Press, 1969), 52–5.
14 The war years witnessed a stunning decline in Canadian criminality: 28,007 indictable offences in 1913 became 24,078 in 1914 (Sessional Papers, vol. 50 (Session 1915), no. 12, "Criminal Statistics 1913–1914"). A further 4.62 per cent decline in charges and 3.69 per cent in convictions followed in 1915 (Sessional Papers, vol. 51 (Session 1916), no. 13, "Criminal Statistics 1915"). The decline in 1916 was 10.38 per cent in charges and 7.10 per cent in convictions, but would have been 21.73 per cent in charges and 21.15 per cent in convictions had "keepers and inmates of bawdy houses" not been reassigned from courts of summary procedure (Sessional Papers, vol. 52 (Session 1917), no. 9, "Criminal Statistics 1916"). In 1917, a further decline of 21.48 per cent in charges and 18.79 in convictions was experienced (Sessional Papers, vol. 52 (Session 1917), no. 9, "Criminal Statistics 1916"). The decline in convictions for drunkenness in the war years was particularly remarkable and mightily assisted, of course, by prohibition. In 1913, 60,975 persons were convicted of drunkenness. In 1917, only 27,882. The greatest rate of decline was experienced in the West, where Alberta experienced a 94.63 per cent, Manitoba a 85.52 per cent, and Saskatchewan a 71.48 per cent decline in this species of criminality in the five years prior to 1917 (Sessional Papers, vol. 53 (Session 1918), no. 10c, "Criminal Statistics 1917"), and during the war years alone, 91.70 per cent in British Columbia, 85.55 per cent in

Alberta, 81.87 per cent in Manitoba, and 79.74 per cent in Saskatchewan. By 1918, things were beginning to return to normal, with an 11.78 per cent increase in charges and 11.63 per cent increase in convictions (Sessional Papers, vol. 54 (Session 1919), no. 3, "Criminal Statistics 1918").

15 For example, *Journal of the Synod of the Church of England in the Diocese of Huron, 59th Session* (London, ON: A. Talbot, 1916), 61–72. Such a future, in fact, was indicated as likely by the very best authorities. See, for example, Robert Borden, *The War and the Future* (London: Hodder and Stoughton, 1917), and Union Government Publicity Bureau, *English Canada and the War* (Ottawa: Dodson-Merrill Press, 1917).
16 Toronto *Globe*, 8 July 1918, 7.
17 Duff Crerar, *Padres in No Man's Land: Canadian Chaplains and the Great War* (Montreal: McGill-Queen's University Press, 1995), 9–10.
18 See for general context Alan Wilkinson, *The Church of England and the First World War* (Southampton: Camelot Press, 1978), and Albert Marrin, *The Last Crusade: The Church of England in the First World War* (Durham, NC: Duke University Press, 1974).
19 See William Katerberg, *Modernity and the Dilemma of North American Anglican Identities, 1880–1950* (Montreal: McGill-Queen's University Press, 2001), esp, 3–19. See also Bishop Williams's 1914 charge to the Diocese of Huron Synod at *Journal of the Synod of the Church of England of the Diocese of Huron, 57th Session* (London, ON: Advertiser, 1914), 65.
20 Neil Semple, *The Lord's Dominion: The History of Canadian Methodism* (Montreal: McGill-Queen's University Press, 1996), 276–305.
21 J.S. Woodsworth, *Strangers within Our Gates; or, Coming Canadians* (Toronto: Methodist Church Missionary Society of Canada, 1909), 290.
22 Semple, *The Lord's Dominion*, 334–62.
23 Ibid., 395–403.
24 Bliss, "The Methodist Church and World War I," 42.
25 Ibid., 43.
26 Robert Rutherdale, *Hometown Horizons: Local Response to Canada's Great War* (Vancouver: University of British Columbia Press, 2004), xvi.
27 *Toronto Star*, 10 February 1916, 2.
28 Toronto *Globe*, 28 March 1916, 6.
29 *Montreal Gazette*, 6 August 1917.
30 *Calgary Herald*, 9 April 1918, 1.
31 Toronto *Globe*, 14 April 1916, 2.
32 Crerar, *Padres in No Man's Land*, 27; and Michael Power, "The Mitred Warrior: Bishop Michael Francis Fallon," *Catholic Insight* 8.3 (April 2000): 20.
33 Ibid.

34 Toronto *Globe*, 1 February 1917, 5
35 J. Castell Hopkins, *The Canadian Annual Review of Public Affairs 1917* (Ottawa: Canadian Annual Review, 1915–19), 412.
36 *Journal of the Synod of the Church of England of the Diocese of Huron, 59th Session* (London, ON: Advertiser, 1916), 59.
37 Leslie Frost, *Fighting Men* (Toronto: Clark, Irwin and Company, 1967), 47.
38 See Jeffrey Keshen, "All the News That Was Fit to Print: Ernest J. Chambers and Information Control in Canada, 1914–1919," *Canadian Historical Review* 73:3 (1992): 328, for the suppression of Lutheran periodicals.
39 *London Free Press*, 8 March 1916.
40 Toronto *Globe*, 27 January 1917, 3, and Ontario Weekly Notes, 417, Supreme Court of Ontario, High Court Division. Curtis Cole discusses this case, but errs in thinking that it was the only time that the WMA was used to suppress verbal expression, in "The War Measures Act, 1914: Aspects of the Emergency Limitation of Freedom of Speech and Personal Liberties in Canada, 1914–1919," MA thesis, University of Western Ontario, 1980, 83–4. See also Patricia Peppin, "Emergency Legislation and Rights in Canada: The War Measures Act and Civil Liberties," *Queen's Law Journal* 18.1 (Spring 1993): 136–7. Fifty dollars was probably rather beyond the means of a Pentecostal preacher in 1916.
41 *Vancouver Sun*, 11 February 1918.
42 Cecil Houston and William Smyth, *The Sash Canada Wore* (Toronto: University of Toronto Press, 1980), 1. R.D. Edwards, *The Faithful Tribe* (London: HarperCollins, 1999), 2.
43 David Wilson, *The Irish in Canada* (Canadian Historical Society, 1989), 11.
44 Ervin, *The Political and Ecclesiastical History of the Anglican Church of Canada*, 83.
45 Houston and Smyth, *The Sash Canada Wore*, 95–6; and P.S. Pennefather, *The Orange and the Black* (Toronto: T.H. Best, 1984), 116.
46 See, for Meighen in general, Roger Graham, *Arthur Meighen* (Toronto: Clark, Irwin and Company, 1960).
47 Houston and Smyth, *The Sash Canada Wore*, 154.
48 R. Miller, "Orangeism in Ontario West, 1896–1917," MA thesis, University of Western Ontario, 1975, 136.
49 Ibid., 137.
50 Ibid., 136.
51 *Sentinel*, 11 June 1914.
52 Pennefather, *The Orange and the Black*, 17.
53 Ibid., 27.

54 R. Miller, "Orangeism in Ontario West, 1896–1917," 139.
55 Desmond Morton, *Minister and Generals: Politics and the Canadian Militia* (Toronto: University of Toronto Press, 1970), 201, table 2, annex A, is particularly eloquent. It charts the presence of militia officers in Parliament, over time.
56 J. Castell Hopkins, *The Canadian Annual Review of Public Affairs 1918* (Ottawa: Canadian Annual Review, 1919), 589.
57 In what is probably the best manpower survey available, Richard Holt excludes quantification by rank and for French/English proportion entirely, as he considers that on these issues in particular the surviving documentation is unreliable. "Filling the Ranks: Recruiting, Training and Reinforcements in the Canadian Expeditionary Force, 1914–1918," PhD dissertation, University of Western Ontario, 2011.
58 PRO CAB 23/1, WC 41, 23 January 1917. In comparison, 17.24 per cent of male Britons were in uniform, 10.7 per cent of Australians, 11.9 per cent of New Zealanders, and 1.7 per cent of South Africans.
59 *Toronto Telegram*, 15 June 1917.
60 PRO CAB 23/40, IWC 6, 30 March 1917. For the spectacular expansion of Canada's war industries, see, for example, LAC MG 26, I, Meighen Papers, vol. 2, J.W. Flavelle, "Memorandum on Shell Production," 4 May 1918.
61 George Emery, "The Origin of the Canadian Methodist Involvement in the Social Gospel Movement, 1890–1914," *Journal of the Canadian Church Historical Society* 19.1 (1977): 104–18. For the role of the Church of England in recruiting suitable immigrants for Canada, see Donald Harris, "The Church of England and Emigration to Canada: Rural Clergy in the County of Shropshire," *Journal of the Canadian Historical Society* 41.1 (Spring 1999): 5–26.
62 *Journal of the Synod of the Church of England of the Diocese of Huron, 59th Session* (London, ON: A. Talbot, 1916), 57–8.
63 Methodists believed that they were under-represented, since soldiers were registered as "Wesleyans" and many Methodists would not accept the name. Neil Smith, "Nationalism and the Canadian Churches," *Canadian Journal of Theology* 9 (1963): 118. Moreover, they claimed, figures did not include as "Methodist" members of Union congregations. Even when allowance is made for these distortions, however, it is clear that the Methodists were under-represented among Protestant denominations, and Roman Catholics more under-represented still. Semple, *The Lord's Dominion*, 398.
64 J. Castell Hopkins, *The Canadian Annual Review of Public Affairs 1918* (Ottawa: Canadian Annual Review, 1919), p. 880.

65 R. Miller, "Orangeism in Ontario West, 1896–1917," 141–2.
66 Donald Avery, "Canadian Immigration Policy and the Alien Question 1896–1919: The Anglo-Canadian Perspective," PhD thesis, University of Western Ontario, 1973, 440.
67 Ibid., 462.
68 Desmond Morton and Glenn Wright, *Winning the Second Battle: Canadian Veterans and the Return to Civilian Life 1915–1920* (Toronto: University of Toronto Press, 1987), 64.
69 Separation allowance for a soldier's family was typically $20 a month. See Desmond Morton's excellent *Fight or Pay: Soldiers' Families and the Great War* (Vancouver: University of British Columbia Press, 2004).
70 LAC MG 26, H, Borden Papers, item 42106, RNWMP commissioner forwarding report from Regina, 12 September 1917; and item 42110, comptroller forwarding D Division Report, 25 August 1917. Police reports followed from an agitation begun by the *Morning Albertan*, which claimed that men were declining work for $4.00 a day as stokers, and $4.50 as binders. This was, the papers considered, obviously an IWW conspiracy, brought north from the US. Not so, the RNWMP concluded. Men would not work for $4.00 because they could get $5.00.
71 Donald Avery, *Dangerous Foreigners: European Immigrant Workers and Labour Radicalism in Canada 1896–1932* (Toronto: McClelland and Stewart, 1979), 68–9.
72 Ibid., 70.
73 LAC MG 26, H, Borden Papers, item 43089, Workman to Borden, 1 February 1917; and item 43110, Workman to Borden, 19 December 1917.
74 Toronto *Globe*, 15 March 1917.
75 Pennefather, *The Orange and the Black*, 103
76 Toronto *Globe*, 13 July 1916, 6.
77 *Montreal Gazette*, 11 July 1917, 5.
78 For the GWVA in general, see Morton and Wright, *Winning the Second Battle*.
79 A "returned man" would have, by definition, been so severely wounded as to have been of no further military use. Wounded men were rare in Canada until 1916. Seventy per cent of Canadian casualties were incurred in the last two years of the war. By the middle of 1917 the trickle was becoming a stream. The GWVA had 16,000 members already, even before the war ended. J. Castell Hopkins, *The Canadian Annual Review of Public Affairs 1918* (Ottawa: Canadian Annual Review, 1919), 580
80 LAC MG 26, I, Meighen Papers, vol. 10, reel C3218, Daly to Meighen, 9 September 1918; and major general to minister of militia, 2 November 1918.

81 DHH (Directorate of History and Heritage), Holly Lane, 325.009 (D281), "Troops Called Out in Aid of Civil Power," Ashton to GOC No. 2, 21 December 1917.
82 G.L. Kristianson, *The Politics of Patriotism: The Pressure Group Activities of the Returned Servicemen's League* (Canberra: Australian National University Press, 1966).
83 LAC MG 26, H, Borden Papers, item 42080, Great War Veterans' Association, Quebec Branch, to Borden, 3 April 1917.
84 Morton and Wright, *Winning the Second Battle*, 70–1.
85 Ibid.
86 Ibid., 120–1.
87 Toronto *Globe*, 18 May 1917.
88 Toronto *Globe*, 1 August 1918, 7.
89 Toronto *Globe*, 5 January 1918. This was also the line of the Orange Lodge. See, for example, *Windsor Record*, 6 March 1918, 2.
90 Toronto *Globe*, 5 February 1918.
91 Morton and Wright, *Winning the Second Battle*, 74.
92 For example, LAC MG 26, 1, Meighen Papers, vol. 1, reel 6314, item 257, Mr J. Stevenson to the Minister of Immigration to Meighen, 24 February 1919.
93 LAC MG 26, 1, Meighen Papers, vol. 1, reel 6314, item 229, Hamilton Bruce to Borden to Meighen, 1 March 1918.
94 J. Castell Hopkins, *The Canadian Annual Review of Public Affairs 1918* (Ottawa: Canadian Annual Review, 1919), 580. The government actually considered this alternative, but felt that internees were too few for this to be any solution, while any coercive action against Alien Enemies more broadly defined was apt to produce reprisal from Germany. LAC MG 26, H, Borden Papers, reel C4331, Statement on Alien Labour, February 1918.
95 J. Castell Hopkins, *The Canadian Annual Review of Public Affairs 1918* (Ottawa: Canadian Annual Review, 1919), 580. Bradbury (Manitoba Conservative) was a veteran himself – a member of the militia since 1885, and a soldier on active service 1915–16 – before being elevated to the Senate in December 1917. Lynch-Stanton (Ontario Conservative) was a Hamilton notable, entering the Senate in January 1917.
96 Toronto *Globe*, 21 February 1918, 6.
97 Toronto *Globe*, 19 April 1918.
98 Toronto *Globe*, 9 May 1918.
99 Toronto *Globe*, 12 April 1918.
100 Toronto *Globe*, 3 July 1918. Recall that the 1918 Spanish Influenza epidemic was then on-going.

101 *Windsor Evening Record*, 10 September 1917, 1.
102 *Windsor Evening Record*, 12 September 1917, 3.
103 *Calgary Herald*, 11 April 1918, 7.
104 Toronto *Globe*, 13 April 1918.
105 Toronto *Globe*, 19 April 1918.
106 Toronto *Globe*, 17 June 1918.

5. "Down with King Borden and His Boches. Long Live the Jails!"

1 *Montreal Gazette*, 13 July 1917.
2 DHH (Directorate of History and Heritage), Holly Lane, 112.3H1.003 (D49), "Report Compiled by WO Marshall, P.R. D Hist, Describing and Listing Occasions since Confederation That Troops Have Been Called Upon to Aid [the] Civil Power, 1870–1914."
3 Toronto *Globe*, 25 August 1916, and *Montreal Gazette*, 24 August 1916.
4 Toronto *Globe*, 4 September 1916, 5
5 *Montreal Gazette*, 26 August 1916, 5.
6 *Montreal Gazette*, 29 August 1916, 6.
7 *Le Devoir*, 11 July 1917, 2.
8 Toronto *Globe*, 26 March 1917.
9 Toronto *Globe*, 8 May 1917.
10 Toronto *Globe*, 25 May 1917.
11 Pierre Vennat, *Les "Poilus" québécois de 1914–1918: Histoires des militaires canadiens-français de la Première Guerre mondiale* (Montreal: Meridian, 1999), 2:55.
12 Toronto *Globe*, 29 May 1917.
13 Toronto *Globe*, 30 May 1917.
14 *Montreal Gazette*, 5 July 1917.
15 Vennat, *Les "Poilus" québécois de 1914–1918*, 2:116.
16 Toronto *Globe*, 1 December 1917.
17 *Le Devoir*, 15 June 1917.
18 *Le Devoir*, 27 June 1917, 3.
19 *Le Devoir*, 29 June 1917, 1.
20 *Montreal Gazette*, 9 July 1917, 4.
21 *Montreal Gazette*, 12 July 1917.
22 *Montreal Gazette*, 13 July 1917.
23 *Montreal Gazette*, 12 July 1917.
24 *Montreal Gazette*, 16 July 1917.
25 Toronto *Globe*, 16 July 1917.
26 *Montreal Gazette*, 16 July 1917.

27 *Montreal Gazette*, 17 July 1917.
28 A. Williams, "Conscription, 1917: A Brief for the Defence," *Canadian Historical Review* 27.4 (December 1956): 10.
29 Criminal Code of Canada, S.C. 1892, chapter 146, para 98.
30 PC 2634, 21 September 1917.
31 *Montreal Gazette*, 17 July 1917.
32 For example, *London Free Press*, 4 March 1916.
33 *Montreal Gazette*, 2 August 1917.
34 *Montreal Gazette*, 3 August 1917.
35 *Montreal Gazette*, 6 August 1917.
36 Toronto *Globe*, *Montreal Gazette*, 10 August 1917. For the *dynomitards* in general, see Gerard Filteau, *Le Québec, le Canada et la Guerre 1914–1918* (Montreal: Les Messageries Prologue, 1977), 117–19.
37 *Montreal Gazette*, 10 August 1917.
38 *Montreal Gazette*, 10 August 1917.
39 Toronto *Globe*, *Montreal Gazette*, 11 August 1917.
40 *Montreal Gazette*, 16 August 1917.
41 Toronto *Globe*, 29 August 1917.
42 Elizabeth Armstrong, *The Crisis of Quebec, 1914–1918* (1937; Montreal: McGill-Queen's University Press, 1974), 196–7.
43 *Montreal Gazette*, 13 August, statement of Paul Lafortune.
44 Toronto *Globe*, 30 August 1917
45 Toronto *Globe*, 31 August 1917
46 Filteau, *Le Québec, le Canada et la Guerre 1914–1918*, 117.
47 Toronto *Globe*, 31 August 1917
48 Toronto *Globe*, 5 and 12 September 1917.
49 *Toronto Star*, 4 September 1917, 4; 5 September, 7.
50 Toronto *Globe*, 15 September 1917, 3.
51 Toronto *Globe*, 20 September 1917, 14.
52 Charles Monette (aka Girard), Joseph Tremblay, Elie Lalumière, Charles Desjardins, Arthur Blackwell, Romeo Wisintainer, Henri Arsenault, J.B. Cyr, Aurele Goyer, A. Chagnon, Joseph Paquette, and E. Bolduc were all arrested. Lalumière, Tremblay, and Goyer were charged with attempted murder of a detective and Conrad Therrien. Cyr, Tremblay, Lalumière, Desjardins, Monette, Goyer, and Wisintainer were charged with the attempted murder of Lord Atholstan. Toronto *Globe*, 7 November 1917.
53 *Toronto Star*, 4 September 1917, 4.
54 Toronto *Globe*, 21 September 1917, 4; 22 and 31 October, 11. See also Filteau, *Le Québec, le Canada et la Guerre 1914–1918*, 118–19.
55 Toronto *Globe*, 16 November 1917, 2.

56 Ibid.
57 Toronto *Globe*, 25 March 1918, 13.
58 Toronto *Globe*, 14 September 1917, 3; and 15 September, 3.
59 Toronto *Globe*, 30 October 1917, 16.
60 Vennat, *Les "Poilus" québécois de 1914–1918*, 2:292.
61 Toronto *Globe*, 26 November 1917.
62 Toronto *Globe*, 3 December 1917.
63 Toronto *Globe*, 25 May 1917.
64 *Montreal Gazette*, 30 June 1917.
65 *Montreal Gazette*, 2 July 1917, 8.
66 *Montreal Gazette*, 9 July 1914.
67 *Montreal Gazette*, 12 July 1917, 4.
68 Toronto *Globe*, 16 October 1917, 3.
69 Marcel Rioux, "The Development of Ideology in Quebec," in *Ethnic Canada: Identities and Inequalities*, ed. Leo Driedger (Toronto: Copp, Clark Pitman, 1987), 198–222.
70 *Montreal Gazette*, 6 August 1917.
71 *Montreal Gazette*, 2 July 1917, statement of T. Bouchard, the Liberal provincial deputy.
72 *Montreal Gazette*, 9 August 1917.
73 *Montreal Gazette*, 18 August 1917.
74 Toronto *Globe*, 10 November 1917.
75 For Tremblay, Toronto *Globe*, 18 March 1918, 2. For Ranger, ibid., 14.
76 *Montreal Gazette*, 11 August 1917; for example, from Mr Eugene Villeneuve, of the city Board of Control, to the effect that the Fernand Villeneuve, notable in recent disturbances, was no relative of his.
77 *Montreal Gazette*, 11 August 1917.
78 *Montreal Gazette*, 15 August 1917.
79 *Montreal Gazette*, 13 August 1917.
80 J. Granatstein and J. Hitsman, *Broken Promises: A History of Conscription in Canada* (Toronto: Oxford University Press, 1977), 94.
81 *Le Devoir*, 11 August 1917.
82 Filteau, *Le Québec, le Canada et la Guerre 1914–1918*, 118.
83 Toronto *Globe*, 22 May 1918.
84 Toronto *Globe*, 13 July 1917, 2.
85 Toronto *Globe*, 26 November 1917.
86 Ibid.
87 Toronto *Globe*, 26 November 1917. The Italian Front had just collapsed. The cause was given throughout the press as being rot established in the army by defeatist socialists.

88 Michael Power, *Bishop Fallon and the Riot at Ford City, 8 September 1917* (Windsor: Essex County Historical Association, 1986).
89 Ibid.
90 DHH, Holly Lane, 112.3H1.003 (D49), "Report Compiled by WO Marshall, P.R. D Hist, Describing and Listing Occasions since Confederation That Troops Have Been Called Upon to Aid [the] Civil Power, 1870–1914."
91 Toronto *Globe*, 16 March 1918, 2.
92 Session Papers, vol 52 (1917), no. 18, report of A.E.C. MacDonnel, N Division, Peace River, Alberta.

6. "We Cheerfully Accept the Burden Laid upon Us"

1 See P.W. Lackenbauer, "The Military and 'Mob Rule': The CEF Riots in Calgary, February 1916," *Canadian Military History* 10.1 (Winter 2001): 31–43; and P.W. Lackenbauer and N. Gardner, "Citizen Soldiers as Liminaries: The CEF Soldier Riots of 1916 Reconsidered," in *Canada's Military History since the 17th Century: Proceedings of the CMH Conference, Ottawa 5–9 May 2000* (CMHC, 2000), 155.
2 Ian Miller, "A Privilege to Serve: Toronto's Experience with Voluntary Enlistment in the Great War," in *Canadian Military History since the 17th Century*, 149.
3 Ian Miller, *Our Glory and Our Grief: Torontonians and the Great War* (Toronto: University of Toronto Press, 2002), 146.
4 The Riot Act. Section 91 of the Criminal Code provided that when twelve or more persons were acting together in riotous assembly, a magistrate was empowered to advise them to disperse on pain of imprisonment for life. If they refused to disperse, then they could be dispersed – all peace officers, or other authorities employed in dispersing them, indemnified against legal action in the event that death or injury resulted from the employment of force. Magistrates and other competent agents of the Crown who did not cause the Riot Act to be read when it was necessary were guilty of an offence themselves and liable to imprisonment for two years. Peace officers or other agents of the government who refused to assist them were liable for imprisonment for a year (para 94, 95).
5 Criminal Code of Canada, S.C. 1892, part 1, chapter 146, para 50.
6 DHH (Directorate of History and Heritage), Holly Lane, 325.009 (D281) "Troops Called Out in Aid of Civil Power," 2MD-34-1-155, 22 August 1918, H.C. Bickford, Comd M.D. No. 2 to Militia Council.

7 See Ian Miller, "A Privilege to Serve," and *Our Glory and Our Grief*, 16–18 for the state of play in 1914.
8 R. Miller, "Orangeism in Ontario West, 1896–1917," MA thesis, University of Western Ontario, 1975, 140.
9 Ian Miller, "A Privilege to Serve," 143–51.
10 See James Wood, *Militia Myths: Ideals of the Canadian Citizen Soldier* (Vancouver: University of British Columbia Press, 2010).
11 Max Foran and Heather MacEwan Foran, *Calgary: Canada's Frontier Metropolis* (Windsor: Windsor Publications, 1982), 156.
12 *Calgary Herald*, 15 January 1916. The battalions were the 31st Battalion, CEF, raised largely in Calgary, and the 3rd Mounted Rifles (Medicine Hat). Two other Western Battalions, the 27th (Winnipeg) and the 28th (Saskatchewan), were hard hit at the same time.
13 *Calgary Herald*, 4 February 1916.
14 *Calgary Herald*, 9 February 1916.
15 Lackenbauer, "The Military and 'Mob Rule,'" 32–3.
16 Nagel was, in fact, an American from Cincinnati, and a naturalized Canadian.
17 DHH, Holly Lane, 74/672, folder 4, "Disturbances in Canada 1916," chapter 8, p. 1. The 89th, then in the process of formation, were quartered at Sarcee.
18 Lackenbauer, "The Military and 'Mob Rule,'" 33.
19 Ibid.
20 Ibid., and DHH Holly Lane, 74/672, folder 4, "Disturbances in Canada," 2.
21 Lackenbauer, "The Military and 'Mob Rule,'" 33.
22 *Calgary Herald*, 11 and 12 February 1916.
23 Lackenbauer, "The Military and 'Mob Rule,'" 37.
24 DHH Holly Lane, 74/672, folder 4, "Disturbances in Canada," 2.
25 Lackenbauer, "The Military and 'Mob Rule,'" 38.
26 *Calgary Herald*, 24 February 1916, 7.
27 Criminal Code of Canada, S.C. 1892, section 3, para 96.
28 Toronto *Globe*, 12 February 1916.
29 DHH, Holly Lane, 74/672, folder 4, "Disturbances in Canada 1916," 2.
30 Ibid., 3.
31 See Patricia P. McKegney, *The Kaiser's Bust: A Study of Wartime Propaganda in Berlin Ontario, 1914–1918* (Wellesley, ON: Bomberg Press, 1991).
32 *Toronto Star*, 9 February 1916, 1 and 4.
33 Ibid.
34 Gottlieb Leibbrandt, *Little Paradise: The Saga of the German Canadians of Waterloo County, Ontario 1800–1975* (Kitchener: Allprint Co., 1980), 252.

35 Philip Morris, *The Canadian Patriotic Fund: A Record of Its Activities from 1914 to 1919* (n.p., n.d.), 9.
36 Cited by the *Kitchener Daily Telegraph*, 1 August 1914, 12.
37 *Kitchener Daily Telegraph*, 24 August 1914, 2.
38 Ibid.
39 *Journal of Parliamentary Debates*, 16 February 1916, 855, statement of Sir Sam Hughes; and DHH, Holly Lane, 74/672, folder 4, "Disturbances in Canada 1916," 3.
40 *Toronto Star*, 9 February 1916, 4.
41 Ibid.
42 Ibid.
43 *Toronto Star*, 10 February 1916, 2.
44 See also Leibbrandt, *Little Paradise*; McKegney, *The Kaiser's Bust*; Lackenbauer, "The Military and 'Mob Rule'"; and W.R. Chadwick, *The Battle for Berlin Ontario: As Historical Drama* (Waterloo: Wilfrid Laurier University Press, 1992), for disturbances in Kitchener in 1916.
45 *Journal of Parliamentary Debates*, 16 February 1916, 855, statement of Sir Sam Hughes; and DHH, Holly Lane, 74/672, folder 4, "Disturbances in Canada 1916," 3.
46 Ibid.
47 *Toronto Star*, 10 February 1915, 1–2.
48 DHH, Holly Lane, 74/672, folder 4, "Disturbances in Canada 1916," 3; and Lackenbauer and Gardner, "Citizen Soldiers as Liminaries," 161.
49 *Journal of Parliamentary Debates*, 6–7 George V, 1916, vol. 122.
50 DHH, Holly Lane, 74/672, folder 4, "Disturbances in Canada 1916," 6.
51 Ibid., 7.
52 Ibid., 9.
53 Toronto *Globe*, 20 April 1916, 2.
54 Toronto *Globe*, 15 December 1917, 11.
55 McKegney, *The Kaiser's Bust*, 166.
56 Ibid., 179–80; and Chadwick, *The Battle for Berlin Ontario*, 160–1.
57 Toronto *Globe*, 2 January 1917, 1; *London Free Press*, 2 January 1917, 1; *Le Devoir*, 2 January 1917, 2, and McKegney, *The Kaiser's Bust*, 179–82, for the 1917 riots. See also Chadwick, *The Battle for Berlin Ontario*, 152–7.
58 Ian Miller, *Our Glory and Our Grief*, 8–9.
59 Toronto *Globe*, 5 and 21 April 1917.
60 The soldiers may have been inspired, as well, by recent American example. The entry of the US to the war had been followed by considerable anti-foreign agitation, a feature of which was the much-publicized expulsion of foreigners from their jobs; indeed, from the

communities in which they lived. In one case, in July 1917, miners in St Francis county, Missouri, rounded up seven hundred foreigners and marched them to the train station, subsequently putting them aboard any outgoing train. *Montreal Gazette*, 16 July 1917.
61 Toronto *Globe*, 13 April 1917.
62 Toronto *Globe*, 14 April 1917.
63 Toronto *Globe*, 19 April 1917.
64 *Toronto Star*, 4 June 1917, 2.
65 Ian Miller, *Our Glory and Our Grief*, 137–8.
66 Ibid., 139. By 1917, under streamlined procedures introduced by Order-in-Council, most wartime offences involving Aliens could be dealt with summarily by any magistrate. There was – no surprise – an explosion of WMA convictions, as we might expect, and as we have seen. Much of this appears to have been directed to silencing expression of provocative opinion.
67 Toronto *Globe*, 22 June 1917.
68 Toronto *Globe*, 20 September 1917, 9.
69 Donald Avery, "Canadian Immigration Policy and the Alien Question 1896–1919: The Anglo-Canadian Perspective," PhD thesis, University of Western Ontario, 1973, 392–3; and "Ethnic and Class Tension in Canada, 1918–1920," in *Loyalties in Conflict: Ukrainians in Canada during the Great War*, ed. Frances Swyripa and John Thompson (Edmonton: University of Alberta Press, 1983), 89.
70 LAC C.P.C. 119-C-1, vol. 19, R.B. Bennett to Chambers, 26 May 1917.
71 Jeffrey Keshen, "All the News That Was Fit to Print: Ernest J. Chambers and Information Control in Canada, 1914–1919," *Canadian Historical Review* 73:3 (1992): 330. For Regina generally, see James Pitsula, *For All We Have and Are: Regina and the Experience of the Great War* (Winnipeg: University of Manitoba Press, 2008).
72 *Journal of Parliamentary Debates*, 15 February 1916, 854–5.
73 Toronto *Globe*, 15 April 1916, 25 and 48.

7. "The Politician Who Attempts to Wander About in No Man's Land Must Be Ruthlessly Destroyed"

1 Roger Graham, *Arthur Meighen* (Toronto: Clarke, Irwin and Company, 1960), 134.
2 R. Matthew Bray, "Fighting as an Ally: The English Canadian Patriotic Response to the Great War," *Canadian Historical Review* 61.2 (1980): 156–7. The Canadian NSL formed when it became apparent that recruitment of

volunteers would never produce the five hundred thousand men Borden had promised in January 1916.
3 LAC MG 30 C11, vol. 1, "The Bonne Entente. How It Began: What It Has Done, and Its Immediate Program"; also, Godfrey to Arthur Hawkes, 4 July 1916.
4 See, for example, an exchange of correspondence in July 1916 between Godfrey and George Van Felson (president of the Association Civile de Recrutement du District de Québec). Van Felson considered that Quebec might possibly accept conscription. His evidence was an address by Colonel Armand Lavergne, reported in *Le Soleil*, in which Lavergne expressed himself as not being against conscription if necessary. Godfrey considered this opinion to be misconstrued. LAC MG 30 C11, vol. 1, Van Felson to Godfrey, 29 June 1916; Godfrey to Van Felson, 3 July 1916.
5 LAC MG 30 C11, vol. 1, Godfrey to Leonard, 15 July 1916; and Godfrey to Judge A.B. Klein, 17 July 1917.
6 LAC MG 30 C11, vol. 1, Godfrey to Van Felson, 15 July 1916. "Registration" meant that men would voluntarily register, and go through some of the steps necessary prior to induction into the army. The army, then, would call them up as needed. Attempted first in the United Kingdom ("the Derby Scheme"), registration was attempted in the Dominions and failed universally.
7 LAC MG 30 C11, vol. 1, Garneau to Godfrey, 12 July 1916. Garneau was looking to attract to the *Entente* a "strong delegation of leading commercial and financial interests, educationalists, and professional men, and especially members of the Bar, newspaper editors, and by no means least, representatives of labour organisations."
8 LAC MG 30 C11, vol. 1, Godfrey to Laurier, 21 June 1916.
9 G.L. Kristianson, *The Politics of Patriotism: The Pressure Group Activities of the Returned Servicemen's League* (Canberra: Australian National University Press, 1966), 5. At about this time, a "win the war" group, under Prime Minister Sir William "Billy" Hughes, had been formed of all parties in 1916 to carry the fight for conscription.
10 The first Ontario Bonne Entente committee included Mr Hewett (chairman of the Toronto Chamber of Commerce); Mr Parsons (president of the Canadian Manufacturers' Association; Dr Lock (president of the Canadian Club); J.P. Bell (general manager of the Bank of Hamilton and president of the Hamilton Canada Club); Colonel Leonard, Colonel Mulloy, Mr Hawkes, and Godfrey himself. LAC MG 30 C11, vol. 1, Godfrey to Neuville Belleau, 4 August 1916.

11 The first Quebec committee consisted of a City of Quebec delegation, including Eustace Leblanc (lieutenant governor); Sir Georges Garneau (chairman of the Quebec Recruiting League); George Van Felson (secretary of the Quebec Recruiting League); Major Vien; N. Le Viguer (mayor of Quebec). M. Picard (president of the allied Chambres de Commerce); and a City of Montreal delegation, including M.K. LaFlamme, KC; Z. Hebert (wholesale grocer); M. Quintall (grain merchant); E. Berthieume (editor of *La Presse*); E. Tarte (editor of *La Patrie*); General Labelle; Comptroller Côté; and O.S. Perault (general manager of the Imperial Tobacco Company). LAC 30 C11, vol. 1, Godfrey to Mullin 30 August 1916.
12 LAC MG 30 C11, vol. 1, Godfrey to Mullin, 18 August 1916.
13 Robert Brown and Ramsay Cook, *Canada 1896–1921: A Nation Transformed* (Toronto: McClelland and Stewart, 1974), 265.
14 MG 30 C11, vol. 1, "History of the *Bonne Entente*, Including a Narrative of the Evidence Leading up Thereto," undated.
15 Toronto *Globe*, 11 January 1917; and Brown and Cook, *Canada 1896–1921*, 265.
16 MG 30 C11, vol. 1, speech of Sir Georges Garneau, 9 January 1917; and *Le Devoir*, 9 January and 9–10 February 1917.
17 LAC MG 26, H, Borden Papers, reel 4324, item 45879, N.F. Davidson, KC to Borden, 1 March 1917.
18 LAC MG 26, H, Borden Papers, item 91928, Godfrey to Borden, 18 February 1917.
19 Bray, "Fighting as an Ally," 167.
20 L.-G. Desjardins, *England, Canada and the Great War* (Quebec: Chronicle, 1918).
21 LAC MG 26, H, Borden Papers, reel 4314, item 35563, Blount from Kemp to Borden, 30 April 1917.
22 Toronto *Globe*, 3 July 1916, 8. Some of the improved atmosphere in Quebec appears to have resulted from the excellent performance of French Canadian troops on the Somme, particularly at Courcelette. An officer of the 75th Battalion opined that "Canada may well be proud of her French-Canadians – excellent troops and fearless officers." Archbishop Bruchesi of Montreal, in reference to the battle, considered that "in this fight Quebec has done, and is doing its share." Toronto *Globe*, 28 October 1916, 6.
23 Brown and Cook, *Canada 1896–1921*, 219–20.
24 A. Williams, "Conscription, 1917: A Brief for the Defence," *Canadian Historical Review* 27.4 (December 1956): 6–7.

25 H. Bowering, *Service: The Story of the Canadian Legion, 1925–1960* (Ottawa: Dominion Command, 1960), 3–4.
26 LAC MG 26, H, Borden Papers, reel C4355, item 71772, Currie to Borden, 23 June 1917.
27 A.M.J. Hyatt, "Sir Arthur Currie and Conscription: A Soldier's View," *Canadian Historical Review* 50.3 (Spring 1969): 286.
28 For the IWC meetings, see B. Millman, *Pessimism and British War Policy 1916–1918* (London: Frank Cass, 2001), 135–8 and 187–92.
29 LAC MG 26, I, vol. 1, reel C3214, Arthur Meighen to R.H. Adams, 26 August 1918.
30 LAC MG 26, H, Borden Papers, reel C4205, "Canada and the United Kingdom," speech in Montreal, 6 December 1916. There appeared to be 287,976 otherwise eligible men, not engaged in some essential occupation. Brown and Cook, *Canada 1896–1921*, 220.
31 Williams, "Conscription 1917," 7.
32 For example, Williams, "Conscription 1917"; *Conscription 1917*, ed. Ramsay Cook, Craig Brown, and Carl Berger (Toronto: University of Toronto Press, 1969), 1: "The cumulative effect of new materials is to show that not only was conscription militarily necessary – that Canada's contribution to the fighting lagged behind that of her principal allies and sister Dominions until conscription was employed – but also that the success of conscription was not achieved at the cost of national tragedy ... Many other historians have tended to accept O.D. Skelton's line that Borden implemented conscription to win an election, or Sir Clifford Sifton's opinion that Borden brought on an election, on this issue, in order to destroy the Liberal Party. Williams is more correct in thinking that Borden fought the election to bring on conscription."
33 Ronald Haycock, *Sam Hughes: The Public Career of a Controversial Canadian* (Waterloo: Wilfrid Laurier University Press, 1986).
34 Robert Borden, *Robert Laird Borden: His Memoirs* (Toronto: Macmillan, 1938), 1:251.
35 Elizabeth Armstrong, *The Crisis of Quebec, 1914–1918* (1937; Montreal: McGill-Queen's University Press, 1974), xvii.
36 Bray, "Fighting as an Ally," 165.
37 *Journal of the Synod of the Church of England of the Diocese of Huron 60th Session* (London, ON: A. Talbot, 1917), 61.
38 Examples: LAC MG 26, H, Borden Papers, reel C4331, item 53540, Newcombe to Borden, 27 March 1918; Toronto *Globe*, 14 March 1917 (the Montreal Board of Trade demanded the immediate enforcement of the Militia Act in order to require every "able-bodied man of military age to

defend his country"); Toronto *Globe*, 15 March 1917 (the LOL agreed, and demanded "immediate enforcement of the Militia Act"). Toronto *Globe* concurred. Toronto *Globe*, 30 April 1917. Otherwise, see Bray, "Fighting as an Ally," 158.

39 Brown and Cook, *Canada 1896–1921*, 270.
40 Graham, *Arthur Meighen*, 121–37.
41 Borden, *Memoirs*, 1:261.
42 LAC MG 26, H, Borden Papers, reel 4205, "Speech Delivered by … in the House of Commons on the IWC and IW Conference, and Compulsory Military Enlistment," 18 May 1917.
43 Borden, *Memoirs*, 2:700.
44 Toronto *Globe*, 24 March 1916, 12, and 2 June 1917, 8, for example.
45 Ian Miller, *Our Glory and Our Grief: Torontonians and the Great War* (Toronto: University of Toronto Press, 2002), 135.
46 *Le Devoir*, 6 June 1917.
47 LAC MG 26, H, Borden Papers, reel 4321.
48 LAC MG 26, H, Borden Papers, reel 4314, item 42360, Kitchener Board of Trade to Borden, 5 July 1917; Toronto *Globe*, 16 May 1917.
49 LAC MG 26, H, Borden Papers, reel 4324, item 45797, Central Committee of Patriotic Organisations to Borden, August 1917.
50 *Le Devoir*, 2 June 1917.
51 *Toronto Star*, 2 June 1917, 2.
52 The Next of Kin Association wanted, in addition to conscription, nationalization of profits in excess of 7 per cent; a fivefold increase in the rate of income tax on incomes over $2,500 p.a.; direct tax on land values, including national resources; a tax on idle land with nationalization as the penalty for default; inheritance taxes on estates over $50,000; removal of tariffs on the necessaries for the duration; price fixing; nationalization of munitions, transport, and communications for the duration. LAC MG 26, H, Borden Papers, reel 4321, item 42410, telegram from the Great War Next of Kin Association, 29 August 1917. For GWVA see Toronto *Globe*, 16 May 1917, 14.
53 Toronto *Globe*, 11 August 1917.
54 Toronto *Globe*, 18 August 1917.
55 LAC MG 26, H, Borden Papers, reel 4314, item 42384, Win the War to Borden, 18 July 1917.
56 *Montreal Gazette*, 23, 24, 25 July, 3 August 1917.
57 LAC MG 30 C11, vol. 1, "Report of Proceedings of the Convention of the 'Win the War' Association, Held in the Arena, Toronto on Thursday and Friday, August 2nd and 3rd 1917." See also Ian Miller, *Our Glory and Our Grief*, 140–1.

58 LAC MG 30 C11, vol. 1, "Report of Proceedings of the Convention of the "Win the War" Association, Held in the Arena, Toronto on Thursday and Friday, August 2nd and 3rd 1917."
59 Ibid.
60 Ibid
61 Ibid.
62 LAC MG 26, H, Borden Papers, item 39992, Godfrey to Borden, 4 October 1917.
63 Toronto *Globe*, 13 November 1917.
64 LAC MG 26, H, vol. 1, reel C3214, H.S. Clement to Borden, 27 December 1917.
65 LAC MG 26, H, Borden Papers, reel 4321, item 42405, ILP Association of Canada to Borden, 8 August 1917.
66 J.F. Thompson, previously a lecturer in England for the Land Nationalisation Society and alderman for Salford, was the leader. Martin Robin, *Radical Politics and Canadian Labour, 1880–1930* (Industrial Relations Centre, Queen's University, 1968), 123. James Simpson, the leader of the peace faction, was a close friend of Ramsay MacDonald, Philip Snowden, and Keir Hardie (ibid., 141). After a meeting with Borden, however, he swung behind the government and became a proponent of conscription. Ian Miller, *Our Glory and Our Grief*, 136.
67 Toronto *Globe*, 6 January 1917, 4; *Le Devoir*, 5 January 1917; and *Montreal Gazette*, 18 August 1916, 6 and 6 January 1917.
68 Toronto *Globe*, 3 January 1916, 24.
69 Toronto *Globe*, 5 January 1917, 3.
70 LAC MG 26, H, Borden Papers, reel 4321, item 42368, "Trade and Labour Congress of Canada. Pronouncement of Organised Labour in Canada on War Problems," 11 June 1917; and item 42371, Steele to Borden, 11 July 1917.
71 Brown and Cook, *Canada 1896–1921*, 309; and Robin, *Radical Politics and Canadian Labour, 1880–1930*, 68. See also Robert Babcock, *Gompers in Canada: A Study in American Continentalism before the First World War* (Toronto: University of Toronto Press, 1974).
72 Robin, *Radical Politics and Canadian Labour, 1880–1930*, 240. For Gompers in Britain, see Brock Millman, *Managing Domestic Dissent in First World War Britain* (London: Frank Cass, 2000), 236–7. Canada provided similar support to allies. Apprised by Beaverbrook that prominent, representative Canadians were required to assist with recruiting in Ireland, Canada appears to have despatched Lord Shaughnessey, and Fitzpatrick and Doherty – members of the government. LAC MG 26, H,

reel 4327, items 48096, 48097, and 48098, Beaverbrook to Borden, 27 June 1917, Borden to Doherty, 28 June 1917, and Borden to Beaverbrook, 28 June 1917.
73 Desmond Morton and Terry Copp, *Working People* (Ottawa: Deneau, 1981), 111.
74 LAC MG 26, H, Borden Papers, Archbishop Mathieson to C.J. Doherty forwarded to Borden, 10, 14 July 1917.
75 *Montreal Gazette*, 31 July 1917.
76 *Montreal Gazette*, 7 July 1917.
77 *Montreal Gazette*, 17 July 1917.
78 Brown and Cook, *Canada 1896–1921*, 272. The powerful Clifford Sifton, a one-time Liberal and minister of the interior, had deserted Laurier in 1905 on the question of Catholic schools in the West. The Siftons were a Methodist, Irish, Orange family originally from Arva, Ontario, just north of London. For the make-up of the new Cabinet, see LAC MG 55/30 no. 135. See also Graham, *Arthur Meighen*, 161.
79 Toronto *Globe*, 6 January 1917, 3.
80 Toronto *Globe*, 14 May 1917, 8. See also *Montreal Gazette*, 12 July 1917, for Rowell at Knox Presbyterian in Harrington, Ontario.
81 Leslie Frost, *Fighting Men* (Toronto: Clark, Irwin and Company, 1967), 41–2.
82 *Brantford Courier*, 20 May 1917.
83 Frost, *Fighting Men*, 121.
84 LAC MG 11 CO 616, item 52208, reel 4009, Devonshire to CO, 24 October 1917.
85 Frost, *Fighting Men*, 122.
86 *Montreal Gazette*, 27 July 1917.
87 LAC Laurier Papers, series A, vol. 715, reel C915, Laurier to Comorthy, 28 November 1917: "one thing, however, I am sure of. It is that if money can defeat us, we will be defeated. At the present stage of the campaign I am pretty sure that that alone can defeat us."
88 *Montreal Gazette*, 9 August 1917.
89 Borden, *Memoirs*, 2:701.
90 Toronto *Globe*, 21 May 1917.
91 *Le Devoir*, 7 April 1917, 7.
92 *Le Devoir*, 27 April 1917, 4.
93 *Le Devoir*, 6 and 14 June 1917, 5.
94 *Le Devoir*, 26 March 1917, 8.
95 *Le Devoir* 2 June 1917, 6.
96 *Le Devoir*, 9 June 1917, 6.

97 *Le Devoir*, 13 June 1917, 4–5.
98 *Le Devoir*, 5, 7, 9, 20 April 1917.
99 *Le Devoir*, 7 June 1917, 2.
100 *Le Devoir*, 8 June 1917.
101 *Le Devoir*, 29 March 1917.
102 Toronto *Globe*, 21 May 1917.
103 *Le Devoir*, 9 June 1917, 6.
104 Borden, *Memoirs*, 2:617–18. Mr J.A. Flavelle to Borden, December 1916.
105 LAC MG 26, H, Borden Papers, reel 4314, item 35455, Borden to Blount, 30 March 1917.
106 LAC MG 26, H, Borden Papers, reel 4329, Laurier in Parliament, 9 April 1918.
107 For example, LAC MG 26, H, Borden Papers, item 41734. In seconding a motion to write a speech of Arthur Balfour (then visiting Canada) into the Parliamentary record, Laurier said: "Mr. Balfour I am sure, would be the first to recognize that the warmth of the reception which he has received, especially in this country, is not due alone to his great name and personality, but is associated with an even greater name, the name of England, the Champion of liberty, the mother of living nations ... England, great at all times, was never greater than at this moment; never was greater, I repeat and because of what? Because today, England is the home of civilisation and the terror of the enemies of civilisation."
108 *Canadian Liberal Monthly*, August 1916.
109 For example, LAC, Laurier Papers, series A, vol. 715, reel C915, Laurier to Blake, 19 November 1917.
110 *Canadian Liberal Monthly*, August 1916.
111 Williams, "Conscription 1917," 3.
112 Graham, *Arthur Meighen*, 146.
113 Sam Hughes, *Correspondence of General Sir Sam Hughes, ex-Minister of the Militia and The Right Hon. Sir Robert Borden GCMG* (Ottawa: Central Liberal Information Office, 1916).
114 Morton and Copp, *Working People*, 102. See also Michael Bliss, *A Canadian Millionaire: The Life and Business Times of Sir Joseph Flavelle, Bart. 1858–1939* (Toronto: Macmillan, 1978), 329–63.
115 For the Flavelle case, for example, LAC MG 26 H1(9), Borden Papers, Northrup to Borden, 21 July 1917.
116 Williams, "Conscription 1917," 2.
117 Joseph Boudreau, "Western Canada's Alien Enemies in World War One," *Alberta Historical Review* 12.1 (Winter 1964): 7–8.
118 Brown and Cook, *Canada 1896–1921*, 268.

119 Ibid., 271.
120 Borden, *Memoirs*, 2:104.
121 Ibid., 2:720.
122 LAC MG 26, I, Meighen Papers, vol. 6, Lieutenant-Colonel W.B. Clayton to Meighen, 3 July 1917.
123 For example, LAC MG 26, I, Meighen Papers, vol. 6, Ed Meighen to Arthur Meighen, 19 December 1917: "Each trip up the line now seems a little livelier and funner than the previous one, but so far I have been lucky. It is simply wonderful how one can get out alive at all."
124 Graham, *Arthur Meighen*, 88.
125 LAC MG 26, H, Borden Papers, reel 4205, "The Electoral Disabilities ... Removal Act."
126 LAC MG 26, H, Borden Papers, reel 4229, "An Act to Enable Canadian Soldiers on Active Military Service during the Present War to Exercise Their Electoral Franchise, 15 April 1915."
127 Borden had suggested that the government prepare this legislation in March against the eventuality that Laurier refused to enter a government or grant further continuances. LAC MG 26, H, Borden Papers, reel 4314, item 55490, Blount from Meighen to Borden, 18 April 1917; and item 35517, Borden to Blount, 20 April 1917.
128 Borden, *Memoirs*, 2:701. Military Voters Act, 7–8 George V, assented 20 September 1917, Statutes of Canada.
129 Graham, *Arthur Meighen*, 165.
130 LAC MG 26, I, Meighen Papers, vol. 1, reel C3214, item 438, "War Time Elections Act." War Time Elections Act, 7–8 George V, assented 20 September 1917, Statutes of Canada.
131 Borden, *Memoirs*, 2:697, diary entry for 8 February 1917: "Bennett came and discussed National Service for more than an hour. Agrees that we should disenfranchise those who have not signed national service cards."
132 Brown and Cook, *Canada 1896–1921*, 271.
133 See, for example, the case of Grace Ritchie-England, president of the Montreal Council of Women, impeached for her criticism of the proceedings and of conscription. Tarah Brookfield, "Divided by the Ballot Box: The Montreal Council of Women and the 1917 Election," *Canadian Historical Review* 89.4 (January 2008).
134 LAC MG 26, H, Borden Papers, reel 4230, circular, 24 October 1917.
135 Robert Borden, *The War and the Future* (London: Hodder and Stoughton, 1917).
136 LAC MG 55/30 no. 135, Union Program.
137 *Toronto Telegram*, 12 June 1917.

138 LAC Laurier Papers, series A, reel 179, Laurier to Thomson, 15 November 1917; Laurier to Frank Hobson, 24 October 1917: the Liberals would lose the election.
139 LAC MG 27, 111, B9, vol. 1, Stevens Papers, A/1/6A, Odlum to Stevens, 1917.
140 Frost, *Fighting Men*, 115.
141 Williams, "Conscription 1917," 10.
142 *Montreal Gazette*, 19 November 1917.
143 Mason Wade, *The French Canadians, 1760–1945* (Toronto: Macmillan, 1955), 752.
144 Sandra Gwyn, *Tapestry of War* (Toronto: HarperCollins, 1992), 415.
145 LAC Laurier Papers, series A, vol. 715, reel C915, W.L. Mackenzie King to Laurier, 21 November 1917.
146 LAC MG 27, 11, F 1–2, Wilfrid Laurier to H.H. Hartley, 11 January 1918.
147 LAC MG 26, H, Borden Papers, reel 4314, item 35445, Blount to Borden, 27 March 1917: "Have thorough understanding with Blondin and am arranging to finance his recruiting campaign. Expect another important French Canadian will retire from public position and support Blondin. Arrangements being made whereby Berthiaume will enthusiastically support Blondin. Plan underway whereby important defection from Bourassa following likely to result. If this materialises whole political complexion Quebec modified and Bourassa movement receives staggering blow. Would be of immense advantage to Blondin and Conservative party in Quebec if you could arrange through proper channels a cable of commendation of Blondin from President of France."
148 Toronto *Globe*, 9 and 17 May 1917.
149 Toronto *Globe*, 18 May 1917.
150 LAC Laurier Papers, series A, vol. 715, reel C915, Laurier to Russell, 27 December 1917.
151 Brown and Cook, *Canada 1896–1921*, 266–8.
152 *Le Canada*, 3 June 1917.
153 LAC MG 26, H, Borden Papers, reel C4229, Major-General J.B. Steel to Borden, 5 July 1917.
154 LAC MG 26, H, Borden Papers, reel C4322, item 42773, Borden to J.R. Robinson, 3 April 1918.
155 LAC MG 30, Currie Papers, E100, vol. 2, Simms to Currie, 3 December 1917.
156 Gwyn, *Tapestry of War*, 416.
157 LAC MG 26, H, Borden Papers, reel 4322, item 42786, Borden to Nickle, 4 September 1918. Of one thousand married men given three months' leave

in 1918, only one-tenth returned promptly at the expiration of their leave. Only 17 per cent returned at all. "Canada leave," therefore, generally led to auto-demobilization.

158 LAC Laurier Papers, series A, vol. 715, reel C915, item 198625.
159 LAC Laurier Papers, series A, vol. 715, reel C915, a soldier to Laurier, 5 December 1917.
160 LAC MG 55/30 no. 135, Union Program.
161 Toronto *Globe*, 11 March 1918, 14.
162 Toronto *Globe*, 3 August 1918.
163 Henry Ferns and Bernard Ostry, *The Age of Mackenzie King* (Toronto: Lorimer, 1976), 228; Brown and Cook, *Canada 1896–1921*, 236.
164 By May 1918, cancellation of the famers' exemption was leading to intense rural unrest, particularly in the West. LAC MG 26, H, Borden Papers, reel C4331, item 53621, Meighen and Doherty to Borden, 4 September 1918
165 LAC MG 26, I, Meighen Papers, vol. 6, Hugh Clark to Meighen, 21 January 1918.
166 LAC MG 26, H, Borden Papers, reel C4375, item 91690, Borden to Long, 20 April 1917. See, for Robertson in general, Morton and Copp, *Working People*, 111.
167 Robin, *Radical Politics and Canadian Labour, 1880–1930*, 138–9.
168 LAC Laurier Papers, series A, vol. 715, reel C915, King to Laurier, 18 December 1917.
169 J. Castell Hopkins, *The Canadian Annual Review of Public Affairs, 1917* (Ottawa: Canadian Annual Review), 414.
170 *Le Devoir*, 2 June 1917, 5.
171 J. Castell Hopkins, *The Canadian Annual Review of Public Affairs, 1917*, 412.
172 1,501,719 Unionist votes were cast to 509,940 Liberal. Williams, "Conscription 1917," 9.
173 John Thompson, "The Alien Enemy and the Canadian General Election of 1917," in *Loyalties in Conflict: Ukrainians in Canada during the Great War*, ed. Frances Swyripa and John Thompson (Edmonton: University of Alberta Press, 1983), 36.
174 Brown and Cook, *Canada 1896–1921*, 309. For labour support for the Unionists, see Robin, *Radical Politics and Canadian Labour, 1880–1930*, 135–6.
175 Thompson, "The Alien Enemy and the Canadian General Election of 1917," 33.
176 LAC MG 26, H, Borden Papers, reel 4327, G.W. Yates to Lloyd Harris, 27 February 1918; and item 48551, 1 March 1918.

177 Brown and Cook, *Canada 1896–1921*, 273.
178 It is doubtful, for example, that the Tory incumbent in Hamilton East needed the help of 3,596 soldier voters, when he could safely count on most of the support of the 15,489 regular voters in his riding: if he did need this help, this proportion of the adult men (and therefore voters) in his district would not have signalled their support for the war by service. Similarly it is doubtful that the Liberal MP for Joliette was much afraid that the three military votes applied to his district would prove decisive in a contest in which most of the 5,712 regular voters could be counted upon, in the main, to support the Liberal platform.
179 Seats: in Ontario, Brant, Bruce South, Essex South, Ottawa (one of two seats) and Perth South; in Nova Scotia, Cape Breton South (two seats), Cumberland, Hants and Pictou; in British Columbia, Skeena; in Prince Edward Island, Kings, and Queens (two seats); in Alberta, Bow River and Edmonton West; and the Yukon. The number of seats in which the Military Voters Act was decisive, therefore, was at least seventeen, and might well have been more. Calculation is that for every soldier who might have voted in a riding, at least one newly enfranchised woman existed (probably, in fact, more than one). When the margin by which a district was carried, therefore, is smaller than the number of military votes locally registered, it is likely that the seat would have been lost without the 1917 innovations. Sessional Paper 13, "Return on the General Election," Sessional Papers, vol. 56 (Session 1920), no. 4.
180 LAC Laurier Papers, series A, vol. 715, reel C915, D.C. Larkin to Laurier, 18 December 1917.
181 LAC Laurier Papers, series A, vol. 715, reel C915, item 198988.
182 LAC Laurier Papers, series A, vol. 715, reel C915, O.D. Skelton to Laurier, 18 December 1917.
183 LAC MG 26, H, reel C4329, item 50095, "Statement of Department of Militia and Defence as of March 18, 1918." See also reel C4331, item 53589, Newcombe to Rowell, 8 May 1918.

8. "Absolute Masters of All Authority"

1 LAC MG 26, H, Borden Papers, reel 4331, item 53550, statement to Parliament, April 1918.
2 LAC MG 26, I, Meighen Papers, reel C3214, Clement to Borden, 27 December 1917.
3 Elizabeth Armstrong, *The Crisis of Quebec, 1914–1918* (1937; Montreal: McGill-Queen's University Press, 1974), 226–31.

4 Robert Brown and Ramsay Cook, *Canada 1896–1921: A Nation Transformed* (Toronto: McClelland and Stewart, 1974), 306. See, for the Easter riots generally, Martin Auger, "On the Brink of Civil War: The Canadian Government and the Suppression of the 1918 Quebec Easter Riots," *Canadian Historical Review* 89.4 (January 2008).
5 Curtis Cole, "The War Measures Act, 1914: Aspects of the Emergency Limitation of Freedom of Speech and Personal Liberties in Canada, 1914–1919," MA thesis, University of Western Ontario, 1980, 42.
6 Armstrong, *The Crisis of Quebec, 1914–1918*, 231. The police do appear to have been quite ruthless in their enforcement of the MSA. Mayor Church, of Toronto, complained as well of "grand stand schemes" which did not produce a single soldier, and which had ruined the CNE that year. Toronto *Globe*, 18 July 1918, 6.
7 Toronto *Globe*, 29 June 1918.
8 Toronto *Globe*, 1 July 1918.
9 Toronto *Globe*, 22 June 1918, 5.
10 *Le Devoir*, 9, 10 February 1917.
11 Toronto *Globe*, 2 August 1918.
12 Toronto *Globe*, 24 July 1918.
13 Toronto *Globe*, 27 July 1918.
14 LAC RG 10, vol. 6767, file 452–16, part 1, Scott to deputy minister militia and defence, 29 May 1917. My thanks to Richard Holt for this reference.
15 LAC MG 26, H, Borden Papers, reel C4333, item 54912, Borden to the press, 3 May 1918.
16 Toronto *Globe*, 14 November 1918.
17 Donald Avery, *Dangerous Foreigners: European Immigrant Workers and Labour Radicalism in Canada 1896–1932* (Toronto: McClelland and Stewart, 1979), 72.
18 Martin Robin, *Radical Politics and Canadian Labour, 1880–1930* (Industrial Relations Centre, Queen's University, 1968), 156. See also LAC MG 26, H, Borden Papers, reel C4332, item 54225, Winnipeg Board of Trade to Borden, 16 May 1918.
19 LAC MG 26, H, Borden Papers, reel C4332, item 54225, Winnipeg Board of Trade to Borden, 16 May 1918.
20 Winnipeg's population was 42,340 in 1901 and 179,087 in 1921. By 1921, one-third of the population was foreign-born. Brown and Cook, *Canada 1896–1921*, 98–9.
21 David Bercuson, *Fools and Wise Men* (Toronto: McGraw-Hill, Ryerson, 1978), 25.

22 Craig Heron and Myer Siemiatycki, "The Great War, the State, and Working Class Canada," in *The Workers Revolt in Canada*, ed. Craig Heron (Toronto: University of Toronto Press, 1998), 22.
23 Avery, *Dangerous Foreigners*, 77, 83–9.
24 Bercuson, *Fools and Wise Men*, 65.
25 Ibid., 88.
26 LAC MG 26, H, Borden Papers, reel C4334, item 56597, Imperial Munitions Board to Borden, 22 February 1918.
27 *Vancouver Sun*, 1 February 1918.
28 LAC RG 13, Justice, series A-2, vol. 237, file 1919–1437.
29 LAC MG 26, H, Borden Papers, reel C4334, item 56617, Davidson to the minister of justice, 19 March 1918.
30 LAC MG 26, H, Borden Papers, reel C4334, minister of militia to Borden, 18 April 1918.
31 LAC MG 26, H, Borden Papers, reel C4334, item 56635, CGS to Borden, 17 April 1918.
32 In Canada, some things truly never change.
33 LAC MG 26, H, Borden Papers, reel C4334, item 56635, CGS to Borden, 17 April 1918.
34 LAC MG 26, H, Borden Papers, reel C4334, item 56611, commissioner of police to minister of justice, 5 March 1918.
35 LAC MG 26, H, Borden Papers, reel C4334, item 56619, Davidson to minister of justice, 21 March 1918.
36 LAC MG 26, H, Borden Papers, reel C4334, item 56620, Temiskaming Mine Managers' Association to Frank Cochrane MP, 22 March 1918; and item 56628, Borden to Cochrane, 22 March 1918.
37 LAC MG 26, H, Borden Papers, reel C4334, item 56632, A.P. Sherwood, chief commissioner of police, to minister of justice, 10 April 1918.
38 LAC MG 26, H, Borden Papers, reel C4334, item 56629, Special Agent R. Allen to A.P. Sherwood, chief commissioner of police, 18 April 1918.
39 Toronto *Globe*, 23 March 1918, 7.
40 LAC MG 26, H, Borden Papers, reel C4334, item 56639, chief commissioner of police to deputy minister of labour, 9 May 1919.
41 Donald Avery, "Canadian Immigration Policy and the Alien Question 1896–1919: The Anglo-Canadian Perspective," PhD thesis, University of Western Ontario, 1973, 448.
42 LAC MG 26, H, Borden Papers, reel C4334, item 56644, Sherwood to minister of justice, 23 May 1918.
43 LAC MG 26, H, Borden Papers, reel C4334, item 56651, Sherwood to minister of justice, 16 June 1918.

44 Robin, *Radical Politics and Canadian Labour, 1880–1930*, 41–6. See, for Western radicalism, Bercuson, *Fools and Wise Men*, and for particular grievances ibid., 15–17.
45 Ibid., 97. For this reason, the Canada First Publicity Association urged the elimination of aliens altogether.
46 Avery, *Dangerous Foreigners*, 81.
47 *Vancouver Sun*, 2 February 1918.
48 *Vancouver Sun*, 7 February 1918.
49 *Vancouver Sun*, 8 February 1918.
50 *Vancouver Sun*, 3 August 1918, 1, 3, and 12.
51 Ibid.
52 *Vancouver Sun*, 4 August 1918. See also Ben Isitt, "The Search for Solidarity:The Industrial and Political Roots of the Cooperative Commonwealth Federation in British Columbia, 1913–1928," MA thesis, University of British Columbia, 2003.
53 *Vancouver Sun*, 6 August 1918.
54 Robin, *Radical Politics and Canadian Labour, 1880–1930*, 152; and Bercuson, *Fools and Wise Men*, 91.
55 *Vancouver Sun*, 11 August 1918.
56 *Vancouver Sun*, 5 August 1918.
57 *Vancouver Sun*, 6 August 1918.
58 *Vancouver Sun*, 8 August 1918.
59 Toronto *Globe*, 15 February 1918.
60 Toronto *Globe*, 9 April 1918.
61 Toronto *Globe*, 12 April 1918.
62 Toronto *Globe*, 8 April 1918.
63 Toronto *Globe*, 1 August 1918.
64 Ian Miller, *Our Glory and Our Grief: Torontonians and the Great War* (Toronto: University of Toronto Press, 2002), 177–8.
65 DHH (Directorate of History and Heritage), Holly Lane, 325.009 (D198), "War Story of the RCAMC," file "The Military Hospitals of Toronto during the Great War."
66 Ibid.
67 DHH, Holly Lane, 325.009 (D281), "Troops Called Out in Aid of Civil Power," 2MD-34-1-155, 22 August 1918, H.C. Bickford to Militia Council.
68 Desmond Morton and Glenn Wright, *Winning the Second Battle: Canadian Veterans and the Return to Civilian Life 1915–1920* (Toronto: University of Toronto Press, 1987), 82.
69 Ian Miller, *Our Glory and Our Grief*, 179.
70 DHH, Holly Lane, 325.009 (D281), "Troops Called Out in Aid of Civil Power," GOC No. 2 to Ashton, 7 August 1918.

71 DHH, Holly Lane, 325.009 (D281), "Troops Called Out in Aid of Civil Power," 2MD 34–1-155, Ashton to GOC No. 2, 12 August 1918. Major Osler, the APM and an eyewitness, considered that only 25 per cent of the rioters were in uniform. Some RAF men and US soldiers were in evidence. SMD-34–1-155, APM MD No. 2 to GOC, 21 August 1918.
72 Toronto *Globe*, 3 August 1918, 1.
73 J. Castell Hopkins, *The Canadian Annual Review of Public Affairs 1918* (Ottawa: Canadian Annual Review, 1919), 587.
74 Toronto *Globe*, 5 August 1918.
75 DHH, Holly Lane, 325.009 (D281), "Troops Called Out in Aid of Civil Power," note on night 3/4 August.
76 DHH, Holly Lane, 325.009 (D281), "Troops Called Out in Aid of Civil Power," 34–1-155, 3 August 1918.
77 Toronto *Globe*, 14 November 1918.
78 Hopkins, *The Canadian Annual Review of Public Affairs 1918*, 587.
79 DHH, Holly Lane, 325.009 (D281), "Troops Called Out in Aid of Civil Power," 34–7-55, 3 August 1918, Major GS to OC O.C. Training Company COTC.
80 DHH, Holly Lane, 325.009 (D281), "Troops Called Out in Aid of Civil Power," 34–1-1155, 5 August 1918, adjutant general to GOC No. 2.
81 DHH, Holly Lane, 325.009 (D281), "Troops Called Out in Aid of Civil Power," 34–1-155, APM MD No. 2 to AAG MD No. 2.
82 Toronto *Globe*, 5 August 1918.
83 DHH, Holly Lane, 325.009 (D281), "Troops Called Out in Aid of Civil Power," MD 2 34–1-155, 4 August 1918, GOC MD No. 2 to OCS.
84 DHH, Holly Lane, 325.009 (D281), "Troops Called Out in Aid of Civil Power," 34–1-155, 23 August 1918, AAG to GOC.
85 DHH, Holly Lane, 325.009 (D281) "Troops Called Out in Aid to the Civil Power," HQ 68–28, 12 September 1918, AG to GOC No. 2, citing PC 834, 4 April 1918. In case there was any doubt, this Order-in-Council was entitled "In Case of a Riot or Other Disturbances the G.O.C. of the District May at His Discretion Use Troops under His Command to Restore Order, the Disturbance in Question to Be under Martial Law. Any Man or Person Found Guilty of Taking Part in Such a Riot or Disturbance in Opposition to the M.S.A. Shall Be Deemed to Be Called Out for Military Service under the Act."
86 Tim Buck, *Canada and the Russian Revolution: The Impact of the World's First Socialist Revolution on Labour and Politics in Canada* (Toronto: Progress Books, 1967), 35.
87 Ibid., 36.
88 Morton and Wright, *Winning the Second Battle*, 121.

330 Notes to pages 203–7

89 LAC MG 26, H, reel 4327, item 48121, GWVA to Borden, 5 September 1918.
90 LAC MG 26, H, reel 4327, item 48135, GWVA (Winnipeg Branch) to Borden, 16 September 1918.
91 PC 25 September 1918; and PC 2693, 13 November 1918. See also Jeffrey Keshen, "All the News That Was Fit to Print: Ernest J. Chambers and Information Control in Canada, 1914–1919," *Canadian Historical Review* 73:3 (1992): 330–1.
92 LAC MG 26, H, Borden Papers, reel C4334, item 56644, A.P. Sherwood, chief commissioner of police, to minister of justice, 23 May 1918.
93 LAC MG 26, H, Borden Papers, reel C4334, item 56698, Public Safety Branch, 21 October 1918.
94 Toronto *Globe*, 11 June 1917.
95 Christopher Hackett, "The Church of England and the Manitoba Schools Question," in *The Anglican Church and the World of Western Canada, 1820–1970*, ed. Barry Ferguson (Regina: University of Regina, 1991), 94–101.
96 Brown and Cook, *Canada 1896–1921*, 254–5.
97 In July 1917, E.B. Devlin, MP, J.C. Walsh, ex-MP, and P. O'Reilly, all prominent Quebec Liberals, joined with Dr Guerin to oppose conscription in St Anne's Hall, Montreal. *Montreal Gazette*, 4 July, 4. For Irishmen involved in the Schools Question, see Michael Fitzpatrick, "The Role of Bishop Michael Francis Fallon and the Conflict between the French Catholics and Irish Catholics in the Ontario Bilingual Schools Question, 1910–1920," MA thesis, University of Western Ontario, 1969, 128.
98 Ibid., 123.
99 LAC MG 26, H, Borden Papers, reel C4358, item 74369, Reverend O'Leary to Borden, 17 November 1917.
100 Robert Borden, *Robert Laird Borden: His Memoirs* (Toronto: Macmillan, 1938), 2:789.
101 LAC MG 26, H, Borden Papers, reels 4330 and 4331.
102 LAC MG 26, H, Borden Papers, reel 4331, item 53242, Congregational Union of Canada to Borden, 5 October 1917.
103 LAC MG 26, H, Borden Papers, reel 4331, item 53245, Ministerial Association, Edmonton, to Borden, 10 October 1917.
104 It did not go away quickly. After the war, in May 1919, Doherty ordered an inquiry into what had occurred (LAC MG 26, H, Borden Papers, reel C4331, item 53276, 21 May 1919). Chief Justice L. Davies (item 53281, Davies to Borden, 31 July 1919) and Justice F.A. Anglin (item 53284, 2 August 1919) both refused to participate as

commissioners, since they felt that an inquiry could only invite controversy and have no good effect.

9. 1919: The War at Home Continues

1 LAC RG 6, E, C.H. Cahan to minister of justice, 6 January 1919.
2 Curtis Cole, "The War Measures Act, 1914: Aspects of the Emergency Limitation of Freedom of Speech and Personal Liberties in Canada, 1914–1919," MA thesis, University of Western Ontario, 1980, 84.
3 Ibid., 85.
4 Toronto *Globe*, 14 November 1918.
5 J.L. Carruthers, "The Great War and Canada's Alien Enemy Policy," *Queen's Law Journal* 4.1 (Summer 1978): 107.
6 Grant Grams, "Karl Respa and German Espionage in Canada during World War One," *Journal of Military and Strategic Studies* 8.1 (Fall 2005).
7 Janet Nicol, "Alvo von Alvensleben: I Am Not 'An Enemy to the People I Have Lived Among,'" *British Columbia History* 40.1 (January 2008).
8 Toronto *Globe*, 16 November 1918.
9 Toronto *Globe*, 18 November 1918.
10 Toronto *Globe*, 23 August 1918.
11 Toronto *Globe*, 6 December 1918.
12 Toronto *Globe*, 21 December 1918.
13 Toronto *Globe*, 25 November and 6 December 1918.
14 LAC RG 13, series A-2, vol. 225, file 1918–1582, Hughes to deputy minister of justice, 2 May 1919.
15 LAC MG 26, I, Meighen Papers, vol. 1, reel C3214, D.A. Ross to Richardson to Meighen, 24 March 1919.
16 LAC MG 26, I, vol. 1, reel C3214, Ross to Richardson to Meighen, 24 March 1919.
17 Robert Brown and Ramsay Cook have January 1919. *Canada 1896–1921: A Nation Transformed* (Toronto: McClelland and Stewart, 1974), 310.
18 LAC MG 26, H, Borden Papers, reel C4334, item 56656, Cahan to minister of justice, 30 July 1918.
19 LAC MG 26, H, Borden Papers, reel C4334, item 56642, Borden to Cahan, 19 May 1918.
20 Robert Borden, *Robert Laird Borden: His Memoirs* (Toronto: Macmillan, 1938), 2:972.
21 LAC MG 26, H, Borden Papers, reel C4334, item 56656, Cahan to minister of justice, 20 July 1918.

22 LAC MG 26, H, Borden Papers, reel C4334, item 56665, Cahan to Doherty, 14 September 1918.
23 LAC MG 26, H, Borden Papers, reel C4334, item 56656, Cahan to minister of justice, 20 July 1918.
24 Ibid.
25 Ibid.
26 LAC MG 26, H, Borden Papers, reel C4334, item 56665, Cahan to Doherty, 14 September 1918. There were, Cahan believed, 1,000–1,200 hard-core members of these organizations in Canada: perhaps 700 in Montreal, with 150–175 each in Sault Ste Marie, Hamilton, Winnipeg, Copper Cliff, and Timmins. Where Cahan obtained these figures, given previous police assurances that no effective revolutionary apparatus existed, can only be conjectured.
27 LAC MG 26, H, Borden Papers, reel C4334, item 56686, Cahan to Doherty, 20 September 1918.
28 LAC MG 26, H, Borden Papers, reel C4334, item 56665, Cahan to Doherty, 14 September 1918.
29 Ibid.
30 J.B. Mackenzie, "Section 98, Criminal Code and Freedom of Expression in Canada," *Queen's Law Journal* 1.4 (November 1972): 470–5.
31 Patricia Peppin, "Emergency Legislation and Rights in Canada: The War Measures Act and Civil Liberties," *Queen's Law Journal* 18.1 (Spring 1993): 139.
32 Criminal Code of Canada, S.C. 1892, Section 97A, "Unlawful Associations." Sections 97A and B were renumbered Section 98 by a statutory revision, in 1927, and are remembered therefore as "Section 98."
33 Criminal Code of Canada, S.C. 1892, Section 97B, "Publishing Seditious Books etc."
34 Criminal Code of Canada, S.C. 1892, Section 134 "Seditious Words."
35 Criminal Code of Canada, S.C. 1892, Section 97A, "Unlawful Associations."
36 LAC MG 26, H, Borden Papers, reel C4334, item 56692, Cahan to Doherty, 26 September 1918.
37 LAC MG 26, H, Borden Papers, reel C4334, item 56698, Cahan to minister of justice, 21 October 1918.
38 Ibid.
39 LAC MG 26, H, Borden Papers, reel C4334, item 56703, Cahan to Doherty, 22 October 1918.
40 Ibid.
41 Ibid.

42 LAC MG 26, H, Borden Papers, reel C4334, item 56708, Rowell to Borden, 29 October 1918. Rowell was an Ontario Liberal who had deserted the party in 1917. He was a member of the government with responsibility for conducting the propaganda war. He would be a future chief justice of Ontario. His views were apt to carry some weight.
43 Ibid.
44 LAC MG 26, H, Borden Papers, reel C4334, item 56710, Rowell to Doherty, 18 October 1918.
45 LAC RG 6, E, Cahan to minister of justice, 6 January 1919.
46 LAC RG 6, E, Chambers to Doherty, 9 January 1919.
47 LAC RG 6, E, Chambers to Cockerill, 18 December 1918.
48 LAC RG 6, E, Cawdron to Chambers, 16 December 1918. Cawdron on censorship: "if restrictions are removed foreigners are left free to print almost anything they like, as none but themselves can read their languages and those who are loyal amongst them would be afraid to give us information."
49 LAC RG 6, E, Gwatkin to Chambers, 16 December 1918. Gwatkin, like Cahan, also feared Chinese nationalism ("there are plots against the Government of our ally, China, which have shown themselves to be very murderous in character, and very difficult to control") and he still had doubts about German intentions ("we have evidence that a new and more subtle German propaganda is in progress of organisation, aiming at depriving the Allies of the fruits of victory, and at enabling the Germans to make fresh attempts to subvert freedom and civilisation").
50 David Bercuson, *Fools and Wise Men* (Toronto: McGraw-Hill, Ryerson, 1978), 99.
51 DHH (Directorate of History and Heritage), Holly Lane, 325.009 (D281), "Troops Called Out in Aid of the Civil Power," for example, C-1–73, 11 February 1919, BGen Comd M.D. No. 2 to Maj P.B. Wilson, 51st Regiment, Sault Ste Marie.
52 DHH, Holly Lane, 325.009 (D281), HQ C2927, 28 January 1919, MGen Ashton to GOC MD No. 2.
53 DHH, Holly Lane, 325.009 (D281), "Troops Called Out in Aid of Civil Power," Ashton to GOC No. 2, 21 December 1917.
54 S.W. Horrall, "The Royal North West Mounted Police and Labour Unrest in Western Canada," *Canadian Historical Review* 61.2 (1980): 169.
55 LAC MG 26, H, reel 4329, item 50770, CIB Office, Secret and Confidential to PM, 30 June 1919.
56 Ibid. While there is not much available for the action of the Canadian police during the war, the records for the RCMP CIB are very full of

334 Notes to pages 221–2

information regarding its war on subversives and suspicious foreigners. LAC RG 18, vols. 6256 and 6257 are particularly valuable.
57 LAC MG 26, H, Borden Papers, reel 4334, item 56611, commissioner of police to minister of justice, 5 March 1918.
58 Jeffrey Keshen, "All the News That Was Fit to Print: Ernest J. Chambers and Information Control in Canada, 1914–1919," *Canadian Historical Review* 73:3 (1992): 319.
59 Horrall, "The Royal North West Mounted Police and Labour Unrest in Western Canada," 176. This organization successfully infiltrated not only radical labour but Hindu separatist and Chinese nationalist organizations as well.
60 LAC RG 9, III, C13, vol. 4597, folder 1, file 11, "Secret Instructions for the Examination of Aliens" [undated]. My thanks to Richard Holt for this reference.
61 LAC MG 26, H, Borden Papers, reel C4334, item 56651, Sherwood to minister of justice, 16 June 1918.
62 LAC MG 26, H, Borden Papers, reel C4334, item 56663, Cahan to Borden, 27 August 1918. With so many agencies in the game, there could not but be occasional comedies. In Alberta, for example, a provincial police detective, operating undercover, arrested a Bolshevist incendiary only to discover that the Red in question was a Mountie. "Good," the commissioner concluded: the arrest would strengthen the Mountie's credibility. Bercuson, *Fools and Wise Men*, 93. On another occasion, W.G. Barber, a telegraph operator at Sault Ste Marie, informed the chief censor of some very odd business. A Mr H.A. Sherman, at the Sault, and a Mr. H.J. Campbell, in Toronto, were in the habit of passing cryptic messages. Sherman also consorted with New Canadians who had odd accents. Subsequent police investigation revealed that Campbell and Sherman both worked for the Thiel detective service, on Dominion contract, and employed Austrian agents to monitor New Canadian munitions workers. Coded messages concerned ongoing company surveillance operations. Keshen, "All the News That Was Fit to Print," 334.
63 LAC RG 18, A2, reel T6527, Office of the Comptroller RCMP, letter book, comptroller to assistant director of military intelligence, 3 April 1919.
64 LAC RG 18, A2, reel T6527, Office of the Comptroller RCMP, letter book, comptroller to superintendent, 3 April 1919.
65 LAC RG 18, A2, reel T6527, Office of the Comptroller RCMP, letter book, comptroller to acting chief of police, 3 April 1919.
66 Horrall, "The Royal North West Mounted Police and Labour Unrest in Western Canada," 175.

67 Mark Leier, *Rebel Life: The Life and Times of Robert Gosden. Revolutionary, Mystic Labour Spy* (Vancouver: New Star, 1999), 86.
68 LAC RG 6, E, 28, Malcolm Reid, immigration inspector, to Sir Percy Sherwood, chief of Dominion Police, copy to chief censor, 5 December 1919.
69 Horrall, "The Royal North West Mounted Police and Labour Unrest in Western Canada," 176.
70 Tim Buck, *Canada and the Russian Revolution: The Impact of the World's First Socialist Revolution on Labour and Politics in Canada* (Toronto: Progress Books, 1967), 85; Martin Robin, *Radical Politics and Canadian Labour, 1880–1930* (Industrial Relations Centre, Queen's University, 1968), 145–6.
71 Buck, *Canada and the Russian Revolution*, 86.
72 Mackenzie, "Section 98, Criminal Code and Freedom of Expression in Canada," 475.
73 For example, LAC RG 18, vols. 6526 and 6527, for RCMP CIB files, and RG 18, A2, reel T6527, Office of the Comptroller, RCMP letter book, volume "Labour Organisation and Communism."
74 Cole, "The War Measures Act, 1914," 84.
75 Toronto *Globe*, 18 December 1918.
76 Donald Avery, *Dangerous Foreigners: European Immigrant Workers and Labour Radicalism in Canada 1896–1932* (Toronto: McClelland and Stewart, 1979), 76–7.
77 LAC MG 26, I, Meighen Papers, vol. 1, reel C3214, Meighen to Richardson, 2 April 1919. Cole, "The War Measures Act, 1914," 85.
78 In August 1914, Colonel J. Hopkinson, working for the immigration branch, was assassinated by a Sikh for refusing to permit the *Komagata Maru* to land on the grounds that it carried pro-German saboteurs. The Chinese minister of the interior, Tang Hui Lui, had been assassinated by followers of Sun Yat Sen in August 1918, during a visit to Victoria. Keshen, "All the News That Was Fit to Print," 334–5.
79 Bercuson, *Fools and Wise Men*, 99. See also Leslie Katz, "Some Legal Consequences of the Winnipeg General Strike of 1919," *Manitoba Law Journal* 4.4 (1970): 47–50.
80 Avery, *Dangerous Foreigners*, 88–92. Deported "incorrigibles" included about 1,600 Germans, including those sent to Canada from elsewhere, and 302 "Austrians." Carruthers, "The Great War and Canada's Alien Enemy Policy," 107.
81 Brown and Cook, *Canada 1896–1921*, 304.
82 LAC Borden Papers, 54538–42, Arthur Meighen to Borden, 1 February 1919.

83 LAC RG 13, vol. 1370, draft Order-in-Council, 22 January 1922.
84 LAC MG 26, I, Meighen Papers, vol. 1, minister of immigration to Meighen, 24 February 1919. Noted by Meighen as "very interesting."
85 Desmond Morton, *A Peculiar Kind of Politics: Canada's Overseas Ministry in the First World War* (Toronto: University of Toronto Press, 1982), 188–92.
86 Max Foran and Heather MacEwan Foran, *Calgary: Canada's Frontier Metropolis* (Windsor: Windsor Publications, 1982), 156.
87 James Eayrs, *In Defence of Canada* (Toronto: University of Toronto Press, 1964), 46–7.
88 G.L. Kristianson, *The Politics of Patriotism: The Pressure Group Activities of the Returned Servicemen's League* (Canberra: Australian National University Press, 1966), 13. Australian veterans rioted against strikers in Adelaide on Peace Day 1918, in Brisbane in March, in Fremantle in May, and in Melbourne in July 1919. Ultimately a two-thousand-man strong "Army to Fight Bolshevism" was founded. Outside Winnipeg, Canadian veterans did not go so far.
89 RCMP assessment, as LAC RG 18, RCMP, F-3, vol. 3314, file HV-1.
90 Donald Avery, "Ethnic and Class Tension in Canada, 1918–1920," in *Loyalties in Conflict: Ukrainians in Canada during the Great War*, ed. Frances Swyripa and John Thompson (Edmonton: University of Alberta Press, 1983), 91–2.
91 Robin, *Radical Politics and Canadian Labour, 1880–1930*, 156.
92 President Weir, of the Manitoba GWVA, confessed himself opposed to strikes, and Reds, but also insisted that the government deal with profiteers, "the original Bolsheviks ... manufacturing in Canada has been caught red-handed in profiteering and the people of this country have a right to demand that similar strong arm action be employed against them.

These profiteers, and all men who belong to their treasonable brood, should be dealt with in a manner exactly similar to that employed against Bolshevists, traitors, and conspirators who, taking advantage of the evils the profiteers bring about, seek to foster revolution and anarchy in this country." *Manitoba Veteran*, 19 June 1919.
93 Eayrs, *In Defence of Canada*, 47.
94 Ibid., 46.
95 Ibid., 47; Bercuson, *Fools and Wise Men*, 91.
96 Eayres, *In Defence of Canada*, 47.
97 Desmond Morton and Glenn Wright, *Winning the Second Battle: Canadian Veterans and the Return to Civilian Life 1915–1920* (Toronto: University of Toronto Press, 1987), 121.

98 Avery, *Dangerous Foreigners*, 82.
99 LAC RG 18, A2, reel T6527, RCMP comptroller to the chief commissioner of police, 20 March 1919.
100 LAC MG 26, I, vol. 1, reel C3214, Meighen to Richardson, 2 April 1919.
101 LAC MG 26, I, vol. 1, reel C3214, Ross to Meighen, 8 April 1919.
102 Kenneth McNaught, "Political Trials and the Canadian Political Tradition," *University of Toronto Law Journal* 24 (1974): 158.
103 Peter MacKinnon, "Conspiracy and Sedition as Canadian Political Crimes," *McGill Law Journal* 23 (1977): 625–6.
104 DHH, Holly Lane, 507.013 (D2), "Aid to the Civil Power" GOC MD No. 10 to Militia Council, 14 May 1919.
105 Ibid.
106 Ibid.
107 DHH, Holly Lane, 507.013 (D2), "Aid to the Civil Power" HQ MD 10 C.69, 31 July 1919, GOC to AG.
108 Donald Avery, "Canadian Immigration Policy and the Alien Question 1896–1919: The Anglo-Canadian Perspective," PhD thesis, University of Western Ontario, 1973, 577.
109 Ibid.
110 Ibid.
111 Horrall, "The Royal North West Mounted Police and Labour Unrest in Western Canada," 169. See also Katz, "Some Legal Consequences of the Winnipeg General Strike of 1919," 41.
112 Barry Cahill, "Howe (1835), Dixon (1920) and McLachlan (1923): Comparative Perspectives on the Legal History of Sedition," *University of New Brunswick Law Journal* 45 (1996): 281–330. That there was commanding recent precedent Cahill denies ... but then he does not look at the war period at all (despite the fact that the war emergency was still ongoing, and most Orders-in-Council remained in effect). The trial, he considers, followed from a much more acute social-political problem, in 1919, than had existed ten years before, and a closer alignment of the government with exploitive finance capitalism. As we have seen, the trial of a labour agitator on a charge of seditious libel was nothing new in Canada at this time.
113 Desmond Morton and Terry Copp, *Working People* (Ottawa: Deneau, 1981), 122.
114 Avery, "Canadian Immigration Policy and the Alien Question 1896–1919," 588–9.
115 Mackenzie, "Section 98, Criminal Code and Freedom of Expression in Canada," 474.

116 MacKinnon, "Conspiracy and Sedition as Canadian Political Crimes," 628.
117 McNaught, "Political Trials and the Canadian Political Tradition," 159.
118 Desmond Brown, "The Craftsmanship of Bias: Sedition and the Winnipeg General Strike," *Manitoba Law Journal* 14.1 (1984).
119 MacKinnon, "Conspiracy and Sedition as Canadian Political Crimes," 630.
120 Brown, "The Craftsmanship of Bias," 5–6.
121 *R. v. Russell*, (1920), 33 C.C.C. Ann. 1, p. 20 (C.A. Man.); cited in Herbert Marx, "The Emergency Power and Civil Liberties in Canada," *McGill Law Journal* 16 (1970): 53; and Katz, "Some Legal Consequences of the Winnipeg General Strike of 1919," 43.
122 Bercuson, *Fools and Wise Men*, 101.
123 Borden, *Memoirs*, 2:940; Bercuson, *Fools and Wise Men*, 94; and Eayrs, *In Defence of Canada*, 48.
124 Bercuson, *Fools and Wise Men*, 97.
125 LAC RG 18, A2, reel T6527, Office of the Comptroller RCMP, letter book, M. Tessler to C. Stephenson, intercepted and subsequently comptroller to chief censor, 31 March 1918.
126 LAC RG 18, A2, reel T6527, special agent from Blairmore to comptroller to assistant director military intelligence, Lieutenant-Colonel M.E. Davis, 14 March 1919.
127 Joseph Boudreau, "Western Canada's Alien Enemies in World War One," *Alberta Historical Review* 12.1 (1964): 4; and Avery, "Canadian Immigration Policy and the Alien Question 1896–1919," 441–2.
128 Bercuson, *Fools and Wise Men*, 119.
129 Ibid., 95.
130 Craig Heron and Myer Siemiatycki, "The Great War, the State, and Working Class Canada," in *The Workers Revolt in Canada*, ed. Craig Heron (Toronto: University of Toronto Press, 1998), 24; and Morton and Wright, *Winning the Second Battle*, 121.
131 Euler was president of the Kitchener Chamber of Commerce, 1916–17, twice mayor of Berlin, and MP for North Waterloo in December 1917. He went on to become Mackenzie King's minister of trade and commerce and later a senator. He is best remembered as a margarine lobbyist after the Second World War. In late 1917, he would have been an object of particular loathing for members of the British League, since he had campaigned in December 1917 as a Laurier loyalist on an anti-conscription platform. Kitchener *Record*, 2 April 2005.
132 *Kitchener News Record*, 12 December 1919.
133 LAC RG 6, E.

134 Clifford Sifton to Dafoe, November 1920: "They are hopelessly incapable of going on farms and succeeding. Pretty nearly all the Great War Veterans Associations that are making trouble are composed of these fellows who enlisted in the Canadian Army when the war came and want the country to support them for the rest of their lives." Avery, *Dangerous Foreigners*, 97.
135 Historical Section GS, *Report No. 22, Reorganisation of the Canadian Militia 1919–1920*, 31 January 1949.
136 Roger Graham, *Arthur Meighen* (Toronto: Clark, Irwin and Company, 1960), 74.
137 Brown and Cook, *Canada 1896–1921*, 336; Bercuson, *Fools and Wise Men*, 90.
138 See J. Vance, *Death So Noble* (Vancouver: University of British Columbia Press, 1997).

Conclusion

1 J. Carruthers, "The Great War and Canada's Alien Enemy Policy," *Queen's Law Journal*, 4.1 (Summer 1978): 109.
2 Robert Borden, *Robert Laird Borden: His Memoirs* (Toronto: Macmillan, 1938), 2:720.
3 Robert Brown, "Whither Are We Being Shoved?" in *Political Leadership in Canada during World War One*, ed. J. Granatstein and R. Cuff (Toronto: Nelson, 1971), 118.

Appendix A

1 *R. v. Felton* (1915), 9 W.W.R. 819, 9 Alta. L.R. 238, 25 C.C.C. 207, 28 D.L.R. 372 (C.A.).
2 Ibid.; also cited in J. Carruthers, "The Great War and Canada's Alien Enemy Policy," *Queen's Law Journal* 4.1 (Summer 1978): 81.
3 *R. v. Felton*, 28 D.L.R. 372, 9 A.L.R. 238, 25 C.C.C. 207, 33 W.L.R. 157, 9 W.W.R 819. For Felton, see also Peter MacKinnon, "Conspiracy and Sedition as Canadian Political Crimes," *McGill Law Journal* 23 (1977): 625–6. This judgment, however, was consistent with the nineteenth-century conviction of Chartists in Britain. They should have known that unrest would have accompanied their meeting, even if they had not advocated "unrest," and even though those attending the meeting were the victims, not the perpetrators, of violence. See Michael Lobban, "From Seditious Libel to Unlawful Assembly: Peterloo and the Changing Face

of Political Crime c1770–1820," *Oxford Journal of Legal Studies* 10.3 (1990): 307–52.
4 *Toronto Star*, 15 October 1916, 7.
5 Sessional Papers, vol. 52 (Session 1916), no. 18, report of Inspector Belcher, Yorkton detachment.
6 Sessional Papers, vol. 52 (Session 1916), no. 18, report of Calgary Division.
7 Joseph Boudreau, "Western Canada's Alien Enemies in World War One," *Alberta Historical Review* 12.1 (1964): 4.
8 *R. v. Cohen* (1916) 10 W.W.R. 333, 9 Alta. L.R. 329, 25 C.C.C. 302, 28 D.L.R. 74 (C.A.); and *R. v. Cohen*, 28 D.L.R., 74, 25 C.C.C. 302, 9 A.L.R 329, 34 W.L.R. 210, 10, W.W.R. 333.
9 Sessional Papers, vol. 52 (Session 1916), no. 18, report of Calgary Division.
10 Ibid.
11 Sessional Papers, vol. 52 (1916), no. 18, RNWMP report for 1916.
12 Sessional Papers, vol. 52 (1916), no. 18, report of Regina Division.
13 *London Advertiser*, 16 March 1916, 4.
14 Toronto *Globe*, 31 May 1918, 13.
15 Toronto *Globe*, 11 April 1917.
16 Toronto *Globe*, 12 April 1917.
17 LAC RG 13, Justice, series A-2, vol. 225, file 1918–1568, July 1918.
18 Toronto *Globe*, 5 July 1918.
19 *Toronto Star*, 25 September 1917, 18.
20 Toronto *Globe*, 12 July 1918, 13.
21 *Hamilton Spectator*, 30 July 1918, 11.
22 Toronto *Globe*, 9 March 1918, 12.
23 RG 18, A2, Office of the Comptroller RCMP, letter book, comptroller to commissioner, 27 February 1919. This letter is confusing, since it refers to a case only part of which is known – other information contained in a file was maintained separately and despatched, this letter attached, for the commissioner's review. This case appears to concern police interception of correspondence between two suspicious characters then under surveillance: Snitzinger ("a dangerous character and requires surveillance") and Mutch ("a hot-headed and extreme Socialist").
24 In May 1917, for example, eight men charged with publishing a subversive leaflet were sentenced to £100 with £10 costs each, or sixty days' imprisonment. Brock Millman, *Managing Domestic Dissent in First World War Britain* (London: Frank Cass, 2000), 190.

Bibliography

Official Papers (by Department)

Colonial Office (Britain)
Chief Censor
Dominion Police
Governor General
Immigration Department
Imperial War Cabinet (Britain)
Justice Department
Militia Department
Royal Canadian Mounted Police
Royal North West Mounted Police

Collections of Private Papers

Borden Papers
Currie Papers
Doherty Papers
Foster Papers
Laurier Papers
Flavelle Papers
Godfrey Papers
Hartley Papers
Meighen Papers
Stevens Papers
White Papers

Published Official Papers

All England Law Reports
Cabinet Command Papers
Canadian Consolidated Ten Year Law Digest
Canadian Supreme Court Reports
The Canadian Annual Digest
Dominion Law Reports
House of Commons Debates
House of Commons Sessional Papers
Ontario Law Reports
Ontario Weekly Notes
The Papers of Woodrow Wilson (Princeton: Princeton University Press, 1980).
Statutes of Canada
United States Statutes at Large
Western Law Reporter
Western Weekly Reports

Monographs

Allen, Richard. *The Social Passion: Religion and Social Reform in Canada, 1914–1928*. Toronto: University of Toronto Press, 1973.
Armstrong, Elizabeth. *The Crisis of Quebec, 1914–1918*. 1937; Montreal: McGill-Queen's University Press, 1974.
Aron, Raymond. *The Century of Total War*. Boston: Beacon Press, 1968.
Atkey, Ronald. "Reconciling Freedom of Expression and National Security." *University of Toronto Law Journal* 41 (1991): 38–59.
Auger, Martin. "On the Brink of Civil War: The Canadian Government and the Suppression of the 1918 Quebec Easter Riots." *Canadian Historical Review* 89.4 (January 2008).
Avakumovic, Ivan. *The Communist Party in Canada: A History*. Toronto: University of Toronto Press, 1975
Avery, Donald. "Canadian Immigration Policy and the Alien Question 1896–1919: The Anglo-Canadian Perspective." PhD thesis, University of Western Ontario, 1973.
– *Dangerous Foreigners: European Immigrant Workers and Labour Radicalism in Canada 1896–1932*. Toronto: McClelland and Stewart, 1979.
Babcock, Robert. *Gompers in Canada: A Study in American Continentalism before the First World War*. Toronto: University of Toronto Press, 1974.
Barber, Marilyn. "The Ontario Bilingual Schools Issue: Sources of Conflict." *Canadian Historical Review* 47.3 (September 1966).

Baxter, Theresa. "The Red Scare: Selected Aspects of Canadian Public Opinion on the Russian Revolution and Its Impact on Canada." MA thesis, University of Western Ontario, 1972.
Bercuson, David. *Fools and Wise Men*. Toronto: McGraw-Hill Ryerson, 1978.
Berger, Carl. *Imperialism and Nationalism 1884–1914: A Conflict in Canadian Thought*. Toronto: Copp Clark, 1969.
– *The Sense of Power: Studies in the Ideas of Canadian Imperialism 1867–1914*. Toronto: University of Toronto Press, 1970.
Cook, Ramsay, Craig Brown, and Carl Berger, eds. *Conscription 1917*. Toronto: University of Toronto Press, 1969.
Bernard, Jean Paul. *Les idéologies québécoises de 19e siècle*. Montreal: Boreal Express, 1973.
Berthoff, Rolland. *British Immigrants to Industrial America*. Cambridge, MA: Harvard University Press, 1953.
Bettelheim, Bruno, and Morris Janowitz. *Social Change and Prejudice*. New York: Free Press of Glencoe, 1964.
Bindon, Kathryn. *More Than Patriotism: Canada at War, 1914–1918*. Toronto: Personal Library Publishers, 1979.
Bliss, Michael. *A Canadian Millionaire: The Life and Business Times of Sir Joseph Flavelle, Bart. 1858–1939*. Toronto: Macmillan, 1978.
Bloustein, Edward. "Criminal Attempts and the 'Clear and Present Danger' Theory of the First Amendment." *Cornell Law Review* 74 (1988–9): 1118–50.
Borden, Robert. *Canada and the Great War*. Ottawa, 1918.
– *Robert Laird Borden. His Memoirs*. Toronto: Macmillan, 1938.
– *The War and the Future*. London: Hodder and Stoughton, 1917.
Boudreau, Joseph. "Western Canada's Alien Enemies in World War One." *Alberta Historical Review* 12.1 (1964): 1–9.
Bowering, H. *Service: The Story of the Canadian Legion, 1925–1960*. Ottawa: Dominion Command, 1960.
Boyle, David. *Unconscious Traitors*. Winnipeg: Saturday Post, 1916.
Bray, R. Matthew. "'Fighting as an Ally': The English Canadian Patriotic Response to the Great War." *Canadian Historical Review* 61.2 (1980): 141–68.
Bright, David. "We Are All Kin: Reconsidering Labour and Class in Calgary, 1919." *Labour* 19 (Spring 1992).
Brookfield, Tarah. "Divided by the Ballot Box: The Montreal Council of Women and the 1917 Election." *Canadian Historical Review* 89.4 (January 2008).
Brown, Robert. "Whither Are We Being Shoved?" In *Political Leadership in Canada during World War One*, ed. J. Granatstein and R. Cuff. Toronto: Nelson, 1971.

Brown, Robert, and Ramsay Cook. *Canada 1896–1921: A Nation Transformed.* Toronto: McClelland and Stewart, 1974.

Brown, R.C., and D.M. Loveridge. "Unrequited Faith: Recruiting the CEF, 1914-1918." *Revue Internationale d'Histoire Militaire* 51 (1982).

Buck, Tim. *Canada and the Russian Revolution: The Impact of the World's First Socialist Revolution on Labour and Politics in Canada.* Toronto: Progress Books, 1967.

Buckner, Philip. *Canada and the British Empire.* Oxford: Oxford University Press, 2008.

Busch, Briton C., ed. *Canada and the Great War.* Montreal and Kingston: McGill-Queen's University Press, 2003.

Cahill, Barry. "Howe (1835), Dixon (1920) and McLachlan (1923): Comparative Perspectives on the Legal History of Sedition." *University of New Brunswick Law Journal* 45 (1996).

Cains, D.S., ed. *The Army and Religion.* London: Macmillan, 1919.

Carnegie, David. *The History of Munitions Supply in Canada.* New York: Longmans, Green, 1925.

Carruthers, J.L. "The Great War and Canada's Alien Enemy Policy." *Queen's Law Journal* 4.1 (Summer 1978).

Carter, David. *Behind Canadian Barbed Wire: Alien, Refugee, and Prisoner of War Camps in Canada 1914–1946.* Calgary: Tumbleweed Press, 1980.

Chadwick, W.R. *The Battle for Berlin, Ontario: As Historical Drama.* Waterloo, ON: Wilfrid Laurier University Press, 1992.

Chafee, Zechariah. *Free Speech in the United States.* Cambridge, MA: Harvard University Press, 1920.

Churchill, Jason. "Of Baymen and Townies – Towards a Reassessment of the Newfoundland Conscription Crisis." *Canadian Military History since the 17th Century: Proceedings of the CMH Conference, Ottawa 5–9 May 2000.* CMHC, 2000.

Clarke, Nic. "Crisis of Conscience: Conscientious Objection in Canada during the First World War." *First World War Studies* 1.2 (October 2010).

Clements, Wallace. *The Canadian Corporate Elite.* Toronto: McClelland and Stewart, 1975.

Cole, Curtis. "The War Measures Act, 1914: Aspects of the Emergency Limitation of Freedom of Speech and Personal Liberties in Canada, 1914–1919." MA thesis, University of Western Ontario, 1980.

Cook, Ramsay, Robert Brown, and Carl Berger, eds. *Imperial Relations in the Age of Laurier.* Toronto: University of Toronto Press, 1969.

Cook, Tim. *Clio's Warriors: Canadian Historians and the Writing of the World Wars.* Vancouver: University of British Columbia Press, 2006.

Creighton, Donald. *The Story of Canada*. London: Faber and Faber, 1959.
Crerar, Duff. *Padres in No Man's Land: Canadian Chaplains and the Great War*. Montreal and Kingston: McGill-Queen's University Press, 1995.
Dahlie, Jorgen, and Tissa Fernando, eds. *Ethnicity, Power, and Politics in Canada*. Toronto: Methuen, 1981.
Desjardins, L.-G. *England, Canada and the Great War*. Quebec: Chronicle, 1918.
Driedger, Leo, ed. *Ethnic Canada: Identities and Inequalities*. Toronto: Copp, Clark Pitman, 1987.
Dumont, Fernand. *Ideologies au Canada francais*. Quebec: PUL, 1971.
Eayrs, James. *In Defence of Canada*. Toronto: University of Toronto Press, 1964.
Edwards, Ruth. *The Faithful Tribe*. London: HarperCollins, 1999.
Emery, George. "The Origins of Canadian Methodist Involvement in the Social Gospel Movement, 1890–1914." *Journal of the Canadian Church Historical Society* 19.1 (1977): 104–18.
Entz, W. "The Suppression of the German Language Press in September 1918." *Canadian Ethnic Studies* 8.2 (1976): 56–70.
Erickson, Charlotte. *Invisible Immigrants: The Adaption of English and Scottish Immigrants to Nineteenth-Century America*. Coral Gables: University of Miami Press, 1972.
– *Leaving England*. Ithaca: Cornell University Press, 1994.
Ervin, Spencer. *The Political and Ecclesiastical History of the Anglican Church of Canada*. Ambler, PA: Trinity Press, 1967.
Ewart, John. *The Disruption of Canada*. Ottawa, 1917.
Farrell, John. "Michael Francis Fallon, Bishop of London, Ontario, Canada: The Man and His Controversies." *Canadian Catholic Historical Association Study Sessions* (1968).
Ferguson, Barry, ed. *The Anglican Church and the World of Western Canada, 1820–1970*. Regina: Canadian Plains Research Centre, 1991.
Filteau, Gerard. *Le Quebec, le Canada et la Guerre 1914–1918*. Montreal: Les Messageries Prologue, 1977.
Fischer, Gerhard. *Alien Enemies' Internment and the Home Front Experience in Australia 1914–1920*. St Lucia: University of Queensland Press, 1989.
Fitzpatrick, David. "The Logic of Collective Sacrifice: Ireland and the British Army, 1914-1918." *Historical Journal* 38.4 (1995): 1017–30.
Fitzpatrick, Michael. "The Role of Bishop Michael Francis Fallon, and the Conflict between the French Catholics and Irish Catholics in the Ontario Bilingual Schools Question, 1910–1920." MA thesis, University of Western Ontario, 1969.
Foran, Max, and Heather Foran. *Calgary: Canada's Frontier Metropolis*. Windsor: Windsor Publications, 1982.

Frost, Leslie. *Fighting Men*. Toronto: Clark, Irwin and Company, 1967.
Frye, Northrop. *Culture and the National Will*. Ottawa: Carleton University, 1957.
Furer, Howard. *The British in America, 1578–1970*. New York: Oceana Press, 1972.
Gagnon, Jean Pierre. *Le 22e Battalion*. Quebec: Les Presses de l'Université Laval, 1986.
Gauvreau, Michael. "War, Culture, and the Problem of Religious Certainty: Methodist and Presbyterian Colleges, 1914–1930." *Journal of the Canadian Church Historical Society* 29.1 (April 1987).
Gould, B.A. *Whither? A Brief Consideration of the Direction in Which by Reason of the War the World May Be Made to Advance*. Toronto: T.H. Best, 1918.
Graham, Roger. *Arthur Meighen*. Toronto: Clark, Irwin and Company, 1960.
Grams, Grant. "Karl Respa and German Espionage in Canada during World War One." *Journal of Military and Strategic Studies* 8.1 (Fall 2005).
Granatstein, J., and J.M. Hitsman. *Broken Promises: A History of Conscription in Canada*. Toronto: Oxford University Press, 1977.
Great Britain, General Statistics Office. *Annual Abstract of Statistics 1903–1919*. London: HMSO, 1919.
Gremond, F.M. "The Drafting and Passage of the War Measures Act in 1914 and 1927: Object Lesson in the Need for Vigilance." In *Canadian Perspectives on Law and Society: Issues in Legal History*, ed. B. Wright. Ottawa: Carleton University Press, 1988.
Hale, James. *Branching Out: The Story of the Royal Canadian Legion*. Ottawa: Royal Canadian Legion, 1995.
Hamburger, Philip. "The Development of the Law of Seditious Libel and the Control of the Press." *Stanford Law Review* 27 (1984–5): 661–765.
Harris, Donald. "The Church of England and Emigration to Canada: Rural Clergy in the County of Shropshire." *Journal of the Canadian Church Historical Society* 41.1 (Spring 1999): 5–26.
Hastings, Paula. "Fellow British Subjects of Colonial Others? Race, Empire and Ambivalence in Canadian Representations of India in the Early Twentieth Century." *American Review of Canadian Studies* 38.1 (January 2008).
Hawkes, Arthur. *Canadian Nationalism and the War*. Montreal, 1916.
Hawkins, Freda. *Canada and Immigration: Public Policy and Public Concern*. Montreal: McGill-Queen's University Press, 1972.
Haycock, Ronald. *Sam Hughes: The Public Career of a Controversial Canadian*. Waterloo: Wilfrid Laurier University Press, 1986.
Henry, Francis, and Carol Tator. "The Ideology of Racism: Democratic Racism." *Canadian Ethnic Studies* 26.2 (1994): 1–14.

Heron, Craig, ed. *The Workers' Revolt in Canada*. Toronto: University of Toronto Press, 1998.
Herridge, W.T. *French and English in Canada and across the Sea*. Ottawa, 1917.
Hewitt, Steve. *Spying 101: The RCMP's Secret Activities at Canadian Universities, 1917–1997*. Toronto: University of Toronto Press, 2002.
Historical Section General Staff. *Report No. 22, Reorganisation of the Canadian Militia 1919–1920 (31 January 1949)*.
Holt, Richard. "Filling the Ranks: Recruiting, Training and Reinforcements in the Canadian Expeditionary Force, 1914-1918." PhD dissertation, University of Western Ontario, 2011.
Hopkins, J. Castell. *Canada at War, 1914–1918*. New York: George H. Doran, 1919.
– *The Canadian Annual Review of Public Affairs* (Ottawa: Canadian Annual Review, 1915–19).
– *The Province of Ontario in the War*. Toronto: Warwick and Ritter, 1919.
Horrall, S.W. "The Royal North West Mounted Police and Labour Unrest in Western Canada, 1919." *Canadian Historical Review* 61.2 (1980): 169–90.
Houston, Cecil, and William Smyth. *The Sash Canada Wore*. Toronto: University of Toronto Press, 1980.
Howard, Taylor. "Forging the Job: A Crisis of 'Modernization' or Redundancy for the Police in England and Wales, 1900–39." *British Journal of Criminology* 39.1 (1999): 113–35.
– "Rationing Crime. The Political Economy of Crime Statistics since the 1850s." *Economic History Review* 50.3 (August 1999): 569–90.
Hughes, Sam. *Correspondence of General Sir Sam Hughes, ex-Minister of the Militia and The Right Hon. Sir Robert Borden GCMG*. Ottawa: Central Liberal Information Office, 1916.
Hyatt, A.M.J. "Sir Arthur Currie and Conscription: A Soldier's View." *Canadian Historical Review* 50.3 (Spring 1969): 285–96.
Isitt, Ben. "The Search for Solidarity: The Industrial and Political Roots of the Cooperative Commonwealth Federation in British Columbia, 1913–1928." MA thesis, University of British Columbia, 2003.
Jones, Katherine. *Accent on Privilege: English Identities and Anglophilia in the United States*. Philadelphia: Temple University Press, 2001.
Journal of the Synod of the Church of England of the Diocese of Huron, 57th Session. London, ON: Advertiser, 1914.
Journal of the Synod of the Church of England of the Diocese of Huron, 58th Session. London, ON: Advertiser, 1915.
Journal of the Synod of the Church of England of the Diocese of Huron 59th Session. London, ON: A. Talbot, 1916.

Journal of the Synod of the Church of England of the Diocese of Huron 60th Session. London, ON: A. Talbot, 1917.
Journal of the Synod of the Church of England of the Diocese of Huron 61st Session. London, ON: A. Talbot, 1918.
Katz, Leslie. "Some Legal Consequences of the Winnipeg General Strike of 1919." *Manitoba Law Journal* 4.4 (1970): 39–52.
Kerr, G. "Canadian Press Censorship in World War One." *Journalism Quarterly* 59.2 (1982): 235–9.
Keshen, Jeffrey. "All the News That Was Fit to Print: Ernest J. Chambers and Information Control in Canada, 1914–1919." *Canadian Historical Review* 73.3 (1992): 313–43.
– *Propaganda and Censorship during Canada's Great War*. Edmonton: University of Alberta Press, 1996.
Kissinger, Henry. *A World Restored*. Boston: Houghton Mifflin, 1957.
Klempa, William. *The Burning Bush and a Few Acres of Snow*. Ottawa: Carleton University Press, 1994.
Kordan, Bohdan. *Enemy Aliens, Prisoners of War: Internment in Canada during the Great War*. Montreal and Kingston: McGill-Queen's University Press, 2002.
Krawchuk, Peter. *The Ukrainian Socialist Movement in Canada, 1907–1918*. Toronto: Progress Books, 1979.
Kristianson, G.L. *The Politics of Patriotism: The Pressure Group Activities of the Returned Servicemen's League*. Canberra: Australian National University Press, 1966.
Lackenbauer, P.W. "The Military and 'Mob Rule': The CEF Riots in Calgary, February 1916." *Canadian Military History* 10.1 (Winter 2001): 31–43.
Lackenbauer, P.W., and Nikolas Gardner. "Soldiers as Liminaries: The CEF Soldier Riots of 1916 Reassessed." In *Canadian Military History since the 17th Century*, ed. Yves Tremblay. Ottawa: National Defence, 2001.
Lawson, Robert. "Joachim von Ribbentrop in Canada, 1910–1914: A Note." *International History Review* 29.4 (January 2007).
Lehmann, Heinz. *The German Canadians 1750–1937: Immigration, Settlement and Culture*. St. John's: Jesperson Press, 1986.
Leier, Mark. *Rebel Life. The Life and Times of Robert Gosden. Revolutionary, Mystic, Labour Spy*. Vancouver: New Star, 1999.
Lighthall, W. "Wartime Experience of Canadian Cities." *National Municipal Review* 7.1 (January 1918).
Lobban, Michael. "From Seditious Libel to Unlawful Assembly: Peterloo and the Changing Face of Political Crime c1770–1820." *Oxford Journal of Legal Studies* 10.3 (1990): 307–52.

Lower, Arthur. *Canadians in the Making*. Toronto: Longmans, Green, and Company, 1958.
Lysenko, Vera. *Men in Sheepskin Coats*. Toronto: Ryerson Press, 1947.
Maher, Lawrence. "The Use and Misuse of Sedition." *Sydney Law Review* 9 (September 1992): 287–316.
Marx, Herbert. "The Emergency Power and Civil Liberties in Canada." *McGill Law Journal* 16 (1970): 39–91.
Mackenzie, J.B. "Section 98, Criminal Code and Freedom of Expression in Canada." *Queen's Law Journal* 1.4 (November 1972): 469–83.
MacKinnon, Peter. "Conspiracy and Sedition as Canadian Political Crimes." *McGill Law Journal* 23 (1977): 622–43.
MacNeil, John. *The Presbyterian Church in Canada 1875–1925*. Toronto: General Board, Presbyterian Church in Canada, 1925.
Macphee, Donald. "The Centralia Incident and the Pamphleteers." *Pacific Northwest Quarterly* 62 (July 1971): 110–16.
Marrin, Albert. *The Last Crusade: The Church of England in the First World War*. Durham, NC: Duke University Press, 1974.
Martynowych, Orest. *Ukrainians in Canada: The Formative Period, 1891–1924*. Edmonton: Canadian Institute of Ukrainian Studies, 1991.
Marwick, Arthur. *Britain in the Century of Total War: War, Peace and Social Change, 1900–1967*. London: Bodley Head, 1968.
– *The Deluge: British Society and the First World War*. Basingstoke: Macmillan, 1991.
– *The Explosion of British Society, 1914–1970*. London: Macmillan, 1971.
– *Total War and Social Change*. Basingstoke: Macmillan, 1988.
McClung, N. *The Next of Kin: Those Who Wait and Wonder*. Toronto: T. Allen, 1917.
McGowan, Mark. "Sharing the Burden of Empire: Toronto's Catholics and the Great War 1914–1918." *Catholics at the "Gathering Place": Historical Essays on the Archdiocese of Toronto 1841–1991*. Toronto: Dundurn Press, 1993, 177–207.
McKegney, Patricia. *The Kaiser's Bust: A Study of Wartime Propaganda in Berlin Ontario, 1914–1918*. Wellesley, ON: Bomberg Press, 1991.
McKernan, Michael, "Clergy in Khaki: The Chaplain in the Australian Imperial Force, 1914–1918." *Journal of the Royal Australian Historical Society* 4.3 (1978): 145–66.
McLaughlin, K.M. *The Germans in Canada*. Ottawa: CHA, 1985.
McNaught, Kenneth. "Political Trials and the Canadian Political Tradition." *University of Toronto Law Journal* 24 (1974): 149–69.
Miller, Ian. *Our Glory and Our Grief: Torontonians and the Great War*. Toronto: University of Toronto Press, 2002.

- "A Privilege to Serve: Toronto's Experience with Voluntary Enlistment in the Great War." *Canadian Military History since the 17th Century. Proceedings of the CMH Conference, Ottawa 5–9 May 2000.* CMHC, 2000.
Miller, R. "Orangeism in Ontario West, 1896–1917." MA thesis, University of Western Ontario, 1975.
Millman, Brock. *Managing Domestic Dissent in First World War Britain.* London: Frank Cass, 2000.
– *Pessimism and British War Policy 1916–1918.* London: Frank Cass, 2001.
Ministry of Overseas Forces. *Report of the Ministry of Overseas Forces.* London, 1918.
Morris, David. *The Canadian Militia.* Erin, ON: Boston Mills Press, 1983.
Morris, Philip. *The Canadian Patriotic Fund: A Record of Its Activities from 1914 to 1919.* N,p., n.d.
Morrison, William. "The Mounted Police on Canada's Northern Frontier, 1895–1940." PhD thesis, University of Western Ontario, 1973.
Morton, Desmond. *Ministers and Generals. Politics and the Canadian Militia.* Toronto: University of Toronto Press, 1970.
– "No More Disagreeable or Onerous Duty." In *Canadians and the Military Aid for the Civil Power, Past, Present and Future,* ed. David Dewitt et al. Scarborough, ON: Prentice Hall, 1995.
– *A Peculiar Kind of Politics: Canada's Overseas Ministry in the First World War.* Toronto: University of Toronto Press, 1982.
Morton, Desmond, and Terry Copp. *Working People.* Ottawa: Deneau, 1981.
Morton, Desmond, and Glenn Wright. *Winning the Second Battle: Canadian Veterans and the Return to Civilian Life 1915–1930.* Toronto: University of Toronto Press, 1987.
Mount, Graeme. *Canada's Enemies.* Toronto: Dundurn Press, 1993.
Murphy, Paul. *World War One and the Origins of Civil Liberties in the United States.* New York: Norton, 1979.
Murray, Robert. *Red Scare: A Study in National Hysteria.* Minneapolis: University of Minnesota Press, 1955.
Nicol, Janet. "Alvo von Alvensleben: I Am Not 'An Enemy to the People I Have Lived Among.'" *British Columbia History* 40.1 (January 2008).
Norris, John. *Strangers Entertained: A History of the Ethnic Groups of British Columbia.* Vancouver: British Columbia Centennial '71 Committee, 1971.
Page, Robert. "The Canadian Response to the Imperial Idea during the Boer War Years." *Journal of Canadian Studies* (February 1960): 33–49.
Panayi, Panikos, ed. *Minorities in Wartime: National and Racial Groupings in Europe, North America and Australia during Two World Wars.* Oxford: Berg, 1993.

Pennefather, P.S. *The Orange and the Black*. Toronto: T.H. Best, 1984.
Peppin, Patricia. "Emergency Legislation and Rights in Canada: The War Measures Act and Civil Liberties." *Queen's Law Journal* 18.1 (Spring 1993).
Pitsula, James. *For All We Have and Are: Regina and the Experience of the Great War*. Winnipeg: University of Manitoba Press, 2008.
Porter, John. *The Vertical Mosaic: An Analysis of Social Class and Power in Canada*. Toronto: University of Toronto Press, 1965.
Powell, Trevor. "The Church of England and the 'Foreigner' in the Diocese of Qu'Appelle and Saskatchewan." *Journal of the Canadian Church Historical Society* 28.1 (April 1986): 31–43.
Power, Michael. "The Mitred Warrior: Bishop Michael Francis Fallon." *Catholic Insight* 8.3 (April 2000): 8–26.
Prang, M. *N.W. Rowell: Ontario Nationalist*. Toronto, 1975.
Reddie, Pennie. "The Crimes of Treason and Sedition in Canada." *Laurentian University Review* 11.1 (November 1978): 7–25.
Resnick, Philip. *The Vertical Mosaic Revisited: The Dynamics of Power in Canada*. Montreal: Our Generation Press, 1971.
Reynolds, Lloyd. *The British Immigrant: His Social and Economic Adjustment in Canada*. Toronto: Oxford University Press, 1935.
Richardson, Alan. *British Immigrants and Australia: A Psycho-Social Inquiry*. Canberra: Australian National University Press, 1974.
Robin, Martin. *Radical Politics and Canadian Labour, 1880–1930*. Industrial Relations Centre, Queen's University, 1968.
– "Registration, Conscription, and Independent Labour Politics, 1916–1917." *Canadian Historical Review* 47 (January 1966): 109.
Rutherdale, Robert. *Hometown Horizons: Local Responses to Canada's Great War*. Vancouver: University of British Columbia Press, 2004.
Semple, Neil. *The Lord's Dominion: The History of Canadian Methodism*. Montreal and Kingston: McGill-Queen's University Press, 1996.
Senior, Hereward. "The Genesis of Canadian Orangeism." *Ontario History* 60 (June 1968): 13–29.
– "Orangeism in Ontario Politics, 1872–1896." In *Oliver Mowat's Ontario*, ed. Donald Swainson. Toronto: Macmillan, 1972.
– *Orangeism: The Canadian Phase*. Toronto: McGraw-Hill Ryerson, 1972.
Shaw, Amy. *Crisis of Conscience: Conscientious Objection in Canada during the First World War*. Vancouver: University of British Columbia Press, 2009.
Shiels, Robert. "The Criminal Trials of John MacLean." *Juridicial Review* 5, pt. 1 (2001): 1–21.
Silver, A. *The French Canadian Ideal of Confederation, 1864–1900*. Toronto: University of Toronto Press, 1982.

Skelton, O.D. *Life and Letters of Sir Wilfrid Laurier*. Toronto: Oxford University Press, 1921.
Smith, David. "Emergency Government in Canada." *Canadian Historical Review* 50.4 (December 1969): 429–48.
Smith, Neil. "Nationalism and the Canadian Churches." *Canadian Journal of Theology* 9 (1963): 112–25.
Sped, Richard. *Prisoners, Diplomats and the Great War*. New York: Greenwood Press, 1990.
Steinhardt, Allan, *Civil Censorship in Canada during the First World War*. Toronto: Unitrade, 1996.
Stern, Paul. "Why Do People Sacrifice for Their Nations?" In *Perspectives on Nationalism and War*, ed. J.L. Comoroff and Paul C. Stern. Amsterdam: Gordon Breach Publishers, 1995.
Stone, Geoffrey. "Judge Learned Hand and the Espionage Act of 1917: A Mystery Unravelled." *University of Chicago Law Review* 70 (2003): 335–58.
Swainger, Jonathan. "Governing the Law: The Canadian Department of Justice in the Early Confederation Era." PhD thesis, University of Western Ontario, 1992.
Swindler, William. "Wartime News Control in Canada." *Public Opinion Quarterly* 6.3 (Autumn 1942): 444–9.
Swyripa, Frances, and John Thompson. *Loyalties in Conflict: Ukrainians in Canada during the Great War*. Edmonton: University of Alberta Press, 1983.
Thompson, John Herd. *The Harvests of War: The Prairie West, 1914–1918*. Toronto: McClelland and Stewart, 1978.
Union Government Publicity Bureau. *English Canada and the War*. Ottawa: Dodson-Merrill Press, 1917.
United States Senate. *Report of the Commission on Protecting and Reducing Government Secrecy (1997)*. Senate Document 105–2. Washington: US Government Printing Office, 1997.
Urquhart, M.C., ed. *Historical Statistics of Canada*. Toronto: Macmillan, 1965.
Vance, Jonathan. *Maple Leaf Empire*. Don Mills, ON: Oxford University Press, 2012.
Van Vugt, William. *Britain to America: Mid-Nineteenth Century Immigrants to the United States*. Chicago: University of Illinois Press, 1999.
Vennat, Pierre. *Les "Poilus" québécois de 1914–1918: Histoire des militaires canadiens-français de la Premiere Guerre mondiale*. 2 vols. Montreal: Meridian, 1999.
Wade, Mason. *The French Canadians, 1760–1945*. Toronto: Macmillan, 1955.
Walker, Barrigton. *The History of Immigration and Racism in Canada*. Toronto: Canadian Scholar's Press, 2008.

Ward, Peter. *White Canada Forever: Popular Attitudes and Public Policy toward Orientals in British Columbia*. Montreal and Kingston: McGill-Queen's University Press, 1990.

White, Clinton. "Pre-World War One Saskatchewan German Catholic Thought Concerning the Perpetuation of Their Language and Religion." *Canadian Ethnic Studies* 26.2 (1994): 14–45.

Wilkinson, Alan. *The Church of England and the First World War*. Southampton: Camelot Press, 1978.

Willis, Robert. "David Williams 1859–1904: The Background of a Bishop." MA thesis, University of Western Ontario, 1957.

Wilson, David. *The Irish in Canada*. Canadian Historical Society, 1989.

Wood, James. *Militia Myths: Ideals of the Canadian Citizen Soldier*. Vancouver: University of British Columbia Press, 2010.

Woodsworth, J.S. *Strangers within Our Gates; or, Coming Canadians*. Toronto: Methodist Church Missionary Society of Canada, 1909.

Wright, Barry. "Sedition in Upper Canada: Contested Legality." *Labour* 29 (Spring 1992).

Zucchi, John. *A History of Ethnic Enclaves in Canada*. Ottawa: CHA, 2007.

Newspapers

Berlin News Record
Brantford Courier
Canada Gazette
Calgary Chronicle
Edmonton Journal
Kitchener Daily Telegraph
Kitchener News Record
London Advertiser
London Free Press
Manchester Guardian
Manitoba Veteran
Montreal Gazette
Le Devoir (Montreal)
La Presse (Montreal)
Sentinel (Loyal Orange Lodge)
Ottawa Evening Journal
Ottawa Free Press
Toronto *Globe*
Toronto *Star*
Toronto *Telegram*

Vancouver Citizen
Vancouver Sun
Veteran
Windsor Record
Winnipeg Evening Tribune
Winnipeg (formerly *Manitoba*) *Free Press*

Index

Alien Enemies, 6–7; definition, 10; repression, 13–14, 18–25, 32, 35, 44, 55; attitude to, 67–88, 99, 100, 104–8, 127–8, 132, 136, 139, 142–4, 157, 189, 199; election (1917), 160–71, 183–4, 197, 198–202; postwar, 210–35, 246–8, 251–3

Alien Restriction Regulations (ARRs), 13, 18–25, 32, 203, 225

Anglican Church, 37, 39, 41, 47, 53, 71, 85–6, 89, 92, 97, 99, 113, 180, 205

Berlin (Kitchener), Ontario, 56, 67, 68, 78–9, 90, 123, 128, 134, 139–43, 157, 240

Bolshevism, 17, 25, 38, 66, 70, 124, 140–4, 107, 190–3, 197, 219, 220–6, 229–30, 234–6, 238

Bonne Entente, 147–50, 157, 162

Borden, Robert (prime minister), 7, 33, 35, 38, 61, 62, 67, 92, 95, 97, 104, 140, 145; and Calgary riots, 145; conscription as "militarily necessary," 153; and conscription in Quebec, 109, 113–17, 154–5; election (1917), 156–80; and German Canadians, 140; in London and France, 150–2; and postwar dissent, 212–13

Bourassa, Henri, 60–4; attitude to violence, 121–3; election (1917), 165, 167, 174, 180; veterans' attitude, 104

Brandon, Manitoba, 4, 156, 165, 240, 246

"British Canada," definition, 8–9

Cahan, C.H. (director of public safety, 1919), 209, 212–15, 217–20, 247

Calgary, Alberta, 42, 127, 128, 133, 219, 221, 235, 238, 240; riots, 128, 134–6, 145

Catholic Church, 8, 37–8, 47, 49, 52–3, 59, 85, 97, 99, 121, 124, 133, 191, 214; importance to government, 204–7; patriotism urged by bishops, 88–9; schools, 62, 70–1

Chambers, F.E. (chief censor), 34, 219

Chown, Dr Samuel, 87

Church, Tommy (mayor of Toronto), 12, 94, 106, 129, 158; riots, 201–2

censorship, 4, 6, 13, 16–18, 23–9, 32, 80, 95, 145, 185, 187, 192, 203, 216–20, 242, 248–50; attitude of government to, 29
Communist Party, 45, 46, 203, 223
communists, 22
conscientious objection, 15, 19, 47, 172, 211
conscription, 4, 6, 12–13, 43, 46, 48, 57, 97, 101, 144, 146, 249; of Alien Enemies, 106; election (1917), 150–82; opposition to, 9, 48, 144, 183–95, 206, 247; repressive practice, 12–25, 33; in Quebec, 109–26; of Ukrainians, 70
constitutionnelles, 114–17, 121–2, 166

Dafoe, J.W., 170, 174, 233
Doherty, C.J. (minister of justice), 113, 206–7
dynomitards, 115–22

Easter riots (Quebec), 183–5, 187, 192
Edmonton, Alberta, 70, 84, 136–9, 207, 221, 240
elections (1911), 61; (1917), 110, 147–82; postwar, 242–3; (1921), 243
Electoral Disabilities Removal Act (1914), 171

Fallon, Bishop Michael, 62; Ford City riot, 124; Ontario Irish leader, 88–9; schools, 205
Fernie, British Columbia, 239
Flavelle, Joseph (Imperial Munitions Board), 117, 166, 168, 170, 190
Ford City, 124
"French Canada," definition, 9

German Canadians, 54, 55–6, 123; identity, 10, 70–2

Godfrey, John, vi, 106; Bonne Entente, 148–50, 162; "win the war" movement, 151, 157–9
Great War Veterans' Association (GWVA), 70, 102–7, 155, 157, 165; postwar violence, 228–41
Guelph, Ontario, 87, 203, 223; Jesuit Noviate, 206–8

Halifax, Nova Scotia, 79–80, 203, 240; explosion, 79
Hughes, Sam (minister of militia), 88, 92, 95, 141, 168, 207

internment, 4, 14, 24, 69, 105, 136, 144, 189, 204, 225; comparison with Britain, 21
Imperial Order Daughters of the Empire (IODE), 91, 95–6
International Workers of the World (IWW), 43, 45, 77, 81; late war fears, 191–6, 204, 215, 217, 222–3

Japanese Canadians, 10, 68; battalion, 73
Jehovah's Witnesses, 48, 91
Jewish community, 46, 48, 97, 143, 191, 192

Kitchener, Ontario: *see* Berlin, Ontario

Lafortune, Paul (anti-conscriptionist), 119, 121, 122
Laurier, Wilfrid (prime minister), 3, 7, 46, 55, 58, 60–3, 68, 78, 120–1, 133, 140, 145, 157, 159; election (1917), 163–81
Lavergne, Armand (Quebec nationalist), 65, 112, 114

London, Ontario, 62, 77, 79, 88, 97, 123, 129
Loyal Orange Order (LOL), 38, 39, 41, 42, 54, 61, 74, 85, 94, 99, 101, 106, 123, 131, 147, 189, 244; and conscription, 154, 156, 159, 166; and Guelph Noviate, 206–7; and GWVA, 104; power, 91–4

Martin, Médéric (mayor of Montreal), 58, 59, 114; reaction to violence, 116, 121, 122
Meighen, Arthur (attorney general, later minister of interior), 67, 74; brother, 170–1; identity, 92–4, 99; and conscription, 113; election gerrymandering, 171, 181; and labour vote, 179; and Guelph Noviate, 207; postwar, 242–3; and veterans, 102; Winnipeg general strike, 231, 233, 237
Migault, Arthur: recruitment of French Canadians, 64
Methodist Church, 37, 47, 54, 85, 101; attitude to aliens, 86–7; and conscription 180; fundraising, 99; and Loyal Orange Order, 92; and military service, 87–9, 97
Military Services Act (MSA, 1917), 14, 15, 33, 47, 77, 102, 129, 155, 158, 163, 164; federalized enforcement, 203, 206–7; postwar, 210–11; resistance in Quebec, 112–22, 183–8, 192
Military Voters Act (1917), 171, 181, 242
Montreal, Quebec, 48, 49, 50, 59, 65, 78, 80, 156; anti-conscription, 110–20, 165–6, 186, 187; and Bonne Entente, 149; and socialism, 191 192, 196

"New Canada," definition, 9–11

Parliament buildings burn (1916), 78–9, 134–6
patriotic fund, 65, 89, 100, 133, 139
Perhuda, John, 77–8
police, 14, 21, 24, 25, 74, 80; American, 76, 77; and Bolsheviks, 25, 192; Dominion Police, 77, 90, 184, 185, 191, 194, 210, 220; and IWW, 191–6, 203, 204; Quebec, 110, 112, 114, 116–19, 122, 124, 187; riots, 130, 136, 139, 144, 184, 186, 189, 200–3; Royal Canadian Mounted Police (RCMP, 1919), 217–21; Royal North West Mounted Police (RNWMP), 125, 221; spying, 221–4, 231; Winnipeg, 234–5
Presbyterian Church, 37, 47, 85, 88, 90, 91, 97, 180

Quebec City, 112; Bonne Entente, 149; Easter riots, 184–7; riots, 114, 119; scepticism concerning socialist action, 192

Red scares, 20, 197, 224, 238–40
Regina, Saskatchewan, 79; riots, 145

sabotage, 76–9, 129, 133, 218
Saskatoon, Saskatchewan, 157, 165, 240
"schools question," 62, 150; Manitoba, 205; Ontario, 65, 206, 214
sedition, 16–19, 22, 78, 91, 158, 216, 235, 240, 248; and Canadian Communist Party, 223; and censorship, 28–9; Calgary, 133; Nova Scotia, 130; Ontario, 139, 140; Quebec, 117, 119, 125, 187

temperance, 17
Toronto, Ontario, 68, 85, 91, 105, 106, 148; conscription, 156–8, 164; and Loyal Orange Lodge, 94, 99, 101; police, 222–3; recruiting, 128–31; riots, 143–4, 198–204; urban railway, 74
trade unions, 42–5, 92, 99, 161–2, 179, 194, 196, 198, 203, 218, 222, 233, 239–40
treason, 18, 29, 117

Ukrainians, 45, 72, 74–5, 105, 180; wartime definition, 67–70
Ukrainian Social Democratic Party (USDP), 195–6, 204, 215
United Kingdom, 21–2, 29–30
United States, 21, 22–3, 25–6, 27, 52, 61, 75, 244, 248

Vancouver, British Columbia, 44, 68, 72–3, 156; Red scare, 238–40; riots 190–1, 197–8, 204; spying, 221, 223
Verville, Alphonse (anti-conscriptionist), 114, 120
Victoria, British Columbia, 80, 106, 107, 221, 238

War Measures Act (WMA), 13, 16, 18, 20, 24, 32, 91, 110, 115, 191, 194, 211, 223, 239, 242
War Times Election Act (1917), 171
Williams, David (Bishop of Huron), 82, 84, 89, 154
"win the war" movement, 46, 106, 109, 142, 147; organization, 150–3, 156–9
Windsor, Ontario, 105; bombing, 75–80; riot, 124–5, 129
Winnipeg, Manitoba, 36, 45, 105, 134, 156, 157, 161, 165, 189–90, 203, 216, 225, 229, 254; strike, 229–38, 240
Woodsworth, J.S., 65, 86, 88, 235